The Dark Side of Discipleship

"The Christian tradition has long recognized the 'three enemies of the soul' as hindrances to spiritual growth: the world, the flesh, and the devil. Tragically, many modern Christians have either demythologized or sensationalized the third enemy. Gary Tyra does neither but proposes that having a sound, biblical understanding of the demonic is indispensable to true discipleship. This book will challenge those who are either dismissive of or fixated on the devil."
—SIMON CHAN, editor of *Asia Journal of Theology*

"Tyra addresses a frequently bypassed theme when talking about Christian discipleship: we have a formidable adversary whose cunning is distracting, derailing, or destroying the faith journeys of countless Christians. He acknowledges the tendency of some to give the devil too much visibility, while others naively act as if the Bible is silent on this 'roaring lion' whose destructive intent is clear. Tyra's alternative replaces an avoidance of the topic, with an empowerment that is a primer on spiritual endurance training."
—BYRON D. KLAUS, President of Assemblies of God Theological Seminary (1999–2015)

"To my own peril I ignored thinking about spiritual warfare for much of my Christian life. Readers of this insightful book can learn, as I have, that following Jesus involves awareness of the enemy of our soul. Gary Tyra provides a welcome orientation to this dark side with sound biblical teaching and encouraging pastoral guidance for endurance training in developing a lifestyle empowered by the Spirit."
—KLAUS ISSLER, Professor of Educational Studies and Theology, Talbot School of Theology, Biola University

"Written from a pastor's heart, informed by a scholar's mind, Gary Tyra's *The Dark Side of Discipleship* speaks with characteristic precision and breadth to a subject rarely addressed, but arguably more needed now than ever before—spiritual warfare. Beginning with a solid biblical foundation, he is able to avoid the extremes of sensationalism and dismissal and provides a theologically sound and pastorally informed study of how the devil seeks to derail and distract the disciples of Jesus. He then turns to a compelling discussion of what might—and must—be done in response. An exceptional work of pastoral theology—recommended without reservation."
—W. H. DOGTEROM, Professor of Pastoral Ministries and Spiritual Formation, Vanguard University

"As a child of the 1980s, the phrase *dark side* easily conjures up images of Darth Vader, the most notorious villain in film history. As Obi Wan Kenobi warned Luke Skywalker in *Episode IV*, there is always a temptation of being seduced by the dark side. Just ask Lord Voldemort of Harry Potter fame, or Thanos in the Marvel universe. But this temptation of the dark side is not reserved for fiction alone. It describes my own experience. It describes my friends' stories. It describes real life. But what do we do with the workings of the *evil one* from the dark side? How do we defend against the attack of the *devil*? Taking us beyond elementary versions of faith and Christianity, Gary Tyra's *The Dark Side of Discipleship* is a much-needed primer on the enemy's modus operandi. Faithfully using Scripture as his foundation, Gary is a veritable code breaker on Satan's schemes. I needed this book, and it will continue to impact and inform my life and pastoral ministry in the local church. Read it and join me in standing firm and holding our ground."

—Brenton Fessler, founding pastor of Refuge, Orange, California

The Dark Side of Discipleship

Why and How the New Testament
Encourages Christians to Deal with the Devil

GARY TYRA

CASCADE Books • Eugene, Oregon

THE DARK SIDE OF DISCIPLESHIP
Why and How the New Testament Encourages Christians to Deal with the Devil

Copyright © 2020 Gary Tyra. All rights reserved. Except for brief quotations in critical publications or reviews, no part of this book may be reproduced in any manner without prior written permission from the publisher. Write: Permissions, Wipf and Stock Publishers, 199 W. 8th Ave., Suite 3, Eugene, OR 97401.

Cascade Books
An Imprint of Wipf and Stock Publishers
199 W. 8th Ave., Suite 3
Eugene, OR 97401

www.wipfandstock.com

PAPERBACK ISBN: 978-1-5326-9121-8
HARDCOVER ISBN: 978-1-5326-9122-5
EBOOK ISBN: 978-1-5326-9123-2

Cataloguing-in-Publication data:

Names: Tyra, Gary, author.

Title: The dark side of discipleship : why and how the New Testament encourages Christians to deal with the devil / Gary Tyra.

Description: Eugene, OR: Cascade Books, 2020 | Includes bibliographical references and index.

Identifiers: ISBN 978-1-5326-9121-8 (paperback) | ISBN 978-1-5326-9122-5 (hardcover) | ISBN 978-1-5326-9123-2 (ebook)

Subjects: LCSH: 1. Spiritual warfare. | 2. Good and evil—Religious aspects—Christianity.

Classification: BS680.G6 T50 2020 (print) | BS680.G6 (ebook)

Manufactured in the U.S.A.   SEPTEMBER 29, 2020

This book is dedicated to all the church members and university students I've had the honor of ministering to over the past forty-five years. It's my hope that reading this work will enable those I've done life with to call to mind some of the biblical/theological themes I felt compelled to emphasize, and did my best to embody. I also pray you will come across some new insights here that will prove empowering in your ongoing walk with Christ. Thank you for your prayers and support. Patti and I love and appreciate you all very much!

Table of Contents

Acknowledgments xi

Introduction | 1

**PART ONE: It's Never Just Us and God:
The Need to Take the Devil Seriously**

Chapter 1 – The Devil's *Reality* and *Origin*:
Avoiding the Mother of All Mistakes, Part 1 | 19

Chapter 2 – The Devil's *Nature* and *Deal*:
Avoiding the Mother of All Mistakes, Part 2 | 37

**PART TWO: Forewarned is Forearmed:
How the Devil Seeks to Derail Christian Discipleship**

Chapter 3 – *Seduction*: The Devil and Christian *Worship* | 61

Chapter 4 – *Deception*: The Devil and Christian *Nurture* | 84

Chapter 5 – *Alienation*: The Devil and Christian *Community* | 114

Chapter 6 – *Temptation*: The Devil and Christian *Mission* | 140

PART THREE: Standing Firm in the Faith:
How the Devil Must Be Dealt with

Chapter 7 – The Full Armor of God:
Putting On, Taking Up, Praying In, and *Praying For* | 163

Chapter 8 – Crucial Close-Quarters Combat Tactics:
Coming Near, Leaning Into, and *Holding Fast* | 197

PART FOUR: Standing Firm in the Faith:
Why the Devil Must be Dealt with

Chapter 9 – Where Angels Fear to Tread:
The Ultimate "Why" Question, Part 1 | 225

Chapter 10 – God's Endgame:
The Ultimate "Why" Question, Part 2 | 253

Conclusion | 277

Bibliography | 281
General Index | 291
Ancient Documents Index | 303

Acknowledgments

Given this book's topic, I didn't think it wise to even begin this publishing endeavor without getting buy-in from my family, and requesting some serious prayer support from as many friends as possible. The year I've spent composing this work has indeed proved eventful, filled with many indications of spiritual opposition. In a sense, I suppose that could be considered a good sign. In any case, as I come to the end of the manuscript-readying process, my heart overflows with gratitude for the grace I've received from God, and the encouragement/support/assistance provided me by many wonderful people.

I'll start by expressing appreciation to my family as a whole (Patti, Megan, Brandon, Lindsay, Jacob, and Raelyn) for not only putting up with my preoccupation, but also for weathering, along with me, not a few spiritual attacks. You never complained. Instead, you routinely inquired about the project's progress and provided some timely words of encouragement. I want to express some special thanks to my beautiful wife Patti for her patience, encouragement, and remarkable proofreading skills, and to my daughter Megan for the way in which one of our conversations significantly impacted the content and structure of the book.

Also deserving of a word of thanks are my faculty colleagues at Vanguard University, especially those who labor with me in the Division of Theology. More than you know, the expressions of interest and words of support and encouragement I received from you this past year provided strength for the day. In particular, I want to voice appreciation to my dear friend, Frank Macchia, for not only his personal support, but his theological partnership as well. While I only refer in this work to the impact that one of our conversations had on it, I'm grateful for them all. You are a treasure, dear friend.

I also want to express my gratitude for the assistance provided me by my teaching/research assistant Brooke Mandagie, who not only provided encouragement, but also some much-appreciated feedback with respect to some of the book's content. Thank you, Brooke. You were and are a gift from God.

Of course, I want to communicate appreciation to everyone at Wipf and Stock who participated in this project. In particular, I offer sincere thanks to Michael Thomson, the acquisitions editor for Wipf and Stock, who was not only instrumental in the project's coming to life, but who also provided ongoing encouragement with respect to it. I'm also deeply appreciative for the privilege of being allowed to work with the venerable Rodney Clapp, a renowned editor of the highest caliber. What a blessing it was, as I worked on this manuscript, to know that someone as wise and as skillful as you, Rodney, would be involved in its formation! Thank you for your partnership in this work.

Finally, I'll give glory to God. In an older version of the NIV, Psalm 50:23 reads: "He who sacrifices thank offerings honors me, and he prepares the way so that I may show him the salvation of God." Throughout the writing process, I've taken this word of exhortation/promise seriously. God has been faithful.

> *You do all things well, Lord. You do all things well. Thank you for calling me to write this book. Thank you for the "assistance" I've experienced along the way. It has been an honor to participate with you in your devil-defeating, evil-ending agenda. I pray this work will contribute, in at least some small way, to the ability of many to render to you the spiritual, moral, and missional faithfulness you desire and deserve.*
>
> *Coram Deo!*

Introduction

There's a dark side to Christian discipleship church members ignore to their peril. We can do better. The authors of the New Testament show us how.

Every semester more than a few students arrive at my Foundations of Christian Life course either frustrated it's required of them, or assuming their lives won't be impacted by the experience. I've discovered, however, there are some things I can do to gain a hearing. For example, early in the semester I'll ask the class: *How many of us want to someday hear Jesus say to us: "Well done, good and faithful servant"* (Matt 25:21)? It's amazing how many hands go up! Even those students who thus far have thought of themselves as "too cool for school" have a hard time not responding humbly to this sobering question. I've also been known to pose this question when preaching in churches. It *always* gets the same result: hands raised all over the worship space! There's something about the query that resonates with most professing Christians, and for good reason.

According to the Bible, *faithfulness* is a big deal. It's a key attribute of God,[1] and something he's looking for in the lives of his people.[2] More specifically, it's my sense that there are three distinct types of faithfulness God both desires and deserves: a *spiritual* faithfulness, a *moral* faithfulness, and a *missional* faithfulness. One of the primary messages of the New Testament seems to be that Jesus not only embodied this threefold faithfulness in his own life and ministry, but is eager to empower his

---

1. For example, see Ps 89:8; 1 Cor 1:9; Heb 10:23.
2. For example, see Josh 24:14; Hos 4:1; Eph 1:1; Col 1:2; Rev 13:10.

followers/apprentices to do the same.[3] There's a sense in which our allowing Jesus to do this is what Christian discipleship is all about!

But this isn't to suggest a lifestyle earmarked by faithfulness is easy to pull off. Unfortunately, the New Testament contains numerous passages which allude to the reality of a spiritual enemy who's committed to bringing about just the opposite: a complete crippling of the disciple's spiritual, moral, and missional faithfulness before God! Moreover, these many biblical texts make clear it's not just the influence of the fallen *world* in which we dwell that's antagonistic to Christian followership (see Rom 12:2; 1 John 2:15–17), or that it's only the disciple's *flesh* (sinful nature) that's opposed to the cultivation of the threefold faithfulness (see Rom 8:5–8; Gal 5:19–21). In addition, the apostolic authors go to great lengths to warn their readers that a personal, spiritual entity referred to variously as the *devil*, *Satan*, and the *evil one* also needs to be taken very seriously![4] *In a nutshell, that's what this book is about: the need to take more seriously than many do something the New Testament authors were careful to include in their writings: practical instruction regarding why and how Christ's followers must deal with the devil.* While paying attention to what the New Testament has to say about why and how the devil must be dealt with is certainly not all that's required for a vibrant, fruitful, enduring walk with Christ, it is necessary. Heeding these much-neglected discipleship instructions is critical if we are to succeed at rendering to God the spiritual, moral, and missional faithfulness he desires and deserves.[5]

Discipleship's Dark Side: A Closer Look

To be more precise, what I will refer to in this work as the *dark side of discipleship* derives from the fact that the New International Version of the New Testament refers to:

---

3. For more on what it means to be spiritually, morally, and missionally faithful, see chs. 3–5 of Tyra, *Getting Real*, 61–118.

4. For a more thorough discussion of how the world, our flesh, and the devil work together to oppose God's work in our lives, and the need, therefore, to maintain a balanced awareness of all three, see Arnold, *3 Crucial Questions*, 32–37.

5. While Satan is also referred to in the Old Testament, and the pertinent passages from there will be considered, the primary focus of this work will be on the distinctive manner in which the New Testament seems to keep referring to the evil one in such a way as to encourage and equip Christian disciples toward a vibrant, fruitful, and enduring walk with Christ.

- *Satan* (37 times);
- the *devil* (35 times);
- the *evil one* (34 times);
- *Beelzebul* (9 times);
- the *serpent* (5 times);
- the *prince of demons* (4 times);
- the *prince of this world* (3 times);
- the *enemy* (3 times);
- the *tempter* (2 times);
- *Belial* (1 time);
- the *ruler of the kingdom of the air* (1 time);
- the *god of this age* (1 time); and
- the *dragon* (1 time).

Moreover, the authors of the New Testament also referred to:

- the reality of *demons* or *the demonic* (92 times);
- *evil spirits* (6 times);
- the *elemental spiritual forces* at work in this world (3 times);
- and the *dominion of darkness* (1 time).

That's 238 times, at least, the authors of the New Testament refer to a spiritual entity that's committed to the debilitation of the Christian's walk with Christ!

Moreover, time and again the apostolic authors exhort their readers to "stand," "stand firm," and "stand against" (or "resist").[6] At the very least, these numerous exhortations suggest the Christian life, rather than being a perpetual picnic, involves a struggle of some kind.[7] But, more than that, the Greek words often translated in the NIV as "stand" and "stand firm" (Greek: *histēmi*) or "stand against" and "resist" (Greek: *anthistēmi*) are

---

6. See Luke 21:19; 1 Cor 10:12; 15:58; 2 Cor 1:21, 24; Gal 5:1; Eph 6:11, 14; Phil 1:27; 4:1; Col 4:12; 1 Thess 3:8; 2 Thess 2:13, 15; Jas 5:8; 1 Pet 5:9.

7. For a succinct but helpful overview of the way the New Testament portrays the reality that the Christian life involves a struggle, see Arnold, *3 Crucial Questions*, 22–23.

often associated with the dynamic of spiritual warfare.[8] This would seem to indicate the intention of the New Testament's authors was not simply to portray the Christian life as a *struggle*, but as a very serious spiritual *battle*.[9] Thus, the apostle Peter felt compelled to provide this pungent warning:

> Be alert and of sober mind. Your enemy the devil prowls around like a roaring lion looking for someone to devour. Resist him, standing firm in the faith, because you know that the family of believers throughout the world is undergoing the same kind of sufferings. (1 Pet 5:8–9)

Likewise, the apostle Paul was careful to conclude his Letter to the Ephesians thusly:

> Finally, be strong in the Lord and in his mighty power. Put on the full armor of God, so that you can take your stand against the devil's schemes. For our struggle is not against flesh and blood, but against the rulers, against the authorities, against the powers of this dark world and against the spiritual forces of evil in the heavenly realms. Therefore put on the full armor of God, so that when the day of evil comes, you may be able to stand your ground, and after you have done everything, to stand. (Eph 6:10–13)

Both of the passages just cited make clear there is indeed a dark side to Christian discipleship. The aim of this book is to enable its readers to experience a vibrant, fruitful, enduring walk with Christ despite this inconvenient reality!

Because What We Don't Know *Can* Hurt Us!

Perhaps you're wondering how a book that focuses on the dark side of anything could be edifying, or whether it wouldn't be wiser to simply ignore this unpleasant, daunting aspect of Christian followership. If so, I understand. But here's the problem: while 1 John 2:13 refers to Christian

---

8. See Matt 12:26; Mark 3:26; Luke 11:18; Eph 6:11–14; 1 Pet 5:8–9.

9. Such an observation might apply as well to the New Testament's use of several Greek verbs and adjectives related to *histemi* and likewise translated in the NIV as "stand firm": *stēkō* (e.g., 1 Cor 16:13; Gal 5:1; Phil 1:27; 4:1; 1 Thess 3:8; 2 Thess 2:15), *stereōma* (e.g., Col 2:5), *stērizō* (e.g., Jas 5:8); *stereos* (e.g., 1 Pet 5:9), and *sthenoō* (e.g., 1 Pet 5:10). For more on the importance of recognizing the Christian life as a struggle against supernatural forces, see Arnold, *3 Crucial Questions*, 37–39.

disciples *overcoming* the evil one, 2 Corinthians 2:11 speaks of the possibility of church members being *outwitted* by him. It's precisely because of the latter possibility that we must take the dark side of discipleship seriously.

As a pastor, I've seen some truly remarkable spiritual and moral transformations occur in the lives of church members and students. I know for a fact overcoming is possible!

But, sad to say, I've also grieved over congregants who, falling prey to Satan's schemes, continually self-sabotaged just about every element of their walk with Christ. I suspect every congregation contains a few members who participate in the life of the church in a hit-and-miss manner. But the sad reality no one really wants to discuss out loud is some eventually stop attending church altogether, and a few actually disavow their commitment to Christ despite the New Testament's repeated encouragement to avoid this terrible possibility![10] Needless to say, this is the opposite of Christian faithfulness!

Having transitioned from the pastorate to the academy, my concern these days has to do with the high number of students who arrive at my Foundations of Christian Life course with virtually no preunderstanding of what the New Testament has to say about why and how Christians need to deal with the devil. For example, many of my students, even those who hail from Christian homes and have some church experience, seem to be somewhat nonplussed when, in a lecture on the problem of evil, I indicate the need to factor the reality and work of Satan into the equation. The upshot seems to be that, whatever spiritual formation these Christian students experienced prior to their going away to college, it did not include a serious discussion of how to deal with the devil. Though some fairly recent polling indicates a majority of Americans still believe in the existence of the devil,[11] such belief is in decline,[12] and my sense is there's a tendency, observable in many, to fail to take this reality seriously in their day-to-day lives. Every semester I interact with students from Christian

---

10. The following references are to New Testament passages which warn of the possibility OF spiritual apostasy and/or encourage an avoidance of it: Matt 24:10–13; Luke 8:13; John 15:1–6; Rom 11:17–22; 1 Cor 9:24—10:12; 15:1–2; 16:13; 2 Cor 1:24; 11:2–3; Gal 4:8–20; 5:2–6; Col 1:21–23; 1 Thess 3:5; 1 Tim 1:18–19; 3:6–7; 4:1–10; 5:8; 6:9–12, 20–21; 2 Tim 2:11–13, 16–21, 24–26; 4:7–8; Heb 2:1–4; 3:6–14; 4:1–2; 6:4–12; 10:26–39; 12:15–17; Jas 5:19–20; 1 Pet 5:8–9; 2 Pet 1:5–11; 3:17; 1 John 2:24–28; 2 John 1:9; Jude 3–5, 20–25; Rev 3:1–6, 11, 15–16.

11. Carter, "Survey," lines 1–3.

12. Shannon-Missal, "Americans' Belief in God," lines 5–6.

homes who, because they've become distracted, discouraged, and defeated in their walk with Christ, have either adopted a post-Christian posture with respect to the faith, or possess a strong inclination to do so. Since there's an essential connection between one's spirituality and morality, these students have a higher-than-normal risk of getting into trouble now that they're away from home. Though I've been a full-time professor for close to two decades now, my pastor's heart can't help but be concerned.

Surely, there are many reasons for this loss of faith in the lives of some students. That said, I'm convinced a major cause is a lack of what I refer to as *spiritual endurance training*. It's not at all uncommon for churches to *evangelize* and *edify* with much intentionality, but then fail to be intentional about helping their members *endure*. This despite the fact the New Testament presents us with many indications of the importance of spiritual endurance![13]

The crucial question is: *Why?* Though in some cases it may be for a theological reason this lack of endurance training occurs (i.e., an extreme emphasis on the sovereignty of God over against any notion of human responsibility), I want to suggest another.

Overcorrections Happen!

I once asked the leader of an international media ministry if he believed in a personal devil. He was unhesitating in his reply, asserting he had witnessed far too many cases of demonic activity in the Majority World to doubt the existence of the evil one. But when I asked him if he believed there are things Christians in the West can and should do to more effectively engage in spiritual warfare, my friend winced and offered that it was probably better to simply ignore the devil and not "give him too much press."

Though I understand the impulse, this strikes me as a classic example of an overcorrection. Overcorrecting to perceived extremes is something we fallen, erratic human beings seem bent on doing. As a result, the pendulum keeps swinging back and forth when it comes to all kinds of philosophical, political, or theological ideas and practices.[14] The

---

13. For example, see Matt 24:10–13; Rom 15:4; Acts 11:23; 14:32; Col 1:9–12; 1 Thess 1:3; 2 Thess 1:3–5; 1 Tim 6:11–12; 2 Tim 2:11–13; Titus 2:1–2; Heb 12:1–3; Rev 1:9; 2:3, 13; 3:8, 10; 13:10; 14:12.

14. For more on the significance of the swinging pendulum for theology and ministry, see Tyra, *Missional Orthodoxy*, 28–34.

problem is overcorrections are, by definition, not the best way to respond to issues of any type. *It strikes me as a particularly dangerous overcorrection for church leaders in the West to simply ignore an aspect of Christian discipleship the New Testament refers to so often.*

Some support for this concern can be found in several sources. For example, in the book *The Evangelical's Guide to Spiritual Warfare*, the author observes:

> Many evangelicals act as if the enemy does not exist. In preaching and teaching and our daily lives, we act as if Satan and his forces are not a problem. We go about our business as if the evil in the world is explainable in some way other than that there is an enemy behind it.[15]

Obviously, it's not a good idea to fixate on or obsess about the reality of the devil. *But isn't it possible a virtual failure on the part of churches to expose members to what the New Testament has to say about the existence of the evil one might make it possible for some members to be outwitted by him?* The same author cited above goes on to offer this frightening observation:

> Though traditional evangelical seminaries and Bible schools claim to be biblical, they usually provide little or no instruction in this important area. Evangelical teachers and pastors, even those who are most critical of the "demythologizing" of liberals, tend to treat anything to do with demons as if they do not exist today. And if teachers do recognize the existence of demons, they have no idea how to deal with them and so ignore them. Ignoring the activity of satanic forces allows them to run rampant within our churches and training institutions.[16]

C. S. Lewis, ever aware of the contemporary church's tendency to overcorrect, spoke to this issue when he observed:

> There are two equal and opposite errors into which our race can fall about the devils. One is to disbelieve in their existence. The other is to believe, and to feel an excessive and unhealthy interest in them. They themselves are equally pleased by both errors and hail a materialist or a magician with the same delight.[17]

---

15. Kraft, *Evangelical's Guide*, 15.
16. Kraft, *Evangelical's Guide*, 32–33.
17. Lewis, *Screwtape Letters*, ix.

Apparently, Lewis believed a third option is available: to believe and, yet, not obsess.

Look, I get it. Who wants to focus on the *dark* side of anything, including discipleship? For that matter, why would anyone *want* to spend a year of their lives researching and writing on what the authors of the New Testament had to say about why and how Christian disciples must take the devil seriously? But here's the thing: my personal and professional experience has been *when people ignore the real devil, we tend to turn God and other people into him.* The pain and suffering we experience in life are real and can't be denied. When we lose sight of who the real source of evil is, it's amazingly easy to conclude it must be either God or our neighbor. Thus, I contend we must resist the perennial temptation to overcorrect, doing our best instead to help our parishioners and students achieve the balanced perspective, with respect to the devil, Lewis was implicitly recommending. Teaching them how to take the devil seriously, without obsessing over him, is simply crucial to providing congregants with the spiritual endurance training they're going to need if they are ever to hear Jesus say to them "Well done, good and faithful servant!"

How This Book Is Different

Over the years many volumes have been devoted to the topic of spiritual warfare. Since some of the more popular works of this sort have been highly speculative in their method, sensationalist in their tone, and triumphalist in their message, this could be a reason why some ministry leaders have decided any book dealing with this topic is likely to do more harm than good.

I'd like to think, however, there are a couple of reasons why this work is different and therefore merits a look. First, the aim here is to meet a very important practical ministry need rather than sell as many books as possible. Second, I've done my best to avoid the overly speculative, sensationalist, and triumphalist approach to this topic that's observable in other books of this type. Instead, I've endeavored to provide careful, responsible discussions of those New Testament passages that not only allude to the reality of the devil, but also indicate how important resisting him is to a vibrant, fruitful, enduring Christian discipleship.[18] Hopefully,

---

18. Put simply, biblical exegesis refers to the process by which biblical scholars attempt to unpack from a biblical text the meaning the biblical author intended it to

the reader will find this no-nonsense investigation has yielded a biblically informed, theologically astute strategy for not only dealing with the devil, but rendering to the risen Christ that spiritual, moral, and missional faithfulness Christian discipleship is ultimately all about.[19]

How This Book Is Built

Part one of the work bears the title "It's Never Just Us and God: The Need to Take the Devil Seriously." The French poet, Charles Baudelaire, once quipped, "The devil's finest trick is to persuade you that he does not exist."[20] Though the Scriptures never encourage God's people to fear the evil one, we are exhorted to reckon with his reality. Not infrequently, I've had to remind hurting, confused parishioners and students it's never just us and God; we simply must take the reality of the evil one into account if we are to make sense of our Christian experience. This pastoral counsel emerges from a no-nonsense overview of the understanding the New Testament authors seem to have had of the devil and the demonic impulse—i.e., what the devil's "deal" is. Providing such an overview is the aim of the first two chapters of the book.

Part two is titled "Forewarned is Forearmed: How the Devil Seeks to Derail Christian Discipleship." According to the apostle Paul, one of the keys to not being outwitted by Satan is to be very aware of his various schemes (2 Cor 2:11; Eph 6:11). As we examine the many New Testament texts which allude to the various devices (Greek: *methodeía*) the devil uses to antagonize Christ's followers, it will become apparent they correspond to four fundamental aspects of one's walk with Christ. Thus, each of the chapters in this section of the book focuses on one of the cardinal components of Christian discipleship—*worship, nurture, community*, and *mission*—examining New Testament passages that explain why and how the devil seeks to disrupt it. It's crucial for Christ's followers to understand how the evil one strives to hinder a dynamic experience of these four key areas of the Christian life. The implication is that

---

convey.

19. Put differently, there's an important difference between a manual for performing exorcisms and a curriculum for endurance training. The marketplace is flooded with the former type of book. This volume aims at being the latter—a book that will help Christian disciples cultivate the threefold faithfulness Jesus modeled for us and wants us to embody ourselves.

20. See Baudelaire, *Prose Poems and La Fanfarlo*, 76.

a key to overcoming rather than being outwitted by Satan is a proactive cultivation of a well-balanced engagement in all four of these discipleship dynamics. *This observation is a game-changer when it comes to both Christian discipleship and spiritual warfare.* Understanding the degree to which the enemy of our souls wants to disrupt these discipleship activities can serve to motivate us with respect to them. Likewise, it's powerfully enabling to know every time we engage in these fundamental dimensions of discipleship, we are saying "yes" to God's Spirit and "no" to the world, our fleshly nature, and the evil one. The devil doesn't like it when we succeed in these endeavors. *Why?* Because this is how disciples cultivate their capacity for a vibrant, fruitful, and enduring walk with Christ! Once again, it's the way this work explores and expounds upon the crucial connection between Christian discipleship and spiritual warfare that sets it apart from others of its kind.

Part three of the work is titled "Standing Firm in the Faith: *How* the Devil Must be Dealt with." Building on the New Testament's call for Christ's apprentices to do more than hope the devil doesn't exist, or won't bother with us, in this section the reader will again be encouraged to be proactive rather than reactive. But the focus in chapter 7 of the book goes beyond the four cardinal components of the Christian life to a consideration of the specific devil-resisting and -defeating activities the apostle Paul refers to in his famous "armor of God" discussion presented in Ephesians 6:10–20. Then, in chapter 8, our focus shifts to three additional "close-quarters" combat tactics prescribed by the New Testament's apostolic authors. It's in these two chapters things really get interesting. This is where we learn to do more than avoid being outwitted by the devil. This is where we learn how to, with the help of the Holy Spirit, actually overcome the evil one, and help our brothers and sisters in Christ do likewise!

Finally, the two chapters that make up part four of the work (which is titled "Standing Firm in the Faith: *Why* the Devil Must be Dealt with") take a turn in terms of both method and message. In them, I humbly attempt to provide a response to the ultimate "why" question which lies behind this entire literary endeavor: *Why did God create a world in which the devil could gain control and wreak so much havoc in the lives of human beings?* The aim of these concluding chapters is to help church members fully process what's known as the problem of evil. The intention is to do so in a way that not only strengthens their personal faith commitment to Christ, but also inspires them to become personally involved in ministry activities that both directly and indirectly serve to promote justice in the face of injustice and mitigate the pain and suffering presently occurring in our world. This too is spiritual warfare, and should be considered the ultimate goal of any serious attempt at Christian endurance training.

My Own Dark-Side Experience

I was reluctant to begin the introduction to this book with a personal story, concerned that doing so might give the impression the work is grounded primarily in one person's experience rather than a careful study of God's word. At the same time, I don't want to conclude this introduction without assuring my readers I've been there. I know what it's like to fight a spiritual battle that seems never-ending. I also know what it feels like to overcome.

I call it my "dark night of the soul" experience.[21] It occurred back in the early eighties, lasted eighteen months, and was defining in terms of my own walk with Christ and ability to minister to others in his name.

I'd been under a lot of stress: pastoring a dysfunctional church in my mid-twenties, while trying to hurry my way through an MDiv degree, be a good husband to my wife Patti, and also be a good dad to my infant son Brandon. Then I experienced a medical problem that thrust me into a year-and-a-half-long battle with a serious anxiety disorder. In general, I guess I was suffering from a condition known as *thanatophobia*—a fear of death or of dying. To be more specific, I developed a phobia related to cancer.

Both of my parents died of cancer at a fairly young age. When a problem with my kidneys didn't clear up immediately, my doctor ordered x-rays without telling me what he was looking for. When I told the x-ray tech my symptoms, he looked worried. That's when I began to suspect the doctor was looking for something serious. While the tests came back negative, the doctor stated in a rather matter-of-fact manner that, given my parents' medical histories, it's more than likely I, too, will someday have to deal with a similar diagnosis.

---

21. The term "dark night of the soul" derives from a devotional classic written by a sixteenth-century Roman Catholic monk named St. John of the Cross, and refers to a season of spiritual desolation that's intended by God to edify the believer despite a painful sense of God's absence and blessing. For more on this, see Coe, "Musings on the Dark Night of the Soul," 293–307.

This simple statement, uttered in such a cavalier manner, was the trigger that produced within me a serious cancer phobia, and thrust me into my most profound dark night of the soul experience. Every time I heard or read the word "cancer" *I would shiver on the inside and my heart would begin to ache.* Every time I visited a sick person in the hospital, especially cancer patients, *I would shiver on the inside and my heart would begin to ache.* Every time I would hear news stories on the radio or television about someone dying, *I would shiver on the inside and my heart would begin to ache.* Patti, Brandon, and I happened to live near a cemetery at the time. Every time I would drive past this cemetery *I would shiver on the inside and my heart would begin to ache.* At this stage in his infancy, Brandon, though weaned, was in the habit of waking up and crying in the middle of the night. Every time I held him in my arms, rocking him back to sleep, I would think that, like my dad, I wouldn't live long enough to see him grow up and begin a family of his own. As a result, *I would shiver on the inside and my heart would begin to ache.*

My phobic fixation on cancer caused me to interpret every little change in my body as a sign the cancer had finally developed. The more I worried about getting cancer, the more weight I lost. The more weight I lost, the more I was convinced I had cancer. I began to have anxiety attacks out of the blue: my esophagus would close while I was trying to eat, or I would begin to hyperventilate while sitting on the couch trying to watch TV with my family.

Are you beginning to get the picture? This was a serious season of suffering in my life I simply didn't have control of. And, the more I prayed, the more confused and bewildered I became. *This dark night of the soul didn't just affect me physically and psychologically, it began to affect me spiritually as well. Yes, there were times when I began to wonder if God was there, and if he was, did he really care?*

The irony is that at a critical moment early on in this experience, I sensed God speaking to me in my heart of hearts.[22] His "message" to me was that the ordeal I was experiencing was purposeful, not random, and the key to overcoming it was to engage in a particular type of spiritual warfare—one I'll describe later on in this work. The problem was that while this prophetic encounter was reassuring and hope-producing at the time, I didn't act upon it in a responsible, faithful, timely manner. So,

---

22. For more on my understanding of the prophetic phenomenon and its role in Christian life and ministry, see Tyra, *Holy Spirit in Mission*; Tyra, *Pursuing Moral Faithfulness*; and Tyra, *Getting Real.*

the dark night continued. My anguished wrestling with a spirit of fear persisted. Self-sabotage happens!

Finally, about a year and a half later, I experienced another prophetic encounter with God that would prove to be monumental. I was away from home attending a pastor's conference. During the night, while I was alone in my hotel room, the *anxiety* demons pounced. Not able to sleep, I sat on the edge of the bed, in the dark, with my head in my hands, my elbows resting on my knees. I remember crying out to God in frustration/anger, "Where are you? Why won't you just say the word and heal me of this spirit of fear?" Then, in the early morning stillness I heard another word from the Lord deep in my heart. The Lord said, "Gary, I told you at the very beginning of this ordeal that it was purposeful, that I wanted to teach you lessons about dealing with the devil, and that the key to your victory was in your hands: your willingness to engage in the spiritual warfare moves I've already made you aware of." In other words, God showed up in that hotel room and sort of got after me. The next day at the conference, God continued to speak to me, but in a powerfully affirming manner. It was my Job moment. I had become crazy-hungry desperate for a personal encounter with God. When he was ready, he showed up, communicating a message of both truth and grace. The effect was profound.

In response to this extended encounter, I returned home and began to engage in those spiritual warfare moves God had previously prescribed. Long story short: it worked! Indeed, it only took a couple of weeks before I realized my year-and-a-half long dark night of the soul experience was over.

How did I know? Well, not surprisingly, this revelation took the form of another prophetic encounter with a speaking God. A single mom in my church needed to talk about her latest problem. I arranged to meet her at a nearby restaurant. As she poured out her problems, I realized I had something to say, *precisely because of the experience I had been through for the past eighteen months.* Then, I heard God speak to my heart in that restaurant saying, "Gary, sometimes my shepherds have to experience things ahead of their flock so they can be prepared to guide them down that same path later on. And, by the way, you need to remember . . . you signed up for this!"

The bottom line is even though my dark night of the soul experience was literally a hellish experience, it ultimately proved to be profoundly formative in my own walk with Christ and ministry to others. When I finally began to heed the biblical exhortations that are elaborated upon in succeeding chapters, I stopped being outwitted by the evil one and experienced what it means to overcome him instead.

Some Additional Good News!

So, yes, speaking as one who's been through the valley of the *shadow* of death, I can affirm that because of Christ's wonderful faithfulness this standing firm business is possible. That's some really good news! And yet, there's more. Also possible, because of God's amazing grace, is a renewal of one's faithfulness before him after having succumbed for a season to the devil's devices!

Earlier in this introduction I referred to a growing number of freshman students who, having been deeply disappointed by life, arrive at my Foundations of Christian Life course already sporting a post-Christian perspective. I also mentioned how even the most spiritually jaded students indicate an eagerness to someday hear Jesus say to them "Well done, good and faithful servant!" Just today (at the time of this writing), I was grading some course journals submitted at the conclusion of a semester. One of my students appended to her journal a personal note addressed to her professor. Since it seems pertinent to this project, I'll share her message here. Her note read:

> Thank You!
>
> I would like to say thank you, Professor Tyra for an amazing theology course this past semester.
>
> I know that I have a long way to go in my spiritual growth and journey, but I can say with tons of confidence, that through engaging in every lecture from this past semester, I have gained so many new things: new skills, new points of views on social issues, new Christian friends, and most importantly a new level of Christian faith.
>
> I really do feel that over this course, I have healed my faith wounds and started moving in the path of building up my spirituality again. And I can't thank you enough for giving me the second chance to hear him say at the gates of heaven, "Well done, good and faithful servant."

This student gets it now: the possibility and importance of what Eugene Peterson referred to as "a long obedience in the same direction."[23] Moreover, she's proof of the fact that with the help of the word, Spirit, and people of God, demoralized disciples can have their faith in, and walk with, the risen Christ renewed. My read of the New Testament causes me to believe Satan absolutely hates when this happens!

It really can be done. Instead of being outwitted by Satan, we can overcome him, rendering to God the spiritual, moral, and missional faithfulness he desires and deserves. But, of course, this devil-defeating lifestyle won't cultivate itself. We must make the decision to stop ignoring the devil and take what the apostolic authors had to say about the dark side of discipleship seriously.

Yes, we can do this! Are you ready to begin? Let's get started!

Reflection/Discussion Questions:

1. To what degree do you think the leaders of local churches should be more intentional about providing members with some spiritual endurance training? Why or why not?

2. Keeping passages like James 4:6 and 1 Corinthians 10:12 in mind, how would you assess the current level of your spiritual, moral, and missional faithfulness before God?

3. Have you ever experienced something similar to what I refer to as my "dark night of the soul" experience? Are you there now? How's it going?

4. Do you know of anyone who might need to be reminded that, because of God's faithfulness, he or she can successfully rebound from a season of distracted, defeated discipleship?

5. What is God's Spirit calling for you to do right now to improve your own ability to stand firm in the faith?

---

23. Peterson, *Long Obedience*.

Part One

It's Never Just Us and God:
The Need to Take the Devil Seriously

1

The Devil's *Reality* and *Origin*
Avoiding the Mother of All Mistakes, Part 1

> Be alert and of sober mind. Your enemy the devil prowls around like a roaring lion looking for someone to devour.
>
> —1 PETER 5:8

Ever since Saddam Hussein claimed in 1991 that the Persian Gulf War would be the "mother of all battles," people have been using the "mother-of-all" idiom to refer to all kinds of things they consider to be "larger, better, worse, etc., than all other things of the same kind."[1] I'm using the phrase here to refer to a huge mistake that's constantly being made by way too many Christian church members and students. Simply put, the serious and recurring *faux pas* I have in mind is this: *the tendency of Christian disciples to keep forgetting to factor the reality of the evil one into whatever adverse circumstances they happen to be experiencing.*

The apostle Peter warned of this tendency in the verse that serves as the epigraph for this chapter. He called Christian disciples to be careful to remain ever mindful of the fact they do indeed have a spiritual adversary who needs to be taken seriously. Not heeding Peter's warning is a very serious mistake that, while extremely common, isn't necessary. Improving the ability of Christ's followers to avoid this mother of all mistakes is what the first section of this book is all about.

---

1. https://www.merriam-webster.com/dictionary/the%20mother%20of%20all.

To be more specific, the first two chapters of this work will provide readers with an overview of what the authors of the New Testament apparently believed to be true about some important matters relating to the devil and the demonic. This chapter will focus on how the apostolic authors understood the *reality* and *origin* of our spiritual adversaries (the devil and his minions). The emphasis in chapter 2 will be on what these authors had to say about their *nature*, as well as what their *deal* (or motivation) is. *The premise behind this two-pronged discussion is that acquiring such a fundamental understanding of the devil and the demonic is a crucial first step in a Christian disciple's endurance training.* How can it not be, given the apostle Peter's fervent warning?

And yet, it has become somewhat fashionable for contemporary scholars and bloggers to suggest that modern, enlightened folks need not take the notion of a personal devil seriously. One reason that's suggested is that a belief in the evil one's existence is irrational in the extreme. Another is, since the traditional Christian take on the devil is actually based on a source other than the Scriptures it can and should be ignored. As we'll soon see, there are ways of responding to both of these trendy arguments; ways that enable Christian church members and students to avoid making the mother of all mistakes, and to do justice to 1 Peter 5:8 instead. The first step in our spiritual endurance training begins now!

The Apostles and the Devil's *Reality*

One of the first and most striking things we discover as we peruse what the apostolic authors had to say about the devil is the categorical nature of their belief in his existence. Nowhere in the New Testament is there any indication any of its authors felt the need to engage in the type of demythologization that earmarks the work of some "modern" scholars.[2] For example, the German theologian Rudolf Bultmann, heavily influenced by the European Enlightenment, famously insisted, "We cannot use electric lights and radios and, in the event of illness, avail ourselves of modern medical and clinical means and at the same time believe in the spirit and wonder world of the New Testament."[3] However, the authors

---

2. In biblical scholarship, demythologization refers to the attempt to provide natural explanations for those things to which the Bible ascribes a supernatural explanation. See Boyd, *God at War*, 59.

3. See Bultmann, *New Testament and Mythology*, 4.

of the New Testament lived in a world that hadn't been impacted yet by the Enlightenment and the modern, anti-supernaturalistic worldview it would produce. So, instead of trying to explain away the notion of a personal devil, the Gospels, Acts, New Testament letters, and Apocalypse (book of Revelation) all portray Jesus and his apostles taking the reality of the evil one very seriously.

And yet, we shouldn't think the only reason for the apostolic authors' conviction regarding the devil's reality was due to their premodern historical context. The fact is not all contemporary scholars feel the need to dismiss the supernatural. For example, consider the work of Richard Gallagher, a board-certified psychiatrist and professor of clinical psychiatry at New York Medical College. A few years ago, Gallagher authored a controversial article in the *Washington Post* that was provocatively titled: "As a Psychiatrist, I Diagnose Mental Illness. Also, I Help Spot Demonic Possession." The article's subtitle is equally ironic: "How a Scientist Learned to Work with Exorcists." The gist of the piece is this: while this Yale-trained psychiatrist maintains demon possession is fairly rare in the United States, he's also convinced it does happen. He states: "Careful observation of the evidence presented to me in my career has led me to believe that certain extremely uncommon cases can be explained no other way."[4]

Gallagher is one of many thoughtful contemporary scholars and scientists who don't feel the need to deny the spiritual dimension of human existence.[5] The reason why? In Gallagher's case it's because he's had some firsthand experience with it! So did Jesus' apostles. Hence their strong conviction regarding the need for church members to reckon with the reality of the evil one![6]

---

4. Gallagher, "As a Psychiatrist," para. 5.

5. Indeed, there's a sense in which Gallagher is following in the footsteps of the noted psychiatrist/author M. Scott Peck. Peck first recounted his own experiences with the phenomena of human evil and demonic possession in his book, *People of the Lie: The Hope for Healing Evil*, and then followed up later with a more detailed account in his *Glimpses of the Devil: A Psychiatrist's Personal Accounts of Possession*. (See Peck, *People of the Lie*, and Peck, *Glimpses of the Devil*.) For more on why many contemporary thinkers in general have, due to the advent of the postmodern perspective, become more open to the notion that "reality is both physical and spiritual, visible and invisible, and that these two dimensions are two sides of the same coin" (Boyd, *God at War*, 61–63).

6. Of course, another reason why many contemporary thinkers have become open to the possibility of the demonic is the world's experience of it in recent history, especially in, though not limited to, the many documented atrocities perpetrated during

This strong apostolic conviction regarding the reality of the devil strikes me as significant. I've come to believe very deeply the Christian Scriptures are a reliable resource for understanding not only who God is and what he's about, but also the way the world works and how to best navigate our way through it. This is why, when discussing with church members and students the reason I personally take the devil seriously, I point out two important factors. First, the reality of the evil one makes the most sense of my personal experience as a human being, Christian disciple, and pastor to others. Second, I also explain my deeply held conviction that since some very spiritually savvy people, including Jesus himself, embraced the notion of personal evil, it only seems wise for me to do so also!

In sum, a biblically informed Christian discipleship can't help but take the devil seriously. One theologian put the matter this way:

> True Christianity is stuck with the Devil, like it or not.... The decision for or against the Devil is a decision for or against the integrity of Christianity as such. We simply cannot subtract the Devil, along with demons, angels, principalities, powers, and elemental spirits, without doing violence to the shape of the Christian faith, as transmitted by Scripture and tradition, our primary sources.[7]

As we continue in our survey, we'll discover just how true it is that both tradition and Scripture simply won't allow us to excise the devil and the demonic from our experience of Christian discipleship. It's because the New Testament takes Satan so very seriously that we should too.

The Apostles and the Devil's *Origin*

As for how the devil came to be, the conventional (traditional) view among Christians is Satan is a fallen angel who led a host of other angels to use their God-given free will in rebellion against their creator. Moreover, these fallen angels now serve as the devil's demonic minions.

Pertinent to our discussion, however, is the fact that some bloggers have suggested the source for this conventional view isn't so much the Bible, but rather the famous literary work, *Paradise Lost*, composed by

---

the Holocaust. See Boyd, *God at War*, 69–71.

7. Carl E. Braaten, as cited in Eddy and Beilby, "Introducing Spiritual Warfare," 21.

the seventeenth-century English poet, John Milton (1608–74).[8] Presented below is a brief summary of this epic poem:

> Paradise Lost is about Adam and Eve: how they came to be created and how they came to lose their place in the Garden of Eden, also called Paradise. It's the same story you find in the first pages of Genesis, expanded by Milton into a very long, detailed, narrative poem. It also includes the story of the origin of Satan. Originally, he was called Lucifer, an angel in heaven who led his followers in a war against God, and was ultimately sent with them to hell. Thirst for revenge led him to cause man's downfall by turning into a serpent and tempting Eve to eat the forbidden fruit.[9]

We must admit, this does sound familiar. That said, some important questions follow: First, *is it true, as some suggest, the conventional view of Satan is entirely based on Milton's poem, or is the poem actually an artistic embellishment of ideas presented in Scripture?* Second, *to what degree did the apostolic authors, long before Milton's time, hold to the idea that the devil was originally an angel who, having led other angels in a rebellion against God, fell from grace and became the evil one?* My task in the next few pages is to address these two questions without getting too deep into the weeds in the process. While this discussion may still strike some as somewhat technical, it's crucial, I believe, to an accurate appraisal of the apostolic understanding of how the devil and his minions came to be.

Old Testament Support for the Conventional View

I will acknowledge straightaway that the Old Testament support for the conventional view is inferential in nature. Though there is a passage in the book of Job that seems to associate the devil with God's angels (Job 1:6), nowhere in the rest of the Old Testament do we find an *explicit* reference to Satan as a fallen angel.[10]

---

8. For example, see Gonzalez, "Your Entire Idea." See also Chastain, "Fall of Satan."

9. Anonymous, "Paradise Lost," lines 1–8.

10. It should be noted that Gregory Boyd has suggested that Job 1:6–7 might indicate that the fall of *Satan* has already occurred. For one thing, says Boyd, the phrase "and Satan also came with them" suggests some irregularity in the event. Second, *Satan's* explanation of where he has come from might indicate that he's already gone "rogue," rather than attending to a specific angelic assignment. See Boyd, *God at War*, 146–47.

What we do, however, find in the Old Testament are a couple of prophetic passages in the books of Isaiah and Ezekiel that seem to *imply* such an origin for the devil. Both of these enigmatic passages can be construed as possessing a double meaning. On the one hand, they both pronounce God's judgment upon a human king. On the other hand, both seem to point to a parallel that exists between the disgrace-precipitating pride of the human king and that of an angelic being that has fallen from grace. Even a casual read of these passages will indicate why some scholars can't rule out the possibility these prophets were led by the Spirit to compare a couple of prideful human leaders to an angelic being whose prideful fall functions as an instructive archetype (or model).[11] In the book that bears his name, the prophet Isaiah articulates this "taunt against the king of Babylon":

> How you have fallen from heaven, morning star, son of the dawn! You have been cast down to the earth, you who once laid low the nations! You said in your heart, "I will ascend to the heavens; I will raise my throne above the stars of God; I will sit enthroned on the mount of assembly, on the utmost heights of Mount Zaphon. I will ascend above the tops of the clouds; I will make myself like the Most High." But you are brought down to the realm of the dead, to the depths of the pit. (Isa 14:12–15)

And then, in his prophecy, Ezekiel seems to be speaking both *to* and *past* the King of Tyre when he announces:

> You were the seal of perfection, full of wisdom and perfect in beauty. You were in Eden, the garden of God; every precious stone adorned you: carnelian, chrysolite and emerald, topaz, onyx and jasper, lapis lazuli, turquoise and beryl. Your settings and mountings were made of gold; on the day you were created they were prepared. You were anointed as a guardian cherub, for so I ordained you. You were on the holy mount of God; you walked among the fiery stones. You were blameless in your ways from the day you were created till wickedness was found in you. Through your widespread trade you were filled with violence, and you sinned. So I drove you in disgrace from the mount of God, and I expelled you, guardian cherub, from among the fiery stones. Your heart became proud on account of your beauty, and you corrupted your wisdom because of your splendor. So I threw you to the earth; I made a spectacle of you before kings. By your many sins and dishonest trade you have desecrated

---

11. For example, see Routledge, "'Evil Spirit,'" 11.

your sanctuaries. So I made a fire come out from you, and it consumed you, and I reduced you to ashes on the ground in the sight of all who were watching. All the nations who knew you are appalled at you; you have come to a horrible end and will be no more. (Ezek 28:12–19)

It's important to note three important themes that are present in both of these passages. First, a central issue in these prophetic passages is the phenomenon of pride and arrogance over against God—a pride and arrogance that precipitated a fall into a state of disgrace (see Prov 11:2; 16:8). Second, in both passages, the hubris of a human king seems to be described in language reflective of a primitive, original archetype. In the Ezekiel passage, this archetype is referred to as a "guardian cherub" or angel (Ezek 28:14) who was present in "Eden, the garden of God" (Ezek 28:13). In the Isaiah passage, the stated goal or ambition of the archetype to make himself "like the Most High" (Isa 14:14) is eerily reminiscent of Genesis 3:4, where we find the serpent tempting the first couple to essentially do the same. Third, in both of these passages it's implied the same type of volitional freedom (free will) the human king possessed was at work in the ancient archetype as well.

All things considered, it certainly seems like something akin to the idiom of *double entendre*, or the practice of double-coding (sending more than one message at a time), is at work in these two passages. The references to an obviously human king make it impossible to say these passages are all about how the devil came to be. But, at the same time, the presence in these passages of some highly symbolic, obviously metaphorical, essentially mystical rhetoric so evocative of the story of the fall presented in Genesis 3 preclude our thinking that they're all about the historical kings of Babylon and Tyre![12]

Still, as compelling as this inferential support might be, it remains true that nowhere in the Old Testament Scriptures is it explicitly stated the devil is a fallen angel who's also the leader of a cohort of fallen angels, all of whom used their God-given free will to rebel against their creator.

---

12. Gregory Boyd arrives at essentially the same conclusion, adding to the discussion the notion that both Isaiah and Ezekiel deliberately used language that would've been evocative of a well-known "Near Eastern cosmic battle motif." For more on this, see Boyd, *God at War*, 157–62. It should also be noted that this interpretation, minus the language of double entendre and double coding, was held by some of the early church fathers. For example, See Origen, as cited in Allison, *Historical Theology*, 302–3.

So, if the conventional view isn't explicitly taught in the Old Testament, where did it come from?

Extrabiblical Support for the Conventional View

Though our ultimate goal is to understand how the authors of the New Testament understood the origin of the devil and the demonic, we must first give some attention to a couple of apocryphal (noncanonical) books that not only address these matters but may have also influenced the way the apostolic authors spoke about them.[13]

The *Book of Enoch* is actually a multivolume work believed to have been written around 200 BC during what scholars refer to as the intertestamental era (the approximately four-hundred-year period between the close of the Old Testament and the beginning of the New Testament).[14] Obviously drawing on Genesis 6:1–8, the *Book of Enoch* speaks of the *fall* of 200 angels (referred to as "watchers") and the devastating effect this *fall* had on the world. Because of the foundational importance of the original Genesis 6 passage, let's first have a look at it:

> When human beings began to increase in number on the earth and daughters were born to them, the sons of God saw that the daughters of humans were beautiful, and they married any of them they chose. Then the LORD said, "My Spirit will not contend with humans forever, for they are mortal; their days will be a hundred and twenty years."
>
> The Nephilim were on the earth in those days—and also afterward—when the sons of God went to the daughters of humans and had children by them. They were the heroes of old, men of renown.
>
> The LORD saw how great the wickedness of the human race had become on the earth, and that every inclination of the thoughts of the human heart was only evil all the time. The LORD regretted that he had made human beings on the earth, and his heart was deeply troubled. So the LORD said, "I will wipe from the face of the earth the human race I have created—and with them the animals, the birds and the creatures that

---

13. The Apocrypha is a collection of documents that, while providing some helpful historical and cultural background for some of the beliefs and practices presented in the New Testament, most Protestant Christians consider to be less inspired than the sixty-six books that make up the biblical canon.

14. Elgvin, "Belial, Beliar, Devil, Satan," 154.

move along the ground—for I regret that I have made them. But Noah found favor in the eyes of the LORD. (Gen 6:1–8)

Now, in a nutshell, chapters 6 and 7 of *1 Enoch* purport to provide the backstory of this biblical passage. In the process, this ostensibly fuller version of the Genesis 6 story not only identifies the "sons of God" (referred to in Genesis 6:2, 4) as "angels," it also provides the reader with much more information about them. For instance, not only are we made aware these angels numbered 200; the names of their leader (Semjaza) and the "chiefs of tens" are also specified.

Moreover, *1 Enoch* takes pains to emphasize *how driven by lust* these angels (or "watchers") were to marry, cohabitate, and procreate with the "beautiful and comely daughters" of humans, and *how very rebellious* in the eyes of God (and his four archangels) the watchers themselves understood this action to be. While the Genesis passage refers to the offspring that resulted from these unions of angels and humans as "Nephilim" and "men of renown," *1 Enoch* describes them as literal giants whose lifestyles became oppressive to the entire ecosystem of the antediluvian (preflood) world. Indeed, chapters 8 and 9 of *1 Enoch* go on to make much more clear than does the Genesis 6 passage that it was the rebellious behavior of these evil, reprobate angels which led to the corruption of the human race and the flood that was designed to deal with it!

Then, in chapter 10 of the work, we find God's response to the rebellion of these insubordinate angels. According to this passage, Michael the archangel was sent to "bind Semjaza and his associates . . . in the valleys of the earth, till the day of their judgement and of their consummation, till the judgement that is for ever and ever is consummated."[15] Eventually, says this document, these fallen angels "shall be led off to the abyss of fire: and to the torment and the prison in which they shall be confined forever. And whosoever shall be condemned and destroyed will from thenceforth be bound together with them to the end of all generations."[16]

The apocryphal volume known as the *Book of Jubilees* (ca. 160–150 BC) also has something to say about the origin of the devil and his angels. However, while the story told here is obviously dependent on the story related in *1 Enoch*,[17] the *Jubilees* version varies a bit. In this account, the fallen angels are bound before the flood rather than afterward. Thus, the

---

15. Anonymous, *Book of Enoch*, 24.
16. Anonymous, *Book of Enoch*, 24.
17. Elgvin, "Belial, Beliar, Devil, Satan," 154.

evil spirits that afflicted the world after the flood are not the imprisoned fallen angels themselves but the spirits of their deceased offspring (the Nephilim or giants).[18] Eventually, God has his archangels bind and imprison these evil spirits (demons) as well. However, their leader, *Mastema* (which, when translated, means "destruction"; see Rev 9:11), asks for and receives permission to preside over one-tenth of these evil spirits so they can, ostensibly, function as accusers and executioners over against a sinful humanity (Jub. 10).[19] According to biblical background scholars Craig Evans and Stanley Porter, "Prince Mastema is a figure close to Satan of the NT [New Testament]. He is the leader of the demonic hosts; he rules the spirits of men and women and opposes God's plans for his people."[20]

In sum, what we have in the *Book of Enoch* and the *Book of Jubilees* are some very explicit accounts of the fall of some angelic creatures that unleashed much evil into the world. Moreover, both of these apocryphal works also indicate, in slightly varying ways, how this story of fallen angels explains something we see in the New Testament: the presence of evil spirits or demons in the world, who, under the command of a prince or chief, actively seek to oppose everything good and holy.[21]

There are several reasons why the stories presented in these two noncanonical documents composed during the intertestamental era are pertinent to our discussion. First, it must be kept in mind that, though the apocryphal accounts of *1 Enoch* and *Jubilees* are highly embellished versions of Genesis 6, their foundation is a story presented in Scripture.

Second, as has already been stated, we know the authors of the New Testament seem to have been familiar with both of these apocryphal works. Indeed, Jude 14-15 is pretty much a direct citation of 1 Enoch 1:9.[22] While it doesn't appear any of the apostolic authors directly quoted

---

18. Elgvin, "Belial, Beliar, Devil, Satan," 154.

19. Elgvin, "Belial, Beliar, Devil, Satan," 154. We should note that, though it's also used as a proper name, the Hebrew term śātān conveys the idea of "opponent," "adversary," "accuser," or "prosecutor," as passages such as Job 1:9; 2:4; 1 Chr 21:1; and Zech 3:1 demonstrate.

20. Elgvin, "Belial, Beliar, Devil, Satan," 154.

21. See 1 En. 15. See also Elgvin, "Belial, Beliar, Devil, Satan," 154; and Anonymous, "Watchers/Nephilim," para. 12.

22. Other indications of apostolic awareness of the *Book of Enoch* is John's references in the Apocalypse (Book of Revelation) to demons emerging from an "abyss" (Rev 9:1-2, 11; 11:7; 17:8; see also Luke 8:31), and Paul's apparently autobiographical reference in 2 Corinthians 12:2 to "a man in Christ who fourteen years ago was caught up to the third heaven." The latter seems to be owing to a discussion in 2 Enoch of

the material found in *Jubilees*, it's possible some New Testament passages might have been influenced by it.[23] Moreover, the fact some Christian authors writing just after the apostolic era were familiar with *Jubilees* would suggest the biblical authors were also.[24]

Third, and of even greater importance to our discussion, is the fact that the New Testament itself contains a number of passages which seem to echo what Isaiah 14:12–15, Ezekiel 28:12–19, Genesis 6:1–8, the *Book of Enoch*, and the *Book of Jubilees* have to say about the fall of Satan and a host of fallen angels. In other words, what we're about to discover is there's also some solid New Testament support for the conventional view—support that seems to build on the Old Testament and apocryphal writings we've just examined.

New Testament Passages that *Seem* to Refer to Fallen Angels

Presented below is a cursory inventory of some New Testament passages which seem to indicate the apostolic authors believed in the existence of some fallen angels, and considered it important to reference them from time to time in their writings.

- In Matthew 25:41, we find Jesus referring to "the devil and his angels":

  Then he will say to those on his left, 'Depart from me, you who are cursed, into the eternal fire prepared for the devil and his angels.' (Matt 25:41)

---

the "ten heavens" that the Enoch of the Bible (Gen 5:24) was escorted through by two angels. See 2 En. 1–22. See also, Anonymous, "2 Enoch," sec. 3, para. 1.

23. For example, it's at least possible that Paul's assertion in 1 Corinthians 10:20 that "the sacrifices of pagans are offered to demons, not to God" (1 Cor 10:20) may have been informed by two passages in the book of Jubilees (1:10; 22:17). As well, there's a story in Jubilees 11 of Mastema, the "prince" of the fallen angels, sending "ravens and birds to devour the seed which was sown in the land, in order to destroy the land, and rob the children of men of their labours. Before they could plough in the seed, the ravens picked (it) from the surface of the ground" (Jub. 11:11). One wonders if there's a relationship between this story and Jesus' reference to the evil one sending birds to gobble up the seed that represents the "message about the Kingdom" in his parable of the sower (see Matt 13:4, 19). Finally, the demons' plea in Luke 8:31 that Jesus not send them to the abyss might reflect an awareness of the story in Jubilees 10 where Mastema/Satan is given permission to preside over a tenth of the demons while the others "descend into the place of condemnation."

24. Charles, *Book of Jubilees*, lxxvii–lxxxvi.

- In Romans 8:38–39, we find the apostle Paul juxtaposing references to angels and demons as if the two types of spiritual beings share some sort of ontological status (state of being):

  For I am convinced that neither death nor life, neither angels nor demons, neither the present nor the future, nor any powers, neither height nor depth, nor anything else in all creation, will be able to separate us from the love of God that is in Christ Jesus our Lord. (Rom 8:38–39)

- Paul asserts in 1 Corinthians 6:3 that Christian disciples will judge angels (While it's possible the apostle had all angels in mind, it makes a bit more sense to think he was referring specifically here to fallen angels):

  Do you not know that we will judge angels? How much more the things of this life! (1 Cor 6:3)

- First Corinthians 11:10—one of the most provocative verses within one of the most provocative passages in the New Testament—contains an enigmatic reference to "angels" (As I explain in the accompanying footnote, I'm suggesting that, however we interpret this passage, Paul had fallen angels in mind):

  It is for this reason that a woman ought to have authority over her own head, because of the angels. (1 Cor 11:10)[25]

---

25. The larger context or discussion in which this reference to angels is found can lead to a couple of interpretations, both of which suggest Paul had the fallen angels described in the book of Enoch in view. First, Paul's desire may have been to simply encourage the women in the Corinthian assembly to, unlike the fallen angels, act with humility rather than pride before God and others. Second, the possibility exists that, when Paul asserted there's something unseemly about a woman appearing in public with her long hair showing, he was encouraging female church members to avoid scandalizing the male members of the congregation (i.e., tempting them to lust). In other words, keeping the angels (of Gen 6:1–2 and 1 En. 6:1–2) in mind, women church members should take care not to put a stumbling stone in the path of their brothers in Christ. Some support for this second interpretation is the fact that a theme running through virtually the entirety of 1 Corinthians is the need for church members, rather than being all about their own rights, to limit their freedom for the good of the other (e.g., 1 Cor 8:1–13; 10:23–33; see also Rom 15:1–2; Phil 2:4).

- Another verse in the Pauline corpus, 2 Corinthians 11:14, likens deceitful workers claiming apostolic status to Satan masquerading as an angel of light (I contend the irony Paul was pointing to in this verse was not that Satan masquerades as an angel, but that he poses as an angel of light):

    And no wonder, for Satan himself masquerades as an angel of light. (2 Cor 11:14)

- It shouldn't escape our notice that in 2 Corinthians 12:8 the apostle Paul famously referred to the thorn in his flesh as a "messenger" (Greek: *angelos*) of Satan:

    ... Therefore, in order to keep me from becoming conceited, I was given a thorn in my flesh, a messenger of Satan, to torment me. (2 Cor 12:8)

- In Ephesians 6:12, Paul explains the Christian disciple's real enemies include *spiritual forces of evil* in the *heavenly realms*:

    For our struggle is not against flesh and blood, but against the rulers, against the authorities, against the powers of this dark world and against the spiritual forces of evil in the heavenly realms. (Eph 6:12)[26]

- Many scholars are of the opinion it's almost certain the apostles Peter and Jude had the *Book of Enoch* in mind when they penned 1 Peter 3:18–20; 2 Peter 2:4; and Jude 6, all of which are cited below:

    For Christ also suffered once for sins, the righteous for the unrighteous, to bring you to God. He was put to death in the body but made alive in the Spirit. After being made alive, he went and made proclamation to the imprisoned spirits—to those who were disobedient long ago when God waited patiently in the days of Noah while the ark was being built.... (1 Pet 3:18–20)

---

26. Furthermore, the reference to "rulers" in this same verse comes from the Greek word *kosmokratoras*, which literally means "world rulers." Some scholars interpret Paul here as referring to "devilish forces, spirit-beings who control parts of the world system." See Huie, "Fallen Angels and Demons," para. 25.

> For if God did not spare angels when they sinned, but sent them to hell, putting them in chains of darkness to be held for judgment... (2 Pet 2:4)

> And the angels who did not keep their positions of authority but abandoned their proper dwelling—these he has kept in darkness, bound with everlasting chains for judgment on the great Day. (Jude 6)

- Finally, it's possible the "angel of the Abyss" mentioned in Revelation 9:11, refers to a dark angel (Satan or a demon) rather than one of God's ambassadors (cf. Rev 20:1; 1 Enoch 10:13)[27]:

  > They had as king over them the angel of the Abyss, whose name in Hebrew is Abaddon and in Greek is Apollyon (that is, Destroyer). (Rev 9:11)

New Testament Passages that *Definitely* Refer to Satan's Fall

We should also take note also of several of New Testament passages which refer, rather explicitly, to the conventional view regarding Satan's own origin.

- Luke 10:17–18 is an interesting passage which combines references to both demons and Satan, and, in the process, refers to Satan experiencing a fall (Moreover, somewhat intriguing is the fact Jesus refers to Satan's fall here as if it were ongoing. The message seems to be the success of the disciples in defeating demons is both suggestive of Satan's original fall and indicative of his ultimate doom.):

  > The seventy-two returned with joy and said, "Lord, even the demons submit to us in your name." He replied, "I saw Satan fall like lightning from heaven." (Luke 10:17–18)

- In 1 Timothy 3:6 the apostle Paul refers to the devil's fall as he discusses with Timothy the qualifications of those who may serve as overseers in the church (We find in this discussion an indication Paul believed it was the devil's conceit that caused him to "fall" under God's judgment.):

---

27. For example, see Boyd, *God at War*, 277.

He must not be a recent convert, or he may become conceited and fall under the same judgment as the devil. (1 Tim 3:6)[28]

- Then, in Revelation 12:7–9, we're presented with a passage which seems to make explicit what is implied in the rest of the Bible: that Satan leads a host of angels who, like him, have rebelled against God and, as a result, have experienced a dreadful fall (Furthermore, this passage is also significant in that it seems to suggest the serpent referred to in Genesis 3 is to be identified as Satan [see Rev 20:2; 2 Cor 11:3].[29] Thus, in this single New Testament passage we seem to find a confluence of themes presented in Genesis 3 and 6, Isaiah 14, and Ezekiel 28!):

> Then war broke out in heaven. Michael and his angels fought against the dragon, and the dragon and his angels fought back. But he was not strong enough, and they lost their place in heaven. The great dragon was hurled down—that ancient serpent called the devil, or Satan, who leads the whole world astray. He was hurled to the earth, and his angels with him. (Rev 12:7–9)

New Testament Passages that Refer to Satan as the "Prince of Demons"

In addition to those passages which refer to the devil's relationship to a host of fallen angels, we should be aware there's another set of verses, each of which alludes to Satan as the "prince of demons" (Matt 9:34; 12:24; Mark 3:22; Luke 11:15). Because of the way these Gospel passages parallel one another, I'll cite only one of them here:

> But when the Pharisees heard this, they said, "It is only by Beelzebul, the prince of demons, that this fellow drives out demons." (Matt 12:24)

The fact each of these parallel verses portrays Christ's antagonists accusing him of being in cahoots with Satan doesn't diminish the fact

---

28. With this thought in mind, we might also want to note how two other New Testament passages juxtapose calls to humility before God (and others) with reminders of the devil's reality: Jas 4:6–10 and 1 Pet 5:5–9.

29. We find a similar suggestion being made in Romans 16:20 when Paul writes: "The God of peace will soon crush Satan under your feet" (see Gen 3:15).

that all of them refer to a demonic prince—an important element of the conventional view.

What's more, the response of Jesus to his critics as reflected in Matthew 12:25-28 and Luke 11:17-26 has the effect of suggesting Jesus himself possessed something akin to what we're referring to as the conventional view of the devil and the demonic. Once again, due to the parallelism present in these passages, I'll cite only one of them here:

> Jesus knew their thoughts and said to them, "Every kingdom divided against itself will be ruined, and every city or household divided against itself will not stand. If Satan drives out Satan, he is divided against himself. How then can his kingdom stand? And if I drive out demons by Beelzebul, by whom do your people drive them out? So then, they will be your judges. But if it is by the Spirit of God that I drive out demons, then the kingdom of God has come upon you. (Matt 12:25-28)

OK, so what do all the New Testament passages we've just surveyed suggest? Taken together they seem to refute the assertion that the conventional view Christians have of the origin of the devil and the demonic is grounded solely (or even primarily) in Milton's poem *Paradise Lost*. Instead, we've found *there's some strong biblical support for the idea that the apostolic authors understood the devil to have originally been an angelic being who rebelled against God and took a host of other angelic beings with him.*

While this is, admittedly, a rudimentary understanding of how the authors of the New Testament viewed the devil's origin, it is significant nevertheless. As will become apparent in the chapter that follows, it can and should inform our understanding of how the apostolic authors viewed two other important topics: the devil's *nature* and his *deal*—i.e., what he's about.

Trendy or not, the idea that contemporary Christian disciples can simply discard the notion of the devil, or simply act as if he doesn't exist, is a huge mistake. It's my hope the material presented in this chapter and the next will enable Christian church members and students to recognize we can and must do better than that! It's never just us and God. Taking the devil seriously always has been and, until Jesus returns, will continue to be crucial to a vibrant, fruitful, enduring walk with Christ!

That said, I recognize how challenging any kind of endurance training can be. So, perhaps a word of encouragement is in order.

The feature film *What About Bob?* popularized the concept of "baby steps" in American culture. The movie shows a psychiatrist, Dr. Leo Marvin (portrayed by Richard Dreyfuss), encouraging a highly neurotic patient named Bob (Bill Murray) to focus on taking small incremental steps rather than stressing over the enormity of any endeavor. This is some very good advice I have often dispensed myself as a pastoral counselor and college professor.

But here's the thing: *no matter how it's conceived, the very first step in any challenging endeavor is going to seem daunting; all the more so if we have reason to believe there may be spiritual forces opposed to our taking it!* Frankly, I suspect that's the situation confronting us as we segue into the second section of our survey of what the New Testament seems to teach about some basic issues relating to the devil and the demonic. *The fact is the latter half of this discussion will be significantly more intense than the first.* But, my awareness of the "greaterness" of God (1 John 4:4), his promise of ultimate victory (Rom 16:20), and the tremendous degree of empowerment this initial step in our endurance training will provide, prompts me to offer readers another piece of well-known advice: *Keep calm and carry on!*

Reflection/Discussion Questions:

1. Some preachers have suggested the message of 1 Peter 5:8 is that there's nothing to worry about: the devil is merely a roaring lion without a bite. How might a careful consideration of the context of this passage affect the way we understand Peter's message?

2. How helpful to you was this chapter's discussion of the argument that modern, rational people need not worry about the notion of a real devil? What else, if anything, might be helpful in responding to this contention?

3. To what degree is it important to you that Jesus and his apostles obviously possessed a very firm belief in the reality of the devil and the danger he represents?

4. How convincing to you was this chapter's argument that the conventional view of the devil and the demonic possesses some strong biblical support after all?

5. Anticipating the discussion that will be presented in chapter 2, what do you think might be some implications of how the information shared in this chapter about the devil and his angels might inform our understanding of his nature and deal (i.e., what they are about)?

2

The Devil's *Nature* and *Deal*
Avoiding the Mother of All Mistakes, Part 2

> But I am afraid that just as Eve was deceived by the serpent's cunning, your minds may somehow be led astray from your sincere and pure devotion to Christ.
>
> —2 CORINTHIANS 11:3

According to the Bible verse cited above, the apostle Paul was genuinely concerned about the possibility of church members being drawn away from their devotion to Christ. Indeed, in another passage Paul lamented: "Some have in fact already turned away to follow Satan" (1 Tim 5:15). The message here is there's a real devil who, à la the serpent of Genesis 3, is eager to disrupt, if not destroy, the disciple's walk with Christ. Passages such as these beg the question we're addressing in this phase of our endurance training: *How did the authors of the New Testament, like Paul, understand who the devil is and what he's about?*

By way of review, in the previous chapter we surveyed what the apostolic authors apparently believed to be true about the *reality* and *origin* of the spiritual adversary the apostle Peter encouraged the readers of his letter to take very seriously. As its subtitle suggests, the focus of this chapter will be on what the New Testament seems to teach with respect to the *nature* of the devil, as well as what his *deal* is.

There's a sense in which that which we learned about the devil's origin in the previous chapter finds its payoff here. And yet, as important as this chapter's discussion of the devil and the demonic is, it's only a relatively "quick, sharp glance" I'll give these important topics. Let me explain why.

Because it seems to those who know me well I'm always at work on a publishing project, I'm often asked about the topic of my next book. To be completely honest, for the past few months I've been a bit reluctant to let people know my current literary endeavor focuses on what the New Testament has to say about the connection between spiritual warfare and a vibrant, fruitful, enduring Christian discipleship. More than once this acknowledgment has produced a quizzical look and then an awkward pause in the conversation. No one has ever actually asked me "Why would you want to write on that?" but I can tell some have wanted to!

However, recently (at the time of this writing) I was chatting with a much-published faculty colleague, Frank Macchia, who also happens to be a formidable expert on the theology of Karl Barth. After discussing his current writing project, Frank inquired as to how my "demonology," as he put it, was coming along. Perhaps sensing some reservation in my sharing, Frank reminded me of how Barth, after suggesting the topic of the demonic was best treated by means of a "quick, sharp glance," did go ahead and address it. I went away from this conversation with Frank as I often do, both encouraged and eager to learn more.

So, later that same day, I looked up the section in the *Church Dogmatics* where Barth treats the demonic. I was struck by the cautious manner in which the eminent Swiss theologian introduced what he obviously considered a necessary but dangerous discussion. Barth wrote:

> And now to conclude our consideration of the kingdom of heaven and the ambassadors of God we must take a brief look at a very different sphere.
>
> Why must our glance be brief? Because we have to do at this point with a sinister matter about which the Christian and the theologian must know but in which he must not linger or become too deeply engrossed, devoting too much attention to it. . . . Sinister matters may be very real, but they must not be contemplated too long or studied too precisely or adopted too intensely. It has never been good for anyone . . . to look too frequently or lengthily or seriously or systematically at demons. . . . It does not make the slightest impression on the demons if we do so, and there is the imminent danger that in so doing

we ourselves might become just a little or more than a little demonic. The very thing the demons are waiting for, especially in theology, is that we should find them dreadfully interesting and give them our serious and perhaps systematic attention. . . . It is not a question of treating them lightly, but of handling them as best befits their nature. *A quick, sharp glance is not only all that is necessary but all that is legitimate in their case.*[1]

I'll elaborate a bit below on what may have been behind Barth's belief the devil and the demonic only deserve a quick, sharp glance. At this point I simply want to make the observation that his counsel for church members and theologians to minimize rather than maximize the time they spend endeavoring to understand the evil one is especially relevant to the discussion that will be presented in this chapter. There's something about a focus on the nature and motive of the devil that takes us to a very dark place. Perhaps that explains why the apostles themselves seem to have treated these matters by means of a quick, sharp glance. I'm referring here to the fact that though there are several references to these topics in the apostolic writings, they are nearly always abrupt, curt, and somewhat oblique. Nowhere in the New Testament do we find a sustained, lengthy, systematic discussion of these two crucial aspects of the devil and the demonic.

That said, there are several very good reasons for us to continue our survey despite the cursory manner in which the New Testament treats these sinister matters. First, it should also be pointed out the way the authors of the New Testament addressed these devil-related issues *does* enable a basic understanding of what they believed to be true about them. And, second, it can be argued the reason why the apostolic authors could be somewhat unsystematic in the way they treated the evil one in their occasional writings was because they could presume, due to these topics having been discussed in church gatherings, their readers already possessed a fundamental understanding of them (see 2 Thess 2:5).

Unfortunately, this work can't presume such a familiarity. And, as a pastor and professor, I've witnessed firsthand the importance of a raised awareness on the part of Christian disciples regarding the matters we'll discuss in this chapter. Thus, we'll press ahead, fully convinced, with all due respect to Barth, we can't be guilty of giving the devil more than his due if we're only endeavoring to improve our understanding of *who* Jesus' apostles believed the devil to be, and *what* his deal is.

1. Barth, *Church Dogmatics* III/3:519 (emphasis added).

The Apostles and the Devil's *Nature*

A closer look at the discussion in *Church Dogmatics* which includes Barth's admonition that the devil deserves only a quick, sharp glance might help us understand a bit more about his concern. Despite the personal, realistic way the biblical authors speak of their origin, Barth insists the devil and the demonic actually derive from "the nothingness" (*das Nichtige*). In other words, the demonic doesn't actually share the same manner of being or existence (ontological status) as the angels, humans, and the rest of creation. Their "existence," so to speak, is made possible by God's creative work, but only indirectly so. The nothingness is the alternative to, or antithesis of, God's good creative work: what God didn't choose to create. Thus, instead of light, evil is darkness; instead of truth, evil is falsehood; instead of love, evil is hate; instead of life, evil is death; etc. And yet, because Barth didn't want to endorse a metaphysical dualism (the idea that all of reality is made up of two eternally equal and opposing forces), he had to admit that the devil and the demonic were created by God who, in his sovereignty, uses them for his purposes. Put simply, while Barth acknowledged the reality of the devil and the demonic, he didn't want to accord them equal status with the angels whom he viewed as the ambassadors of a good and holy God.[2]

But here's the problem, the biblical authors not only seemed to use personal and realistic language when referring to the devil, they ascribed some specific creaturely attributes and behaviors to him as well.[3] While the chief prefall characteristic of the devil, according to the conventional view, would have to be *pride* (e.g., Isa 14:12–15; Ezek 28:12–19; see also 1 Tim 3:6; Rev 13:4–6), the biblical writings suggest some other attributes of the devil can also be deduced. For instance, we've already seen how Isaiah 14:13–14 seems to provide implicit support for the idea that the

---

2. See Barth, *Church Dogmatics* III/3:519–31. It should be noted that Barth's attempt to deny evil any ontological status has met with some significant critique. For example, see the summary and evaluation of Barth's view presented in Warren, *Cleansing the Cosmos*, 62–65.

3. N. T. Wright seems to indicate a qualified support for a Barthian description of the devil when he asserts that "it is wrong to think of the satan as 'personal' in the same way that God or Jesus is 'personal'—which is not to say that the satan is a vague or nebulous force. Quite the reverse: I prefer to use the term 'subpersonal' or 'quasi-personal' as a way of refusing to accord the satan the full dignity of personhood while recognizing that the concentration of activity (its subtle schemes and devices) can and does strike us as very much like that which we associate with personhood" (Wright, *Evil and the Justice of God*, 111–12).

devil's pride was accompanied by a raging sense of *envy* and *selfish ambition*. In the New Testament's Letter of James we find a passage that seems to affirm this association:

> Who is wise and understanding among you? Let them show it by their good life, by deeds done in the humility that comes from wisdom. But if you harbor bitter envy and selfish ambition in your hearts, do not boast about it or deny the truth. Such "wisdom" does not come down from heaven but is earthly, unspiritual, demonic. For where you have envy and selfish ambition, there you find disorder and every evil practice. (Jas 3:13–16)

Going further, it should concern all of us that in 2 Corinthians 11:3 the apostle Paul refers to Satan as being quite *cunning*. The Greek word here, *panourgia*, connotes the idea the devil should be considered crafty, creative, adroit, subtle, tricky.[4] It's hard *not* to think of the devil in personal terms when he's described in such a manner. This observation reminds me of a famous quote by Mark Twain in which he too uses personal and realistic language of the devil. Hopefully, it was with an impish grin on his face that Twain, speaking of Satan, wrote:

> We may not pay him reverence, for that would be indiscreet, but we can at least respect his talents. A person who has, for untold centuries, maintained the imposing position of spiritual head of four-fifths of the human race, and political head of the whole of it, must be granted the possession of executive abilities of the loftiest order.[5]

All jesting aside, the fact is the New Testament portrays the devil as a scheming, cunning foe, someone to be taken very seriously lest we be outwitted by him (see 2 Cor 2:11). Indeed, even more distressing than his crafty nature is the fact Jesus himself ascribed to the devil not only an abject *dishonesty*, but also a *thirst for blood* (or *murderous heart*)! In what should be considered a key passage regarding the devil's nature, Jesus says about him:

---

4. According to biblical scholar Linda Belleville, "Eve's thorough deception is attributed to the serpent's cunning. The basic meaning of the noun *panourgia* is 'capable of all work' (*pan* + *ergon*). In the New Testament it refers to someone who uses his ability unscrupulously and resorts to trickery and slyness" (Belleville, *2 Corinthians*, 271).

5. Twain, *Mysterious Stranger*, 18.

> He was a murderer from the beginning, not holding to the truth, for there is no truth in him. When he lies, he speaks his native language, for he is a liar and the father of lies. (John 8:44)

Actually, this is only one of several passages which indicate the devil and the demonic are by nature both *anti-truth* (e.g., 2 Cor 11:14; 2 Tim 2:25–26; Rev 12:9; 20:3, 8, 10) and *anti-life* (e.g., 1 Pet 5:8; see also Rev 2:10; 12:3–4, 17; 13:4–10). Given the biblical support for this two-pronged understanding of the devil's nature, we could probably conclude our discussion of it here. However, I'll go on to point out the way the authors of the New Testament define the devil by what he's against (*anti*) is reminiscent of Barth's suggestion that Satan and his host have their very being in "the nothingness"—that which God personally is not and did not choose to bring into existence. This observation is too significant for us to ignore. Again, I'll have more to say about Barth's concept of *das Nichtige* (the nothingness) below. Right now the point is, regardless of whether we fully embrace his understanding of the devil's ontology (being), we haven't begun to fully understand the nature of the devil until we've reckoned with the possibility the reason why the devil is anti-truth and anti-life is because he is thoroughly and ultimately *anti-God*. Satan is the personification of evil, the antithesis of who God is and what he's about!

And yet, while this anti-God understanding of the devil's nature is technically correct and possesses much implicit biblical and theological support, I've found it's still a bit too general for my students to be able to wrap their heads around. So, I'm in the habit of going further to suggest the evil one's being anti-God means he is, by nature, radically antagonistic to everything God exudes (e.g., love, peace, and joy), and everything he values (e.g., justice, mercy, community, and *shalom*). Going further still, I tie this discussion together with this summary statement: The Bible as a whole seems to indicate that for the devil to be anti-God means he is *anti-human flourishing*. This is because, according to Genesis 1:26–31, the crowning achievement of God's creative work are those creatures that bear his very image. This theologically loaded passage reads:

> Then God said, "Let us make mankind in our image, in our likeness, so that they may rule over the fish in the sea and the birds in the sky, over the livestock and all the wild animals, and over all the creatures that move along the ground." So God created mankind in his own image, in the image of God he created them; male and female he created them. God blessed them and

said to them, "Be fruitful and increase in number; fill the earth and subdue it. Rule over the fish in the sea and the birds in the sky and over every living creature that moves on the ground." . . . God saw all that he had made, and it was very good. And there was evening, and there was morning—the sixth day. (Gen 1:26-28, 31)

Interestingly, there's a passage in the book of Job which seems to indicate God's angels witnessed the act of creation described in Genesis 1. This passage reads:

> Where were you when I laid the earth's foundation? Tell me, if you understand. Who marked off its dimensions? Surely you know! Who stretched a measuring line across it? On what were its footings set, or who laid its cornerstone—while the morning stars sang together and all the angels shouted for joy? (Job 38:4-7)

One line of thought is Satan, as one of the morning stars (angels), referred to in Job 38:7 (see also Isa 14:12), was envious of the special devotion God exhibited toward his human image-bearers upon their creation. Saint Cyprian of Carthage, an early (third-century) church father, said of Satan: "When he saw human beings made in the image of God, he broke forth into jealousy and malevolent envy. . . . How great an evil is that by which an angel fell!"[6] According to this reading, it's precisely because we human beings are so very important to God that the one whose very nature is to be anti-God, is supremely antagonistic to anything that bespeaks of, earmarks, or contributes to human flourishing!

The Apostles and the Devil's *Deal*

Now, if it's true the nature of the devil is to oppose God at absolutely every turn, we shouldn't be surprised to find passages in the New Testament which describe Satan as a usurper king who, having wrested authority over creation away from those to whom God originally gave it (Gen 1:26-28), is now doing the opposite of what God called his image-bearers to do. Instead of imaging the Creator to the creation in a caring, responsible manner, he's corrupting it instead. Moreover, if it's also accurate to say the evil one is stridently, incorrigibly against everything God is for—especially the flourishing of human beings—we should expect to

---

6. Cyprian, *Treatise* 10.4, 303.

find some passages in the New Testament that reflect his brutality against our species. Unfortunately, the two types of passages just described are precisely what we do find in the writings of the apostolic authors!

Satan's Deal Per the New Testament in General

In his book, *God at War*, Gregory Boyd surveys what the New Testament has to say about the role the devil plays in our world at present, as well as some of the specific activities he and his minions routinely engage in. To begin, Boyd explains that even though "Satan, demons and the hostile cosmic powers were understood in the New Testament to be in principle defeated through Christ's ministry, death and resurrection," this victory had not yet been "fully applied to the world at large." Thus, Boyd suggests, the New Testament understands the current age as an "in-between time," during which "Satan is still viewed as 'the god of this world' (2 Cor 4:4), 'the ruler of the power of the air' (Eph 2:2) who heads up a rebel kingdom (Rev 9:7–11) and still controls 'the whole world' (1 John 5:19)."[7]

Drilling down a bit deeper, Boyd draws attention to the fact the New Testament portrays this demonic kingdom "as being directly or indirectly behind much of the evil in the world."[8] Passages such as Romans 8:34–39 suggest "demonic powers can bring about 'hardship, or distress, or persecution, or famine, or nakedness, or peril, or sword (death).'" Moreover, after commenting on the way Paul described the thorn in his flesh as "a messenger of Satan," Boyd states, "[c]learly, for Paul, Satan is an ever-present reality ready to inflict physical suffering whenever able to do so."[9] Indeed, Boyd goes on to point out, "in the apocalyptic vision of Revelation, Satan is named 'Abaddon' and 'Apollyon' (Rev 9:11)—the 'destroyer'—who in the last days is permitted to head up a vicious attack of demonic forces (symbolized as locusts) upon the earth, using plagues, fire, 'natural' catastrophes and death as their weapons (Rev 9; 6:12–17)."[10] In sum, Boyd's overview confirms our suspicions regarding the devil's deal, affirming the New Testament does indeed emphasize the desire of the devil and the demonic to not only rule over, but also to hurt, torment, and even destroy human beings.

---

7. Boyd, *God at War*, 276.
8. Boyd, *God at War*, 277.
9. Boyd, *God at War*, 277.
10. Boyd, *God at War*, 277.

Satan's Deal Per a Few Passages in Particular

It's my contention that Boyd's observations regarding the devil's desire to tyrannize God's creation finds some support in several passages located in the Gospels. For example, in the exorcism story presented in Mark 5:1–20, we discover that the self-destructive behaviors which the legion of demons influenced their host to engage in tells us something very important about the demonic impulse writ large—i.e., what the devil and his demons are up to. *Under the influence of the demons who possessed him, the man in Mark 5 was slowly but surely killing himself.* He had alienated himself from any semblance of family or community. He didn't simply surround himself with symbols of death and destruction, his abode was literally among the dead. Finally, he was in the habit of cutting himself with sharp stones.[11] The poor guy was his own worst enemy: one bad decision after another. His self-sabotaging behaviors must have perplexed his family and friends and frightened the neighbors to no end. He was beyond human help. In reality, the demons were slow-playing him, killing him by degrees, and terrorizing everyone around him in the process. An all-too-common scenario has such a host actually killing himself, or acting so aggressively toward those around him that he precipitates a violent end at the hands of fellow humans. Sadly, it happens, and if Jesus hadn't intervened when he did, this story might have had just such an ending!

I'm suggesting, therefore, this biblical tale is paradigmatic, and one of the theological truths it communicates is that *the demonic impulse is ultimately about the destruction of the host.* The demise of the man in this story was taking a while, perhaps because humans bear the image of God and possess free will.[12] Worth noting is the fact when Jesus allows the same cadre of demons to invade a herd of pigs the hapless creatures immediately end themselves. It's hard to imagine more dramatic evidence of the anti-life aspect of the demonic impulse!

And yet, chapter 9 of Mark's Gospel comes close. Here we find another exorcism story which links demonic possession and the destruction of the host. A father had begged Jesus to cast a demon out of his son.

---

11. Some Old Testament passages that refer to this as a pagan practice include Deuteronomy 14:1 and 1 Kings 18:28.

12. See M. Scott Peck's discussion of the importance of free will to the possession and exorcism dynamics in Peck, *Glimpses of the Devil*, 125–26.

As the boy was brought to Jesus, he asked the father how long his son had been symptomatic. The father's reply is telling:

> "From childhood," he answered. "It has often thrown him into fire or water *to kill him*." (Mark 9:21–22)

Finally, it's true many biblical scholars are quick to dismiss the idea that Jesus had the devil in mind when he stated in John 10:10, "[t]he thief comes only to steal and kill and destroy." Still, my question is this: Why isn't it possible the same type of Spirit-prompted *double entendre* and double-coding some scholars believe is discernible in Isaiah 14 and Ezekiel 28 might also be at work in John 10?[13]

In sum, these three Gospel passages seem to indicate the demonic impulse is ultimately about the destruction of the host. I'll go further to suggest a reason why: afflicting, tormenting, and killing human beings is at the heart of the devil's deal because the prince and his minions know, very well, how much the death of those he desperately loves grieves the heart of God (see Ps 116:15; John 11:32–35).

Das Nichtige Revisited

What I'm hinting at is the viability of a nuanced version of the teaching that the devil's very essence has to do with "the nothingness" (*das Nichtige*). Such a suggestion calls for a closer look at this provocative proposal. The iconic theologian, Karl Barth, defined sin (or evil) as that which "God has not willed and does not will and will not will."[14] The essence of evil is to affirm, embrace, do, and be what God has said "no" to, rather than what God is into.

It's hard not to see in Scripture some support for this understanding of the devil's nature. Such an understanding has implications for the devil's deal. Once again, it's because he's anti-God that the evil one is also anti-life: resolutely, violently opposed to any sort of human flourishing,

---

13. For example, Craig Keener, correctly, I believe, argues that the larger context would seem to indicate Jesus probably had the religious authorities referred to in John 9 in mind when he referred to the thief in John 10 (See Keener, "Who Comes to Steal?," paras. 10–11). As someone who has written about the pronounced antagonism that existed between Jesus and the religious leaders of his day, I have no problem with Keener's exegesis. Again, my question is: Why isn't it possible that the text could've also been suggesting that behind the actions of the religious leaders was the evil one whom Jesus named as their father (see John 8:44)?

14. Barth, *Church Dogmatics* IV/1:409.

either in this age or the age to come.[15] If he had his way, every human being—every creature bearing the image of God, and cherished by him—would die a slow, horrible death while God in heaven watches, heartbroken. This is why many theologians insist the problem of evil in the world—whether it be those grotesque acts of human cruelty (moral evil), or those natural disasters and calamities that produce so much human misery (natural evil)—can't be adequately explained apart from an acknowledgment of what the Bible has to say about a personification of evil and its consistent opposition to the will of God.[16] For example, in a powerful book titled *Evil and the Justice of God*, biblical theologian N. T. Wright explains:

> The satan, it seems, is opposed not only to humankind, to Israel and to Jesus but to creation itself. It is constantly pressing to undo the project of God, the world which God said was very good (Genesis 1:31), when what that world needs—according to the biblical authors—is remaking. The height of satan's aim in other words, is death: the death of humans and the death of creation itself. The means that the satan has chosen to bring the world and humans to death is sin; and sin is the rebellion of humankind against the vocation to reflect God's image into the world, the refusal to worship God the Creator, and the replacement of that worship and that vocation with the worship of elements of the created order, and the loss of image-bearing humanness which inevitably results. Death is not an arbitrary punishment for sin; it is its necessary consequence, since the turning away from the living God which constitutes idolatry is the spiritual equivalent of a diver cutting off his own breathing

---

15. Jeffrey Burton Russell has referred to his belief "in the existence of a personal devil, a mighty being with intelligence and will whose energies are bent on creating human misery and death" (Russell, as cited in Arnold, *3 Crucial Questions*, 30–31). Likewise, N. T. Wright has suggested: "Evil is the force of anti-creation, anti-life, the force which opposes and seeks to deface and destroy God's good world of space, time and matter, and above all God's image-bearing human creatures" (Wright, *Evil and the Justice of God*, 89).

16. For example, see Bilezikian, *Christianity 101*, 39–40. For a book-length treatment of this thesis see Boyd, *Satan and the Problem of Evil*. Note: near the end of the publishing process of this work, an allegation of moral misconduct against Gilbert Bilezikian that was originally made years ago, became public. Though disturbing, the publishers and I made the decision not to excise from this book the several references to Bilezikian's scholarship it contains. Our prayers are for everyone concerned in the matter referred to above: that truth will win out and that all the principals will experience the spiritual and moral freedom that Christ's truth imparts (John 8:32).

tube. The biblical picture of the satan is thus of a non-human and non-divine quasi-personal force which seems bent on attacking and destroying creation in general and humankind in particular, and above all on thwarting God's project of remaking the world and human beings in and through Jesus Christ and the Holy Spirit.[17]

The last lines of this excerpt indicate how determined the devil is to sabotage the goal of God to fix the fall that has occurred to us humans and the world we were originally called to steward on God's behalf. A final discussion focuses our attention on how adept our cunning spiritual enemy is at getting human beings to self-sabotage—i.e., to develop the habit of cutting themselves with sharp stones, eventually destroying themselves in the process.

Satan and the Phenomenon of Self-Sabotage

Thank God, because of his sovereignty and protective mercy, the devil can't simply *devour* all human beings despite how much he'd like to (John 17:11, 15; 2 Thess 3:3; cf. 1 Pet 5:8). That failing, the devil does his best to antagonize God by afflicting and tormenting as many image-bearers as possible. In his book, *Walking with God through Pain and Suffering*, Tim Keller explains:

> Satan hates the good, and he hates God. And so his motives are completely evil. He enjoys inflicting pain and he wants to see people suffer. And he knows the heart of love God has for the human race, so he wants to defeat God's purpose to turn them into joy-filled worshippers of him. He wants to frustrate the great desire of God's heart.[18]

To be more specific, the oppressing activities of the devil play out in slightly different ways depending upon whether the person is a professing Christian or someone who has yet to come to Christ. Let's take a quick look at both scenarios.

---

17. Wright, *Evil and the Justice of God*, 109.
18. Keller, *Walking with God*, 273.

Satan, Self-Sabotage, and the Non-Christian

First, the apostolic authors clearly understood one of the devil's main goals is to keep as many people as possible in the dark with respect to the liberating power of the gospel of Jesus. The apostle Paul explained:

> And even if our gospel is veiled, it is veiled to those who are perishing. The god of this age has blinded the minds of unbelievers, so that they cannot see the light of the gospel that displays the glory of Christ, who is the image of God. (2 Cor 4:3–4)

I'll make the bold suggestion that one of the ways the evil one "blinds" people in such a way as to keep them from entering into a life-giving relationship with God is by deceiving them into thinking other pursuits will provide the type of soul-satisfaction we have reason to believe all humans are looking for.[19] In other words, both Keller and Wright have it right: Satan can and does seek to grieve the heart of God by encouraging his image-bearers to engage in various types of *idolatry*. The apostle explains that human beings break the heart of God in this way any time they exchange the truth of God for a lie, and worship and serve created things rather than the Creator (Rom 1:25). Moreover, in his Letter to the Ephesians, Paul pulls out all the stops and utters this bold exhortation:

> So I tell you this, and insist on it in the Lord, that you must no longer live as the Gentiles do, in the futility of their thinking. They are darkened in their understanding and separated from the life of God because of the ignorance that is in them due to the hardening of their hearts. Having lost all sensitivity, they have given themselves over to sensuality so as to indulge in every kind of impurity, with a continual lust for more. (Eph 4:17–19, NIV, 1984)

The references in Romans 1:26 to "shameful lusts" and in Ephesians 4:19 to a "continual lust for more" suggest to me that idolatry in the modern world doesn't have to involve a ceremony at a pagan shrine. No, the cunning of the devil in our age is to incite an idolatry that takes the form of a *driven lifestyle*: people questing voraciously for a soul-satisfying sensual experience of the transcendent but never quite getting there. Why? Precisely because they are foolishly seeking to find this connection with

---

19. Saint Augustine famously acknowledged this universal longing for a connection with God in this written prayer: "You stir man to take pleasure in praising you, because you have made us for yourself, and our heart is restless until it rests in you" (See Augustine of Hippo, *Confessions*, 3).

God in some aspect of the created world rather than the Creator himself. This thesis finds even more support in Titus 3:3, which reads: "At one time we too were foolish, disobedient, *deceived and enslaved by all kinds of passions and pleasures*. . . ."[20]

Put plainly, what I'm suggesting is perhaps the devil is ultimately behind the phenomenon of addictive lifestyles that become so all-consuming that the hearts of those driven by them are rendered virtually blind and deaf—stubbornly insensitive—to the life-giving message of the gospel. If this is true, then missional Christian disciples must understand something very important: some of their peers who have yet to come to Christ may never do so on the basis of presentations of the gospel message that aren't also empowered by the type of prayer and fasting Jesus once indicated are necessary when the demonic is involved (Mark 9:29). To be sure, I'm *not* saying all addicts are demon-possessed. But I am suggesting it may be that there's something spiritual as well as psychological at work in some people's addictive lifestyles. When this is the case, something other than the best intellectual argument or counseling technique will be necessary for any kind of deliverance to occur. People addicted to self-sabotaging behaviors (cutting themselves with sharp stones) need more than a good talking to!

Some support for this bold suggestion can be found in that fascinating letter sent by the famous psychiatrist, Carl Jung, to Bill W., one of the founders of Alcoholics Anonymous. In that letter Jung described an alcoholic client he had sent away to find help in a religious experience. Writing to Bill W. about this former client, Roland H., Jung explained: "His craving for alcohol was the equivalent, on a low level, of the spiritual thirst of our being for wholeness, expressed in medieval language: the union with God." He went on to make the following assertion: "An ordinary man, not protected by an action from above and isolated in society, cannot resist the power of evil, which is called very aptly the Devil." The way Jung concluded the letter is especially interesting. He explained to Bill W.: "You see, 'alcohol' in Latin is 'spiritus' and you use the same word

20. It should be noted that, commenting on Jude 6, an early church father, Clement of Alexandria, offered that the "everlasting chains" currently binding the original angels referred to in Genesis 6, who "did not keep their positions of authority but abandoned their proper dwelling," symbolizes the "loss of honor in which they had stood, and *the lust of feeble things*" (see Clement of Alexandria, as cited in Allison, *Historical Theology*, 302; emphasis added). Clement's reference to the "lust of feeble things" might be understood as an indication that it's the lustful, driven nature of demons themselves that motivates them to replicate this behavior in God's image-bearers.

for the highest religious experience as well as for the most depraving poison. The helpful formula therefore is: *spiritus contra spiritum*." A rough but contextually sensitive translation of what Jung meant by this Latin phrase might be: *It requires the Spirit to conquer the spirits*. Finally, Jung's postscript shouldn't go unnoticed. Under his signature he wrote: "'As the hart panteth after the water brooks, so panteth my soul after thee, O God' (Psalms 42:1)."[21]

Could it be that one of the ways the devil oppresses people is by enticing them into lifestyles of blinding addictions, and the first step toward genuine deliverance occurs when the afflicted person, with the help of Christ's Spirit, turns to God and surrenders the control of his or her life over to him? If so, we now know reaching them with the gospel will require some spiritual warfare as well as some training in apologetics and friendship evangelism.

Satan, Self-Sabotage, and the Almost Christian

I'm using the term "almost Christian" to refer to church members who, though they profess faith in Christ, are nevertheless not fully committed followers of him. In Revelation 3:14–18, we discover it's possible to be lukewarm in our devotion to Christ rather than devoted to him with the enduring fervency he expects:

> To the angel of the church in Laodicea write: These are the words of the Amen, the faithful and true witness, the ruler of God's creation. I know your deeds, that you are neither cold nor hot. I wish you were either one or the other! So, because you are lukewarm—neither hot nor cold—I am about to spit you out of my mouth. You say, 'I am rich; I have acquired wealth and do not need a thing.' But you do not realize that you are wretched, pitiful, poor, blind and naked. I counsel you to buy from me gold refined in the fire, so you can become rich; and white clothes to wear, so you can cover your shameful nakedness; and salve to put on your eyes, so you can see. (Rev 3:14–18)

This passage also suggests, since the condition of being spiritually lukewarm is something we church members might need to repent of, we are in some sense responsible for it. In other words, allowing ourselves to become lukewarm in our commitment to Christ is an act of

---

21. See Anonymous, "History of Alcoholics Anonymous," sec. 3, paras. 3, 5, 7, and 11.

self-sabotage. Moreover, the many references to the devil/Satan/serpent/dragon in the immediate context of this warning passage (Rev 2:9, 10, 13, 24; 3:9), and in the rest of Revelation as a whole (Rev 12:1–17; 20:2, 7, 10), strongly suggest the evil one is *ultimately* behind this truly tragic act of self-sabotage. In other words, it would seem when the devil doesn't succeed at blinding people to the gospel of Christ (see Matt 13:18–19), his next move is to entice them into such a lukewarm response to it that they either eventually fall away from it (see Matt 13:20–21; 2 Cor 11:3), or become so distracted in their discipleship that they never succeed at rendering to God the spiritual, moral, and missional faithfulness he desires and deserves (see Matt 13:22).

I alluded to the importance of these three forms of faithfulness (spiritual, moral, and missional) in the book's introduction. Here I'll go a step further and draw attention to the dynamic interconnectivity between this threefold faithfulness and the *discipleship fruitfulness* we have reason to believe God expects of us (see Matt 13:22–23; 21:33–44; John 15:1–8, 16; 1 Cor 3:9; Titus 3:14). Simply put, my contention is the discipleship fruitfulness the New Testament keeps referring to assumes a *missional faithfulness* on the part of Christian disciples, that is supported (rather than subverted) by a *moral faithfulness*, which in turn flows out of a foundational *spiritual faithfulness*.[22] At the risk of stating the obvious, I'll assert here that *the reason why the endurance training this work aims to provide is so crucial is precisely because a big part of the devil's deal is to make sure Christ's followers fail to cultivate a lifestyle earmarked by a faithfulness/fruitfulness before God!* Mark it down: if the devil can't keep us from coming to faith, or cause us to renounce our faith (more about this in chapter 4), he'll do the best he can to make sure our discipleship is as fruitless as possible. He doesn't want us to have the experience of hearing Jesus say to us, "Well done, good and faithful servant!" Neither does he want Jesus to experience the joy of rewarding us for having borne the fruit that derives from a long obedience to him in the same direction (Matt 25:21, 23; 2 Tim 4:7–8).

The chapters that make up part two of this book will provide an elaborate discussion of the various ways Satan attempts to subvert the ability of Christian church members and students to embody the kind of spiritual, moral, and missional faithfulness Christ modeled for his apprentices. Still, I'll briefly discuss here an example of one very subtle but

---

22. See Tyra, *Getting Real*, 61–118.

effective way the evil one goes about this nefarious task. In his excellent book, *The Life You've Always Wanted: Spiritual Disciplines for Ordinary People*, John Ortberg devotes a chapter to the practice of slowing, presenting it as an antidote to a spiritual malady many Americans suffer from. In brief, the "hurry sickness" is the mistaken belief that hurrying through our days will somehow afford us more time. The problem is that just the opposite nearly always occurs when we feel compelled to hurry: we end up making a mess of things or leaving some truly important things undone.

The reason why Ortberg's treatment of the hurry sickness is pertinent to our discussion is his suggestion there's something devilish, demonic at its core. He explains:

> Hurry is the great enemy of spiritual life in our day. Hurry can destroy our souls. Hurry can keep us from living well. As Carl Jung wrote, "Hurry is not of the devil; hurry is the devil."
>
> Again and again, as we pursue spiritual life, we must do battle with hurry. For many of us the great danger is not that we will renounce our faith. It is that we will become so distracted and rushed and preoccupied that we will settle for a mediocre version of it. We will just skim our lives instead of actually living them.[23]

The implication here is there's something insidious about the hurry sickness. It's a way the evil one can, with great cunning, corrupt our ability to live faithfully and fruitfully before God. He's fully aware two critical discipleship endowments are forfeited when we rush frenetically through our days: our capacity to experience the empowering presence of Christ in our lives; and our ability to love our neighbors as ourselves—to treat them the way they deserve to be treated as fellow image-bearers of God and those for whom Christ died. Ortberg pretty much bottom-lines his readers when he makes this insightful observation:

> Following Jesus cannot be done at a sprint. If we want to follow someone, we can't go faster than the one who is leading.
>
> We must ruthlessly eliminate hurry from our lives. This does not mean we will never be busy. Jesus often had much to do, but he never did it in a way that severed the life-giving connection between him and his Father. He never did it in a way that interfered with his ability to give love when love was called for. He observed a regular practice of withdrawing from

---

23. Ortberg, *Life You've Always Wanted*, 77.

> activity for the sake of solitude and prayer. Jesus was often busy, but never hurried.
>
> Hurry is not just a disordered schedule. Hurry is a disordered heart.[24]

In other words, giving in to the hurry sickness is a way the devil and the demonic succeed at causing people who *aren't* possessed by demons to, nevertheless, cut themselves with sharp stones. It's one of many self-sabotaging, self-destructive, discipleship-disrupting behaviors normal rank-and-file Christian church members and students engage in without realizing how they're being played.

Indeed, it's the insidious nature of the hurry sickness which convinces me the devil is ultimately behind it. Think of it: our churches are filled with congregants who are completely oblivious to the fact there's a drivenness to their existence that's significantly compromising their spiritual, moral, and missional faithfulness before God. I've come to believe this cluelessness on the part of some otherwise intelligent and spiritually sincere believers is a telltale sign the hurry sickness pandemic is due to the crafty work of the evil one.

If my suspicion is true, then there are two critical takeaways: first, we must awaken to the fact there's more than one way to cut ourselves with stones; and second, it's going to take more than our simply trying harder to overcome our self-sabotaging compulsions (like the one to hurry). We're going to need to master the four discipleship dynamics discussed in part two of this work, and the seven close-quarters combat tactics presented in part three. In other words, our endurance training must continue.

The premise of this chapter and the one preceding have been that acquiring a biblically informed sense of the devil's reality, origin, nature, and deal (what he's about) is an important first step toward becoming the kind of disciples who can overcome rather than be played by him. I've attempted in this chapter to heed the admonition of Karl Barth to avoid giving the devil and the demonic much more than a quick, sharp glance. At the same time, I've endeavored to raise the reader's awareness of some important aspects of *das Nichtige*—"the nothingness"—about which the New Testament authors had, ironically, more than a little to say.

In sum, we've discovered the devil is anti-life, anti-truth, anti-God by nature, and he's about grieving God by hurting the people he loves.

---

24. Ortberg, *Life You've Always Wanted*, 79.

Having succeeded at effecting the breach between God and his image-bearers that's described in Genesis 3, Satan's primary goal is to keep human beings from entering into, and then enduring in, a restored, intimate, interactive, life-story-shaping, fruit-bearing relationship with their creator. Sometimes he does this directly by blinding folks to the gospel. Other times he accomplishes his goal by surreptitiously distracting disciples, drawing them away from a solid spiritual faithfulness that in turn affects their ability to be morally and missionally faithful before God. It really does seem to be true: *we don't have to literally be demon-possessed to be in the habit of cutting ourselves with stones!*

The good news, however, is God is greater (1 John 4:4) and grace abounds (Rom 5:20)! I recently received an email from a former student. After saying some nice things about the course as a whole, she commented on one lecture in particular. She wrote:

> Your lesson on taking sin seriously really got to me and I realize I have not been. I feel extremely lukewarm in my faith and feel that I'm walking completely out of purpose with what God has for me, even though I don't know the exact plan. I do know however, that I have not been taking sin seriously and I was just asking for some prayer. I want to be a fully devoted follower of Christ but as of right now I feel completely lost and feel like I've messed up too much for God to even welcome me back, because He has showed me His grace after grace and I feel as if I mess up by sinning. If you could please just pray for my faith and my relationship with God. Thank you so much and I hope you have a great summer.

After praying for this young woman, I felt led to send her a reply that included these words of encouragement:

> Let me encourage you not to project onto God our human incapacity to act in grace. God is bigger and better than us. What makes God's grace so remarkable, so amazing, is the fact that it provides us with a never-ending supply of new beginnings in our relationship with him. That's how committed God is to being in relationship with you. Your concern should not be that God will give up on you, but that you will give up on yourself. Keep loving God and being radically, brutally honest with him. Keep asking the Holy Spirit to fill you and influence you. Slowly but surely, an ability and desire to say "yes" to God and "no" to sin will become strong in you. The process will often be one of "three steps forward, two steps back," but over time progress

will occur. Someday you'll hear Jesus say: "Well done, good and faithful servant!"

But that wasn't all. I then proceeded to provide this student with this important reminder:

> Also, don't forget that one of the main devices of the devil is discouragement. He's so good at getting into our heads and enticing us to give up on ourselves. Don't allow the evil one to have his way with you! OK?

This exchange illustrates an important truth: one of the biggest mistakes Christian students and church members make is to forget the fact it's never just us and God. There's a real devil at work behind the scenes, doing his best to hurt God by hurting the people he so magnificently loves. I've found simply being reminded of this spiritual reality can be incredibly empowering. It can produce within the most beleaguered believer a fresh sense of spiritual resolve!

Now that we've completed the first phase of our endurance training, my hope is we'll continue it together. As I wrote to my student: "Let's not allow the evil one to have his way with us! OK?"

Reflection/Discussion Questions:

1. Having completed this first step in your spiritual endurance training, to what degree do you feel more empowered to maintain a sincere and pure devotion to Christ?

2. Have you had any personal experiences with the evil one that might cause you to suggest some personal attributes not referred to in this chapter? Care to share? What biblical support do these additional attributes possess?

3. Have you had any personal experiences with the evil one that would support the idea that he's essentially anti-life, anti-truth, anti-God? Care to share?

4. To what degree do you wrestle with the "hurry sickness?" Are there any other ways in which you might be guilty of "cutting yourself with sharp stones?"

5. To what degree do you think it's important for Christians to remember it's never just us and God? How would you explain this concept to someone who has yet to read this book?

Part Two

Forewarned is Forearmed: How the Devil Seeks to Derail Christian Discipleship

3

Seduction

The Devil and Christian *Worship*

> Jesus said to him, "Away from me, Satan! For it is written: 'Worship the Lord your God, and serve him only.'"
>
> —MATTHEW 4:11

We've already taken note of the fact the apostle Paul considered it important for Christ's followers to be fully aware of the devil's various schemes (2 Cor 2:11). The thought I'll develop in this section of the book is that the way the apostolic authors referred to the evil one in their writings makes it apparent his devices or methods (Greek: *methodeía*) correspond to what I refer to as the cardinal components of Christian discipleship—*worship, nurture, community* and *mission. My contention is that a key to overcoming Satan, rather than being outwitted by him, is a proactive cultivation of a well-balanced, ongoing, and theologically real engagement in all four of these discipleship dynamics.* In other words, it's possible for Christian disciples to cultivate what I refer to as a *lifestyle spirituality*—an ongoing, day-by-day, hour-by-hour, even moment-by-moment, empowering communion with God the Father and Christ the Son by means of the Holy Spirit (see Col 3:1–17).[1]

---

1. For more on the notion that Christian discipleship/spirituality can and should involve a moment-by-moment mentoring relationship with the risen Christ by means of the Holy Spirit, see the entirety of Tyra, *Christ's Empowering Presence*, and Tyra,

I'll have more to say about the nature and importance of a lifestyle spirituality later on. For now, it's enough to observe that it's hard to overstate how opposed the evil one is to our succeeding in the four formational practices the next few chapters address. It's precisely by doing so that we cultivate the type of spirituality that makes possible a vibrant, fruitful, and enduring walk with Christ!

Let's begin our survey of the four cardinal components of the Christian life with a discussion of Christian worship. Every semester I encourage my Foundations of Christian Life students to meditate a bit on this powerful observation I ran across many years ago:

> Most middle-class Americans tend to worship their work, to work at their play and to play at their worship. As a result, their meanings and values are distorted, their relationships disintegrate faster than they can keep them in repair, and their lifestyles resemble a cast of characters in search of a plot.[2]

I'm convinced that this neglect of worship isn't simply a result of the press of culture—something our society models for us—but is actually the work of the evil one. Make no mistake, one of the main ways the devil seeks to derail the devotion of Christian disciples is by waging warfare on their experience of worship.

What Worship Is

At the risk of oversimplifying, worship occurs when human beings pause to honor and adore God for who he is, and to give thanks to him for our existence and other blessings he's already allowed to come our way or for blessings we hope to experience. One thing which the Hebrew word *shachah* and the Greek word *proskuneo* have in common is the idea of bowing low before God in humble submission and adoration, acknowledging both his lordship and "worthship." At the heart of worship, then, is a willingness to honor God as our Creator and the source of every goodness we've experienced in this life (Jas 1:16–18). The alternative is to credit ourselves for these blessings, to offer thanks or praise to someone or something else, or to simply chalk them up to chance. It's not because God is egocentric that we find so much encouragement in the Scriptures to worship him and him alone; it's because, as our Creator, he deserves

---

Getting Real, 61–80.

2. Dahl, *Work, Play and Worship*, 12.

this acknowledgment (i.e., it's the right thing to do), and because, as our sustainer, it's to our benefit to experience an ongoing communion with a life-giving, wisdom-imparting, sovereign God (Ps 36:9).

What *Theologically Real Worship* Is

As will soon become apparent, at the heart of my understanding of Christian discipleship is the dynamic of *theological realism*. This is a theme I consider so important to Christian discipleship that I've written about it elsewhere at some length.[3] Thus, I'll simply point out here that theological realism is the belief that the incarnation of Christ and the outpouring of the Holy Spirit make it possible for human beings to know and interact with God in ways that are real, phenomenal (immediate and evident to the senses), and existentially impactful (life-story-shaping). There is an empowering alternative to a Christianity that is *merely* conceptual, theoretical, or formalistic.[4] Perhaps a key phrase to keep in mind is "real presence." It's one thing to interact with the *idea of God*; it's another to interact with *God himself*.

Applied to worship, this means that we must recognize the tremendous difference between interacting with God himself during our worship experiences, as opposed to merely singing, speaking, gesturing, or acting toward the idea of God. What a difference a theologically real engagement in worship makes! It's the real presence of God that's empowering, liberating, transforming, etc. It's an embrace of, and commitment to, a theologically real worship of God that infuses this first cardinal component of the Christian life with a special degree of significance.

---

3. See Tyra, *Getting Real*, ix, x, 5n5, 24–25, 28, 28–29n32, 30, 32–33, 36, 53–54, 82n1, 87, 143, 154, 154n41, 155; Tyra, *Holy Spirit in Mission*, 33, 104, 112–13, 115, 121, 127, 164, 170; Tyra, *Missional Orthodoxy*, 15, 45n50, 66, 77n39, 85n67, 110–11, 118–23, 132, 137, 146, 157, 162, 164, 167, 169, 179, 206, 220–27, 238, 240, 279, 327, 354, 366; Tyra, *Pursuing Moral Faithfulness*, 19–23, 25, 28, 136, 150, 158, 167, 179, 183, 186, 188–89, 201–3, 206, 218, 230, 236, 247–48, 262, 271, 275, 284, 286, 294.

4. As I'm using the term, "formalism" is the prioritizing of external forms over inner meaning, essence, and purpose. In religion, it manifests as *obsessive* and *myopic* rule-keeping and ritual observance, which ends up functioning as a substitute for a Spirit-enabled, genuinely interactive, life-story-shaping relationship with God.

Why the Devil Assaults Our Experience of Worship

Just over two decades ago, when something known as the "praise and worship revolution" was hitting its stride,[5] Richard Foster, a prominent spiritual life author, made the following observation:

> Today God is calling his Church back to worship. This can be seen in high church circles where there is a renewed interest in intimacy with God. It can be seen in low church circles where there is a renewed interest in liturgy. It can be seen everywhere in between these two. It is as if God is saying, "I want the hearts of my people back!" And if we long to go where God is going and do what God is doing, we will move into deeper, more authentic worship.[6]

The Bible is filled with passages which speak of the critical importance of worship. For example, according to the apostle Paul, the refusal to worship the Creator, and to revere creation instead, is what brings God's wrath upon the pagan (those who engage in the worship of nature). In Romans 1 we read:

> The wrath of God is being revealed from heaven against all the godlessness and wickedness of people, who suppress the truth by their wickedness, since what may be known about God is plain to them, because God has made it plain to them. For since the creation of the world God's invisible qualities—his eternal power and divine nature—have been clearly seen, being understood from what has been made, so that people are without excuse. For although they knew God, they neither glorified him as God nor gave thanks to him, but their thinking became futile and their foolish hearts were darkened. Although they claimed to be wise, they became fools and exchanged the glory of the immortal God for images made to look like a mortal human being and birds and animals and reptiles. Therefore God gave them over in the sinful desires of their hearts to sexual impurity for the degrading of their bodies with one another. They exchanged the truth about God for a lie, and worshiped and served created things rather than the Creator—who is forever praised. Amen. (Rom 1:18–25)

---

5. See Eskridge, "'Praise and Worship' Revolution," lines 1–3.
6. Foster, *Celebration of Discipline*, 61.

On the other hand, according to passages like Psalm 50:23, true worship will result in an outpouring of grace upon those who offer sincere thanks to the true God:

> Those who sacrifice thank offerings honor me, and to the blameless [sincere] I will show my salvation. (Ps 50:23)

More specifically, sincere, theologically real worship carries with it the potential for an intimate, interactive, existentially impactful (life-story-shaping) encounter with the living God. For example, if the worship scene depicted in Isaiah 6:1–8 is any indication, such a worship encounter will not only result in personal moral transformation, but a robust commitment to engage in mission as well. It's precisely because of the impact our worship experience can have on our willingness and ability to render to God the spiritual, moral, and missional faithfulness he desires and deserves, that the devil is so committed to sabotaging our experience of it. Time and again, the Scriptures portray the evil one endeavoring to interfere with the intimacy between God and his people, doing his best to diminish, or sever entirely, the spiritual lifeline between the risen Christ and his followers.

How the Devil Wages War on Our Worship

Having defined worship as an intimate, spiritual encounter with God resulting from the act of humbly acknowledging his loving lordship and personal involvement in our lives, we can proceed to survey several ways the evil one tries to assault our worship. The several methods I'll discuss here fall into two broad categories: Satan's primary and secondary maneuvers.

Satan's Primary Worship-Wrecking Maneuver:
He Tries to *Seduce* Us

"Seduction" is a strong word. It's also an appropriate way of referring to Satan's chief ambition with respect to the worship life of human beings. The classic example of the devil interfering with the intimacy between God and his people is found in Genesis 3. Here we find Satan successfully seducing the "first Adam" (1 Cor 15:45a) and his wife Eve away from an intimate, trust-based relationship with their Creator:

> Now the serpent was more crafty than any of the wild animals the Lord God had made. He said to the woman, "Did God really say, 'You must not eat from any tree in the garden'?"
>
> The woman said to the serpent, "We may eat fruit from the trees in the garden, but God did say, 'You must not eat fruit from the tree that is in the middle of the garden, and you must not touch it, or you will die.'"
>
> "You will not certainly die," the serpent said to the woman. "For God knows that when you eat from it your eyes will be opened, and you will be like God, knowing good and evil."
>
> When the woman saw that the fruit of the tree was good for food and pleasing to the eye, and also desirable for gaining wisdom, she took some and ate it. She also gave some to her husband, who was with her, and he ate it. Then the eyes of both of them were opened, and they realized they were naked; so they sewed fig leaves together and made coverings for themselves.
>
> Then the man and his wife heard the sound of the Lord God as he was walking in the garden in the cool of the day, and they hid from the Lord God among the trees of the garden. But the Lord God called to the man, "Where are you?"
>
> He answered, "I heard you in the garden, and I was afraid because I was naked; so I hid."
>
> And he said, "Who told you that you were naked? Have you eaten from the tree that I commanded you not to eat from?"
>
> The man said, "The woman you put here with me—she gave me some fruit from the tree, and I ate it."
>
> Then the Lord God said to the woman, "What is this you have done?" The woman said, "The serpent deceived me, and I ate." (Gen 3:1–13)

It's important for us to pay some careful attention to how this archetypal act of spiritual seduction played out. There were really three temptations effected by the serpent. First, there was the temptation to *doubt the promise of God*. Satan, in the form of the serpent, suggested that God's promise that the man and woman would die if they ate of the tree in the middle of the garden was not to be believed. Second, though it was not overt, the story implies that there followed a temptation to *disobey the instruction of God*. One way or another, the serpent enticed them to go ahead and eat of the fruit God had warned them not to eat. Third, the rationale provided by the serpent suggests that inseparably connected to the temptation to disobey the instruction of God was and is the temptation to *defect from the service of God*. The tree in the middle of the garden represented the knowledge of good and evil (right and wrong). In other words, the tree represented spiritual and moral autonomy. According to Genesis 3:5, the serpent promised the first couple that if they ate of this tree's fruit they would become as gods themselves (knowing good and evil) rather than continue in a discipling relationship with their Creator. Thus, the temptation was, essentially, to declare their independence from someone the serpent portrayed as a manipulative, domineering God.[7]

The consequences were catastrophic. The intimacy between God and the first couple was lost, and the rest of Genesis 3 and the chapters which follow (Genesis 4–11) indicate how the sense of *shalom* (peace, well-being, wholeness) the first couple had previously enjoyed in their relationships with God, each other, themselves, and the rest of creation morphed into conflict and estrangement.[8]

What a tragic story! Even more tragic is the fact that it has been repeated many times over. The Old Testament is filled with accounts of people being successfully seduced away from a personal, trust-based relationship with God. Indeed, we see Satan attempting the same maneuver in the life of someone the New Testament refers to as the "last Adam"— Jesus Christ (1 Cor 15:45b).

The story of Jesus' wilderness warfare with the devil is related in the Gospels of Matthew, Mark, and Luke. Since I'll discuss this crucial event in the life of Jesus at length in chapter 6, all I'll do here is point out that one way of looking at the three temptations Satan put to the last Adam at the outset of his public ministry is to recognize them as identical to the ones he put to the original Adam. First, he tempted Jesus to *doubt the value of God's promise* to provide for him by enticing him to turn stones into bread (Matt 4:2–3; see Deut 8:3). Second, he tempted Jesus to *disobey the instruction of God* by enticing him to violate the biblical command not to put God to the test (Matt 4:5–7; see Deut 6:16). Third, he tempted Jesus to *defect from the service of God* by enticing him to worship someone other than God (Matt 4:8–9; see Deut 6:13).

As we've already discovered, this is the ultimate desire of the devil: to cause people to give up on God and worship something, anything else. Why? We need to keep in mind what Paul had to say about the sacrifices which pagans offer to their idols: the worship really does go somewhere; it's received by demons (1 Cor 10:20)!

---

7. See Lewis, *Mere Christianity*, 49.
8. See Lewis, *Mere Christianity*, 49.

Thank God, while this particular worship-wrecking device of the devil succeeded with respect to the "first Adam," it failed with respect to the "last Adam." It's for this reason that Jesus could proceed in his public ministry to wreak havoc upon Satan's kingdom (Acts 10:36–38; see also Matt 12:29), and eventually triumph over him through his sacrificial death on the cross (Col 2:15; see also Heb 2:14; 1 John 3:8). What's more, because of his resurrection, the risen Christ can and will help his followers (disciples) resist the seductive endeavors of the evil one in their own lives (Heb 2:17–18; 4:15–16). So, there are two questions we must rather routinely ask ourselves. The first is this: *How's the devil doing right now in his ongoing attempt to interfere with our experience of intimacy with God?* Make no mistake, he *will* tempt us to doubt the promises of God, to disobey the instruction of God, and to defect from the service of God. This is the devil's deal. He continues to be a seductive serpent enticing people away from a personal, trust-based relationship with God. This leads us to consider the second question we need to be continually asking ourselves: *Will we follow in the footsteps of the first Adam or the last?* Does this sound alarmist? Paranoid? Overly cautious or defensive? Perhaps this is a good time to be reminded of the warning penned by the apostle Peter:

> Be alert and of sober mind. Your enemy the devil prowls around like a roaring lion looking for someone to devour. Resist him, standing firm in the faith, because you know that the family of believers throughout the world is undergoing the same kind of sufferings. (1 Pet 5:8–9)

So, when we develop the righteous habit (Rom 6:18) of *routinely* asking ourselves the two questions presented above, we're not only being shrewd (rather than paranoid), we're engaging in spiritual warfare (see Matt 10:16)!

Satan's Secondary Worship-Wrecking Maneuvers: Secluding, Sidelining, Sidetracking, and Secularizing

Though Satan's greatest desire is to seduce people away from a felt-need to render to God a spiritual, moral, missional faithfulness, he doesn't simply give up on them if they persist in their profession of faith and worship activities. There are other means by which he can and will attempt to interfere with our experience of intimacy with God. *In other words, if the devil can't keep us from worshiping God altogether, he'll do what he can to diminish the degree to which we do so, and the effect it has upon us.* Unfortunately for us, he can be quite successful at this. Presented below is a concise survey of just some of his secondary tactics. I've found that by raising the awareness of church members to the various ways the devil seeks to diminish their worship, they become increasingly able to recognize them for what they are and empowered to push back against them.

He Tries to Seclude Us

With respect to the issue of frequency, another device the evil one will use against our engagement in worship is seclusion or isolation. In other words, he strives to separate us from the worship gathering.

On his way to be martyred in Rome, an early-second-century church leader, Ignatius of Antioch, wrote these words of warning and exhortation to the members of the Ephesian church:

> Take heed, then, often to come together to give thanks to God, and show forth his praise. For when ye come frequently together in the same place, the powers of Satan are destroyed, and his "fiery darts" urging to sin fall back ineffectual. For your concord and harmonious faith prove his destruction, and the torment of his assistants.[9]

While, ultimately, all worship should be personal (rather than impersonal), the New Testament encourages Christian disciples to be active participants in a worship community. In other words, biblical worship will be both *personal* and *corporate*. (While I'll have more to say about the importance of personal worship to the cultivation of a lifestyle spirituality later in this chapter, the focus of the next few pages will be on the phenomenon of corporate worship.)

With respect to the practice of corporate worship, it's amazing how many things can go wrong when we're trying to get ourselves (and our families) to a corporate worship gathering. Seriously, has it never seemed that your best effort at forging a consistent participation in the worship life of a community of believers was being fiercely resisted by spiritual forces nefarious in nature? While a desire to engage in corporate worship with the believers in Thessalonica wasn't the only item on the apostle Paul's ministry agenda, I'm not at all surprised to find him blaming the evil one for his inability to get to them. He explained his absence thusly:

9. Ignatius, "Epistle of Ignatius to the Ephesians," 55.

> But, brothers and sisters, when we were orphaned by being separated from you for a short time (in person, not in thought), out of our intense longing we made every effort to see you. For we wanted to come to you—certainly I, Paul, did, again and again—but Satan blocked our way. (1 Thess 2:17–18)

It's no wonder then that we find in the writing of Saint Ignatius the suggestion that corporate worship possesses some serious devil-defeating potential. As we will discover in chapter 5 of this work, Christian unity is anathema to the evil one. We need, therefore, to take seriously the notion that when rank-and-file church members succeed in forging the righteous habit of becoming active participants in the corporate worship life of a Christian community—celebrating, embodying, and strengthening the dynamic of Christian unity in the process—they are engaging in spiritual warfare! I'm absolutely convinced that the devil really does work hard at secluding us: keeping us isolated, insulated, segregated from the church gathered. I've seen the toll that an inconsistent participation in corporate worship can take on the ability of church members to maintain a vibrant, fruitful, and enduring walk with Christ. We simply must keep the connection between worship consistency and spiritual warfare in mind when we feel "tempted" to skip the corporate worship gathering for just any reason.

He Tries to Sideline Us

As previously indicated, the evil one not only endeavors to mitigate the frequency of our engagement in corporate worship, he aims to diminish its impact as well. One of the ways he does this is by attempting to *sideline* us so we become spectators rather than active participants during the worship gatherings we do attend.

It's not at all uncommon for churchgoers to approach a corporate worship event in much the same way they would a concert, comedy show, or theater production. All the action is on the stage (or platform) and performed by a select few folks who possess either a priestly status or various kinds of liturgical expertise: musical, dramatic, rhetorical, even comedic! The bulk of the church family makes up the audience whose role is to witness the spectacle. Hopefully, the members of the audience observe the onstage action in an attentive, prayerful, worshipful manner. Sadly, however, this isn't always the case. Indeed, a telltale sign church members have adopted a spectator mentality and the consumerist mindset it produces is they begin running all over town looking for the *perfect worship experience*. In his book, *The Screwtape Letters*—a fictional correspondence between a demon named Wormwood and his uncle/mentor Screwtape—C. S. Lewis has Screwtape instructing his nephew thusly: "Surely you know that if a man can't be cured of churchgoing, the next best thing is to send him all over the neighborhood looking for the church that 'suits' him until he becomes a taster or connoisseur of churches."[10] This exchange between Screwtape and Wormwood suggests the problem with our approaching worship with a spectator mentality is we almost inevitably tend to become picky, demanding, snooty evaluators of worship rather than humble doers of it. The exchange also suggests that behind the consumerist mindset that seems to earmark the worship expectation of growing numbers of contemporary Christians (church members as finicky consumers of religious goods and services) is the insidious influence of the evil one.

The good news is, of course, we can do better than this. Rather than remain bedeviled by a consumerist and spectator mentality, we can, with the help of the Holy Spirit, come back to the heart of worship. We can do our best, despite the either pageant- or concert-like milieu of the worship event, to make it personal—to participate in the singing, speaking, gesturing, and doing in a theologically real manner. Personally, I've found it helpful, in any kind of worship setting, to close my eyes and recite these words: "May my prayer be set before you like incense; may the lifting up of my hands be like the evening sacrifice" (Ps 141:1–2). Of course, I then have to actually do it: pray and lift my hands, offering God the incense/sacrifice inherent in my expressions of praise, adoration, and thanksgiving. When I do, I find it increases the likelihood I'll experience a genuine encounter with God. Oh, and it doesn't hurt that I've developed the habit of reminding myself, as I enter into worship in this personal, theologically real way, I'm also engaging in spiritual warfare.

He Tries to Sidetrack Us

To be clear, I'm not suggesting that experiencing worship merely as a spectator can't be *inspirational*. It most certainly can. But we must take seriously the possibility that a consistent worship experience that's less

---

10. Lewis, *Screwtape Letters*, 81.

than genuinely personal will, in the long run, fail to be *transformational*. And that's a big, big problem!

According to the apostle Paul, the Christian life isn't simply about having our sins managed so we can go to heaven someday. Neither is Christian worship about occasionally attending inspirational worship services in order to receive the kind of religio-emotional fix that's required for us to hang in there in the meantime. Instead, the Christian life is all about transformation—our becoming new creatures in Christ (2 Cor 5:17). And in genuine Christian worship, Jesus' disciples are enabled by the Spirit of Jesus to enter into the very presence of God and encounter his glory, with the result that, little by little, "we are being transformed into his image with ever increasing glory" (2 Cor 3:17-18). In other words, genuine Christian worship is about growing in godliness.

Obviously, the devil is going to be fervently opposed to the phenomenon of transformational worship. A truly sacred, encounter-producing, existentially impactful worship experience is his worst nightmare. This explains his eagerness to keep church members worshiping in a manner that's less than theologically real. As I've already indicated, one of the prime ways he accomplishes this is by encouraging us to sing, speak, and act toward the idea of God rather than God himself. He will also attempt to steer us toward a devotion to, or a preoccupation with, various religious rules and rituals that, if we're not careful, can function as *substitutes* for the real presence of God in our lives. In other words, it's possible for our worship to be sidetracked—to become something other than authentic. When this happens, it's the devil who's ultimately behind it.

In John 4 we read of a ministry conversation Jesus had one day with a Samaritan woman. Sensing there was something special about Jesus, and perhaps not altogether comfortable with this fact, the woman seems to have deliberately steered the conversation toward a controversial topic—the proper location for the worship of God:

> "Sir," the woman said, "I can see that you are a prophet. Our ancestors worshiped on this mountain, but you Jews claim that the place where we must worship is in Jerusalem." (John 4:19-20)

One of the significant features of Jesus' response to the woman's implied question is he seems to indicate that there is such a thing as authentic, God-honoring, God-pleasing worship:

> "Woman," Jesus replied, "believe me, a time is coming when you will worship the Father neither on this mountain nor in

> Jerusalem. You Samaritans worship what you do not know; we worship what we do know, for salvation is from the Jews. Yet a time is coming and has now come when the true worshipers will worship the Father in the Spirit and in truth, for they are the kind of worshipers the Father seeks. God is spirit, and his worshipers must worship in the Spirit and in truth." (John 4:21–24)

Though scholars quibble over the best way to interpret Jesus' clarification, I'm going to suggest, at the very least, Jesus seems to have been insisting an authentic worship of God must be spiritual in nature (rather than governed by its geographical location) and theologically real (rather than overly conceptual or formalistic).

There is, I believe, some biblical support for the idea that one of Satan's devices is to encourage Christian disciples to approach worship in an *overly* formalistic manner. For example, in 1 Timothy 4:2–3, Paul expresses a concern that his readers, rather than focusing on that which brings about a transformation into genuine godliness (see Titus 1:1), would become distracted by the teachings of those who insist that honoring God has to do with legalistic and ritualistic matters such as abstaining from marriage and avoiding certain foods. Paul prefaces this stated concern with this warning: "The Spirit clearly says that in later times some will abandon the faith and follow deceiving spirits and things taught by demons" (1 Tim 4:1).

Furthermore, the idea that Paul was concerned that Christian disciples not reduce the Christian life to rules and rituals is also indicated by a similar passage found in his Letter to the Colossians. In chapter 2 of that missive he wrote:

> Therefore do not let anyone judge you by what you eat or drink, or with regard to a religious festival, a New Moon celebration or a Sabbath day. These are a shadow of the things that were to come; the reality, however, is found in Christ. Do not let anyone who delights in false humility and the worship of angels disqualify you. Such a person also goes into great detail about what they have seen; they are puffed up with idle notions by their unspiritual mind. They have lost connection with the head, from whom the whole body, supported and held together by its ligaments and sinews, grows as God causes it to grow.
>
> Since you died with Christ to the elemental spiritual forces of this world, why, as though you still belonged to the world, do you submit to its rules: "Do not handle! Do not taste! Do not touch!"? These rules, which have to do with things that

are all destined to perish with use, are based on merely human commands and teachings. Such regulations indeed have an appearance of wisdom, with their self-imposed worship, their false humility and their harsh treatment of the body, but they lack any value in restraining sensual indulgence. (Col 2:16–23)

In his book, *Powers of Darkness: Principalities and Powers in Paul's Letters*, Clinton Arnold links the passage just cited with the warning Paul provided in 1 Timothy 4:1–3. He does this by asserting the "elemental forces" referred to in Colossians 2:20 are demonic in nature. They are part of the "dominion of darkness" referred to in Colossians 1:13, the "powers and authorities" referred to in Colossians 2:15, and the "principalities and powers" he specifically associates with Satan in Ephesians 6:10–12.[11] So, we have good reason to believe if Satan can't keep people from worshiping God altogether, he will at least try to pervert its focus so its effect is something other than *an authentic spiritual encounter that leads to genuine life transformation*. Trite or not, it needs to be said: there's a significant difference between a real relationship with God and a religion that focuses *solely* on religious rules and rituals. Certainly, the Holy Spirit can be experienced through a theologically real engagement in liturgical worship.[12] That said, it's also true that our being careful to avoid being sidetracked by the devil toward an unbiblical devotion to, preoccupation with, and dependency upon religious rule- and tradition-keeping is important to the experience of transformational worship. It's also spiritual warfare.

He Tries to Secularize Us

To secularize something is the opposite of making it sacred. The secular has to do with the temporal and mundane, with the here-and-now of this world as opposed to the spiritual dimension that extends into eternity. Thus, yet another way the enemy attempts to interfere with our intimacy with God is by secularizing our experience of worship. Our expectations are dramatically lowered: instead of real, transformative encounters with God that result in growth toward godliness, we settle for much less—an

---

11. Arnold, *Powers of Darkness*, 111, 115, 132.

12. Advocating for what I would refer to as a theologically real approach to liturgical worship, Paul Anderson writes: "The issue is not structure or freedom, but Spirit. God has no preference for formless spiritualism or Spiritless formalism—he rejects both" (Anderson, "Balancing Form and Freedom," para. 3.)

emotional high that leaves the spiritual, moral, and missional dimensions of our lives unaffected.

In my book, *Getting Real: Pneumatological Realism and the Spiritual, Moral, and Ministry Formation of Contemporary Christians*, I share a story which pastor and author Jim Wilson included in his book *Future Church: Ministry in a Post-Seeker Age*. Because of its pertinence to this discussion, I'll share the same story here. It goes like this:

> Sitting in a window seat, Roger Williams III was looking forward to thumbing through a magazine on a short flight from Sacramento to attend a national youth ministry conference in San Diego. He'd fastened his seatbelt, made sure his chair was in the full upright position, his tray table locked, and his luggage properly stowed, when two well-dressed Ally McBeal look-alikes sat down next to him.
>
> Their conversation competed for attention with his magazine. They talked about the club scene—what they enjoyed drinking, who they were dating, their intimate relationships with men, both single and married. Then it turned into a gripe session.
>
> Why do guys have such a hard time committing?" one asked. "And why don't they ever leave their wives like they promise to?" another complained. They talked about work for a while, and about the time Williams was tuning out, one of them said, "But you know, if it wasn't for church, my life would really be hell."
>
> By now Williams was only pretending to read his magazine. They had his full attention.
>
> "Wow, you go to church too. I know exactly how you feel. If it wasn't for church, I don't know where I'd be."
>
> "Yeah, I know what you mean," the other woman said. "If I miss more than two weeks of church, everything in my life goes nuts."
>
> The plane started its descent into San Diego, and everything got quiet. Williams sat still—stunned by what he'd just heard. These women weren't genuine seekers—people looking for the truth. Instead they were going to church to get their religious fix.[13]

I go on in *Getting Real* to clarify that Wilson's concern goes beyond the consumerist mindset with which some "seekers" approach worship. Ultimately, he lays the blame for this secularization of worship on the

---

13. Wilson, as cited in Tyra, *Getting Real*, 48–49.

churches themselves. At what point, if ever, do the "seekers" attending our churches become aware the invitation to them is not simply to obtain an occasional "religious fix," but to become part of a genuine Christian community that will enable them to experience spiritual and moral transformation into men and women of God? According to Wilson:

> These women on the plane didn't need a sermon on five steps to success. They didn't need a Band-Aid. They needed transformation. They were getting a faith inoculation when they needed an antidote for sin. They needed a church that would confront them, not accommodate them. They needed a church that would get past their felt needs and speak to their greatest need, to confess their sin and turn to Christ.[14]

I'm going to add here that something else these women needed was a church that would help them approach worship with a sense of "holy expectancy." We really can't blame churchgoers for attending worship gatherings with a secularized, overly therapeutic understanding of the nature of worship in place if pastors and worship leaders aren't effectively communicating to them that so much more can and should be expected.

Though he doesn't use the terms, Richard Foster describes the phenomenon of "theologically real worship" or "worship as encounter" when he writes:

> A striking feature of worship in the Bible is that people gathered in what we could only call a "holy expectancy." They believed they would actually hear the *Kol Yahweh*, the voice of God. When Moses went into the Tabernacle, he knew he was entering the presence of God. The same was true of the early Church. It was not surprising to them that the building in which they met shook with the power of God. It had happened before (Acts 2:2, 4:31). When some dropped dead and others were raised from the dead by the word of the Lord, the people knew that God was in their midst (Acts 5:1–11, 9:36–43, 20:7–10). As those early believers gathered they were keenly aware that the veil had been ripped in two, and, like Moses and Aaron, they were entering the Holy of Holies. No intermediaries were needed. They were coming into the awful, glorious, gracious presence of the living God. They gathered with anticipation, knowing that Christ was present among them and would teach them and touch them with his living power. . . . When more than one or two come into public worship with a holy expectancy, it can change the atmosphere

---

14. Wilson, as cited in Tyra, *Getting Real*, 49.

of a room. People who enter harried and distracted are drawn quickly into a sense of the silent Presence. Hearts and minds are lifted upward. The air becomes charged with expectancy.[15]

My suggested takeaway from this discussion is two-pronged. First, pastors and worship leaders must do a better job of promoting among those attending their worship gatherings a sense of "holy expectancy." Second, it's the responsibility of every Christian disciple not to allow ourselves to be so secularized by the world, the flesh, and the devil that we attend worship gatherings with a mindset that's closed rather than open to the possibility of a very real, life-story-shaping encounter with the risen Christ.

The story of the apostle John at the empty tomb of Jesus on Easter morning (see John 20:1–10) powerfully illustrates how a changed perspective can lead to a deepened spiritual experience. According to this passage, though John outran Peter to the tomb, he lingered at its entrance. When Peter arrived at the tomb a few moments later he burst right into it. Perhaps John was reluctant to enter in because of traditional rules about contact with dead bodies (see Num 19:11–22). Or maybe his reticence was simply due to an understandable fear of the unknown. Regardless, as long as John stood at the entrance to the tomb, merely peering into the dark interior, it appears he assumed someone had stolen the body of Jesus. The linen wrappings lying in disarray on the floor mandated no other explanation. According to the Fourth Gospel, it was not until John pressed in, actually entering the tomb, that he saw the head cloth "folded by itself, separate from the linen" and encountered that which produced within him the seeds of what would become resurrection faith.

Likewise, you and I need to get *beyond the linen wrappings* (so to speak) if we are to truly experience the supernatural in our worship. As long as we, for whatever reason, stand at a distance, merely looking on, we will miss the opportunity for encounter that exists whenever two or three gather together in Christ's name. Every time we engage in worship we need to remember the need to *press in*, to overcome our fear of the unknown, and dare to draw near with a sense of holy expectation in place. It's this type of worship that leads to existentially impactful (life-story-shaping) encounters with the risen Christ. It's this type of worship that constitutes an important but often overlooked dimension of spiritual warfare.

---

15. Foster, *Celebration of Discipline*, 161–63.

Excursus: A Lifestyle Spirituality and the Role of Worship in It

Before I conclude this first chapter of the second section of the book, I want to drill down a bit more deeply into the notion of a lifestyle spirituality. Since I believe such a spirituality is critical to a vibrant, fruitful, and enduring walk with Christ, I consider it imperative we understand what it is and how it works. What's more, this sidebar discussion will also indicate why the theologically real, encounter-oriented type of worship we've discussed in this chapter is at the heart of a Christian spirituality that's devil-defeating in effect.

Behind the concept of a *lifestyle* spirituality is the realization that our engagement in the spiritual disciplines Jesus himself practiced and promoted can, with the help of the Holy Spirit, allow Christ to be formed in us in such a way that the entirety of our lives is impacted. Furthermore, such a spirituality can and should be something we pursue perpetually rather than occasionally after becoming fully devoted followers (apprentices) of Jesus. As it happens, the act of worship is at the very center of such a pervasive, highly impactful spirituality. Though this chapter has focused mainly on the practice of *corporate* worship, I want to emphasize here the huge significance of an ongoing engagement in *personal* worship to a Christian life well lived.

In a work titled *Christ's Empowering Presence: The Pursuit of God through the Ages*, I not only draw attention to the *theology of presence* that's presented in the Old and New Testaments, I also interact with the writings of many spiritual masters in the Christian tradition, from the desert fathers to the contemporary era. These discussions suggest the various spiritual disciplines referred to in Scripture and by various spiritual masters (e.g., prayer, fasting, study, worship, service, solitude, silence, celebration, etc.), can, when engaged in for the right reasons and in the right way (see Matt 6:1–18), have the effect of bringing us face to face, so to speak, with the real presence of God via the risen Jesus.[16] In other words, it's my contention that at the heart of Christian spirituality is the perpetual "pursuit" of Christ's empowering presence, and that the payoff of this "pursuit" will be an ongoing, moment-by-moment, mentoring relationship with him. Though I didn't make use of the term "lifestyle spirituality" when writing *Christ's Empowering Presence*, I've come to believe this is precisely what the "pursuit" constitutes.

16. For more on this see Tyra, *Defeating Pharisaism*, 151–60.

The significance of this for our current discussion derives from the fact that, given the emphasis on the real *presence* of God in this understanding of spirituality, the spiritual discipline of worship is especially critical to it. Therefore, a *personal* and *theologically real* experience of worship is fundamental to the God-honoring, Christ-centered, Spirit-empowered *lifestyle spirituality* I believe to be crucial to overcoming the evil one!

While I don't want this discussion to become too technical in the process, I'll point out here that some serious support for my contention that a theologically real worship of God is integral to a lifestyle spirituality can be adduced from the writings of the spiritual masters alluded to above. For example, the two passages below were penned by a seventeenth-century French monk, Nicholas Herman (better known as Brother Lawrence of the Resurrection), author of the spiritual classic, *The Practice of the Presence of God*. In these passages he argues for the propriety of pausing periodically throughout each day in order to interact with God. These passages remind me of Romans 12:1-2 where we're encouraged by the apostle Paul to render to God the worship he deserves. The good brother writes:

> Since you cannot but know that God is with you in all you undertake, that He is at the very depth and centre of your soul, why should you not thus pause an instant from time to time in your outward business, and even in the act of prayer, to worship Him within your soul, to praise Him, to entreat His aid, to offer Him the service of your heart, and give Him thanks for all His loving-kindnesses and tender-mercies?
>
> What offering is there more acceptable to God than thus throughout the day to quit the things of outward sense, and to withdraw to worship Him within the secret places of the soul?[17]
>
> In very truth we can render to God no greater or more signal proofs of our trust and faithfulness, than by thus turning from things created to find our joy, though for a single moment, in the Creator.[18]

About the same time Brother Lawrence was writing *The Practice of the Presence of God*, an Anglican churchman named Jeremy Taylor was composing a work titled *The Rule and Exercises of Holy Living*, which

---

17. Herman, *Practice of the Presence of God*, 71–72.
18. Herman, *Practice of the Presence of God*, 72.

contains a section titled "The Practice of the Presence of God." In a couple of passages from this section, Taylor emphasizes the connection between worship and the experience of God's presence. For example, in one passage Taylor suggests as we begin our quiet times we should spend a few moments in worship: picturing God with the eyes of faith; rehearsing the reasons why he is worthy of our time, attention, and praise; imagining ourselves in his very presence. According to Taylor, this simple act of connecting with God in a theologically real way will have a tremendously positive effect upon our devotional exercises. He writes:

> In the beginning of actions of religion, make an act of adoration, that is, solemnly worship God, and place thyself in God's presence, and behold Him with the eye of faith; and let thy desires actually fix on Him as the object of thy worship, and the reason of thy hope, and the fountain of thy blessing. For when thou hast placed thyself before Him and kneelest in His presence, it is most likely all the following parts of thy devotion will be answerable to the wisdom of such an apprehension, and the glory of such a presence.[19]

But it's not just during our quiet times that we should focus on God's presence. Taylor goes on to indicate this should be happening throughout the day. Though Taylor's style of speech is archaic, his tone stern, and his focus on the fear of God, what he ends up saying is true: remaining mindful of God's holy presence throughout the day will empower us to say "yes" to God and "no" to sin. Says Taylor:

> Let this actual thought often return, that God is omnipresent, filling every place; and say with David, "Whither shall I go from Thy spirit, or whither shall I flee from Thy presence? If I ascend up into heaven, Thou art there..." (Psalm 139:7, 8). This thought by being frequent will make an habitual dread and reverence towards God, and fear, in all actions. For it is a great necessity and engagement to do unblameably when we act before the Judge who is infallible in His sentence, all-knowing in His information, severe in His anger, powerful in His providence, and intolerable in His wrath and indignation.[20]

Yet another sixteenth-/seventeenth-century spiritual life master, a spiritual director named Francis de Sales, offered his readers four

---

19. Herman, *Practice of the Presence of God*, 62–63.
20. Taylor, "Holy Living," 62.

methods by which they might "place themselves in God's presence." Paraphrased, these methods are:

1. reflect upon the fact that God is everywhere around you;
2. reflect upon the fact that God lives in your heart, your spirit;
3. reflect upon the fact that Christ, who sits at the right hand of God in heaven, is constantly watching over his people; and
4. use your imagination when in prayer or worship, picturing Christ being right next to you.[21]

Remember, what we're focusing on here is the way in which some of the church's spiritual masters have connected a perpetual awareness of the presence of God with worship, and the role this theologically real worship plays in what I'm referring to as a lifestyle spirituality. Toward that end, I'll also refer here to the work of some contemporary spiritual life authors. For instance, Thomas Kelly, a twentieth-century Quaker missionary, scholar, and teacher, included the following passage in this work, *A Testament of Devotion:*

> There is a way of ordering our mental life on more than one level at once. On one level we may be thinking, discussing, seeing, calculating, meeting all the demands of external affairs. But deep within, behind the scenes, at a profounder level, we may also be in prayer and adoration, song and worship and a gentle receptiveness to divine breathings.[22]

One of my favorite passages of this type comes from the work of a gifted friend, Jan Johnson. I met Jan in the summer of 2002 at a Fuller Seminary Doctor of Ministry course taught by the late Dallas Willard. Jan connects all the dots in a powerful way when she writes:

> An awareness of God can flow through our day the way blood circulates through the body, replenishing it with nutrients and oxygen. We pay attention to God, conscious that He may be speaking to us. His presence begins to permeate our lives—through thoughts, feelings, dreams, activities, and in-between moments.
>
> Practicing God's presence moves His companionship beyond church gatherings, before-meal graces, and quiet times to

21. de Sales, *Introduction to the Devout Life*, 84–85.
22. de Sales, *Introduction to the Devout Life*, 124–25. Kelly, *Testament of Devotion*, 35.

infiltrate the ordinary moments of life. Keeping company with God this way transforms tasks such as building circuit boards into acts of worship because we know at whose feet we sit for the rest of our lives.[23]

Finally, I'll underscore the fact that a theologically real worship of God in Christ is not only beneficial to a vibrant Christian spirituality, it's also an act of spiritual warfare. Once again, there are allusions to this fact in the writings of Christianity's spiritual masters. I'll cite but a couple of examples here. According to Brother Lawrence:

> We must go about our labors quietly, calmly, and lovingly, entreating Him to prosper the works of our hands; by thus keeping heart and mind fixed on God, we shall bruise the head of the evil one, and beat down his weapons to the ground.[24]

Another favorite quote of mine from the spiritual masters comes from the work of British preacher and theologian Leslie Weatherhead, whose many references to the vital importance of a transforming and liberating fellowship with Christ suggests a real experience with a risen Lord that is devil-defeating in its effect. According to Weatherhead:

> There is no greater need in our time than that those who teach religion should concern themselves, not with tightening up the machinery, developing organization, or arranging more meetings; but rather to make Jesus real to men; to invite them into that transforming fellowship which cannot be proved save by personal experience, but which, when realized, brings men that glorious exhilaration, that sense of ineffable peace, and that escape from all bondage which are promised in the New Testament.[25]

It's no wonder, then, that Satan is so feverishly committed to interfering with our sense of intimacy with God. And now that we know why the devil desperately wants us to stumble in our worship, and how he goes about causing us to do so, we can become proactive in making sure we don't. But this doesn't simply mean we take a stab at worshiping better and more often. The call is for us to, with the help of the Holy Spirit, cultivate a lifestyle spirituality, at the heart of which is some intimate, theologically real interaction with God the Father through Christ the Son.

---

23. Johnson, *Enjoying the Presence of God*, 14.
24. Herman, *Practice of the Presence of God*, 71.
25. Weatherhead, *Transforming Friendship*, 37.

Game on!

Reflection/Discussion Questions:

1. What's your understanding of what the second phase of our endurance training will focus on and why?
2. To what degree have you ever been guilty of worshiping your work, working at your play, and playing at your worship? What effect did this have?
3. How would you explain to someone what a *theologically real* experience of worship is? To what degree do you consider this distinction to be an important one to keep in mind? Why or why not?
4. Has the evil one ever utilized any of the devices described in this chapter (seducing, secluding, sidelining, sidetracking, or secularizing) to try to interfere with your experience of intimacy with God? Care to share?
5. How would you explain to someone what a "lifestyle spirituality" is, and its importance to a vibrant, enduring, fruitful walk with Christ? How committed are you to cultivating such a spirituality?

4

Deception

The Devil and Christian *Nurture*

> The Spirit clearly says that in later times some will abandon the faith and follow deceiving spirits and things taught by demons.
>
> —1 TIMOTHY 4:1

Unfortunately, it happens: sometimes church members abandon the faith. Indeed, the church in America is currently experiencing something of an epidemic in this regard, especially among the emerging generations. In his book, *unchristian: What a New Generation Really Thinks about Christianity . . . and Why it Matters*, Christian researcher David Kinnaman reports, "the vast majority of outsiders in this country, particularly among young generations, are actually *de-* churched individuals."[1] The "outsiders" Kinnaman refers to are young adults who are currently *outside* both the church and the Christian faith. The point he's making is it wasn't always like this. They used to be *inside* both the faith and the church but, for a variety of reasons, they have, as it were, "left the building."

Building on this distressing insight, author Drew Dyck, in his *Generation Ex-Christian: Why Young Adults are Leaving the Faith . . . and How to Bring them Back*, further clarifies the identity of these "outsiders" thusly:

---

1. Kinnaman and Lyons, *unchristian*, 74.

> In other words, these are not strangers, some mysterious denizens of a heathen underworld. Rather most unbelieving outsiders are old friends, yesterday's worshipers, children who once prayed to Jesus, even if they didn't fully grasp what they were saying. Strictly speaking, they are not an "unreached people group." They are our brothers, sisters, sons and daughters, and our friends. They have dwelt among us.[2]

Historically, church leaders and Christian apologists (those who specialize in defending the faith) have focused on the phenomenon of disciples rejecting orthodox (biblical, historical) Christianity for an unorthodox version of the faith (e.g., Mormonism, Jehovah's Witnesses, the New Age), or a non-Christian religion (e.g., Judaism, Buddhism, Hinduism, Islam). But most recently, the concern in apologetics has shifted to the phenomenon of Christian church members leaving the faith in favor of no religion at all. Though Dyck's *Generation Ex-Christian* was written in 2010, in a recent interview, the author cited a much more current statistic, stating that

> [t]here has definitely been an acceleration in the number of people in the West claiming to have no religion. When I wrote my book in 2010, 22 percent in the younger cohort of 18 to 30 claimed to have no religion. Many of those had grown up in Christian homes. And that was a huge spike because the numbers before that were from 1990 that showed 11 percent. Today, it's at 34 to 36 percent.[3]

In sum, let's make sure we understand what's going on in our current ministry context. Of the growing number of American young adults who now claim to have no religion, the vast majority are actually de-churched ex-Christians. Such a realization brings to mind the line from the film *Apollo 13*: "Houston, we have a problem!" To be clear, the problem we're presently discussing has a name. I refer to it as the "post-Christian dynamic"—young adults who've grown up in a "Christian environment" coming to a place where they declare to family and friends that they are "over" Christianity and "done" with the church.[4]

The technical term for the dynamic of a genuine Christian disciple defecting, departing, falling away from, or abandoning the Christian

2. Dyck, *Generation Ex-Christian*, 33–34.
3. Lee, "Responding to Josh Harris's Announcement," para. 30.
4. For a rather thorough survey of reporting regarding the post-Christian dynamic, especially among young people, see Wallace, "Updated."

faith is *apostasy*. "The English word 'apostasy' is derived from a Greek word (*apostasia*) that means, 'to stand away from.'"[5] Though at the time of this writing two rather high-profile Christian leaders have just recently publicly announced that they no longer consider themselves Christians,[6] I'll offer here an important observation: while genuine apostasy does happen, I'm not convinced that all our post-Christian peers, including the two high-profile former ministry leaders just referred to, have actually committed apostasy. As I've stated elsewhere, my experience in the university classroom tells me very few of the post-Christians I've interacted with have actually rejected Christianity. What most post-Christians are reacting adversely to is not Christianity per se, but "churchianity"—the sometimes egregiously imperfect manner in which many church members tend to represent the faith to one another and those outside the ecclesial community.[7]

That said, the post-Christian dynamic is still a very serious development. Only the evil one is pleased whenever genuine apostasy or the borderline version of it occurs! Apostasy in any form is the very antithesis to the *spiritual endurance* which, as we've seen, numerous New Testament passages not only refer to but in one way or another encourage.[8]

So, what's up? Given what the New Testament has to say about the importance of spiritual endurance, how do we explain increasing numbers of Christians, especially young adults, declaring they've had enough, that they're over Christianity and done with the church?

In this book's introduction I suggested the post-Christian dynamic is reflective of a lack of endurance training going on in churches. This diagnosis is based not only on my awareness of how students belonging to the emerging generations are arriving at college having experienced less and less formal spiritual and moral formation, but also on the findings of some reputable sociological studies which confirm this observation.[9]

---

5. Fink, "Apostasy," 87.

6. See Aaron, "'Losing My Religion,'" lines 1–2.

7. For more on this distinction, see Tyra, *Getting Real*, 76–80.

8. For example, see Matt 24:10–13; Rom 15:4; Col 1:9–12; 1 Thess 1:3; 2 Thess 1:3–5; 1 Tim 6:11–12; 2 Tim 2:11–13; Titus 2:1–2; Heb 12:1–3; Rev 1:9; 2:3; 3:10; 13:10; 14:12.

9. Principally, I have in mind here the National Study of Youth and Religion (NSYR), a research project directed by Christian Smith, Professor of Sociology at the University of Notre Dame, and Lisa Pearce, Assistant Professor of Sociology at the University of North Carolina at Chapel Hill. The findings of this multi-stage study are reported on in Smith and Denton, *Soul Searching*; Smith and Smith, *Souls in Transition*;

I'm also convinced, however, that the apostolic authors would insist that, in addition to any other ecclesial and cultural factors that might be in play, *behind any person's act of apostasy (greater or lesser) is the loss of a head-and-heart connection with Christ that's ultimately caused by the evil one.* Some support for this assertion is provided in Clinton Arnold's *Powers of Darkness: Principalities and Powers in Paul's Letters.* Arnold writes:

> Ever since the garden of Eden, Satan has continued to use his diabolical method of deception, causing people to believe a lie. This was particularly true in Paul's churches with regard to the proliferation of false teaching and the deceitful work of false teachers. In writing to the Galatians, Corinthians and the Colossians, Paul warned these believers about the influence of false teaching, In all three cases he explicitly connects the false teaching with the work of Satan and his powers. Paul also instructed Timothy on how to deal with false teachers at Ephesus, who essentially were pawns in Satan's hands.[10]

What Arnold says about these letters penned by Paul also applies to the Epistles composed by Peter, Jude, and John. Later in this chapter we will survey several polemical passages in which we find an apostle confronting a false teaching inspired by the devil. For now, the message not to be missed is that, according to the apostolic authors, apostasy happens, and when it does, the devil is ultimately behind it.

Moreover, I have reason to believe the same New Testament authors who warned the early church about the dangers of false teaching would likewise encourage the contemporary church to keep this hazard in mind when developing its nurturing (discipling) ministries. As we will soon see, the apostolic authors considered the experience of Christian nurture to be of extreme importance when it comes to spiritual warfare. *The premise of this chapter is that it's precisely because a church's nurturing ministry is so very crucial to the ability of church members to endure in the faith that the devil is so desperate to negate it.* But this doesn't have to happen; local churches can implement nurturing/discipling ministries that

---

and Smith et al., *Lost in Transition.* Kenda Creasy Dean, an NSYR research team member and Associate Professor of Youth, Church and Culture at Princeton University, has provided a book-length discussion of the significance of the NSYR for youth ministry in Dean, *Almost Christian.* I provide some rather thorough discussions of the implications of this study for the spiritual, moral, and missional formation of church members in Tyra, *Getting Real,* 36–57, and Tyra, *Pursuing Moral Faithfulness,* 127–58.

10. Arnold, *Powers of Darkness,* 129–30.

enable church members to render to Jesus the long obedience in the same direction he's looking for in the lives of his followers. Moreover, it's not just professional clergy who are to nurture and disciple. Fully equipped church members are to, likewise, serve the body of Christ in these critical endeavors (Rom 12:6–8; Eph 4:11–16; Col 3:16; 2 Tim 2:2)!

The Nature of Christian Nurture

To begin, the word *nurture*, when used as a noun, refers to "the process of caring for and encouraging the growth or development of someone or something."[11] As a verb, *to nurture* is to "care for and encourage the growth or development of" someone or something.[12] Christian nurture, then, has to do with the way churches strive to encourage the growth and development of their members toward full maturity in Christ.

Because of the rise of the megachurch model of doing church, and the phenomenon of multisite churches where the weekend message is transmitted via satellite to several locations, we might be tempted to equate a church's nurturing ministry with its pulpit ministry. However, it's best to talk about the importance of a nurturing/discipling *environment* which possesses multiple inputs. In other words, the most effective nurturing experience will be a holistic one that's contributed to by all four of the cardinal components of the Christian life.[13] In the previous chapter we discovered theologically real *worship* contributes mightily to one's spiritual formation. In succeeding chapters we'll learn genuine Christian *community* and *mission* are likewise absolutely critical to spiritual growth (chapters 5 and 6, respectively). The focus of this chapter will be on the kind of *teaching ministry* that's critical to the nurture of Christian disciples, whether it occurs in the worship space, a classroom, or the living rooms of parishioners' homes.[14]

11. Anonymous, "Nurture," lines 5–6.

12. Anonymous, "Nurture," line 2.

13. For more on the need for a holistic, multifaceted discipling *environment* in the local church, see Tyra, *Defeating Pharisaism*, 200, 205–6.

14. While the primary focus of this chapter will be on the corporate teaching ministry of the church, it should be pointed out that a holistic nurturing ministry will seek to enable church members to, on their own, read, study, and admonish one another from God's word in a way that's faithful to the self-revelation of God that's presented in Scripture. In other words, a teaching ministry that's successful at being endurance-enabling will be one that's equipping rather than excusing. Rather than congregants

The Apostles and the Importance of a "Head-and-Heart" Connection to Christ

We've already established if the devil can't succeed in either killing us or causing us to self-destruct, his ambition is to keep us from entering into an intimate, interactive, life-story-shaping relationship with God.[15] That failing, he will do his best to stymie our cooperation with the Holy Spirit, whose goal is to enable us to render to God the spiritual, moral, and missional faithfulness he desires and deserves.[16] This explains why some of the passages in the New Testament that encourage the cultivation of spiritual endurance also refer to the phenomenon of Christian faithfulness (e.g., Rev 13:10; 14:12).

As well, we've already noted the dynamic interconnectivity that's at work in the threefold faithfulness God is looking for. A disciple's *missional faithfulness* is supported by his or her *moral faithfulness*, which in turn flows out of a foundational *spiritual faithfulness* present in his or her walk with Christ. It's because of the foundational nature of the disciple's spiritual faithfulness that the devil works so hard at destroying it. This observation begs the question: *What does it mean for Christ's followers to be spiritually faithful to God?* The answer to this question will help us understand not only why Satan is so antagonistic to the nurturing/discipling ministries of the local church, but also how he comes at them.

As I've discussed elsewhere, the phenomenon of spiritual faithfulness in the Old Testament required that the people of Israel remain loyal to the Mosaic covenant they had entered into with God (see Ps 25:8–10; 78:32–37). Similarly, the New Testament also speaks of a covenant—a *new* covenant which centers in the sacrifice of Christ (see Luke 22:20; 1 Cor 11:25; Heb 8:6–13; 9:15–28). Faithfulness to this new covenant

---

becoming dependent upon the leadership of the church, they will be empowered to read, study, and share God's word themselves, and do so in a spiritually healthy manner. A helpful resource for teaching members how to properly interpret the Scriptures in their personal study of it is Fee and Stuart, *How to Read the Bible*.

15. This explains why, when Elymas the sorcerer (Bar-Jesus) attempted to interfere with Paul's sharing of the gospel with the proconsul Sergius Paulus, Paul prophetically referred to Elymas as a "child of the devil" (Acts 13:6–11).

16. Unfortunately, though Paul calls for Christian disciples to "keep in step with the Spirit" (Gal 5:25), the rest of the New Testament and Christian history clearly indicate that it's possible for the enabling work of the Spirit to be *resisted* (Acts 7:51), *grieved* (Eph 4:30), *rejected* (1 Thess 4:8), and *quenched* (1 Thess 5:19) by those who formally profess the faith! For more on the role the Holy Spirit plays in our cultivation of the threefold faithfulness, see Tyra, *Getting Real*, 61–118.

requires that disciples *remain steadfast in their devotion to Jesus*, God's Son (see Col 1:21–23; 2:6; Heb 3:1–6, 12–14; 4:14; 10:19–39). The crucial question is: *What does this steadfast, ongoing devotion to Jesus involve?*[17]

John 15 is a key New Testament passage which famously articulates the call for Christian disciples to *remain connected* to Christ. In this passage we hear Jesus say:

> I am the true vine, and my Father is the gardener. He cuts off every branch in me that bears no fruit, while every branch that does bear fruit he prunes so that it will be even more fruitful. You are already clean because of the word I have spoken to you. Remain in me, and I will remain in you. No branch can bear fruit by itself; it must remain in the vine. Neither can you bear fruit unless you remain in me.
>
> I am the vine; you are the branches. If a man remains in me and I in him, he will bear much fruit; apart from me you can do nothing. If anyone does not remain in me, he is like a branch that is thrown away and withers; such branches are picked up, thrown into the fire and burned. If you remain in me and my words remain in you, ask whatever you wish, and it will be given you. This is to my Father's glory, that you bear much fruit, showing yourselves to be my disciples. (John 15:1–8)

According to this passage it's imperative that Christ's followers "continue," "remain," or "abide" (Greek: *menō*) in him. *But what does this mean?* On the one hand, this can be interpreted as a call for Christian disciples to maintain a *volitional-intellectual commitment* to Christ. In other words, to continue in Christ is to be careful to maintain an orthodox understanding/profession of who Jesus is and what he's about. On the other hand, there's also some support for the idea that it's important for Christians to maintain a *mystical-experiential communion* with the risen Jesus—to interact with him daily in a spiritual/devotional manner.[18] So, which is it? *Does a steadfast devotion to Christ involve a volitional-intellectual commitment or a mystical-experiential communion?* The answer is: it involves both! Though some theologians suggest *believing* is overrated and *beloving* is the only thing that matters when it comes to

---

17. For more on what constitutes a spiritual faithfulness before God and the importance of the Holy Spirit to it, see Tyra, *Getting Real*, 61–80.

18. For more on the way Christians have, through the years, pursued the cultivation of this mystical experiential communion with Christ, see Tyra, *Christ's Empowering Presence*.

remaining connected to Jesus, it's actually both a head and heart connection to Christ the New Testament calls for us to maintain.[19]

In the previous chapter's discussion of the importance of a lifestyle spirituality to Christian endurance, the focus was on the believer's ongoing experience of a mystical-experiential communion with Jesus. In this chapter, we'll observe that the New Testament also evidences an equally fierce apostolic concern that Christian believers stand strong in their faith—i.e., maintain a steadfast volitional-intellectual commitment to Christ. That this is a legitimate interpretation of John 15 finds some support from the fact that just such a concern is especially apparent in the Johannine writings. Indeed, passages such as John 20:30–31, 1 John 4:1–6, and 2 John 1:7–11 indicate the apostle John was especially *on* about this issue! Put simply, it's because a spiritual faithfulness before God requires we maintain a *volitional-intellectual commitment* to Christ that the devil is so committed to using various forms of *doctrinal deception* to short-circuit it. Thus, the message of this chapter is that a primary way the local church enables its members to resist the devil's faith-adulterating devices is to make available to them a holistic, theologically real, discipleship-enhancing nurturing/teaching ministry/environment (1 Tim 4:6).

Now, before we begin this important discussion, I want to acknowledge in advance that in addition to being a bit lengthy, it is also somewhat technical in nature, and is bursting with biblical references. And yet, it's my hope that readers will diligently make their way through it, keeping in mind its importance to our endurance training, and the fact that a little attempted precision, especially when dealing with important biblical theological matters, never hurt anyone!

The Apostles and the Need for a Teaching Ministry

Let's establish the fact, straightaway, that local churches simply must provide their members with both preaching (faith-instilling) and teaching (faith-informing) ministries. There's certainly nothing wrong with seeker-friendly, inspirational, essentially therapeutic (how to be and live well) sermons. But this type of "teaching," even if it is presented in the context of small groups meeting in homes, can't be all that's involved in a

---

19. For more on this proposed antithesis and the need to choose between a Christianity of the head or of the heart, see the discussion titled "Christian Orthodoxy and the Swing of the Proverbial Pendulum" in Tyra, *Missional Orthodoxy*, 28–34.

church's nurturing/discipling ministry. As I'll indicate later in this chapter, a biblically faithful nurturing/discipling ministry will also discuss some theological and practical matters that, while they aren't necessarily seeker-friendly, are critical to the cultivation of the threefold faithfulness God is looking for. This explains why the New Testament portrays the apostles as fervently engaged in a teaching/nurturing ministry (as well as a preaching ministry) as they launched the Christian movement (see Acts 5:42; 14:21–22; Col 1:28–29).

Moreover, we must not overlook those passages in which we find the apostle Paul exhorting church leaders (Timothy and Titus) to be careful to engage in the spiritual nurture of their members by means of a bold and doctrinally faithful teaching ministry (see 1 Tim 1:3–5; 4:6, 11–16; 2 Tim 2:1–2, 24–25; 3:16; Titus 2:1, 15). It's hard not to find in these passages some strong support for the notion that the apostolic authors considered faithful biblical teaching to be critical to the dynamic of Christian nurture.

The Apostles and the Need for a Teaching Ministry that Enables Endurance

Pressing further, the premise of this chapter is not simply that the dynamic of Christian nurture is an important component of the Christian life, but that it's critical to the endurance training of church members. What I'm suggesting is the New Testament documents provide us with good reason to believe the kind of Christian nurture the apostolic authors would be looking for in contemporary churches, especially in light of the post-Christian dynamic we're currently experiencing, is a strong teaching ministry that's *intentional* about *helping church members overcome the evil one*. Can such an assertion be backed up? Let's see.

I'll begin by pointing out the New Testament refers to several apostasy triggers. These include: "persecution (Matt 24:9, 10); false teachers (Matt 24:11); temptation (Luke 8:13); worldliness (2 Tim 4:4); defective knowledge of Christ (1 John 2:19); moral lapse (Heb 6:4–6); forsaking worship and spiritual living (10:25–31); unbelief (3:12)."[20] I contend that behind all these scenarios is the loss of a head-and-heart connection to Christ that's precipitated by the church member's loss of confidence in the apostolic message concerning him. This explains the presence in the

---

20. Pratt, "Apostasy," 202.

New Testament of many passages emphasizing the need for Christian believers to remain strong in the faith delivered by means of apostolic preaching.[21]

Moreover, this concern that Christian disciples maintain a firm faith-connection to Christ is also evident in some passages warning against the phenomenon of false teachers seeking to introduce false, faith-busting doctrines into the community of believers.[22]

Finally, we must also pay attention to some passages in the New Testament that point to the evil one as the ultimate cause of Christians defecting from the faith. I've referred to a couple of these passages already (1 Pet 5:8-9; 2 Cor 11:2-4, 13-15). Not surprisingly, the epigraph on the title page of this chapter is also pertinent to this discussion (1 Tim 4:1). Indeed, this passage can and should inform our understanding of two other passages from Paul's pen. First, to the church in Colossae, Paul wrote this word of warning:

> See to it that no one takes you captive through hollow and deceptive philosophy, which depends on human tradition and the elemental spiritual forces of this world rather than on Christ. (Col 2:8)

And to his ministry protégé, Timothy, Paul gave this word of instruction:

> Opponents must be gently instructed, in the hope that God will grant them repentance leading them to a knowledge of the truth, and that they will come to their senses and escape from the trap of the devil, who has taken them captive to do his will. (2 Tim 2:25-26)

In addition, some of the letters penned by the apostles Peter, John, and Jude also seem to point to the evil one as the ultimate source of the false teachings that lead to the loss of a faith connection with Christ (e.g., 2 Pet 2:1-22; 3:14-18; 1 John 4:1-6; 2 John 1:7-11; Jude 3-24). We will focus even more on these passages in the pages that follow, but, for now, what's important is the observation that, considered together, *all the passages referred to above suggest the endurance training provided by churches*

---

21. For example, see Acts 14:21-22; 1 Cor 15:1-2; 16:13; 2 Cor 13:5; Gal 1:6-9; Phil 1:27; Col 2:6-7; 2 Thess 2:15; 1 Tim 1:18-19; 3:8-9; 4:1; 6:12, 20-21; 2 Tim 1:13-14; Heb 3:12-14; 4:14; 1 Pet 5:8-9; 2 Pet 3:17-18; Jude 3.

22. For example, see Matt 7:15; 24:10-13; 2 Cor 11:13; Gal 2:1-5; Col 2:17-19; 1 Tim 1:3-7; 6:3-5, 9-10; 2 Tim 2:14-18; 2 Pet 2:1-3; 1 John 4:1; Rev 2:2.

should include a teaching ministry that's intentional about enabling disciples to maintain a strong faith connection to the risen Christ.

The Apostles and the *Earmarks* of a Teaching Ministry that Is Endurance Enabling

It's one thing to provide church members with a teaching ministry; it's another to provide a teaching ministry that actually enables church members to grow in their ability to stand firm against the wiles of the evil one. I contend the latter type of teaching ministry will be *biblically grounded, Christ-honoring,* and *Spirit-empowered.* Put differently, this teaching ministry will be fiercely faithful to the apostolic witness to the word of God fulfilled in Christ (2 Pet 1:1–21; 1 John 1:1–3). It will also be christologically orthodox (right believing in its understanding of who Christ is and what he's about). Finally, because it is also genuinely enlivened by the Spirit of Christ, it will produce ongoing personal encounters with the risen Jesus. Add to this a commitment to make the aim of the teaching ministry not only edifying in a therapeutic manner but specifically devil-defeating, and you have a nurturing/discipling ministry the apostles would approve of. Let's take a closer look at each of these earmarks one at a time.

A Teaching Ministry that Is *Biblically Grounded*

Apparently, the authors of the New Testament were concerned about first-century church members being led astray by "false doctrines" (1 Tim 1:3), "destructive heresies" (2 Pet 2:1), and "things taught by demons" (1 Tim 4:1) that were being promoted by "false teachers" (2 Pet 2:1), "false apostles" (2 Cor 11:13; Rev 2:2), and "antichrists" (1 John 2:18, 22). More specifically, these spiritually dangerous teachings are referred to in the New Testament as: "cleverly devised stories" (2 Pet 1:16), "godless myths and old wives' tales" (1 Tim 4:7), "myths and endless genealogies" (1 Tim 1:4), "godless chatter" (1 Tim 6:20; 2 Tim 2:16), and "the opposing ideas of what is falsely called knowledge" (1 Tim 6:20).

Over against these extrabiblical, nonapostolic sources of spiritual knowledge (Greek: *gnōsis*), the New Testament encourages its readers to focus on what Jesus' true apostles had to say about the gospel. The apostle John did this by reminding his readers of the up-close and personal nature of the apostolic witness to Jesus that derived from their having literally walked and talked with him (1 John 1:1–3)! The apostle Peter made essentially the same point (2 Pet 1:16–18), but then went on to also emphasize the continuity between the apostolic version of the Jesus story and the prophetic passages in the Old Testament that witnessed to it in advance (2 Pet 1:19; see also 1 Pet 1:10–12). In other words, Peter's argument was the apostolic version of the gospel enjoyed biblical support while the other versions didn't!

For his part, the apostle Paul encouraged church members to be very careful to remain faithful to the gospel he had delivered to them (e.g., Gal 1:6–9). We can consider this, too, an endorsement of the apostolic witness to the gospel even though Paul himself wasn't a part of the original apostolic community. This confidence derives from Paul's insistence that: he too was an apostle chosen by Christ (Gal 1:1); he had received his gospel directly from the risen Christ (Gal 1:11–12); and his understanding of the gospel had been validated by Jesus' original apostles (Gal 1:13—2:10).[23] Also, like Peter, Paul emphasized the support his gospel enjoyed from the Old Testament prophecies regarding the Jewish messiah (Acts 9:22; 17:2–3; Rom 16:25–26). In sum, there's simply no doubting the apostolic authors would've maintained that a strong, effective nurturing ministry, in any era, will be one that, because it's faithful to the apostolic witness to Christ, will, by extension, also be faithful to the Scriptures as a whole.

And why is being grounded in the Scriptures so important? We should also note how, in the process of encouraging their readers to stay true to the apostolic version of the gospel, both Peter and Paul also imply the importance of church members maintaining a high rather than low view of Scripture. One critical component of a high view of Scripture concerns its origin: whether we consider it merely a human product or also inspired by God. The other defining characteristic of a high view of Scripture is an awareness of its transformational capacity—its ability to make a genuine difference in the lives of those who hear, read, and study it.

We find the apostle Peter promoting a high view of Scripture when he makes the bold assertion that the Old Testament prophetic passages,

---

23. Though Paul would've probably argued that his ministry didn't really require the approval of the original apostles, the fact is that he did take care to assert that this was the case.

though originally uttered and eventually inscribed by human authors, were also inspired by the Holy Spirit. He writes:

> Above all, you must understand that no prophecy of Scripture came about by the prophet's own interpretation of things. For prophecy never had its origin in the human will, but prophets, though human, spoke from God as they were carried along by the Holy Spirit. (2 Pet 1:20–21)

The apostle Paul's high view of Scripture is evident when he not only affirms the Scriptures are divinely inspired (literally God-breathed), but also their usefulness in the formation of Christian disciples. He writes:

> All Scripture is God-breathed and is useful for teaching, rebuking, correcting and training in righteousness, so that the servant of God may be thoroughly equipped for every good work. (2 Tim 3:16–17)

So, while Peter's message seems to have been that it's precisely because the Scriptures are inspired by God that any Christian teaching that's supported by them should be preferred over that which is not, Paul went on to also assert the transformational capacity of teachings grounded in the inspired Scriptures. It's this type of teaching, Paul affirms, that has what it takes to successfully nurture disciples in the faith!

So, the biblically grounded nurturing ministry the apostles engaged in and advocated for was birthed out of a high view of Scripture which emphasized both the divine inspiration of the Bible and its transformational capacity. And yet, I want to suggest two further clarifications are necessary regarding this initial earmark.

Toward a Theologically Nuanced Understanding of Biblical Inspiration

First, I'll draw attention to the need for preaching/teaching ministers to provide church members with a nuanced understanding of biblical inspiration. Every semester I have the students taking my religion capstone course work through an unpublished essay written a few years ago by a person who has become a post-Christian and wants others to know why. A big takeaway from the essay is, because he'd never been taught anything at all on the topic, the essay writer had embraced a *divine dictation* view of biblical inspiration that was somewhat naive. Throughout his time in the faith he assumed the Bible sort of fell out of heaven—that every word of it had been dictated by God to human stenographers. The reason the preacher and elders in his fundamentalist church referred to the Bible as the "word of God," he concluded, was because it's an entirely divine product with no human aspect to it.

However, when he came into contact with some nonfundamentalist biblical scholarship, he became aware of the humanity of the Scriptures—that the Bible actually bears the fingerprints of the human authors: their vocabulary, cultural perspectives, and premodern worldviews, etc. Not knowing what to make of this new information, and having no one in his church that could help him understand how the Bible could be both divinely inspired and yet bear the fingerprints of the human authors God used in the inscripturation process, he felt the need to either assassinate his brains and continue to embrace the divine dictation theory of biblical inspiration, or reject the idea that the Bible is the word of God at all. Encouraged by the writings of some progressive (liberal) Christian scholars, and some that were intentionally atheism-promoting, he eventually chose to do the latter. As a result, his Christian faith collapsed like a house of cards.

Of course, it didn't have to be this way. He could have been taught that, even as the *living* Word of God, Jesus himself, is both human and divine (John 1:1, 14), the *written* word of God can also be thought of as having come into existence in a way that's roughly analogous to Christ's incarnation. This is not to say the Bible is inherently divine and deserving of worship the way Jesus is. It simply means the inscripturation process included both divine and human activity. I tell my students if someone had been able, early on, to help this essay writer understand how an incarnational, "both-and" understanding of the inscripturation dynamic represents a third option with respect to the doctrine of biblical inspiration, he might still be a follower of Christ today!

What's really disturbing is most of my freshman students tell me they've never had anyone explain to them how biblical inspiration works. In truth, many Christian students arrive at the university having simply assumed the Bible somehow fell out of heaven, every word divinely dictated and immediately written down by human scribes. As a result, they are, in effect, potential post-Christians, capable of the same tragic choice made by the essay writer referred to above.

I realize how difficult it is to tackle a topic like this in the local church, especially if the bulk, if not all, of the church's teaching is presented during the main worship gathering each week. But a nurturing/discipling ministry that's going to succeed at steeling church members against the deceptive work of Satan will have to create a setting where some theologically nuanced teaching can be delivered, and some thoughtful discussion of it engaged in. The supposed need to choose between the idea that the Bible is entirely a divine product with no human involvement at all, or it must be an entirely human product with no divine inspiration at work in it, is one of many false choices our spiritual enemy is eager to present to the members of our churches![24]

Toward a Theologically Real Understanding of the Bible's Transformational Capacity

Second, I'll also proffer what I consider to be a needed clarification with respect to the transformational capacity of Scripture Paul alluded to in 2 Timothy 3:16 (see also Heb 4:12–13). Though it's true the hearing, reading, and studying of the Bible can have a transformational impact on those who engage in these activities, this impact will not occur unless the Scriptures are experienced in a theologically real manner. Put differently, I've found that church members and university students need to be made aware the transformational capacity of the sacred Scriptures is determined by the manner in which they approach them. There are two main ways we can relate to the Scriptures: either with an "I-It" mentality in place, or with an "I-Thou" expectation in mind. Put differently, we can study the Bible as an it—something to be mastered by us—or we can approach it more reverently and relationally, allowing the God of the Bible to have his way with us, to keep encountering us in a transformational manner through it. In other words, we're back to the dynamic of "holy expectancy." Just as a sense of spiritual expectancy is crucial to the sense of *encounter* we can experience in *worship*, it's also critical to the sense of *encounter* we can experience as we *read, study, hear, and share the Scriptures*. The youth of our churches need to know this. Indeed, everyone in our churches, regardless of their generational status, needs to be made aware of how an ongoing, theologically real engagement with God's word will enable us to be transformed into the people God created us to be

---

24. For more on the many false choices the enemy uses to confuse church members with respect to their faith, see Tyra, *Missional Orthodoxy*. For more on how the incarnational model of biblical inspiration presents us with a third option with respect to bibliology (our doctrine of the Bible) in particular, Tyra, *Missional Orthodoxy*, 135–38. See also Enns, *Inspiration and Incarnation*.

(Rom 12:2; 2 Cor 3:18; see also Heb 4:12–13)! It is, very simply, another critical component of the kind of lifestyle spirituality that will empower us to keep saying "yes" to God, and "no" to the evil one.

A Teaching Ministry that Is *Christ-Honoring*

The second earmark of a nurturing ministry that's endurance-enabling comes into focus when we consider the way the apostles warned their readers to steer clear of "false doctrines," "destructive heresies," and "things taught by demons" (1 Tim 4:1). Apparently, there existed even in the apostolic era *alternative* versions of the Christian faith that didn't align with the apostolic presentation of who Jesus is and what he's about. Eventually, some of these alternative iterations of the Jesus story would be written down and included in a collection known as the "apocryphal" or "noncanonical" Gospels.[25] However, long before the publication of these false Gospels, there were both *legalistic* and *antinomian* perversions of the true gospel attempting to invade Christian assemblies. The legalistic versions encouraged disciples to adhere closely to religious rules and ceremonies, while the antinomian version so emphasized the disciples' freedom from the Mosaic law that they tended to promote sinful behavior. All of these alternative, nonapostolic versions of Christianity differed from the real deal in their conception of: (1) Jesus' *ontology* (i.e., his nature or being); (2) Jesus' *ministry* (i.e., what he came into the world to accomplish and how he did so); and (3) the *spirituality* Jesus modeled for his disciples, and that his apostles then prescribed for his followers. Clinton Arnold sums up this matter well when, in a discussion of the false teaching referred to in the New Testament, he makes the observation that "[a]ll these forms of false teaching characteristically impugn the true nature of the gospel and the person of the Lord Jesus Christ—always leading to the wrong kind of lifestyle and behavior."[26]

It's no wonder, then, that the New Testament provides us with a significant number of passages in which we find the apostles adamantly admonishing their readers to reject the legalistic (law-promoting) and antinomian (law-rejecting) versions of the Jesus story that had emerged

---

25. The designation "non-canonical" means that they were excluded from the New Testament canon (the twenty-seven documents that make up our New Testament). The biggest reasons for this exclusion was their non-apostolic authorship and the dramatically different Jesus and Christian faith they heralded.

26. Arnold, *Powers of Darkness*, 130.

even in their day. These very important polemical (confrontational) passages include: 2 Corinthians 11:1–15; virtually the entirety of Paul's letters to the Galatians and Colossians; selected passages from his two letters to his ministry protégé Timothy; selected passages from 2 Peter 2–3; and virtually the entirety of the Epistle of Jude, and 1 and 2 John. A careful survey of these polemical passages will make apparent why the devil is so eager for these false teachings, and others like them, to invade the church. *A distorted understanding of who Jesus is and what he's about leads to a deficient experience with the risen Christ, and either a spirituality that's rule- and ceremony-constrained, or one that produces the opposite of genuine godliness.*[27]

Of the several polemical passages referred to above, I've chosen to focus primarily here on only two. The first is a passage from the pen of the apostle Paul which refers to a false teaching that seems to have encouraged a *legalistic* and/or *overly mystical* approach to the Christian faith (2 Corinthians 11:1–15). Second, we'll also have a look at the way

27. To be even more specific, elsewhere I refer to four "christological verities" or doctrines that, because of their soteriological (saving) significance as indicated in the Bible, are at the very heart of the Christian faith and should be considered dogma (non-negotiable Christian beliefs). These four verities are: Jesus is both God and man (John 20:31; 1 John 5:5, 11–12; 2 John 1:7–9); Jesus' death on the cross possessed an atoning significance (1 Cor 15:1–3; 1 John 2:2; 4:10); Jesus rose bodily from the grave (Rom 10:9–10; 1 Cor 15:1–5); and Jesus is now Lord of all (Rom 10:9–10; see also Rom 14:9–12; 1 Cor 12:3; Phil 2:9–11; Heb 3:1, 15). There are, of course, other biblical doctrines that are basic to or that derive from the four listed above (e.g., the virgin birth; Jesus' miracles, the return of Christ, the final judgment, etc.). These other beliefs are important and should be included in our preaching and teaching. Together, all these doctrines fill out a biblically informed vision of the Christian faith. However, we should note that it's the four christological verities referred to above that the apostles consistently emphasized in their refutation of various versions of false teaching. I believe this is due to the fact that these four christological doctrines seem to underwrite, so to speak, the gospel or story of Jesus in such a way that without them, the gospel loses its impact, and the story of Jesus its significance. Put differently, for Jesus' twin ministries of revelation and reconciliation to be theologically coherent and actually productive of genuine transformation in the lives of his followers, these four christological doctrines would seem to be necessary. Moreover, I contend that it's when these four christological doctrines are either denied or downplayed that we find the result to be a version of the Christian faith that leads to either a soul-killing legalism or a sin-promoting antinomianism. Thus, I suggest that any nurturing/discipling ministry that seeks to be endurance-enabling will have at its core a solid commitment to these four Christ-honoring doctrines. For more on this see Tyra, *Missional Orthodoxy*, 49–50, 180–213. For a discussion of why the doctrine of Christ's atoning death should be considered an element of Christian dogma despite the fact that it is not a formal article in the Nicene Creed, see DeVine, "Can the Church Emerge?," 190–95.

the apostle John referred to a faux version of the faith that promoted a very dangerous *antinomian* understanding of the gospel (1 and 2 John). Along the way, we'll glance at how the other polemical passages cited above contribute to the discussion.

The Polemic Inherent in 2 Corinthians 11:1–15

We've already noted how in 2 Corinthians 11:1–3 Paul expressed his concern that Satan might succeed in leading at least some of the members of that church into apostasy. By way of review, this passage reads:

> I hope you will put up with me in a little foolishness. Yes, please put up with me! I am jealous for you with a godly jealousy. I promised you to one husband, to Christ, so that I might present you as a pure virgin to him. But I am afraid that just as Eve was deceived by the serpent's cunning, your minds may somehow be led astray from your sincere and pure devotion to Christ. (2 Cor 11:1–3)

Though in the verses that follow (2 Cor 11:4–15), Paul doesn't go into detail about the nature of the false teaching that had surfaced in Corinth, he does describe the false teachers. Clinton Arnold summarizes Paul's description of them thusly:

> The Corinthians were giving credence to a group of polished orators who had described themselves as apostles and missionaries (2 Cor 11:13). They publicly disdained Paul and tried to present themselves as having a higher level of spiritual authority over the Corinthians. While they apparently claimed to possess authority from Jerusalem, Paul implied that they were teaching a different Jesus and a different gospel than he had proclaimed to them (2 Cor 11:4). Paul charged them with being "false apostles, deceitful workmen, masquerading as apostles of Christ." Finally, he unmasked their true identity: They are servants of Satan masquerading as Christians. Paul regarded Satan as the master of masquerade and deceit. Paul said that Satan can even disguise himself as an angel of light (2 Cor 11:14).[28]

What we actually find in 2 Corinthians 11 and 12 is an extended discussion in which Paul defends his ministry authority over against these "false apostles." But our concern here is the substance of the heresy these

---

28. Arnold, *Powers of Darkness*, 130.

false teachers, as unwitting agents of Satan, were proclaiming. Authority issues aside, what were these ministry usurpers teaching that, according to Paul, threatened to lead the Corinthian church members astray in their faith?

The way Paul prefaces his description of the false apostles makes clear their teaching was, from his perspective, anything but Christ-honoring (see 2 Cor 11:3). The false teaching would, if accepted, cause church members to stray from their sincere and pure devotion to Jesus. OK, but how?

It's certainly possible to see a similarity between the false apostles referred to in 2 Corinthians 11:13 and the disrupters referred to in Acts 15:1 and 15:24. These agitators are described as Jewish Christians who had traveled "from Judea to Antioch" and then announced to the gentile believers there: "'Unless you are circumcised, according to the custom taught by Moses, you cannot be saved'" (Acts 15:1; see also verse 5). We know Paul confronted this bold but errant claim in several other letters (Gal 2:12; 6:12; Phil 3:2–3, Titus 1:10–11). However, the fact 2 Corinthians 11 doesn't refer explicitly to the practice of circumcision or the need to keep the law of Moses per se causes some commentators to be reluctant to assert the false teachers in Corinth were the same as the Judaizers at work in Galatia and possibly elsewhere.[29]

The scholarly reticence to identify the false apostles in Corinth with the Judaizers referred to in Galatia is also supported by the fact that we find Paul confronting a slightly different kind of legalism/ritualism in some of his other letters (e.g., Colossians, 1 and 2 Timothy). In these missives, Paul seems to refer to a legalism/ritualism which, while still retaining some Jewish emphasis on the Mosaic law (Col 2:11–14),[30] also contained some elements that were based on philosophical and mystical traditions (Col 2:8).[31] The source for these traditions ranged beyond

---

29. For example, see Kruse, *2 Corinthians*, 179–80; Belleville, *2 Corinthians*, 273. This, despite the fact that the Jewish character of the false teachers in Corinth is indicated by Paul's defensive comments in 2 Corinthians 11:22, and that in both 2 Corinthians 11:4 and Galatians 1:6 Paul states that the false teachers in question were guilty of promoting a "different gospel."

30. For more on this, see Melick, *Philippians, Colossians, Philemon*, 262–65.

31. Melick, *Philippians, Colossians, Philemon*, 252–54. Referring to the false teaching Paul instructed Timothy to deal with in Ephesus, Donald Guthrie writes: "The false teachers insisted on two prohibitions: marriage and the eating of certain foods. There is no doubt that these point to an incipient Gnosticism with its dualistic view of matter, which found its climax in the heretical teachers of the early second century (cf.

the Old Testament Scriptures to dreams and visions (Col 2:18), "godless myths," and "old wives' tales" (1 Tim 4:7).

Regardless, I contend that whether the heresy promoted by the false teachers referred to in 2 Corinthians was strictly Mosaic in nature or contained some more mystical elements really makes no difference. The way Paul refuted the tendency of religious legalism/ritualism was the same in either case. A careful look at the polemic inherent in Paul's letters to the Galatians and Colossians makes it clear Paul had a huge problem with the way both of these errant approaches to the faith *underemphasized* the importance of Christ's death on the cross, and *overemphasized* the significance of religious rules and rituals for Christian spirituality.[32] Thus, Paul's refutation of the heresy promoted by the false teachers in Corinth would likely have been the same as his message to the Galatians and Colossians: Christ is everything! The real key to being righteous before God is not to embrace a spirituality of rules and rituals, but to allow the Holy Spirit to produce in them the character of Christ (Gal 5:5–6, 13–14, 16, 22–25). Put differently, what is needed is not more religion (Col 2:16–17, 20–22), but a steadfast devotion to the crucified (and risen) Jesus (Col 2:6–8, 3:1–4) that will produce within Christian disciples a new way of being in the world (Gal 6:14–16; Col 3:5–17). It's because Paul understood that the serpent's aim was to cause Christ's followers to stray from their sincere and pure devotion to him that the apostle wrote in such a strident manner, passionately calling for them to do the very opposite.

The Polemic Inherent in 1 and 2 John

At the opposite end of the spectrum is a perversion of the gospel that's anything but obsessed with religious rules and rituals. Ironically, the apostolic authors were insistent that the evil one is behind this heresy as well. The problem of false teachers promoting an antinomian (libertine or sin-promoting) version of Christianity, and seeking to infiltrate

---

Introduction, 45ff.). The apostle's strong opposition to these practices is due to their dangerous implications. He argues that prohibitions such as these are in conflict with the divine ordinance. Here he strikes at the roots of dualistic Gnosticism, which denied that God created matter. Quite apart from this the forbidding of marriage could never lead to a healthy society as God had planned it, and food-taboos were in direct opposition to the bountiful provision of God and could only lead to legalism" (Guthrie, *Pastoral Epistles*, 106–7). See also Towner, *1–2 Timothy & Titus*, 103.

32. Melick, *Philippians, Colossians, Philemon*, 253–54.

orthodox Christian churches with it, shows up in several New Testament documents. While the most vivid descriptions of the antinomian heresy and those promoting it are presented in 2 Peter 2 and the Epistle of Jude, the most extensive treatment of this false teaching is found in the first two Epistles attributed to the apostle John.[33] We've already seen that John begins his first letter with an exhortation for his readers to remain connected to the apostolic rather than nonapostolic version of the Jesus story (1 John 1:1–3). What a good number of contemporary church members may not realize, however, is one of the main goals of John's first two Epistles was to combat an unorthodox, heretical, nonapostolic version of Christianity that was producing a serious schism (split or division) amongst the various churches of Asia Minor (modern-day Turkey).[34] Indeed, John states this explicitly in his letter when he writes: "I am writing these things to you about those who are trying to lead you astray" (1 John 2:26). What this means is, like Paul's Letter to the Galatians and the Epistle of Jude, the entirety of the letters we know as 1 and 2 John are polemical in nature, calling for readers to reject some false teaching that, if embraced, could have devastating effects upon their relationship with God and each other! Biblical commentator Daniel Akin explains:

> First John was written to a church or group of churches in crisis—churches who were being attacked by false teaching (see 2:18–28; 4:1–6; 5:6–7). Some individuals who had once been associated with the Christian community had adopted heretical doctrine, particularly as it related to Christology, and had left the church (2:19). Evidently, after their departure they continued to spread their teachings to those who remained within the Johannine churches. They went so far as to organize and send out

---

33. As with 2 Peter and Jude, scholarly debate surrounds the authorship of 1, 2, and 3 John. Rather than wade into that debate here, I'll simply refer to the author of these Epistles as the apostle John. Some support for this expositional move can be found in the work of biblical commentator David Jackman, who writes of the Epistles: "It is very probable that the author of these letters was also the author of the Fourth Gospel and that he was the apostle John. There are so many parallels of thought and expression in these documents that few scholars have been prepared to follow the suggestion that more than one author was involved" (Jackman, *Message of John's Letters*, 11).

34. According to biblical commentator Colin Kruse, 3 John, though similar in some ways to 2 John, differs in that while 2 John was "a letter written to a church," it was "written to an individual, Gaius." Kruse continues: "The letter has little theological content, but it is nevertheless of significant interest because of the insight it provides concerning the life and tensions of an early Christian community" (Kruse, *Letters of John*, 219).

itinerant teachers/missionaries who moved among the churches with the goal of converting those in the churches to their beliefs (see 2:26; 4:1–3; 2 John 7). Undoubtedly, this theological assault created confusion and crisis within the believing community.[35]

Akin goes on to indicate that, in the process of combatting the false teaching that threatened to divide the churches in Asia Minor, 1 John argued the false teachers were not "genuine believers." They lacked the "marks of authentic Christianity" in three key ways: doctrinally, morally, and socially.[36]

Doctrinally, the false teachers possessed a deficient Christology. For one thing, they had "compromised the person and work of Jesus Christ." They did not "confess Jesus of Nazareth as the Christ (1 John 2:22)" and they "denied that Jesus had come in the flesh (4:2–3)." In other words, they rejected the orthodox teaching that the historical Jesus was and is the God-man—the incarnate Son of God (1 John 4:15; 5:5–12).[37]

Moreover, this deficient understanding of who Christ is produced a deficient view of what he's about (1 John 3:8)—particularly his death on the cross. Put simply, this false teaching denied Jesus' cross-work possessed atoning significance. This is why, says Akin, 1 John strongly emphasizes the "atoning results of Christ's death" (1 John 2:2; 4:10). Even "as John highlights the importance of the incarnation, he also stresses the distinctive nature of Christ's work of atonement."[38]

Morally, Akin continues by pointing out that "the false teachers minimized the seriousness of sin (1 John 1:6–10)." He then explains:

> Apparently, due to their embrace of the Greek philosophical ideas that spirit and matter don't mix, and that only the spiritual really matters, they insisted that their fellowship with God didn't

---

35. See Akin, *1, 2, 3 John*, 29.
36. Akin, *1, 2, 3 John*, 29.
37. After explaining that the false teaching John is responding to in his letters seems to have been "influenced by early Gnostic ideas," Akin explains: "Gnosticism was a heretical movement that became prominent in the second century A.D. Although Gnosticism took many forms, it usually emphasized the essential goodness of spirit and the inherent evil or inferiority of all matter. Influenced by this type of understanding, these false teachers may have viewed Christ as some type of spirit, perhaps a spirit who had come upon the man Jesus during part of his ministry (from his baptism until his crucifixion; cf. 5:6–8). They refused, however, to directly associate 'the Christ' with the human Jesus; this refusal led to a rejection of Jesus of Nazareth as the Christ, the unique God-man" (Akin, *1, 2, 3 John*, 29).
38. Akin, *1, 2, 3 John*, 29.

depend, one way or the other, on how they lived out their bodily existence (see 1 John 1:6). This explains why John is so insistent in this letter that "one's relationship to God has serious ethical implications" (see 1 John 2:3-4, 28-29; 3:7-8).[39]

Once again, we find the biblical authors making the point that genuine Christianity is all about church members actually becoming more and more like Christ (1 John 2:5-6, 28-29)!

Socially, the false teaching 1 John is combatting also failed to produce in its disciples the loving community Jesus called his followers to (e.g., John 13:34-35). Instead of promoting brotherly love, it precipitated in its devotees an elitist mentality that in turn produced spiritual pride and an attitude of indifference toward others who weren't as enlightened as they (1 John 2:9, 11). According to Akin, this explains why John argues in such a persistent manner that "love for other believers is a manifestation of genuine Christianity" (3:10-11, 14, 16-18; 4:7-21).[40]

Now, as helpful as this overview of the main contours of the false teaching referred to in 1 and 2 John is, there are several additional distinctive features of John's polemic that shouldn't go unnoticed. For instance, it's only the apostle John who refers to false teachers as "antichrists" (1 John 2:18, 22-23; 4:2-3; 2 John 1:7). This profoundly pejorative designation highlights for us the importance John placed on our maintaining a high Christology. Indeed, it explains why John goes on to exhort Christian disciples to be very careful not to, even indirectly, support the work of those who deny that Jesus is fully God and fully man (2 John 1:8-10).

Finally, in a way other New Testament polemical passages don't, John refers to the role of the Holy Spirit in: (1) validating the truthfulness of any teaching (1 John 2:20, 26-27); (2) enabling church members to arrive at an orthodox (Christ-honoring) understanding of the faith (1 John 4:1-6; 5:6-8); and, (3) ultimately, assuring them of their inclusion in Christ (see 1 John 3:24; 4:13). For sure, Jude boldly asserts the false teachers are without the Spirit (v. 19), and indicates the importance of church members praying in the Spirit (v. 20). Still, John's treatment of the role of the Spirit in combatting false teaching seems to be even more extensive.

The bottom line is that what 2 Peter, Jude, and 1 and 2 John all have in common is the Christ-centered cure they prescribe for the spiritual disease that is antinomianism. According to 2 Peter:

---

39. Akin, *1, 2, 3 John*, 29.
40. Akin, *1, 2, 3 John*, 30.

> Therefore, dear friends, since you have been forewarned, be on your guard so that you may not be carried away by the error of the lawless and fall from your secure position. *But grow in the grace and knowledge of our Lord and Savior Jesus Christ.* To him be glory both now and forever! Amen. (2 Pet 3:17–18)

According to the Epistle of Jude:

> But you, dear friends, by building yourselves up in your most holy faith and praying in the Holy Spirit, keep yourselves in God's love *as you wait for the mercy of our Lord Jesus Christ to bring you to eternal life.* (Jude 20–21)

According to 1 John:

> We know that we are children of God, and that the whole world is under the control of the evil one. We know also that *the Son of God has come and has given us understanding, so that we may know him who is true. And we are in him who is true by being in his Son Jesus Christ. He is the true God and eternal life.* (1 John 5:19–20)

Like Paul, the apostles Peter, Jude, and John were convinced Christ is everything! If our teaching/nurturing ministries are going to imitate those we find in the New Testament, they will need to be Christ-honoring.

This brings us to the third earmark of an endurance-enabling teaching ministry—a Spirit-empowered approach to the preaching and teaching of God's word that results in sermons/teachings that are sacramental (encounter-effecting) in nature.

A Teaching Ministry that Is *Spirit-Empowered*

My thesis (proposal) here is that when we Christians talk about *anointed* preaching and teaching we can have more in mind than the presenter's style or the presentation's length. We can be referring instead to sermons and teachings that are highly transformational in their effect precisely because they facilitate an existentially impactful (life-story-shaping) encounter with the living God. In other words, truly anointed (Spirit-empowered) preaching and teaching has the effect of causing hearers to sense they've been in the presence of the risen Christ, and have experienced him speaking into their lives in a personal and powerful manner.[41]

---

41. For a much more thorough discussion of this nurturing phenomenon, see my

Some support for my thesis can be found in this quote from author/blogger John Frye who explains that:

> Preaching, in some traditions, is a sacrament or comparable to a sacrament. . . . Preaching is a *holy event* when the preacher and the preached to *encounter the living God together*. The aim of preaching is community-encounter with the living, eyes-blazing Christ Who walks in the community's ordinary, particular midst. Revelation chapters 2–3 are not just about the living Christ showing up a long time ago to seven churches in Asia Minor. The glorified Jesus, as Lord of his church, still walks around in the midst of local gatherings.[42]

Moreover, while being careful to not become too technical here, I'll point out the eminent Swiss theologian, Karl Barth, seems to have been open to the type of anointed preaching or "Christian proclamation" I'm advocating for. Early in his career, Barth spoke of the preaching moment thusly: "On Sunday morning when the bells ring to call the congregation and minister to church, there is in the air an *expectancy* that something great, crucial, and even momentous is to *happen*."[43] What expectation did Barth have in mind? In a word: *encounter*. Barth was convinced that truly anointed preaching, or what he referred to as real Christian proclamation, had a prophetic quality about it. According to Barth:

> Proclamation is human speech in and by which God Himself speaks like a king through the mouth of his herald, and which is meant to be heard and accepted as speech in and by which God Himself speaks, and therefore heard and accepted in faith as divine decision concerning life and death, as divine judgment and pardon, eternal Law and eternal Gospel both together.[44]

---

essay titled "From Sola Scriptura to the Sacramental Sermon: Karl Barth and the Phenomenon of Prophetic Preaching" in Tyra, *Getting Real*, 141–81.

42. McKnight, "From the Shepherd's Nook," para. 3.

43. Barth, "Need and Promise," 104, emphasis original.

44. Barth, *Church Dogmatics* I/1:52. Indeed, speaking specifically of the prophetic aspect of preaching, Barth offers preachers an important clarification, some encouragement, and then a warning when he states: "Our preaching today differs from that of the prophets and apostles who saw and touched Christ. To be sure, it does not differ qualitatively, but it differs inasmuch as it is done in a different place. If, however, God speaks through our word, then the prophets and apostles are actually there even though it be a simple pastor that speaks. Yet we should not be self-conscious about this, nor listen for our own prophetic booming, for even though Christ be present, it is by God's own action. Preachers are under a constraint, and *anankē* (1 Cor. 9:16) that strips them of all their own proposals and programs" (Barth, *Homiletics*, 48–49).

Just think of it: preaching and teaching empowered by the Spirit in such a way as to be encounter-facilitating in its effect! Truly anointed preaching occurs when we sense that somehow the risen Christ has been in the room with us, speaking to us through the sermon/teaching in strengthening, encouraging, comforting, and, sometimes, challenging ways (1 Cor 14:3, 24–25).

Let's assume for the sake of argument the phenomenon Frye, Barth, and I are describing is real. Cutting to the chase, the questions that follow would be: (1) *What would the effect of this kind of preaching/teaching be?*, and (2) *What, if anything, can we Christian preachers, teachers, and congregants do to increase the frequency with which the sermons and teachings we experience in the church are truly anointed by the Spirit of God?*

The Effect of Spirit-Empowered Preaching and Teaching

For the sake of both brevity and clarity, let's focus our attention in this discussion on the phenomenon of anointed preaching. It has been my experience that truly anointed preaching occurs within the church when:

- the theme of the sermon is due to a special prompting of the Spirit;
- the study of the pertinent biblical text(s) seems to possess an unusually insightful quality;
- the dynamic of serendipity occurs during the acquisition of illustrative material; and
- the Holy Spirit seems to "speak through" the preacher during the preaching event, sometimes even articulating sermonic content the preacher had no intention of, or the natural capacity to, deliver.

And yet, the ultimate indication that prophetic preaching has occurred, I propose, is when we find that:

- the Spirit has impressed the sermon's message upon the minds and hearts of those listening in an especially powerful manner.

In other words, *genuine transformation occurs.*

Barth was famous for his assertion that the ultimate test of real proclamation—what I'm referring to as anointed preaching—is its effect. Proclamation is real, said Barth, when it is "talk which has to be listened to and which rightly demands obedience."⁴⁵ Barth's assumption seems to have been when God speaks those with ears to hear know it and can't help but take it seriously (see Jer 23:29; Isa 55:10–11).⁴⁶ Put differently, Barth seems to have had in mind the possibility of encounter-facilitating preaching that leaves a mark, the kind of mark the real presence of a holy God leaves on people who truly experience him during the worship gathering.

I can't help but think of the dramatic encounter depicted in Isaiah 6:1–8. If Isaiah's experience in the temple is any indication, the only appropriate response to the manifest presence of God in the worship space is a sincere turning away from sin, toward an eager engagement in the *missio Dei* (God's mission). This is the effect of truly anointed preaching: sincere repentance and an eagerness to serve. According to Barth scholar Thomas Currie:

> It is in the church's attempt to proclaim and hear the gospel, that the risen Christ comes and comes again, speaking the Word of God through broken human words, *freeing* the Christian community to *get up and follow in discipleship*, and *sending* the Christian community to *engage the world* in correspondence to the life and activity of Jesus Christ at work in their midst.⁴⁷

For sure, the Holy Spirit is at work in anointed preaching to awaken and strengthen faith in the risen Jesus. But he is also doing more. He is graciously drawing those who have ears to hear deeper and deeper into the reality of an intimate, interactive, existentially impactful relationship with the living God. Indeed, it has been my experience that, at times, he may even provide specific disciples, or the community as a whole, with some spiritual, moral, or ministry guidance that is amazingly timely and specific.

The Three Keys to Spirit-Empowered Preaching and Teaching

In a nutshell, three things are necessary if we are to experience truly anointed preaching and teaching. These three things are: a sense of holy expectancy; theologically real prayer; and the phenomenon of spiritual agreement (Greek: *symphōnēsis*).

---

45. Barth, *Church Dogmatics* I/1:93.
46. Barth, *Church Dogmatics* I/1:92–93.
47. Currie, *Only Sacrament*, xiii, emphasis added.

First, as we've seen, Barth was convinced it's only normal for a profound sense of expectancy to animate the congregation each Sunday morning. In the introduction he provided for Barth's published lectures on homiletics, David Buttrick indicates Barth's contention that if this corporate sense of expectancy is to occur, it needs to begin with the preacher. Buttrick explains:

> Those who preach the Scriptures will not be pontificating clerics or detached visionaries or merely dull. For, again and again, the Scriptures will speak God's *new* word. "The proper attitude of preachers," Barth says, "does not depend on whether they hold on to the doctrine of inspiration but on whether or not they expect God to speak to them. . . ." Barth calls ministers to "active expectation" and "ongoing submission" in their study of the Bible.[48]

I will humbly add that this holy expectation that God can and will encounter us through his preached word is not just for the preacher, but for the congregation as well. My experience has been that when church members approach the preaching/teaching moment open to, and hopeful for, a sense of encounter with the risen Christ, it's much more likely to happen. Evangelical theologian Gilbert Bilezikian has made the following observation: "Every instance of the intervention of the Holy Spirit reported in the New Testament indicates that he cooperates actively in situations where he is expected and wanted."[49] What Bilezikian seems to be suggesting here is when it comes to the work of the Spirit in the lives of believers, *a sense of eager expectancy tends to precede, perhaps even precipitate, experience.*

Second, with this thought in mind, there is also a need for some theologically real prayer. Barth insisted the key to effective Christian preaching is prayer. He wrote: "it is prayer that puts us in rapport with God and permits us to collaborate with him."[50] And yet, what I'm advocating for is a special kind of prayer.

As I've already indicated, a realist understanding of God maintains he is much more than a philosophical concept or impersonal spiritual force. The testimony of the New Testament Scriptures is that the God who is revealed to us in Jesus Christ is a personal, relational, and responsive

---

48. Buttrick, "Foreword," 9, emphasis original.
49. Bilezikian, *Christianity 101*, 109.
50. Barth, as cited in Currie, *Only Sacrament*, 113.

"heavenly Father" who can be experienced in ways that are intimate and interactive. Put simply, there's a huge difference between *praying to God* and *praying toward the idea of God*. The kind of prayer that empowers anointed preaching occurs when both preachers and church members are in the habit of actually conversing with God rather than merely talking at him: prayerfully waiting upon him, pleading for his anointing, and actually anticipating a response (e.g., Acts 13:1–3).

Third, since I'll have much to say about the phenomenon of *symphōnēsis* (spiritual agreement) in the following chapter, I'll simply indicate here that there's something very powerful about Christian disciples *agreeing with one another* in prayer. It's not magical, but its effect is something we can count on. Jesus shows up in an empowering way when his followers experience spiritual agreement and then speak to God from it. Question: *What would happen if more congregations, filled with holy expectation, were in the habit of praying together in a theologically real way for an anointing to rest upon their church's nurturing ministries?* Answer: *Some Spirit-empowered preaching and teaching that would greatly enhance the ability of good-hearted congregants to render to Christ a long obedience in the same direction!* If there's even a chance what I've just suggested is true, don't we need to give it a try?

At the heart of this chapter has been the message that the apostles Paul, Peter, Jude, and John felt the need to advocate for a nurturing ministry in the church that intentionally addresses the dynamic of false teaching. They were convinced a primary way in which the devil attempts to negate this second component of Christian discipleship is to introduce into the church a low rather than high view of: the Scriptures, the person and work of Jesus, and the importance of the Holy Spirit to the formational ministries of the church.

But Satan doesn't have to succeed in his deceptive attempts to negate our experience of Christian nurture. Imitating the apostles, local churches in our place and day can be careful to create a nurturing environment that's intentional about enabling church members to endure in the faith rather than join the ranks of post-Christians. With respect to a church's teaching ministry, in particular, it needs to be biblically grounded, Christ-honoring, and Spirit-empowered in order to do the best job of enabling endurance.

We can do this! Why am I so sure? My confidence is founded on the fact that God the Father, Christ the Son, and the Holy Spirit are on our side! Or, as the apostle John put it, "You, dear children, are from God and have overcome them, because the one who is in you is greater than the one who is in the world" (1 John 4:4).[51]

Reflection/Discussion Questions:

1. Do you know any post-Christians? Do you have a sense of what caused them to decide they're over Christianity and done with the church?

2. How would you explain to someone the importance of both a *volitional-intellectual commitment* to Christ and *mystical-experiential communion* with Christ? How holistic is your devotion to Christ?

3. Have you personally experienced the transformational capacity inherent in the sacred Scriptures? Care to share?

4. To what degree do you believe you'd notice if you heard or read a teaching that wasn't sufficiently Christ-honoring? How motivated are you to improve your understanding of the essence and importance of a high Christology?

5. Have you ever felt that Jesus seemed to speak to you in a personal way through a sermon or teaching? How might you improve your ability to approach preaching/teaching events with a sense of holy expectancy in place?

---

51. For an inspirational discussion on the proper way to interpret and apply this verse, see Mays, "Greater Is He."

5

Alienation

The Devil and Christian *Community*

"In your anger do not sin": Do not let the sun go down
while you are still angry, and do not give the devil a foothold.
—EPHESIANS 4:26–27

You should see the look on my students' faces when I make them aware it's possible for Christians to fool around and provide the devil with a spiritual foothold from which he can undermine a crucial aspect of their walk with Christ. Remember what we discovered in chapter 2 about the self-sabotage that earmarks the demonic impulse? It happens! By not being careful to resist the evil one's attempts to alienate us from our brothers and sisters in Christ, we allow him to stymie one of the primary ways the Holy Spirit seeks to bring us to full spiritual, moral, and missional maturity. The third cardinal component of Christian discipleship is genuine Christian community and, according to the New Testament, a steadfast commitment to it is vitally important to our rendering to Christ the long obedience in the same direction he's expecting from us. In this chapter I'll attempt to provide some biblically informed answers to four key questions: *What does Christian community look like? What makes Christian community especially important to Christian discipleship? How can we expect the evil one to attack our experience of community? What are the earmarks of a truly healthy Christian community?*

What Christian Community Looks Like

The phenomenon of Christian community or fellowship (Greek: *koinōnia*) is what happens when a group of people who possess the shared conviction that Jesus is Lord decide to do life together rather than apart. From a biblical perspective, this togetherness involves our speaking and acting into each other's lives in some remarkable ways. To be more specific, Christian community is what's experienced when church members obey the many "one another" commands we find in the New Testament. Listed below are some of the ways the apostles exhorted Christian disciples to speak and act into one another's lives. I encourage you to take your time and focus for a moment on each item on this list:

- Love one another (John 13:34; Rom 13:8; Heb 13:1; 1 Pet 1:22; 3:8; 1 John 3:11, 23; 4:7, 11; 2 John 1:5)
- Be devoted to one another (Rom 12:10)
- Honor one another (Rom 12:10)
- Live in harmony with one another (Rom 12:16)
- Stop passing judgment on one another (Rom 14:13)
- Accept one another (Rom 15:7)
- Instruct one another (Rom 15:14)
- Greet one another with a holy kiss (Rom 16:16; 1 Cor 16:20; 2 Cor 13:12; 1 Thess 5:26; 1 Pet 5:14)
- Encourage one another (2 Cor 13:11; 1 Thess 4:18; 5:11; Heb 3:13; 10:25)
- Serve one another (Gal 5:13)
- Bear with one another in love (Eph 4:2)
- Be compassionate to one another (Eph 4:32)
- Speak to one another with psalms, hymns, and songs from the Spirit (Eph 5:19)
- Submit to one another (Eph 5:21)
- Forgive one another (Col 3:13)
- Admonish one another (Col 3:16)
- Build each other up (1 Thess 5:11)

- Spur one another on toward love and good deeds (Heb 10:24)
- Do not slander one another (Jas 4:11)
- Don't grumble against one another (Jas 5:9)
- Offer hospitality to one another (1 Pet 4:9)
- Clothe yourselves with humility toward one another (1 Pet 5:5)

This is an amazing collection of apostolic prescriptions! It serves as both a rather detailed indication of the shape of Christian community, and as a not-so-subtle call to it. We get the impression that, from the perspective of the apostles, community is critical—yet another vital component of the type of lifestyle spirituality that makes possible a long obedience in the same direction. Put simply, trying to follow Christ in an individualistic rather than communal manner simply isn't an option!

That said, let's try now to imagine what it would be like to exist in an ecclesial (church or small group) environment where these kinds of interpersonal behaviors are routinely being engaged in. Notice how two dynamics in particular seem to be at the heart of Christian community: *support* (in the form of both instruction and affirmation) and *accountability* (in the form of loving, caring, and mercy-saturated admonishment when necessary). I'll have more to say about these two relational dynamics in the concluding section of this chapter. For now, I simply want to encourage readers to ask themselves this provocative question: *What would an ecclesial environment rich with both Spirit-enabled support and Christ-honoring accountability do to us?*

Why Christian Community Is Especially Important to Christian Discipleship

In my book *Getting Real*, I tell the story of a post-Christian student who had her faith in the risen Christ renewed as a result of her having encountered him in a theologically real way through a prayerful reading of one of the biblical Gospels.[1] Here's a detail of that story I've not shared in print until now. The first thing I did, now that her heart was open to Jesus once again, was to encourage her to begin asking God to bring into her life some "spiritual friends"—some fellow Christ-followers she could meet with on a regular basis so she might *continue to experience the risen*

---

1. See Tyra, *Getting Real*, 78–79.

Christ by means of genuine Christian community. This pastoral move on my part is an indication of how very important I consider this component of Christian discipleship to be. Indeed, I'll state my position even more clearly: it's my conviction that the ongoing, Spirit-enabled, theologically real encounters with Christ we experience in genuine Christian community are simply critical to a vibrant, fruitful, and enduring walk with him!

I'll begin to make my case for the special significance of the third component of Christian discipleship by pointing out that as important as the "one another" commands are to any discussion of Christian community they are not the only passages which speak to us about the importance of this discipleship dynamic. In truth, the apostolic writings are replete with indications there's something very special about Christian disciples doing life together rather than in isolation. Let's take a look at several ways I see the New Testament emphasizing how very important Christian community is to Christian discipleship.

The Way Jesus Emphasized the Importance of Community

First, we must reckon with the way the Gospel of Matthew portrays Jesus laying the foundation for the special emphasis on community we find in the rest of the New Testament. Well known is the fact that when teaching his disciples how to pray in Matthew 6, Jesus assumes (or prescribes) a corporate rather than private prayer environment. Here's a rendition of Jesus' model prayer with the first-person *plural* pronouns highlighted:

> This, then, is how you should pray: "*Our* Father in heaven, hallowed be your name, your kingdom come, your will be done, on earth as it is in heaven. Give *us* today *our* daily bread. And forgive *us our* debts, as *we* also have forgiven *our* debtors. And lead *us* not into temptation, but deliver *us* from the evil one." (Matt 6:9–13)

Biblical scholars insist the presence of these plural pronouns in this model prayer are significant. Leon Morris writes: "Jesus starts with the address, '*Our Father in heaven*' . . . . *Our* links the praying person to other believers; while the prayer may be used in private it is meant to be prayed in community . . . ."[2] Likewise, Craig Blomberg suggests, "[t]he use of the first-person plural pronouns throughout the prayer reminds us that our praying ought to reflect the corporate unity, desires, and needs of the

---

2. Morris, *Gospel According to Matthew*, 143–44, emphasis original.

entire church. The Lord's Prayer is not simply a private utterance."[3] Nothing is more basic to Christian discipleship than prayer. It's significant, therefore, that when Jesus taught his disciples how to pray, the model he gave them implies they will be doing so not as lone-ranger Christians, but as part of a spiritual family.[4]

Building on this insight, let's go on to reflect upon the way that later in Matthew's Gospel we find Jesus indicating the tremendous importance of community to his future church. In Matthew 18:15–18 we hear Jesus say:

> If your brother or sister sins, go and point out their fault, just between the two of you. If they listen to you, you have won them over. But if they will not listen, take one or two others along, so that "every matter may be established by the testimony of two or three witnesses." If they still refuse to listen, tell it to the church; and if they refuse to listen even to the church, treat them as you would a pagan or a tax collector.
>
> Truly I tell you, whatever you bind on earth will be bound in heaven, and whatever you loose on earth will be loosed in heaven.
>
> Again, truly I tell you that if two of you on earth agree about anything they ask for, it will be done for them by my Father in heaven. For where two or three gather in my name, there am I with them. (Matt 18:15–20)

The importance of community is emphasized in this very challenging passage in several ways. First, on a positive note, Jesus suggests his followers should think of one another as "brothers and sisters"—i.e., spiritual family members. But then, second, Jesus indicates one of the ways we are to care for spiritual family members is to gently, lovingly admonish them to come correct if some type of sinfulness begins to manifest itself in them (see Gal 6:1–2).[5] Third, if necessary, the entire community

---

3. Blomberg, *Matthew*, 119.

4. But there are other emphases in this model prayer as well: *intimacy* – God is to be addressed as "*Father*"; *humility* – "*Hallowed by your name*"; *surrender* – "*Your* kingdom come, *your* will be done"; *dependency* – "*Give* us," "*forgive* us," "*lead* us," "*deliver* us"; *responsibility* – "As we also . . . "; and *hope* – "For yours is the kingdom and the power and glory forever. Amen." All these prompts suggest that it's not simply the idea of God we're talking to, but God himself. In other words, it's a theologically real way to pray that Jesus provided his followers.

5. Having pointed out that there's reason to wonder whether the sin in the brother's life we're being called upon to confront was simply a sin, or a sin against us in particular, Morris goes on to explain that the manner of the confrontation should be gentle

of faith must become involved if it becomes apparent that Satan has succeeded in turning a member's heart to the dark side. To get the sinful brother to recognize the seriousness of his sin and the perilous spiritual trajectory it has placed him on, the church may have to disfellowship him (see 1 Cor 5: 1–13). Hopefully, however, this act of ecclesial discipline will be temporary and the erring brother can eventually be readmitted to fellowship (2 Cor 2:5–7).[6] Finally, Jesus underscores the importance of a dynamic I briefly referred to in the previous chapter. Jesus speaks of

---

and loving rather than harsh. He writes: "Jesus seems to be saying that the first thing the believer should do is try to get the offender to see his sin for what it is. He is not advocating the harsh attitude his people sometimes take up nor the very light attitude that is also common. Jesus specifies that this should be done "between you and him alone." There should be no attempt to bring all this out into the open. It is a matter between the offender, the offended, and God, and if the sinner can be persuaded to repent and seek forgiveness, the whole affair is over. 'If he listens to you, you have won your brother.' The brotherly relationship was disrupted by the sin; now it is restored. Instead of a lost brother there is a restored brotherhood" (Morris, *Gospel According to Matthew*, 467).

6. According to Morris: "This appears to be another attempt to win the offender over. . . . Jesus envisages the brother who initiated the process as telling the local church as a whole what had happened. . . . Yet this is still by way of appeal, for Jesus goes on to what is to be done if he does not heed the church. The implication is that the church will try to bring him to his senses. When the offender sees that the whole group of believers opposes his behavior, surely he will repent? But the possibility remains that he will not. In that case he has cut himself off from the group of people who have eschewed the kind of conduct that he has followed and from which he refuses to depart" (Morris, *Gospel According to Matthew*, 468–69).

Michael Green's take on this topic is also worth citing. He writes: "A word about discipline. When a person has to be ejected from leadership or, temporarily at least, from membership of the church, he or she is to be treated like a pagan or a tax collector (17). Is this pure vitriol on the lips of Jesus? Some commentators think so. Are Matthew's old prejudices coming out? This is how he would have thought in his pre-conversion days.

"I believe the answer is both simpler and more profound. There is realism and there is hope in that phrase *a pagan or a tax collector*—the realism of recognizing that there is at present an impenetrable barrier separating us from him; and the hope of forgiveness and a new start. The person will not listen, we are told three times. It takes two parties to make reconciliation; and therefore exclusion must follow and the barrier must stand. But what did Jesus do with tax collectors and sinners? He loved them into repentance and new hope. Matthew had good reason to remember that. He had been one of them. So this instruction is saying that love and patient caring for the straying individual should always accompany Christian discipline. As Paul subsequently put it, 'hand this man over to Satan so that the sinful nature [literally, "flesh," the self-centred life] may be destroyed and his spirit saved'. The aim should always be restoration" (Green, *Message of Matthew*, 196).

a *spiritual agreement* (Greek: *symphōnēsis*) that can occur among church members as they endeavor together to discern and do God's will. Such an agreement, says Jesus, can and will result in an ability to function with his authority and empowerment in important ecclesial matters. Let's look at the culmination of this passage again:

> Again, truly I tell you that if two of you on earth *agree* about anything they ask for, it will be done for them by my Father in heaven. For where two or three gather in my name, there am I with them. (Matt 18:19–20)

Now, it's possible what the disciples heard Jesus saying in Matthew 18:19–20 was simply: "Going forward, anytime you find yourselves in agreement concerning a matter about which you've been praying, you can presume your agreed-upon course of action has the blessing of heaven." On the other hand, Leon Morris provides some cultural background information that suggests a different, more theologically real possibility. Morris explains:

> The [Jewish] rabbis could say, "if two sit together and words of the Law (are spoken) between them, the Divine Presence rests between them" ('Abot 3:2). For Christians, coming together in the name of Jesus replaces coming to study the law, and the presence of Jesus is "the Divine Presence."[7]

In other words, it's also possible the disciples understood Jesus to be saying something like this: "I know this instruction regarding how to deal with an erring brother will seem daunting, but you need to know that something special occurs when you guys come together to prayerfully discern and do God's will here on earth. It's possible for you to experience a *symphōnēsis* that's sacramental in nature. A prayerful agreement with one another can result in a Spirit-enabled experience of my empowering presence in your midst that will allow you to faithfully hear and honor God's heart in this or that situation!"

What we're talking about here is a Spirit-empowered, theologically real kind of Christian community in which disciples end up interacting with not simply the idea of God but God himself. It's not my sense that most local churches are sufficiently aware of the sacramental potential of spiritual agreement. Needless to say, such an awareness would be huge for our understanding of the importance of community. It would mean

---

7. Morris, *Gospel According to Matthew*, 470–71. See also Keener, *Matthew*, 290.

Christians coming together in a theologically real manner to discern and do the will of the risen Christ (rather than operating as lone-ranger believers) is critical to the cultivation of a corporate spiritual, moral, and missional faithfulness before God!

But, if this is true, we should expect to find some support for this bold thesis in the rest of the New Testament. Let's see if that support is there.

The Way the Apostles Experienced the Importance of Community

Let's have a look now at some passages found in the rest of the New Testament which indicate the serious manner in which Jesus' first followers sought to practice this dynamic of agreement (*symphōnēsis*) in their life together as his church. While space won't permit an exhaustive survey, even a cursory examination will reveal numerous incidences of the apostles experiencing Christian community in the Spirit-empowered, theologically real manner described above.

Theologically Real Community in Acts 2

First, it probably goes without saying that we should consider it significant that Christ's church was launched out of a corporate prayer meeting that was nothing if not theologically real. Early on in the book of Acts we read:

> When the day of Pentecost came, they were all together in one place. Suddenly a sound like the blowing of a violent wind came from heaven and filled the whole house where they were sitting. They saw what seemed to be tongues of fire that separated and came to rest on each of them. All of them were filled with the Holy Spirit and began to speak in other tongues as the Spirit enabled them. (Acts 2:1–4)

Jesus had instructed his disciples to wait in Jerusalem until they experienced a divine empowerment that would underwrite their apostolic ministry to the world (Luke 24:49; Acts 1:8). Thus, the extended prayer gathering described in Acts 2:1–4 (see also Acts 1:14) would seem to indicate the seriousness with which the apostles took Jesus' promise concerning theologically real experiences of prayerful agreement.

Though we'll soon view some other New Testament passages which seem to portray early Christians experiencing community in Spirit-empowered ways,[8] let's focus first on another passage from Acts 2. This prototypical passage appears to have been intended to provide the readers of this biblical book with a compelling overview of what life was like for members of the church in Jerusalem in the hours, days, and weeks following the outpouring of the Holy Spirit. The passage I have in mind is Acts 2:42–47. While this passage famously alludes to all the cardinal components of Christian discipleship (worship, nurture, community, and mission), an emphasis on community is especially apparent. There are several indications in this ideal passage that these very first members of Christ's church were careful to do discipleship *together* rather than in isolation. Theirs was a lifestyle spirituality that was earmarked by a special commitment to community. Luke tells us:

> *They* devoted themselves to the apostles' teaching and to *fellowship*, to the breaking of bread and to prayer. *Everyone* was filled with awe at the many wonders and signs performed by the apostles. *All the believers* were *together* and had everything in common. *They* sold property and possessions to give to anyone who had need. Every day *they* continued to meet *together* in the temple courts. *They* broke bread in their homes and ate *together* with glad and sincere hearts, praising God and enjoying the favor of all the people. And the Lord added to *their* number daily those who were being saved. (Acts 2:42–47)

We should also take note of what this paradigmatic passage has to say about the theologically real nature of this Christian community—i.e., how involved the Lord was in the life of this church. In various ways the

---

8. It's my contention that the New Testament promotes something I refer to as a *pneumatological realism*. The word "pneumatology" refers to our understanding (doctrine of) the Holy Spirit. A pneumatological realism occurs when Christians stop treating the Holy Spirit as simply a force or concept and begin interacting with him in personal, phenomenal, life-story-shaping ways. A realist understanding of the Spirit also encourages a sense of pneumatological *expectancy* in Christian congregations rather than an attitude of pneumatological *presumption* (or even *indifference*). In other words, church members stop presuming that the Holy Spirit is at work in their lives (or being indifferent to whether he is or not) and take seriously Paul's call to continually be being filled with him (Eph 5:18) and to "keep in step" with him (Gal 5:25)! For more on the dynamic of pneumatological realism—its relationship to theological realism and importance to the life of the church—see Tyra, *Getting Real*. For more on the need for Christians to leave themselves "open to be filled constantly and repeatedly by the divine Spirit," see Foulkes, *Ephesians*, 152.

risen Christ was there blessing—anointing what was going on—with the result that new disciples were continually being made. The point is that these early Christians were not interacting with simply the idea of God or the risen Jesus. It was theologically real teaching, prayer, worship, fellowship, and sharing that was occurring among them, with some remarkable ministry fruitfulness occurring as a result.

This anointing should come as no surprise. When commenting on Acts 2:42–47, more than one commentator has proposed that it's an apt description of a "Spirit-filled church."[9] In other words, they're suggesting this is what a church that's genuinely being guided by the Holy Spirit into theologically real experiences of worship, nurture, community, and mission looks like. It would appear, then, that Luke intended the passage to serve as a paradigm, prototype, or pattern the readers of Acts should prayerfully emulate. If this is true, then this church's commitment to Christian community, experienced in a theologically real manner, will be something all Christians should take seriously![10]

Theologically Real Community in the Rest of Acts

This is precisely what we see happening throughout the book of Acts: not simply "pie and coffee" social events, but incidents of a sacramental, encounter-effecting kind of community that dramatically affected the emergence of the church.

For instance, in Acts 4:23–31 we read of a subsequent corporate prayer meeting that resulted in yet another experience of Spirit-infilling. This prayer gathering proved critical to the Jerusalem church's ability to stay the course despite an attempt by its antagonists to intimidate it into submission.

In addition, Luke goes on to describe a couple of other theologically real times of corporate prayer and worship that hugely impacted the mission of the first-century church. The ones I'm referring to occurred in the city of Antioch, among disciples who were being led by the apostle Paul and his ministry companion Barnabas. Because the Antiochene church was made up of both Jews and gentiles it was already somewhat missional

---

9. For example, see Stott, *Message of Acts*, 81; Larkin, *Acts*, 61.

10. I'll have more to say in chapter 7 about why other New Testament churches, though generous in the financial assistance they rendered to the churches in Judea, didn't seem to embrace the practice of having "everything in common."

in its orientation. However, the corporate times of waiting upon the Lord reported on in Acts 11 and 13 demonstrate how and why this church (in ancient Syria) became even more missional in its orientation. First, Acts 11:27–29 tells us it was during a corporate, Spirit-empowered worship gathering that the disciples in Antioch sensed God calling them to launch a relief ministry to aid the churches in Judea. And then, two chapters later we find that the result of another Spirit-sensitive experience of communal prayer, worship, and waiting on the Lord was the sending of Paul and Barnabas on their first missionary journey (Acts 13:1–4)!

Then, in Acts 15 we discover it was during yet another time of corporate, prayerful, theologically real deliberation that the mother church in Jerusalem made a decision that would shape the missional approach of the entire Christian movement. The issue was whether gentile Christians should be compelled to be circumcised and obey all the ceremonial commands in the Law of Moses in order to become followers of Jesus (Acts 15:1–5). A careful read of Acts 15:6–29 will reveal that this deliberation process was highly impacted by a theologically real experience of community. To be more specific, in this lengthy passage we find such community-connoting phrases as:

- "met to consider" (v. 6);
- "After much discussion" (v. 7);
- "whole assembly" (v. 12);
- "with the whole church" (v. 22);
- "so we all agreed" (v. 25); and, importantly,
- "It seemed good to the *Holy Spirit* and to *us*" (v. 28).

It's obvious this was a communal, theologically real (Spirit-empowered) deliberation process!

The point of this collection of literary snapshots from the book of Acts is to indicate how committed to a theologically real experience of Christian community the very first followers of Jesus were, and how impactful their experiences of agreement were for the emergence of his church. Apparently, what we read of Jesus saying in Matthew 18 about an encounter-effecting agreement among his disciples was taken seriously by them.

But what about the other New Testament documents? Do they also bear witness to the importance of a theologically real experience of

Christian community to the spiritual, moral, and ministry formation of Christian disciples? They do.

Theologically Real Community in the Rest of the New Testament

Since we've previously taken note of the "one another" commands that permeate the letters of the apostles, we know already how important doing life together was to them. This brief survey will focus on some passages which indicate the value they placed on a communal, Spirit-empowered approach to the dynamics of worship, nurture, and mission in particular.

For instance, in his correspondence with the Corinthian church, Paul advocates for a communal, theologically real approach to their *worship* gathering that he says may cause even unbelievers in attendance to recognize the real presence of God. After referring to the phenomenon of unbelievers coming correct spiritually because of the Spirit-empowered (prophetic) preaching/teaching/sharing that has taken place (1 Cor 14:24–25), Paul goes on to *prescribe* a worship gathering that is highly communal in its mode: "What then shall we say, brothers and sisters? When you come together, each of you has a hymn, or a word of instruction, a revelation, a tongue or an interpretation. Everything must be done so that the church may be built up" (1 Cor 14:26). This is not to say all worship services must be conducted in this specific manner. But it does beg the questions: *How often in our worship gatherings or small group meetings are those in attendance experiencing the palpable presence of the risen Christ that Paul indicates is possible? What's the role of synergy in truly anointed worship gatherings? Could it be that Christian community plays a significant role in theologically real, encounter-effecting worship?* At the least, this passage presents us with an explanation for a phenomenon many of us have experienced: God speaking to us through other members of the body of Christ in ways that are remarkably strengthening, encouraging, comforting, and at times challenging (see 1 Cor 14:3, 25).

Pressing further, Paul also advocated for a communal approach to Christian *nurture*. In Ephesians 4:15–16, we discover the spiritual formation of individual disciples really can't occur apart from a mutually impactful participation in the body of Christ. The apostle explains that

> speaking the truth in love, we will in all things grow up into him who is the Head, that is, Christ. *From him the whole body, joined*

> *and held together by every supporting ligament, grows and builds itself up in love, as each part does its work.* (Eph 4:15-16)

Paul says something very similar to this in his Letter to the Colossians where he also encourages a communal, theologically real approach to Christian nurture. The passage I have in mind reads: "Let the message of Christ dwell among you richly as you teach and admonish one another with all wisdom through psalms, hymns, and songs from the Spirit, singing to God with gratitude in your hearts" (Col 3:16).

In both of the nurture-themed passages just cited, Paul teaches that the vertical connection of individual disciples to Christ, the head of the body, requires a horizontal, cooperative, reciprocal, mutually impactful connection with other members of his body! This theme is also emphasized by Paul in 1 Corinthians 12:7-20 and Romans 12:4-8, and by Peter in 1 Peter 4:10-11. In sum, the apostles seem to have held that the best kind of Christian nurture occurs in the context of Christian community.

I never tire of referring to an incident that occurred many years ago in a small group meeting my wife and I were leading. Long story short, a young wife who had just received news she was pregnant, and who had come to this meeting having already made plans to have the pregnancy terminated, chose to do otherwise as a result of the theologically real experience of Christian community she experienced that night. No one besides her husband and I knew what was going on in this woman's life. And yet, as the group simply checked in with each other at the beginning of the meeting, something dramatic, prophetic occurred. Our process was to go around the room, each person indicating briefly what they sensed God had been saying to them since the last meeting, and what he seemed to be up to in their lives. On this occasion, the Holy Spirit used the innocent, naive sharing of each of the group members to speak to this young wife's heart. By the time it was her turn to share, she tearfully indicated God had spoken to her through the sharing, and was telling her she needed to have this baby. Today, there's a young woman in her early thirties who owes her existence to the fact that her mom and dad once attended a small group meeting during which Jesus chose to reveal himself to her parents through the guileless sharing of the other members of the group. Such is the power of a Christian community!

Finally, any survey of New Testament passages that purports to highlight how committed the apostles were to a theologically real experience of Christian community cannot avoid citing this well-known set of *pastoral care* instructions presented by James, the brother of Jesus:

> Is anyone among you sick? Let them call the elders of the church to pray over them and anoint them with oil in the name of the Lord. And the prayer offered in faith will make the sick person well; the Lord will raise them up. If they have sinned, they will be forgiven. Therefore confess your sins to each other and pray for each other so that you may be healed. The prayer of a righteous person is powerful and effective. (Jas 5:14–16)

What do Christian disciples do when illness persists despite their having cried out to God for healing many times on their own? How do Christian disciples deal with habitual sins that persist despite their having privately repented of them before the Lord? According to James, we don't continue to bear these burdens alone. Instead, we call upon the elders of the church and confess our sins to them. What's more, we do this with Matthew 18:19–20 ringing in our ears—i.e., with the hope that, having entered into a prayerful agreement (*symphōnēsis*) with one another, we might then engage in some especially powerful, theologically real interaction with the risen Jesus.

I'll have more to say later about why the dynamics of honest confession and then heartfelt prayer for one another are essential earmarks of genuine Christian community. But for now I'll simply assert the point of all the passages cited in this survey is that the very last thing we want to do as Christian disciples is go it alone. As new creations in Christ (see 2 Cor 5:17) we are literally made for community. There's something powerful about our approaching God in prayerful agreement. *Indeed, this third cardinal component of Christian discipleship is especially critical to the cultivation of a spiritual, moral, and missional faithfulness before God because of the role it plays in making possible theologically real experiences of worship, nurture, and mission!*

How the Devil Seeks to Destroy Christian Community

Given the importance of community to Christian discipleship, is it any wonder Satan is so eager to poison the well? As the title of this chapter suggests, one of the main ways the evil one endeavors to put the kibosh on our experience of community is to so alienate us from one another that an encounter-effecting agreement (*symphōnēsis*) doesn't occur. As

I survey the New Testament Scriptures, I'm able to discern three kinds of distance the devil tries to put between Christian disciples with this alienation objective in mind.

The *Geographical* Distance the Devil Encourages

> But, brothers and sisters, when we were orphaned by being separated from you for a short time (in person, not in thought), out of our intense longing we made every effort to see you. For we wanted to come to you—certainly I, Paul, did, again and again—but Satan blocked our way. (1 Thess 2:17–18)

In chapter 3 we took note of how the enemy will endeavor to keep us physically distant from the rest of the body of Christ to keep us from engaging in theologically real corporate worship. The same tactic is used by Satan to negatively impact our experience of Christian community. While life in the digital era makes possible a certain amount of connectivity that's not dependent on physical proximity, there's something special about literally being in the same room with fellow brothers and sisters in Christ. While it's true that with God all things are possible (Matt 19:26), it's hard for me to conceive of the prayer meeting that launched the church (Acts 2:1–4) occurring in a digital manner. We simply must take seriously the idea that one of the devil's schemes (Eph 6:11) is to put physical distance between disciples.

Paul's reference to the church members in Thessalonica as "brothers and sisters," and his assertion that he felt "orphaned" (Greek: *aporphanizō*) as a result of the geographical distance that separated him from them, implies he considered them family. This is reinforced by his speaking of the "intense longing" he had for their company. Obviously, there are times when some geographical distance between us and our "family of faith" can't be helped—as in Paul's estrangement from the disciples in Thessalonica (see Acts 17:1–15). Often, however, it can be. The question is: Are we as careful as we need to be to not allow the evil one to put physical space between us and our circle of spiritual friends when it's in our power to resist his effort to do so?

For example, I've seen church members elect to move away from a community of faith that was really helping them cultivate a spiritual, moral, and missional faithfulness, even though there was no family-, employment-, education-, or health-related reason for them to do so. It was simply a matter of wanderlust or a hankering to change things up. Such a move is fine when God is in it. But it can be catastrophic when he's not.

Several years ago, a young couple became Christ-followers as a result of having accepted an invitation from their next-door neighbors to visit their church. Tom and Susan (not their real names) were super excited about their new life in Christ and began to flourish spiritually and in their relationship with each other.

A huge hiccup in their spiritual journey occurred, however, when the neighbors who had invited Tom and Susan to church felt the need to move to another part of the state for employment-related reasons. Tom and Susan began to think about how nice it would be to live in that part of the state themselves. They longed to live in a more rural, green, clean, pristine locale.

The problem was several fact-finding visits to the region failed to produce any evidence that God was opening doors there for Tom and Susan in terms of employment, housing, or a new church home. Despite this, and the fact that several spiritual friends where they currently lived felt led of the Lord to virtually plead with them not to press ahead anyway, they made the decision to sell their home and move to the new locale. Even though God seemed to be sending them a signal when the escrow of the home they were selling fell through at the last minute, they persisted. They simply presumed that, in any case, they would be able to find in their new location work, housing, and, most importantly, a new circle of spiritual friends who could help them continue to grow spiritually and maritally.

Sadly, that didn't occur. This couple, still young in the Lord and somewhat naïve in their expectation that providential miracles would simply have to materialize if they were courageous enough to "act in faith," weren't prepared to deal with some significant "closed doors" and the spiritual dryness they experienced as a result of them. Specifically, the lack of a job made it impossible to qualify for a new home. Tom took a job driving a truck up and down the state. His long absences away from home and the fact that they never did find a new church family to belong to put a strain on their marriage. Tragically, the bottom line is that the enemy succeeded in driving a wedge between them and God, and each other. The last we heard, Tom and Susan both fell away from the faith, and their marriage ended in divorce.

This terribly sad story serves as a cautionary tale regarding the evil one's ability to at times outwit professing Christians who, though sincere, haven't experienced a sufficient degree of endurance training. Having done my best to pastor Tom and Susan through this experience, I can attest to the fact that a significant factor was their electing to distance themselves from a circle of spiritual friends that really was helping them grow toward Christian maturity. Despite some attempts by those friends to encourage Tom and Susan to slow down and wait a bit more on the Lord before making this move, they pressed ahead, disregarding their friends' counsel and ignoring one closed door after another. So, here's my take on the moral of this story: *given the importance of Christian community to our walk with Christ, we simply must think twice before electing to put geographical distance between ourselves and a truly healthy circle of spiritual friends.*

The *Relational* Distance the Devil Exploits

When the devil can't keep Christian disciples apart physically, he will endeavor to put distance between them relationally. The truth is: any kind of community involving fallen humans is going to include some misunderstandings, conflicts, slights, offenses, hurt feelings, anger, and even bitterness. It's no different with Christian community. There's a great need, therefore, for the phenomenon of forgiveness. It's not for nothing that one of the "one another" commands is all over this: "Bear with each other and forgive one another if any of you has a grievance against someone. Forgive as the Lord forgave you" (Col 3:13).

What's more, according to Jesus, forgiveness is not just nice but necessary if we ourselves want to experience the forgiveness God offers us (Matt 16:14–15; 18:21–35). Perhaps it was his awareness of this Jesus-teaching that motivated the apostle Paul to warn in both Ephesians 4:26–27 and 2 Corinthians 2:10–11 that an unwillingness on our part to forgive others can result in our leaving a door wide open whereby the evil one can gain a foothold in our lives! These passages read thusly:

> "In your anger do not sin": Do not let the sun go down while you are still angry, and do not give the devil a foothold. (Eph 4:26–27)

> Anyone you forgive, I also forgive. . . . in order that Satan might not outwit us. For we are not unaware of his schemes. (2 Cor 2:10–11)

In his book, *Satan and the Problem of Evil*, Gregory Boyd tells a story about the self-sabotaging, self-damning effects of ignoring Paul's counsel in the passages presented above, choosing instead to hold on to our bitterness toward others. While working as a volunteer for a charity organization that delivered presents to shut-ins during the holiday season, Boyd interacted with an elderly lady whose life story was so tragic and pathetic he never forgot it.

This lady told Boyd that sixty years earlier she had been betrayed by her fiancé and her sister. Having fallen in love, they ran off together and were married just days before she and her fiancé were supposed to say their vows. Boyd writes:

> Her heart was understandably broken. But even more wounded was her pride. She had been an exceptionally beautiful woman and, as she put it, "could have had any beau in the country." (Portraits of herself as a young woman hanging on the wall confirmed her claim.) But the one she had chosen to give her heart to had rejected her.[11]

Most of us would probably agree the woman's sense of pain after this betrayal was understandable. The question is: What do we do with feelings of resentment? Nurse them or eventually find a way to let them go? Boyd continues his retelling of the woman's story, explaining:

> Her heart and her pride were so wounded that she never again seriously considered the possibility of marriage, though many men attempted to convince her otherwise. Nor did she seriously consider the possibility of forgiveness. Some time after their marriage, her ex fiancé and sister sought forgiveness from her, but she refused. Indeed, she resolved never to speak to them again, and despite repeated efforts on their part to reconcile with her over the course of the next six decades, she never wavered from this commitment period. Indeed, in time her bitterness so possessed her that she managed to alienate all of her friends and relatives because they continued to have relationships with these two.[12]

The self-sabotaging effect of the woman's community-rejecting choices are beginning to become apparent. But Boyd has more to share:

---

11. Boyd, *Satan and the Problem of Evil*, 348.
12. Boyd, *Satan and the Problem of Evil*, 348–49.

Now this bitter old woman sat alone on Christmas Eve without a person in the world who even knew, let alone cared, that she existed. With a scornful, jaw-stiffened, pridefully triumphant tone, this pitiful woman boasted to me how her sister and ex fiancé had gone to their graves never having heard her voice again. With an air of victory she told me how "so many times" people had encouraged her to let her hatred go only to have her mock their pleas and eventually disdain them personally as well.[13]

After comparing this woman to "the Satan of Milton's *Paradise Lost*" whose credo was "Better to reign in Hell, than serve in Heav'n," Boyd concludes this real-life tale of self-damnation with this observation: "For more than sixty years this woman chose bitterness over forgiveness, war over love. The result was a life (if one could call it such) that was completely curved in on itself, shut off from the land of the living."[14]

Boyd tells the story in order to illustrate his theory regarding the "self-enclosed nature of hell."[15] While I'll have more to say about that topic in a later chapter, a takeaway from this story that's relevant for our current discussion is this: *people don't have to wait until the afterlife to experience hell. By holding on to anger and bitterness—by intentionally choosing to live among the tombs and cut ourselves with sharp stones—we can allow the evil one to put us in a hellish place here and now!*

But this doesn't have to happen. Instead of allowing lingering feelings of anger and bitterness/unforgiveness to open the door for the devil and the demonic to work woe in our lives, we can prayerfully take those who've hurt us deeply to the cross and picture Jesus praying over them: "Father, forgive them." We can allow the grace we so desperately need and appreciate to flow out of us to other imperfect people. While a perfectly renewed relationship won't be possible until some repentance has been expressed, we can at least let go of our right to damn these people on the day when we will all stand before God. It's a first step toward complete forgiveness—an important step that keeps the door of our heart closed rather than open to the evil one.

---

13. Boyd, *Satan and the Problem of Evil*, 349.
14. Boyd, *Satan and the Problem of Evil*, 349.
15. Boyd, *Satan and the Problem of Evil*, 349.

The *Spiritual* Distance the Devil Engenders

For lack of a better word, I'm going to use the word "spiritual" to describe a third kind of devil-devised alienation between disciples I've witnessed over the years. By *spiritual* distance I have in mind the separation between disciples that occurs when one disciple veers from the path of a biblically informed, Christ-honoring, Spirit-empowered Christian discipleship without having renounced the Christian faith per se. The problem is even a subtle shift in the way a disciple understands what God is up to in Christ can create a new faith trajectory that will, over time, alienate the affected disciple from those who are staying the course as laid out by the New Testament's witness to Christ. The result, ironically, is the need for the community of faith to engage in the heart-wrenching work of putting some disciplinary distance between the errant disciple and itself.

The apostle Paul seems to describe this phenomenon in several letters. For example, in his letter to the church in Philippi, Paul encouraged his readers to recognize and avoid the beliefs and behaviors of some professing believers whose agenda and ambitions were clearly not in step with the apostolic understanding of what Christian discipleship entails. Paul wrote:

> Further, my brothers and sisters, rejoice in the Lord! It is no trouble for me to write the same things to you again, and it is a safeguard for you. Watch out for those dogs, those evildoers, those mutilators of the flesh. (Phil 3:1–2)

> Join together in following my example, brothers and sisters, and just as you have us as a model, keep your eyes on those who live as we do. For, as I have often told you before and now tell you again even with tears, many live as enemies of the cross of Christ. Their destiny is destruction, their god is their stomach, and their glory is in their shame. Their mind is set on earthly things. But our citizenship is in heaven. And we eagerly await a Savior from there, the Lord Jesus Christ, who, by the power that enables him to bring everything under his control, will transform our lowly bodies so that they will be like his glorious body. (Phil 3:17–21)

Likewise, in his concluding remarks to the readers of his Epistle to the Romans, Paul issues this sobering warning:

> Greet one another with a holy kiss. All the churches of Christ send greetings. I urge you, brothers and sisters, to watch out for those who cause divisions and put obstacles in your way that are contrary to the teaching you have learned. Keep away from them. For such people are not serving our Lord Christ, but their own appetites. By smooth talk and flattery they deceive the minds of naive people. (Rom 16:16–18)

In yet another passage, Paul goes further, instructing the church in Corinth to formally disfellowship a sinful, unrepentant member whose lifestyle choice (incest with his father's wife) had not only put his own soul in danger, but posed a serious threat to the spiritual, moral, and missional well-being of the church as well. Too long to cite in full here, I'll simply point out that this passage (1 Cor 5:1–13) presents us with some of the most distressing words in the New Testament.

Finally, in his letters to Timothy and Titus, Paul discusses the correct way for the leaders of a church to deal with someone who is not only divergent in their beliefs, but is divisive and disruptive in their behavior as well. Paul wrote to Timothy, saying:

> Don't have anything to do with foolish and stupid arguments, because you know they produce quarrels. And the Lord's servant must not be quarrelsome but must be kind to everyone, able to teach, not resentful. Opponents must be gently instructed, in the hope that God will grant them repentance leading them to a knowledge of the truth, and that they will come to their senses and escape from the trap of the devil, who has taken them captive to do his will. (2 Tim 2:23–26)

Finally, the apostle provided his pastoral emissary to Crete, Titus, these instructions:

> But avoid foolish controversies and genealogies and arguments and quarrels about the law, because these are unprofitable and useless. Warn a divisive person once, and then warn them a second time. After that, have nothing to do with them. You may be sure that such people are warped and sinful; they are self-condemned. (Titus 3:9–11)

The point is a third type of distance the devil delights in creating between disciples is spiritual in nature. It begins with a subtle divergence away from what the apostles taught regarding who Jesus is and what God is up to in and through him, and ends up with significant amounts of division and disruption in the body of Christ (see Jas 3:13–16). More specifically, we're talking about another form of self-sabotage that, if it's not dealt with in the manner Paul prescribes, will not only subvert the errant disciple's spiritual, moral, and missional faithfulness, but that of the church he or she belongs to as well.

The good news is, every once in a while, what Paul had to say about these wayward disciples coming to their senses and escaping the trap of the devil actually happens! If it does, it's because a community of faith has succeeded in interacting with him or her in the way of Jesus—in both grace and truth (John 1:7), or as Paul prescribed, by "speaking the truth in love" (Eph 4:14–15). I've even seen disciples who've been disciplined bounce back and experience a renewal of their "sincere and pure devotion to Christ" (2 Cor 11:3). Such is the power of an ecclesial environment earmarked by both grace and truth, support and accountability. The last section of this chapter will explore these dynamics a bit more.

The Twin Earmarks of Genuine Christian Community

I've made repeated references in this chapter to *genuine* Christian community. This implies there's such a thing as pseudo-community. How can we tell the difference?

Over the course of four decades of pastoral and professorial ministry I've not only maintained the importance of Christian community to a vibrant, fruitful, and enduring Christian discipleship, I've done my best to model a commitment to it as well. Literally thousands of hours spent leading whole congregations and small groups of church members toward the experience of community have taught me the most fundamental characteristics of authentic Christian community are these: *support* (in the form of both instruction and affirmation) and *accountability*. Put differently, for a theologically real experience of the risen Christ to be realized within a circle of disciples, each needs to have his or her life spoken into and acted upon in wise, affirming, Spirit-enabled ways. At precisely the same time, all must be held accountable, in a loving, gracious manner, to the promises they make to themselves, the group, and Jesus. There's something remarkable about the way the experience of both support and accountability within a small group of Christian friends empowers personal transformation.

Support in the form of verbal affirmation is especially powerful. In a book on marriage I co-authored with my wife Patti several years ago, we included an inspirational story that, while well-worn, some of the readers of this book might not be familiar with.[16] It goes like this:

> In her memoir *The Whisper Test*, Mary Ann Bird tells of the power of words of acceptance in her own life. She was born with multiple birth defects: deaf in one ear, a cleft palate, a disfigured face, a crooked nose, lopsided feet. As a child, Mary Ann suffered not only the physical impairments but also the emotional damage inflicted by other children. "Oh, Mary Ann," her classmates would say, "what happened to your lip?"
>
> "I cut it on a piece of glass," she would lie.
>
> One of the worst experiences at school, she reported, was the day of the annual hearing test. The teacher would call each child to her desk, and the child would cover first one ear, and then the other. The teacher would whisper something to the child like "The sky is blue" or "You have new shoes." This was "the whisper test;" if the teacher's phrase was heard and repeated, the child passed the test. To avoid the humiliation of failure, Mary Ann would always cheat on the test, secretly cupping her hand over her one good ear so that she could still hear what the teacher said.
>
> One year Mary Ann was in the class of Miss Leonard, one of the most beloved teachers in the school. Every student, including Mary Ann, wanted to be noticed by her, wanted to be her pet. Then came the day of the dreaded hearing test. When her turn came, Mary Ann was called to the teacher's desk. As Mary Ann cupped her hand over her good ear, Miss Leonard leaned forward to whisper. "I waited for those words," Mary Ann wrote, "which God must have put into her mouth, those seven words which changed my life." Miss Leonard did not say "The sky is blue" or "You have new shoes." What she whispered was "I wish you were my little girl." Mary Ann went on to become a teacher herself, a person of inner beauty and great kindness.[17]

Words of affirmation can indeed empower personal growth and transformation. So can the dynamic of accountability. Several years ago, I was passing through a difficult season in my own spiritual and ministry journey. I won't go into detail here, but will simply indicate that for several weeks I seemed to be especially prone to becoming angry.

---

16. Tyra and Tyra, *Beyond the Bliss*, 203–5.

17. As cited in Long, *Testimony*, 85–86.

In truth, I felt like I was a powder keg about to explode. I knew for sure this intense predisposition toward aggravation wasn't due to the influence of the Spirit in my life (Gal 5:16–17). After a verbal altercation with a stranger in a parking lot, I became concerned I might actually act out in a ministry-sabotaging manner. I began to pray, asking God to deliver me, to save me from myself. The way he answered that prayer was literally life-changing!

Besides Patti, my closest spiritual friend is a former parishioner named Mike. Mike and I routinely meet to check in with each other, discussing not only what's going on in our families and professional lives, but our spiritual lives as well.[18] At one such meeting several years ago, I felt I was being prompted by the Holy Spirit to share with Mike how my life seemed to be filled with a pervading sense of frustration, and how losing my temper with my son the night before sounded an alarm within me. Obviously, my praying about my increasingly temperamental state of mind wasn't, by itself, solving the problem.

But, after asking Mike to pray with me about my anger issues, I felt the need to go further. I gave him permission to ask me how I was doing in this regard any time he felt led to do so. I promised him I'd always respond honestly, and would never be offended. In sum, I became accountable to my spiritual friend regarding an issue I knew I couldn't control on my own.

The result was truly amazing. The back of the dangerous dynamic I had been experiencing in my life had been broken. Whether it was literally a demonic "spirit of anger" I was dealing with, or some sort of deep-seated psychological pathology that was being enlivened by my current circumstances, I can't say for sure. All I know is my becoming accountable to someone whose support for me was without question served to raise my awareness in a way that proved to be liberating. Instead of merely *reacting* to frustrating circumstances, I felt a freedom to *respond* to them instead. This experience was more than life-changing for me; it was ministry-altering as well. I became a pastor who was thoroughly

---

18. These one-on-one meetings can be understood as a version of the "band" meeting that John Wesley encouraged Christian disciples to participate in. Much smaller in number than the "society" and "class" meetings, and gender specific, these meetings were occasions when disciples could discuss heart issues in an environment rich with both support and accountability. For more on the role Wesley's interlocking groups can play in Christian discipleship, and the influence of the same on my disciple-making practice in particular, see Tyra, *Defeating Pharisaism*, 222–32.

convinced genuine Christian community isn't simply nice; it's necessary. We really do need each other![19]

This chapter has endeavored to indicate why the apostles were so insistent that Christian disciples not do life alone, and why the devil is just as eager for us to avoid Christian community at all costs. This third cardinal component of Christian discipleship is especially important because it makes possible a theologically real experience of the other three. But not all forms of Christian community are created equal. The two earmarks of genuine Christian community are support (fellow Christians who speak and act into our lives in instructive and affirming ways) and accountability (fellow Christians keeping us honest in a loving, merciful manner).

Sadly, however, the truth is many Christian small groups are rife with support but no accountability, others provide members with much accountability but not much support. Tragically, some Christian small groups don't provide their members with either support or accountability! The fact is genuine Christian community is rare. But it does exist and the Holy Spirit is eager to enable it whenever and wherever there are disciples who insist on it. This is why every semester I tell all my students in all my classes that one of the most important things they can do to enhance their walk with Christ is to find (or cultivate) a small circle of friends with whom they can experience some authentic, biblically grounded, Christ-honoring, and Spirit-empowered support and accountability. It's the balance, the synergy between these two interpersonal dynamics that makes genuine transformation possible. We must not settle for anything less than genuine Christian community if we want to effectively deal with the devil.

---

19. Only recently did an internet search on "support and accountability" make me aware of a program named Circles of Support and Accountability (COSA) that has proved to be remarkably effective at reducing recidivism (reoffending) in the lives of convicted sex offenders returning to society after a period of incarceration. The success of this program would seem to bolster my contention regarding the transformational potential that exists within a relational environment rich with both support and accountability. For more on COSA see Anonymous, "Circles of Support and Accountability."

Reflection/Discussion Questions:

1. Which of the "one another" commands presented in the New Testament is the most striking to you? Why?

2. Have you ever experienced a special sense of Christ's empowering presence among gathered church members engaging in prayer, worship, study, or service in his name? Care to share?

3. Has the evil one ever attempted to insert geographical, relational, and/or spiritual distance between you and other church family members? Have you seen him do this in the life of someone you know? Do you suspect he may be trying to do so now?

4. Have you ever experienced the transformational power this chapter attributes to the presence of both support and accountability in a small group of Christian disciples?

5. What is one thing the Holy Spirit may be calling you to do in order to take your commitment to Christian community to the next level? Will you do so? Will you give us permission to hold you accountable for this in a loving, merciful manner?

6

Temptation

The Devil and Christian *Mission*

> Jesus turned and said to Peter, "Get behind me, Satan! You are a stumbling block to me; you do not have in mind the concerns of God, but merely human concerns."
>
> —MATTHEW 16:23

Something I'm afraid not all Christian church members recognize is the God of the Bible is a missionary God.[1] As I've emphasized elsewhere, according to some of the best theological minds, mission is not just something God does, it is who he is. There is a "sendingness of God" that is "evident within the trinity itself."[2] Indeed, not only has God sent the Son and the Spirit into the world to achieve his purposes, but angels, prophets, his word, *and the church as well*.[3] This explains why missiologist Christopher Wright has famously asserted: "Mission is not just one of a

---

1. See Stott, as cited in Wright, *Mission of God*, 24. See also Van Gelder and Zscheile, *Missional Church in Perspective*, 27, 32–33, 52; and Bosch, *Transforming Mission*, 400.

2. See Hunsberger, "Starting Points." See also Van Gelder and Zscheile, *Missional Church in Perspective*, 52–53; Flett, *Witness of God*, 5.

3. Flett, *Witness of God*, 42. See also Bosch, *Transforming Mission*, 399; Hastings, *Missional God*, 77–78.

list of things that the Bible happens to talk about, only a bit more urgently than some. Mission is, in that much-abused phrase, 'what it's all about.'"[4]

Now, if the *missio Dei* (mission of God) is what the Bible is all about, then it shouldn't surprise us to discover passages in the New Testament which portray it as a cardinal component of Christian discipleship that simply must not be neglected. For example, in 1 Corinthians 15:58 we read: "Therefore, my dear brothers and sisters, stand firm. Let nothing move you. Always give yourselves fully to the work of the Lord, because you know that your labor in the Lord is not in vain" (1 Cor 15:58). A missional faithfulness is another critical component of the lifestyle spirituality that enables a long obedience in the same direction. Thus, the focus of this chapter is on why and how the devil comes at this fourth cardinal component of Christian discipleship. Toward that end it will include discussions of four pertinent topics: (1) what Jesus' own mission was; (2) why the dynamic of spiritual warfare was at the heart of it; (3) how the devil did his best to *tempt* Jesus to go off mission; and (4) the way the apostolic authors encouraged their readers to deal with these same diabolical temptations. Let's have a look at these four New Testament themes one at a time. It's my hope that doing so will enable contemporary church members to overcome the evil one by staying on mission!

What Jesus' Mission Was

According to the New Testament, the mission of Jesus can be thought of as essentially two-pronged: *revelation* and *redemption (which, in turn, involves the dynamics of reconciliation and restoration)*. Jesus' ministry of revelation involved his revealing to humankind who God truly is and what he's really about. John's Gospel and the book of Hebrews in particular present us with numerous passages which emphasize this first aspect of Jesus' mission and the significance of it (John 1:14, 18; 12:44–46; 17:3–6; Heb 1:1–3).

However, in addition to *revealing* God to humankind, Jesus' redemptive mission was to *reconcile* fallen, sinful humankind (and all creation) to its Creator. While Jesus himself spoke of this aspect of his ministry (Mark 10:45), his apostles did as well, many times (Rom 3:21–24; 5:10–11; 1 Cor 1:30; 2 Cor 5:18–20; Gal 4:4–5; Eph 1:7; Col 1:13–14, 19–22; Titus 2:13–14; Heb 9:12, 15).

---

4. Wright, *Mission of God*, 22.

Furthermore, the full *redemption* of human beings (and all creation) also requires their eventual *restoration*. This explains why yet another manner in which both Jesus and his apostles referred to his mission was by means of the phrase: *kingdom of God*.

According to many scholars, God's kingdom as spoken of in the Old Testament and by Jesus can be thought of as a future world order characterized by peace, justice, and celebration under God's loving lordship and compassionate rule.[5] In other words, the mission of Jesus was ultimately about *restoration*—a better day when all of the wrongs currently at work in God's world will be put to right.

Jesus spoke of this restorative aspect of his ministry at the very beginning of it: in the sermon he delivered in the synagogue of his hometown, Nazareth. Quoting the words of the prophet Isaiah and applying them to himself, Jesus boldly asserted:

> The Spirit of the Lord is on me, because he has anointed me to proclaim good news to the poor. He has sent me to proclaim freedom for the prisoners and recovery of sight for the blind, to set the oppressed free, to proclaim the year of the Lord's favor. (Luke 4:18–19)

Then, as the Jesus story unfolds we discover the "kingdom of God" was a prominent theme in Jesus' public ministry as these passages from the Gospels of Mark and Luke make clear:

> After John was put in prison, Jesus went into Galilee, proclaiming the good news of God. "The time has come," he said. "The kingdom of God has come near. Repent and believe the good news!" (Mark 1:14–15)

> But he said, "I must proclaim the good news of the kingdom of God to the other towns also, because that is why I was sent." (Luke 4:43)

Indeed, the four Gospels reveal Jesus using this phrase no less than fifty-two times! The prominence of this theme in the Jesus story would suggest that in order to even begin to understand Jesus' mission, we simply must recognize how important the restoration of God's kingdom was to it.

---

5. See Guder, *Missional Church*, 91.

Why the Dynamic of Spiritual Warfare Was at the Heart of Jesus' Mission

What we also need to understand is that the entirety of Jesus' ministry of kingdom restoration was an act of spiritual warfare. John's Gospel portrays Jesus referring repeatedly to the evil one as the "prince of this world" (John 12:31; 14:30).[6] The other three Gospels portray Jesus not only *proclaiming* the good news concerning the kingdom of God, but then *demonstrating* it by means of physical healings, exorcisms, and raising the dead to life (e.g., see Matt 4:23; 9:35; 11:1-6; 12:28). These passages give the impression that Jesus' message was that the arrival of the kingdom of God spells the end of Satan's tyranny over creation. While disease, demonic oppression, and death are the devil's stock and trade, we're given to believe there won't be any disease, demonic oppression, or death in the coming kingdom of God (see Rev 21:1-4; 22:1-5). For sure, the full arrival (or consummation) of the kingdom will require the return of Christ (Acts 3:19-21; Rev 19:11-16).[7] But even during Jesus' earthly ministry its nature and future certainty was being manifested in advance (or in seed form). Thus, after announcing the arrival of the kingdom of God in himself (Luke 17:21), Jesus proceeded to demonstrate its present and future reality by graciously and powerfully healing someone, delivering someone, raising someone from the dead (see Mark 5)!

Furthermore, the fact that spiritual warfare was at the heart of Jesus' ministry was made crystal clear when, in a discussion with the Pharisees regarding his ministry of casting out demons, he spoke of the need to first bind the strong man before attempting to plunder his house (Matt 12:29). Commenting on this passage, New Testament scholar Craig Blomberg writes: "One cannot attack a well-protected home without first rendering the guard powerless. So, too, Jesus must first bind Satan before he can plunder . . . his house, i.e., cast out his demons. The exorcisms demonstrate that God in Christ is decisively defeating the devil."[8]

Finally, in 1 John 3:8 we read: "The reason the Son of God appeared was to destroy the devil's work." We need to get this right: it's precisely because Jesus' mission was to release the stranglehold the devil had on humanity (Heb 2:14-15) that Satan was so committed to derailing it!

---

6. I'll have more to say about this theory of how the devil became the "prince of this world" in chapter 9 of this book.

7. Ladd, *Theology of the New Testament*, 373.

8. Blomberg, *Matthew*, 203.

How the Devil Did His Best to Get Jesus to Go Off Mission

This recognition that Jesus' ministry of redemption (i.e., reconciliation and restoration) would mean the cosmic and eternal defeat of the devil helps us understand why he was so eager to cause Jesus to, if possible, go off mission. In this section, we'll ponder several additional passages which seem to indicate the way Satan attempted to do this.

Jesus' Wilderness Warfare

The Gospels attributed to Matthew, Mark, and Luke (referred to by scholars as the *synoptic* Gospels because they can be viewed together) present their readers with an account of Jesus engaged in a duel, so to speak, with the devil out in the desert (Matt 4:1–11; Mark 1:12–13; Luke 4:1–13). The insinuation is that this encounter was not just a prelude to Jesus' public ministry, but was pivotal to it. All three Gospels indicate that the Holy Spirit either sent or led Jesus into this encounter. All three Gospels state that the encounter involved Satan tempting Jesus. Mark doesn't specify the number and nature of the temptations, but Matthew and Luke stipulate there were three. Though Matthew and Luke present these three temptations in a slightly different order, they both agree on their nature. Most importantly, all three accounts portray Jesus successfully fending off these three significant, potentially mission-busting temptations proffered by Satan at the very beginning of his ministry career. Matthew's version reads thusly:

> Then Jesus was led by the Spirit into the wilderness to be tempted by the devil. After fasting forty days and forty nights, he was hungry. The tempter came to him and said, "If you are the Son of God, tell these stones to become bread."
>
> Jesus answered, "It is written: 'Man shall not live on bread alone, but on every word that comes from the mouth of God.'"
>
> Then the devil took him to the holy city and had him stand on the highest point of the temple. "If you are the Son of God," he said, "throw yourself down. For it is written: 'He will command his angels concerning you, and they will lift you up in their hands, so that you will not strike your foot against a stone.'"
>
> Jesus answered him, "It is also written: 'Do not put the Lord your God to the test.'"
>
> Again, the devil took him to a very high mountain and showed him all the kingdoms of the world and their splendor.

"All this I will give you," he said, "if you will bow down and worship me."

Jesus said to him, "Away from me, Satan! For it is written: 'Worship the Lord your God, and serve him only.'"

Then the devil left him, and angels came and attended him. (Matt 4:1–11)

Scholars vary in their understanding of what the devil's goal was in this set of temptations. The fact that the temptations thrown at Jesus seem to correspond to the ones the Israelites failed miserably at during their wilderness wanderings has caused not a few scholars to conclude the devil was attempting to see Jesus spiritually disqualified at the very outset of his ministry.[9] According to Leon Morris, "Each temptation was defeated by citing a passage of Scripture that had reference to the temptations that confronted Israel in the wilderness. Again we have the thought that Jesus fulfilled Israel's vocation. Where Israel failed in the wilderness Jesus succeeded in the wilderness."[10]

Though an entire chapter could be devoted to the nature and significance of these three temptations, I'm going to hasten to suggest that the devil's ultimate goal was to create doubt in Jesus' mind about whether he should proceed with the mission at all. Craig Blomberg seems to agree. He writes:

> One might expect the main, central period of Jesus' public ministry to unfold at once, but one more crucial preparatory event must occur. Jesus could well have perverted the nature of his messianic sonship and bypassed the way of the cross in favor of some more glamorous political or military role as liberator of Israel. But refusing to die for the sins of the world would have given the devil rather than God the victory. So Jesus' resolve to fulfill God's plans for him must be tested and proved right at the outset of his ministry.[11]

This take on the devil's ultimate goal in the temptations finds support in the way Jesus responded to each of them. Apparently, Jesus knew precisely what the evil one was up to. Let's look ever so briefly at each one and I'll show you what I mean.

---

9. For example, see France, *Matthew*, 102.
10. Morris, *Gospel According to Matthew*, 71.
11. Blomberg, *Matthew*, 82–83.

Are You Sure You Can Trust God to Provide for You?

This was the first question Satan put to Jesus. Both Matthew and Luke seem to go out of their way to alert their readers to the fact that Jesus, in his very real assumed humanity (Heb 2:14–18), was hungry. The first temptation was to serve himself—to use his powers to meet his own physical needs. It was a subtle temptation, but one Jesus considered significant. Refusing to be influenced by Satan away from a single-minded devotion to the service of others,[12] Jesus parried this first thrust by Satan by quoting Deuteronomy 8:3, which was part of a speech Moses delivered to the Israelites just before they began a crucial God-given assignment:

> Be careful to follow every command I am giving you today, so that you may live and increase and may enter and possess the land the LORD promised on oath to your ancestors. Remember how the LORD your God led you all the way in the wilderness these forty years, to humble and test you in order to know what was in your heart, whether or not you would keep his commands. He humbled you, causing you to hunger and then feeding you with manna, which neither you nor your ancestors had known, to teach you that *man does not live on bread alone but on every word that comes from the mouth of the LORD*. Your clothes did not wear out and your feet did not swell during these forty years. Know then in your heart that as a man disciplines his son, so the LORD your God disciplines you. (Deut 8:1–5)

Nice try, Satan, but Jesus wasn't having it. He wouldn't be driven by some devil-induced doubt regarding God's ability to provide for him to go off mission. He would trust God instead![13]

---

12. Morris clarifies the likely significance of this first temptation thusly: "At a later time, it is true, Jesus did use his powers to provide food for multitudes (14:15–21; 15:32–38), but these were special and exceptional occasions. There was no use of his powers for his own gratification or as a means of impressing people. His multiplication of loaves on those occasions was consistent with his God-ordained mission, just as was his refusal to do it here. He had come to take a lowly place and in the end die on a cross to save others; to use his powers to satisfy personal needs would be to deny all this" (Morris, *Gospel According to Matthew*, 74–75).

13. Weber, *Matthew*, 41.

Are You Sure You Can Trust God to Protect You?

This was the second question which, according to Matthew's Gospel, Satan used to tempt Jesus to go off mission. While some commentators have suggested the temptation was really for Jesus to try to gain a following by pulling off a spectacular stunt (i.e., jumping off the highest point of the Temple in Jerusalem and surviving it),[14] I believe Jesus' response indicates he understood the temptation differently. Jesus fended off this attempt to produce some mission-defeating doubt in his heart by, again, quoting Moses. Specifically, Jesus cited Deuteronomy 6:16, which reads simply, "Do not put the LORD your God to the test as you did at Massah." But the immediate literary context of this verse (Deut 6:10–25) is crucial. It's filled with references to God's ability to both provide for and protect his people, enabling them to succeed in their looming mission. Given this, it was imperative, said Moses, for the Israelites to be scrupulously careful to obey the commands of the Lord rather than go off script. Once again, it appears Jesus understood the devil was trying to get him to disqualify himself before his ministry even commenced. And, once again, Jesus wasn't having it. He wouldn't feel the need to make God prove himself. He'd trust him instead![15]

Are You Sure You Can Really Trust God's Plan for You?

Simply put, I'm convinced the *ultimate* goal of Satan's tempting Jesus in the wilderness was to try to get him to go off mission by suggesting it was unnecessary for him to die on the cross. Again, Craig Blomberg seems to concur. Referring to this third temptation, he explains: "Here the devil tries to seduce him with instant power, authority, and wealth apart from the way of the cross."[16] In other words, the first two temptations were, so to speak, warm-ups. It was in his third pitch to Jesus that Satan really brought the heat.

At the heart of this final temptation was the suggestion that Jesus could gain his objective—a more just, peaceful world—without all the bleeding. Satan's claim to be able to provide Jesus with "all the kingdoms of the world and their splendor" went uncontested by Jesus. It seems

---

14. Weber, *Matthew*, 41.
15. See France, *Matthew*, 104.
16. Blomberg, *Matthew*, 85.

this was a serious possibility, given the manner in which the creation's original vice-regents (Gen 1:28) had, in their own time of temptation, surrendered their authority to him.

About the third temptation Jesus faced, Morris writes:

> Satan holds out before him the prospect of a mighty empire, one that would embrace the whole world. When we contemplate the evils that flourish in even the best states we know and the wickedness that abounds in high places, we can see that to establish a worldwide empire that would be ruled with perfect justice was a real temptation, not a sham parade.[17]

A real temptation. The kingdom without the cross. Hmmm?

But, there was a catch; one that Jesus was fully aware of. Citing another New Testament scholar in the process, Morris explains the crux of this third temptation thusly:

> "Serve the devil and rule the world. In modern terms, be practical, realistic, ready to compromise; 'the end justifies the means.' To help people you must get position and power." The expression signifies not a passing gesture but a real acceptance of Satan's ways; it means yielding the chief place to Satan. It meant that if Jesus was to obtain these kingdoms he would have to accord to the evil one the place that belongs to God alone. Jesus would obtain the mighty empire only by doing what Satan wanted.[18]

In other words, the problem was this would put Jesus off mission. Why? Because his twin ministries of revelation and redemption required he remain faithful to God the Father. To do otherwise would have scuttled everything. It was a clever, sneaky temptation that, on its face, seemed very attractive: Jesus could make the world a much better place and not have to suffer and die in the process. The devil was trying to get into Jesus' head. *Are you sure you can trust the plan of God for your life? Doesn't this offer of mine prove otherwise? Let's make a deal!*

Jesus saw this for what it was: a nonstarter. Again citing the Old Testament Scriptures (Deut 6:13), Jesus' response to this diabolical offer was a hard pass. Matthew tells us:

---

17. Morris, *Gospel According to Matthew*, 77.

18. Morris, *Gospel According to Matthew*, 77. The citation is from Filson, *Commentary on the Gospel According to St. Matthew* (page number not provided). See also Blomberg, *Matthew*, 85.

Jesus said to him, "Away from me, Satan! For it is written: 'Worship the Lord your God, and serve him only.'" (Matt 4:10)

Jesus stayed on mission by maintaining his personal integrity and remaining faithful to his Father. The world will never be the same as a result.

Now, while Matthew's account of this spiritual wrestling match between Jesus and Satan could seem to be a one-off, Luke's version indicates otherwise. Luke tells us: "When the devil had finished all this tempting, he left him until an opportune time (Luke 4:13). Ironically, it's Matthew's Gospel that does the best job of providing us with some proof that Satan's effort to get Jesus to go off mission, rather than one and done, was ongoing.

Jesus' Rebuke of Peter

The verse that serves as the epigraph for this chapter—Matthew 16:23—portrays Jesus rebuking the apostle Peter as a tool of Satan! The reason for this rebuke is instructive.

To review, this verse reads: "Jesus turned and said to Peter, "Get behind me, Satan! You are a stumbling block to me; you do not have in mind the concerns of God, but merely human concerns." The irony is just a few verses earlier, we read of Jesus affirming Peter as someone who was hearing from heaven:

> When Jesus came to the region of Caesarea Philippi, he asked his disciples, "Who do people say the Son of Man is?"
>
> They replied, "Some say John the Baptist; others say Elijah; and still others, Jeremiah or one of the prophets."
>
> "But what about you?" he asked. "Who do you say I am?"
>
> Simon Peter answered, "You are the Messiah, the Son of the living God."
>
> Jesus replied, "Blessed are you, Simon son of Jonah, for this was not revealed to you by flesh and blood, but by my Father in heaven. (Matt 16:13–17)

But then, after affirming Peter's answer to the question he had posed to his disciples, Jesus went on to discuss the future in a way Peter and the other disciples had a hard time understanding, given their militaristic understanding of what Israel's messiah would be and do. According to Matthew:

> From that time on Jesus began to explain to his disciples that he must go to Jerusalem and suffer many things at the hands of the elders, the chief priests and the teachers of the law, and that he must be killed and on the third day be raised to life. (Matt 16:21)

The problem was Peter, like most Jews of his day, conceived of the Jewish messiah as a militaristic hero who would lead Israel to victory over her military opponents (i.e., the Romans). Thus, he virtually took Jesus in hand, insisting there was no way he and the other disciples were going to allow what Jesus had just foretold to come true.

Peter meant well, but it was because his preferred future actually had Jesus going off mission (see Heb 2:14–15) that he immediately received a stinging rebuke, with Jesus referring to him as Satan in the process! In other words, though Peter had heard from heaven previously, he was now doing the devil's work.[19]

Jesus' Life of Prayer

How many times Jesus had to deal with this kind of temptation during his public ministry, we don't know for sure. We do know Jesus routinely took time to be alone with God in prayer (Matt 14:23; Mark 1:35; 6:46; Luke 5:16; 6:12; 9:28; 11:1). We also know the model prayer Jesus provided his disciples included this petition: "And lead us not into temptation, but deliver us from the evil one" (Matt 6:13). As well, we're aware on the night of his betrayal, Jesus prayed for his disciples thusly: "My prayer is not that you take them out of the world but that you protect them from the evil one" (John 17:15). Finally, how can we forget what occurred in the garden of Gethsemane just before Jesus' passion commenced? Matthew tells us:

> Then Jesus went with his disciples to a place called Gethsemane, and he said to them, "Sit here while I go over there and pray." He took Peter and the two sons of Zebedee along with him, and he began to be sorrowful and troubled. Then he said to them, "My soul is overwhelmed with sorrow to the point of death. Stay here and keep watch with me."
> Going a little farther, he fell with his face to the ground and prayed, "My Father, if it is possible, may this cup be taken from me. Yet not as I will, but as you will."

---

19. For some support for this interpretation, see Keener, *Matthew*, 93.

Then he returned to his disciples and found them sleeping. "Couldn't you men keep watch with me for one hour?" he asked Peter. "Watch and pray so that you will not fall into temptation. The spirit is willing, but the flesh is weak."

He went away a second time and prayed, "My Father, if it is not possible for this cup to be taken away unless I drink it, may your will be done."

When he came back, he again found them sleeping, because their eyes were heavy. So he left them and went away once more and prayed the third time, saying the same thing.

Then he returned to the disciples and said to them, "Are you still sleeping and resting? Look, the hour has come, and the Son of Man is delivered into the hands of sinners. Rise! Let us go! Here comes my betrayer!" (Matt 26:36–46)

What I'm suggesting is we have some reason to believe one of the reasons why Jesus' lifestyle spirituality included so many hours spent in prayer is because it was in prayer he received the spiritual strength even he needed in order to stand up against the devil's relentless antagonism and to stay on mission. Before we pass this idea off as insulting to Jesus' divine nature, we must take note of the fact that a genuinely high, orthodox Christology (doctrine of Christ) requires we affirm he is both fully divine and fully human at the same time.[20] We should also keep in mind this mysterious, profoundly important passage from the Letter to the Hebrews:

> During the days of Jesus' life on earth, he offered up prayers and petitions with fervent cries and tears to the one who could save him from death, and he was heard because of his reverent submission. Son though he was, he learned obedience from what he suffered and, once made perfect, he became the source of eternal salvation for all who obey him and was designated by God to be high priest in the order of Melchizedek. (Heb 5:7–10)

The way this enigmatic passage refers to "the days of Jesus' life on earth" may very well provide some poignant support for the idea that the spiritual wrestling match between Jesus and Satan wasn't one and done, but was ongoing.[21] At the very least, it suggests the contest that took place in Gethsemane was crucial.[22] Here, apparently, was one last

---

20. See McGuckin, *Westminster Handbook to Patristic Theology*, 80.
21. See Guthrie, *Hebrews*, 134.
22. Guthrie, *Hebrews*, 135.

opportunity for the devil to succeed at getting Jesus to go off mission. This interpretation is buttressed by a detail Luke included in his version of the Gethsemane affair: "An angel from heaven appeared to him and strengthened him" (Luke 22:43). The only other time we read of an angel attending to Jesus was in the aftermath of his wilderness warfare with Satan (Matt 4:11; Mark 1:13)!

Having surveyed what the New Testament has to say about what Jesus' mission was and why and how the devil did his best to derail it, let's turn our attention now to another important issue related to the fourth cardinal component of Christian discipleship. It's one thing to argue Satan used the tactic of temptation to try and get Jesus to go off mission. It's another to assert he does the same thing with us.

The Apostles on the Need for Christ's Followers to Overcome the Temptation to Go Off Mission

My thesis here is the New Testament also presents us with passages which indicate Jesus' followers can expect to deal with the same kind of temptation to go off mission that Jesus himself had to endure. Some of these passages portray the apostles wrestling with the same three questions Satan put to Jesus. Other passages indicate the way the apostolic authors encouraged their readers to overcome these three temptations to go off mission. The next several pages are some of the most important in this book. Together, they help us understand what a lifestyle spirituality that does justice to the fourth cardinal component of Christian discipleship will look like.

Can We Be Sure God Will Provide for Us?

A comprehensive engagement in Christian mission requires we become good stewards of not only our time and talents, but our treasure as well. Sometimes the missional prompting of the Spirit is for us to speak and act into the lives of hurting people. Other times, the Spirit may prompt us to resource others who are being led to do so. Regardless, the devil knows if we are reluctant to invest our time, talent, and treasure into the work of the kingdom, he has us right where he wants us—not being fully faithful! This is why we can expect the evil one to keep putting the question to us throughout our spiritual/ministry journey: *Can you really be sure God will provide for you?*

A story from the book of Acts vividly illustrates how such a doubt can be devil-inspired. We read in Acts 4:32–35 of an apparently ad hoc relief ministry that arose, I'm going to suggest, as a result of a missional need that developed in the life of the rapidly expanding Jerusalem church. The practical question confronting this growing congregation was how to make it possible for those who had become Christ followers on the day of Pentecost to extend their stay in Jerusalem. These new converts had been visiting Jerusalem as pilgrims observing the feast of Pentecost. Having heard Peter preach on the day of Pentecost, these pilgrims had submitted to Christian baptism and become part of the community of disciples (Acts 2:37–41). Eventually, their limited resources ran out. Without some assistance they would have been forced to return to their homelands less than fully formed in their faith. So, the church made a missional move. Individuals such as Barnabas who owned property sold it and put the proceeds into the hands of the apostles to be distributed as they saw fit (Acts 4:36–37).[23]

In Acts 5, however, we read of a couple named Ananias and Sapphira who apparently couldn't bring themselves to donate the full proceeds of the piece of property they'd sold as part of the relief effort (Acts 5:1–2). Though Peter made it clear that while Ananias and Sapphira had not been under any compulsion to sell the property, or, having done so, to give any of the money to the missional endeavor, they had erred greatly by having boldly lied to the Holy Spirit—i.e., to God himself (Acts 5:3–4). In the process, Peter referred to Satan's role in enticing Ananias and Sapphira to engage in this act of subterfuge: "Ananias, how is it that Satan has so filled your heart that you have lied to the Holy Spirit and have kept for yourself some of the money you received for the land?" (Acts 5:3).

This is a terribly sad and sobering story, which seems to indicate it's not beyond the devil to put to Jesus' followers the same question he put to Jesus himself: *Can you be sure God will provide for you?* Luke is careful to tell his readers this episode had a profound effect upon the first

---

23. Some implicit support for this interpretation can be found in Larkin, *Acts*, 83. Larkin writes: "Jerusalem's tenuous local economy and Palestine's famines and political unrest placed some members in economic need. The displacement of the Galilean apostles and other members of the church's central core away from their normal means of livelihood, together with social and economic persecution, necessitated a ministry to meet economic needs (Longenecker 1981:310)." The parenthetical reference is to Longenecker, "Acts."

followers of Jesus. "Great fear seized the whole church and all who heard about these events" (Acts 5:11). Certainly it raised everyone's awareness regarding the theologically real nature of their walk with Christ. But, I suggest, it also served to make it clear an inability to fully trust God to provide for them would make them hesitant to fully obey the missional promptings of the Holy Spirit to invest their time, talents, and treasure into the work of the Lord.

The Gospels indicate Jesus made it a point to warn his hearers of the need to avoid greed (Matt 23:25; Mark 7:22; Luke 11:39; 12:15), and to trust instead in God's ability to provide for them (Matt 6:2-4, 19-34; Luke 6:38). It was probably because he was aware of Jesus' teaching about stewardship (see Acts 20:35) that the apostle Paul likewise penned passages which warned against greed (Rom 1:29; 1 Cor 5:9-11; 6:9-11; Eph 4:17-19; 5:3-5; Col 3:5; 1 Tim 6:10). He was also careful to encourage a Christian stewardship grounded in a remarkable trust in God (2 Cor 9:6-10; Phil 4:12-13). Here's the bottom line: according to the New Testament, a big part of Christian discipleship is learning to, like Jesus, trust that God will provide for us. A failure to do this will put us at risk to go off mission and be disqualified for the prize (see 2 Tim 4:6-8).

Can We Be Sure God Will Protect Us?

The truth is, however, in addition to being costly in terms of our resources, engaging in mission can be precarious socially, emotionally, and physically as well. Jesus was up-front with his disciples about there being a cost to discipleship (Luke 14:25-27). I'm convinced any attempt at endurance training that doesn't force church members to reckon with the dangers inherent in a fully faithful engagement in Christian mission is bound to founder. Here are just some of the words of warning Jesus forthrightly provided his apostles:

> Blessed are you when people insult you, persecute you and falsely say all kinds of evil against you because of me. Rejoice and be glad, because great is your reward in heaven, for in the same way they persecuted the prophets who were before you. (Matt 5:11-12)

> If the world hates you, keep in mind that it hated me first. If you belonged to the world, it would love you as its own. As it is, you do not belong to the world, but I have chosen you out of the

world. That is why the world hates you. Remember what I told you: 'A servant is not greater than his master.' If they persecuted me, they will persecute you also. If they obeyed my teaching, they will obey yours also. They will treat you this way because of my name, for they do not know the one who sent me. (John 15:18–21)

I am sending you out like sheep among wolves. Therefore be as shrewd as snakes and as innocent as doves. Be on your guard; you will be handed over to the local councils and be flogged in the synagogues. On my account you will be brought before governors and kings as witnesses to them and to the gentiles. But when they arrest you, do not worry about what to say or how to say it. At that time you will be given what to say, for it will not be you speaking, but the Spirit of your Father speaking through you. Brother will betray brother to death, and a father his child; children will rebel against their parents and have them put to death. You will be hated by everyone because of me, but the one who stands firm to the end will be saved. (Matt 10:16–22)

The book of Acts contains many passages that indicate how Jesus' warnings played out in the lives of his apostles (e.g., Acts 12:1–4). Likewise, the letters of the apostles present us with several frank assertions regarding the dangers of discipleship. For instance, the apostle Paul not only describes in some detail the persecution he himself experienced (2 Cor 11:23–28), but also boldly alerts his ministry assistant Timothy to the fact that "everyone who wants to live a godly life in Christ Jesus will be persecuted" (2 Tim 3:12). Similarly, the book of Hebrews warns its readers of the need to, like Jesus, endure in the face of persecution (Heb 12:1–3), and the apostle Peter does the same, saying:

> Dear friends, do not be surprised at the fiery ordeal that has come on you to test you, as though something strange were happening to you. But rejoice inasmuch as you participate in the sufferings of Christ, so that you may be overjoyed when his glory is revealed. (1 Pet 4:12–13)

At the same time, the apostolic writings also provide us with some encouragement regarding God's ultimate protection. For example, Luke tells us of several occasions when God's ability to protect his people was on display (Acts 12:5–11; 16:22–34; 18:9–11; 27:21–25). Likewise, Paul, who would occasionally request prayer from the churches regarding his safety (e.g., Rom 15:30–33; 2 Thess 3:1–2), would also provide his readers with testimonies of God's deliverance. One such passage reads:

> You, however, know all about my teaching, my way of life, my purpose, faith, patience, love, endurance, persecutions, sufferings—what kinds of things happened to me in Antioch, Iconium and Lystra, the persecutions I endured. Yet the Lord rescued me from all of them. (2 Tim 3:10–11)

Finally, we also find in the New Testament passages intended to assure Christ's followers they can count on God to protect them. For example, in one of the letters to the church in Thessalonica, Paul wrote: "But the Lord is faithful, and he will strengthen you and protect you from the evil one" (2 Thess 3:3).

In sum, it appears the apostolic authors were concerned to provide their readers with both the truth about the dangers inherent in genuine Christian discipleship and some reasons to stay on mission anyway. When it comes to our personal safety, the New Testament's call is for us to, like Jesus, keep trusting in God and stay the course, rather than allow the devil to get into our heads!

Can We Really Be Sure of God's Plan for Us?

And yet, what happens when, though we know God *can* protect us from Satan-initiated pain and suffering, we're also aware *he doesn't intend to*? Genuine endurance training aims to help church members process this possibility. This was Jesus' ultimate test. In ways that vary from disciple to disciple, it is ours as well.[24]

Whatever else its purpose was, the book of Revelation was intended to provide strength and encouragement for its original readers. The call, enunciated over and over again, was to be victorious—to stand firm in the faith no matter what—to render to Christ a long obedience in the same direction (Rev 2:7, 11, 17, 26; 3:5, 12, 21). But these were Christians who were either about to or who had already begun to experience some serious physical persecution. I sometimes wonder what they were supposed to do with passages like these:

---

24. My addressing this topic in greater length in chapter 8 means that this discussion can be relatively brief and introductory in nature. Given its importance to our endurance training, I consider this issue to be worthy of two treatments!

> Do not be afraid of what you are about to suffer. I tell you, the devil will put some of you in prison to test you, and you will suffer persecution for ten days. Be faithful, even to the point of death, and I will give you life as your victor's crown. (Rev 2:10)

> Whoever has ears, let them hear. "If anyone is to go into captivity, into captivity they will go. If anyone is to be killed with the sword, with the sword they will be killed." This calls for patient endurance and faithfulness on the part of God's people. (Rev 13:9-10)

> This calls for patient endurance on the part of the people of God who keep his commands and remain faithful to Jesus. Then I heard a voice from heaven say, "Write this: Blessed are the dead who die in the Lord from now on." "Yes," says the Spirit, "they will rest from their labor, for their deeds will follow them." (Rev 14:12-13)

Of course, we know what the original readers of these passages were supposed to do. Like Jesus, they were to pray hard for strength, resist the temptation to doubt the goodness of God, and stay on mission no matter what the cost!

This was precisely the message of the apostle Paul, who also models for us a steadfast missional faithfulness despite some significant, unrelieved distress. In a couple of very poignant passages, Paul is frank about how, though God had allowed him to suffer, he was resolute in his decision to lean into this suffering for the sake of the mission. It's because meditating upon both passages has value for our endurance training that I've cited them in full below. In one passage, Paul wrote:

> Therefore, in order to keep me from becoming conceited, I was given a thorn in my flesh, a messenger of Satan, to torment me. Three times I pleaded with the Lord to take it away from me. But he said to me, "My grace is sufficient for you, for my power is made perfect in weakness." Therefore I will boast all the more gladly about my weaknesses, so that Christ's power may rest on me. That is why, for Christ's sake, I delight in weaknesses, in insults, in hardships, in persecutions, in difficulties. For when I am weak, then I am strong. (2 Cor 12:7-10)

In another very moving passage, Paul seems to be engaging in a personal catharsis and counseling his readers at the same time. In the process, he provides historical evidence for the veracity of something C. S.

Lewis has Mr. Beaver say about the lion Aslan, the Christ character in his famous children's story, *The Lion, the Witch and the Wardrobe*: "'Safe?' . . . 'Who said anything about safe? 'Course he isn't safe. But he's good.'"[25] For his part, the apostle Paul wrote:

> But we have this treasure in jars of clay to show that this all-surpassing power is from God and not from us. We are hard pressed on every side, but not crushed; perplexed, but not in despair; persecuted, but not abandoned; struck down, but not destroyed. We always carry around in our body the death of Jesus, so that the life of Jesus may also be revealed in our body. For we who are alive are always being given over to death for Jesus' sake, so that his life may also be revealed in our mortal body. . . . Therefore we do not lose heart. Though outwardly we are wasting away, yet inwardly we are being renewed day by day. For our light and momentary troubles are achieving for us an eternal glory that far outweighs them all. So we fix our eyes not on what is seen, but on what is unseen, since what is seen is temporary, but what is unseen is eternal. (2 Cor 4:7–11, 16–18)

In the conclusion of *Pursuing Moral Faithfulness: Ethics and Christian Discipleship*, I refer to a *Christianity Today* article, the focus of which is the kind of radical obedience we disciples of Jesus are sometimes required to render. In that article, Alec Hill, president of InterVarsity Christian Fellowship, shares the following story:

> When Martin Luther King Jr. was 26, fellow clergy urged him to lead the Birmingham bus boycott. After agreeing to do so, he received regular death threats. Late one night, a caller threatened to bomb his house and kill him, his wife, and their infant daughter.
> As King prayed past midnight, he heard: "Martin Luther, stand up for righteousness. Stand up for justice. Stand up for truth. And lo, I will be with you, even until the end of the world." He said, "I heard the voice of Jesus saying still to fight on."
> King went to bed peacefully, no longer worried about death. That night changed his life. That night he accepted his duty. Whatever the cost might be to him or his family, he would be faithful to his calling.[26]

---

25. Lewis, *Lion, the Witch and the Wardrobe*, 80.
26. Hill, "Most Troubling Parable," 79.

To be faithful to our calling is critical to a missional faithfulness, a long obedience in the same direction, defeating the devil. But make no mistake: *the ways the devil tempts Christ's followers to go off mission can and will be quite intense.* Paul's reference in one of his letters to the ministry defection of one of his trusted ministry associates serves as yet another cautionary tale (see 2 Tim 4:10). None of us should simply presume we have what it takes (in our own strength) to emulate the radical ministry faithfulness of Jesus and his apostles.

Still, this is what staying on mission requires: our trusting God's provision, protection, and plan despite the doubts the devil tries to foster, and any actual pain and suffering God allows him to foist. Paul's call is for us to live by faith rather than by sight (2 Cor 5:7), manifesting a missional faithfulness in the process (2 Cor 5:14–15). When we do this, we overcome the devil, even if, at times, it might appear to others (and ourselves) that just the opposite is occurring. It's precisely because the Christian life can involve mystery and agony, as well as peace and joy, that it requires a significant amount of spiritual endurance.

I will have more to say about what constitutes the defeat of the devil and how it occurs in part three of this work. Specifically, in the next two chapters, our focus will be on seven specific spiritual warfare moves the apostolic authors call for us to make. In other words, the third phase of our endurance training is much too important not to participate in. It begins with a turn of the page.

Reflection/Discussion Questions:

1. How would you explain to someone the significance of the missionary nature of God?

2. How would you explain to someone the mission of Jesus, and why the devil was so eager to get him to go off mission?

3. How would you explain to someone the manner in which Satan tried to get Jesus to go off mission?

4. Which of the temptations Satan put to Jesus has he put to you? Care to share about how things turned out?

5. Do you possess a personal, specific sense of mission? Are you currently on mission? How open are you to any fresh ministry

promptings the Holy Spirit may decide to provide? How can we be praying for you?

Part Three

Standing Firm in the Faith:
How the Devil Must Be Dealt with

7

The Full Armor of God

Putting On, Taking Up, Praying In, and *Praying For*

> Put on the full armor of God, so that you can take your stand
> against the devil's schemes.
> —EPHESIANS 6:11

There are literally dozens of New Testament passages that allude to the reality and necessity of spiritual warfare. How ironic that the one best known is also the least bothered about (actually put into practice)! Then again, given the cunning, deceptive nature of Satan, perhaps this is to be expected. I'm referring to Paul's "Armor of God" discussion presented in Ephesians 6:10–20. This single biblical text, referred to by some scholars as the "classic spiritual warfare passage,"[1] will be our sole focus in this chapter as we begin the third phase of our endurance training.[2]

As he brought his letter to the Ephesian Christians to a close, the apostle Paul exhorted his readers thusly:

> Finally, be strong in the Lord and in his mighty power. Put on the full armor of God, so that you can take your stand against the devil's schemes. For our struggle is not against flesh and blood, but against the rulers, against the authorities, against the

---

1. Arnold, *3 Crucial Questions*, 37, 120. See also Powlison, "Classical Model," 92.
2. A prior version of some aspects of this chapter can be found in Tyra, "Paul's 'Armor of God' Discussion." Permission received.

> powers of this dark world and against the spiritual forces of evil in the heavenly realms. Therefore put on the full armor of God, so that when the day of evil comes, you may be able to stand your ground, and after you have done everything, to stand. Stand firm then, with the belt of truth buckled around your waist, with the breastplate of righteousness in place, and with your feet fitted with the readiness that comes from the gospel of peace. In addition to all this, take up the shield of faith, with which you can extinguish all the flaming arrows of the evil one. Take the helmet of salvation and the sword of the Spirit, which is the word of God. And pray in the Spirit on all occasions with all kinds of prayers and requests. With this in mind, be alert and always keep on praying for all the Lord's people.
>
> Pray also for me, that whenever I speak, words may be given me so that I will fearlessly make known the mystery of the gospel, for which I am an ambassador in chains. Pray that I may declare it fearlessly, as I should.

Many biblical scholars are convinced this passage is important not only because it seems to summarize the Letter to the Ephesians as a whole—or at least the *paraenesis* (practical moral and ministry application) section of the letter (4:1—6:9)[3]—but also because it provides the most elaborate discussion of spiritual warfare to be found in the New Testament.[4] This is why it's so important that Christian disciples do their best to understand and apply this discussion to their lives.

The problem is nearly all the freshman students enrolled in my THEO 101, Foundations of Christian Life course come to it each semester with virtually no preunderstanding of what it means to accomplish what Paul was calling for his readers to do in this famous passage. It's hard for me not to conclude that whatever spiritual formation these Christian students have experienced prior to their going away to college it did not include a serious discussion of how to put on the full armor of God. If this is true, it begs an important question: *What would such a discussion look like?*

I'm certain most preachers and teachers approach Ephesians 6:10–20 with a deep desire that their presentation of it be both *exegetically responsible* and *existentially impactful* (i.e., life-story-shaping). In other

---

3. For example, see Mitton, *Ephesians*, 218; Arnold, *Power and Magic*, 103, 105; Lincoln, *Ephesians*, 432, 438, 456; and O'Brien, *Letter to the Ephesians*, 457.

4. See Murphy, *Handbook for Spiritual Warfare*, 402. See also Arnold, *3 Crucial Questions*, 37.

words, their goal is to do a good job of accurately unpacking what Paul was saying in this passage, while also aiming for a presentation that's inspirational as well as informational. But achieving this balance is no easy task. Trust me: I know from experience that busy pastors need all the help they can get. It's not easy being informational and inspirational at the same time week after week!

And it doesn't help that many of the scholarly discussions of Ephesians 6:10–20 that diligent pastors are careful to consult, don't, in my opinion, make it any easier to present this passage in a way that inspires parishioners to actually put on the full armor of God. For example, at the risk of sounding a bit technical, I'll suggest that some commentaries on this important spiritual and ministry formation text may be guilty of overemphasizing the notion that the "armor of God" discussion was intended by Paul to function as a *peroratio* (a motivational summary of what had already been discussed in the letter).[5] Though I'm supportive of the exegetical theory that there's a significant connection between Paul's epistle-ending discussion and what has come before, an *overemphasis* on this theory can result in an interpretation of Ephesians 6:10–20 that's essentially redundant, void of any sense that Paul was saying anything new or important in it.[6] For sure, many scholars will acknowledge Paul was breaking some new ground here with his brief but instructive description of his readers' spiritual enemy and the seriousness of the conflict before them. But I wonder if an interpretation of Paul's "armor of God" discussion that doesn't present anything new to the message of Ephesians in terms of specific behaviors to be employed might not lead some pastors to preach and teach this text in a way that, while exegetically responsible, lacks existential (life-story-shaping) impact. *Is it possible that viewing this important passage as simply a motivational summary can, ironically, have the effect of lessening rather increasing the sense of urgency with which some preaching pastors present this text to their congregations, and the way their congregants respond to it?*

As well, it may be the commentary a pastor consults when preparing his or her presentation on Paul's "armor of God" discussion doesn't adequately indicate the role and importance of the Holy Spirit to the process of standing firm in the faith. This, too, could lead to a less than fully careful and compelling preaching of this text.

---

5. See Lincoln, *Ephesians*, 432, 438–40; O'Brien, *Letter to the Ephesians*, 458, 490.
6. See Powlison, "Classical Model," 92.

I've hinted in earlier chapters at the need for contemporary churches to recover a robust, fully Trinitarian, *realist rather than nonrealist* doctrine of the Holy Spirit.[7] Once again, a *pneumatological realism* insists that, rather than conceive of the Holy Spirit as a philosophical concept or impersonal force that is simply *presumed* to be at work in believers' lives, he can and should be known and interacted with in ways that are *personal, phenomenal,* and *life-story-shaping.* Thus, a pneumatological realism produces among church members an important sense of pneumatological *expectancy* rather than *presumption.* Paul's call in Galatians 5:25 for Christian disciples to "keep in step" with the Spirit seems to require a realist rather than nonrealist understanding and experience of the Spirit—an ongoing act of prayerful surrender to the leadership of the Spirit that I'm convinced is crucial to putting on and keeping on the full armor of God.

All of this leads me to suggest the need for a treatment of Ephesians 6:10–20 that is both exegetically responsible and existentially impactful precisely because it's Spirit-sensitive (pneumatologically real) in its approach. Identifying the basic contours of what a careful and compelling understanding of Paul's "armor of God" discussion might look like is what this chapter aims to accomplish. After identifying some of the key earmarks of what I consider to be an exegetically responsible handling of this passage, I will discuss what a Spirit-sensitive (pneumatologically real) interpretation of, and approach to, putting on the full armor of God might look like. In the process, we will witness the apostle Paul prescribing for his readers several spiritual warfare moves that are crucial to the defeat of the devil. As well, the critical importance of the lifestyle spirituality referred to several times in part two of this work will become crystal clear. *Ultimately, I'm hopeful the interpretation of Ephesians 6:10–20 presented in this chapter might encourage its readers to, much to the devil's chagrin, really do it: put on (and keep on) the full armor of God!*

Some Earmarks of an Exegetically Responsible Approach to Ephesians 6:10–20

My aim in this section is to lay out what I consider to be some key features of a responsible (careful/competent) exegetical approach to Paul's

---

7. For more on what a pneumatological realism is and its importance to contemporary Christianity, see Tyra, *Getting Real.*

"armor of God" discussion. Though I'll try not to become too technical, it's important we approach this biblical passage with the thoughtfulness it deserves. Five earmarks are worth noting.

First, we must take seriously the opinion of some scholars that this epistle-ending discussion was intended by Paul not only to *summarize* his Letter to the Ephesians, but to *complete* it. For example, New Testament scholar Gordon Fee writes: "Paul's placing this material in the emphatic final position suggests that he has been intentionally building the letter to this climax right along."[8] There most definitely is a connection between Paul's "armor of God" discussion and the rest of the epistle (especially 4:1—6:9). But Ephesians 6:10–20 is more than a rousing recapitulation of what had already been articulated; some new, vitally important pastoral exhortations are enunciated here! Indeed, my contention is that in his epistle-ending discussion, Paul provided his readers with the key to actualizing all the spiritual, moral, and ministry exhortations the letter contains! If this is so, how could we not take it seriously?

Second, without getting too bogged down in the process, we *should* do our best to discern the Old Testament (and apocryphal) passages Paul likely had in mind when he penned his armor of God discussion.[9] Scholars are aware that Paul's references in this discussion to the various pieces of armor and weaponry that need to be put on and taken up (e.g., belt, breastplate, helmet, shield, etc.) were inspired by passages in the Old Testament (and Apocrypha). As will be indicated below, there are some important theological truths communicated in these influential passages which can help us discern what Paul was up to in Ephesians 6:10–20.

Third, at the same time we should avoid the mistake of focusing too much attention on the armor rhetoric.[10] I fear some commentaries run the risk of wearying readers with overly thorough, essentially speculative discussions of the size, shape, and function of each piece of armor. Over against this approach, I contend there are several reasons why a thoughtful interpretation of Paul's "armor of God" discussion will, ironically, not be preoccupied with the armor rhetoric. First, the rhetoric is not original with Paul but is borrowed from various Old Testament passages.[11] Second, the virtue associated with each piece of armor differs from one Old

8. See Fee, *God's Empowering Presence*, 723.

9. See Barth, *Ephesians*, 768.

10. Support for this suggestion can be found in Arnold, *3 Crucial Questions*, 42; Dean and Ice, *What the Bible Teaches*, 156.

11. For example, some principal passages include Isaiah 11:5, 52:7, and 57:19.

Testament passage to another.[12] Third, Paul himself is not consistent in the way he describes the spiritual significance of the various pieces of spiritual armor he encourages the readers of his letters to put on (see Eph 6:14, 17; cf. 1 Thess 5:8). I'm not suggesting we should completely ignore the armor rhetoric; only that we devote the bulk of our attention to the actual virtues and behaviors Paul prescribes in his "armor of God" discussion (e.g., truth, righteousness, readiness, etc.). Biblical scholar Rudolf Schnackenburg implies the need for this type of approach when he writes: "The author is less concerned with the weapons or articles of clothing themselves than with the function which is indicated for each of them. . . It is a symbolic representation of the battle of the Christians against the evil in the world."[13]

Fourth, while always keeping in view the Old Testament passages Paul seems to have been inspired by,[14] our primary method, as we attempt to interpret the virtues and behaviors Paul wanted his readers to focus on, should be to examine what he had to say about these themes in earlier parts of Ephesians and other letters written by him. What did Paul have in mind when he encouraged his readers to *put on* the virtues of truth, righteousness, and the readiness that comes from the gospel of peace? What was he thinking when he instructed them to *take up* such things as faith, salvation, and the word of God? How did the missionary apostle refer to these virtues and behaviors elsewhere in his letters, especially his Epistle to the Ephesians? These questions, I contend, are at the very center of a responsible approach to Paul's "armor of God" discussion.

Fifth, and perhaps most importantly, given the way Paul refers to the Holy Spirit in Ephesians 6:10–20, elsewhere in the Ephesian letter, and in the rest of his letters, we simply must take seriously the strong possibility that the Spirit plays a pivotal role when it comes to Christian disciples resisting Satan and standing firm in the faith. This suggestion finds some significant support in the works of biblical scholars such as George Ladd and Gordon Fee. These eminent biblical theologians indicate the pneumatological realism inherent in Paul's theology by drawing attention to:

---

12. See Barth, *Ephesians*, 775n106; Muddiman, *Epistle to the Ephesians*, 291.

13. See Schnackenburg, *Epistle to the Ephesians*, 276–77. See also Lincoln, *Ephesians*, 436.

14. See Lincoln, *Ephesians*, 436–37.

(1) the many and striking ways the apostle referred to the personhood of the Spirit;[15]

(2) the apostle's many references to the vital importance of the Holy Spirit to the Christian experience in general;[16] and

(3) the way Paul seemed to conceive of the *existential significance* of the indwelling of the Holy Spirit in particular.

For example, presented below is a passage in which Fee contends the apostle had *experienced* the Spirit of Christ as a personal, life-story-shaping reality, and encouraged his readers to do likewise:

> The Spirit is God's way of being present, powerfully present, in our lives and communities as we await the consummation of the kingdom of God. Precisely because he understood the Spirit as God's personal presence, Paul also understood the Spirit always in terms of an empowering presence; whatever else, for Paul the Spirit was an *experienced* reality.[17]

We should also note that Fee's writings in particular contain some rather emphatic assertions of the profound importance of the Holy Spirit to Paul's theology. For example, Fee writes: "*One reads Paul poorly who does not recognize that for him the presence of the Spirit, as an experienced and living reality, was the crucial matter for Christian life, from beginning to end.*"[18]

As we will soon see, there's reason to believe Paul's notion of a Spirit-enabled experience of God's empowering presence played a crucial role in his understanding of what it means to put on the armor of God. Thus, anything other than a Spirit-sensitive (pneumatologically real) approach to this important text will not only fail at being exegetically responsible but will likely fall short of being existentially impactful (life-story-shaping) as well!

---

15. Fee, *God's Empowering Presence*, 830.
16. Ladd, *Theology of the New Testament*, 534.
17. Fee, *God's Empowering Presence*, xxi, emphasis original.
18. Fee, *Paul*, xiii, emphasis original.

Toward an Existentially Impactful Interpretation of Ephesians 6:10–20

OK, so what does a Spirit-sensitive approach to Paul's "armor of God" discussion look like? And what real difference will such an exegetical approach make? These are precisely the questions I'll focus on in the rest of this chapter. Having noted the importance of the Spirit to Paul's theology as a whole, my goal now is to explain why our understanding the importance of the Spirit to putting on the armor of God will increase the likelihood that we will treat this teaching with the seriousness it deserves. For the sake of expediency, I won't provide here an exhaustive, verse-by-verse commentary. Rather, my tack will be to survey the main sections of the passage before us, highlighting an importance of the Holy Spirit to it that many scholars have acknowledged. The end goal is, once again, an understanding and presentation of Paul's "armor of God" teaching that will be compelling as well as coherent.

The Call to Arms (6:10–11)

> Finally, be strong in the Lord and in his mighty power. Put on the full armor of God, so that you can take your stand against the devil's schemes.

The first thing we see Paul doing in this passage is emphasizing the need for Christian disciples to find strength in the Lord rather than rely on their own.[19] A theme that runs throughout Paul's Letter to the Ephesians is the Christian disciple's experience of divine empowerment (see 1:15–21; 3:14–19).[20] In keeping with this, at the outset of what I refer to as the Ephesian letter's "*peroratio*-plus" (or pregnant summary), Paul exhorts his readers to experience divine empowerment by putting on the "armor of God."[21]

Most scholars suggest, given Paul's apparent familiarity with passages such as Isaiah 11:5; 52:7; and 57:19, the idea connoted here is *it's God's very own armor—armor also worn by Jesus himself—that Christian*

---

19. See Barth, *Ephesians*, 760–61; Lincoln, *Ephesians*, xli–xliii, 432–33; Mitton, *Ephesians*, 220.

20. See Arnold, *Power and Magic*, 107; Hoehner, *Ephesians*, 820–21. See also Muddiman, *Epistle to the Ephesians*, 286–87.

21. See O'Brien, *Letter to the Ephesians*, 460; Foulkes, *Ephesians*, 170.

disciples are to don.[22] When we also take into account passages such as Ephesians 4:24, Colossians 3:1–10, and Romans 13:14, it becomes apparent that a rather consistent theme in Paul's letters is a call for Christian disciples to clothe themselves in a spiritually empowering manner. It also appears the apostle meant for his readers to understand this "suiting up" is not a one-time experience, but something to be engaged in repeatedly.[23] Therefore, Paul seems to have been calling for a *spirituality that enables the followers of Christ, through the work of Christ's Spirit,* to embody in themselves the virtues and behaviors Jesus himself embodied in his life and ministry (see Gal 5:22–23, 25).[24] This is huge! It's when we recognize how very important an ongoing partnership with the Spirit is to our "putting on Christ," and how important "putting on Christ" is to our putting on and keeping on the full armor of God, that we allow Ephesians 6:10–20 to pack the life-story-shaping punch Paul intended when he penned it![25]

The Nature of the Struggle (6:12–13)

> For our struggle is not against flesh and blood, but against the rulers, against the authorities, against the powers of this dark world and against the spiritual forces of evil in the heavenly realms. Therefore put on the full armor of God, so that when the day of evil comes, you may be able to stand your ground, and after you have done everything, to stand.

Another takeaway from this text that will motivate us to take it seriously derives from this exegetical question: *What did Paul have in mind when he suggested the goal of the believer's engagement in spiritual warfare is to "stand?"*

Keeping in mind the concern for moral integrity Paul has evidenced earlier in this letter (e.g., 4:1, 17–32), it would be easy to conclude that, for Paul, to stand firm is simply to avoid the temptation to sin. But Paul

---

22. For example, see Lincoln, *Ephesians*, 437, 441–42; O'Brien, *Letter to the Ephesians*, 457, 463, 473; Barth, *Ephesians*, 769; Hoehner, *Ephesians*, 821; Schnackenburg, *Epistle to the Ephesians*, 277; Foulkes, *Ephesians*, 171. Dean and Ice, *What the Bible Teaches*, 157.

23. See Mitton, *Ephesians*, 220; Foulkes, *Ephesians*, 170.

24. Arnold, *3 Crucial Questions*, 27.

25. See Barth, *Ephesians*, 762.

also evidenced a concern in this letter that the Ephesian disciples stand firm in the sense of not being "tossed back and forth by the waves, and blown here and there by every wind of teaching and by the cunning and craftiness of people in their deceitful scheming" (Eph 4:14; see Col 2:1–8).[26] Moreover, we can also find in Paul's letters calls for his readers to stand firm in a missional sense, to remain fruitfully engaged in kingdom ministry—i.e., to stay on mission (e.g., 1 Cor 15:58; Phil 1:27)!

Furthermore, not only does Paul exhort his readers to prove faithful in the spiritual, moral, and missional dimensions of their lives, this is precisely how he prays for them (see Eph 3:16–19; Col 1:9–12; 1 Thess 3:12–13). I've written extensively elsewhere about the role of the Holy Spirit in the cultivation of a spiritual, moral, and missional faithfulness before God, and, therefore, the importance of a pneumatological realism to the spiritual, moral, and ministry formation of contemporary Christians.[27] But I'm not the only one to suggest such a thing. New Testament scholar Clinton Arnold provides some implicit support for a pneumatological realism when he emphasizes the role of the Spirit in our being empowered to "stand against the devil's schemes." According to Arnold:

> God has not left us without the resources for fulfilling his will. As Jesus said in John's Gospel, "I will not leave you as orphans, I will come to you" (14:8). He promises his own presence through the Holy Spirit: "But you know him, for he lives with you and will be in you" (14:17). Thus, Paul can encourage the Ephesians to be filled with the Spirit (Eph. 5:18). We find our strength in the presence of the indwelling Lord, who empowers us to stand against the devil's schemes.[28]

I'm going to suggest that, for Paul, putting on and keeping on the full armor of God is critical to the cultivation of the threefold faithfulness God desires and deserves. I suspect virtually all church members would say they want to someday hear Jesus say to them: "Well done, good and *faithful* servant!" (Matt 25:21, 23). Because of the way the Scriptures connect standing firm and the threefold faithfulness Christ is looking for in us, we simply must take Ephesians 6:10–20 seriously!

---

26. See also 1 Cor 16:13; 2 Cor 1:24; Gal 5:1; Col 2:6–7; and 2 Thess 2:13, 15.
27. See Tyra, *Getting Real*, 61–120.
28. Arnold, *3 Crucial Questions*, 41–42.

The Nature of the Armor/Weaponry (6:14–17)

> Stand firm then, with the belt of truth buckled around your waist, with the breastplate of righteousness in place, and with your feet fitted with the readiness that comes from the gospel of peace. In addition to all this, take up the shield of faith, with which you can extinguish all the flaming arrows of the evil one. Take the helmet of salvation and the sword of the Spirit, which is the word of God.

In these four verses of his *peroratio*-plus, Paul continues his overarching call to stand firm, while also indicating the way his readers are to do so. The six exhortations presented in this portion of Paul's "armor of God" discussion (we will treat the call to pray in verse 18 separately) are obviously very important. Each one focuses on a commitment to be cultivated (truth, righteousness, readiness/peace) or a provision to be employed (faith, hope, word of God). According to Paul, these commitments and provisions are critical to a successful engagement in spiritual warfare. Though each exhortation merits a chapter-length if not book-length discussion, I'm going to present here only a cursory treatment of each, but one that I hope will prove to be both careful and compelling.

Toward this end, I want to underscore how important it is to approach this Pauline passage, being careful to keep three Pauline perspectives in mind:

1. The importance Paul placed on the Holy Spirit in Christian experience;

2. How crucial to Christian discipleship Paul considered the cultivation of a spiritual, moral, and missional faithfulness before God to be; and

3. The likelihood Paul meant for the virtues prescribed in this passage to be understood in both their objective and subjective senses—i.e., as attributes and actions of Christ himself that are to be gratefully *embraced* by his followers, and then, with the help of his Spirit, *embodied* by them.

In other words, Paul meant for the six exhortations presented in this section of his Letter to the Ephesians to be actualized rather than merely acknowledged. These exhortations are at the heart of a Spirit-empowered Christian discipleship that defeats the devil. It's only by approaching them with these three Pauline perspectives in mind that we will arrive at an understanding of Paul's "armor of God" discussion that actually makes a difference in our everyday lives.

Paul's Calls to "Put On"

The first three exhortations enunciated by Paul focus on three divine virtues which, if embraced and then embodied, will make church members a force to be reckoned with in the spiritual realm. Thus, Paul calls for his readers to cultivate a commitment to truth, righteousness, and the readiness that comes from the gospel of peace.

PAUL AND *TRUTH*

> Stand firm then, with the belt of truth buckled around your waist . . . (Eph 6:14a)

The very first virtue Paul prescribes in his "armor of God" discussion is *truth*. What did Paul have in mind here? How are Christian disciples to put on truth?

The Old Testament passage that may have inspired Paul to exhort the Ephesians to put on *truth* as a belt was almost certainly Isaiah 11:5, which reads:

> Righteousness will be his *belt* and faithfulness the *sash* around his waist.

Though some commentators insist it's the objective truth of the gospel Paul had in mind when he exhorted the church members in Ephesus to gird themselves with this initial virtue,[29] others contend he was actually encouraging them to live with integrity or "truth in the inward parts" (Ps 51:6, KJV).[30] Still other scholars suggest the way Paul referred to the virtue of truth in the earlier sections of the Ephesian letter indicates he may have had both aspects of truth in view (see Eph 1:13; 4:14–15, 20–21; 5:8–10)! One commentator observes that:

> As believers buckle on this piece of the Messiah's armour, they will be strengthened by God's truth revealed in the gospel, as a

---

29. Dean and Ice, *What the Bible Teaches*, 158; Rankin, *Spiritual Warfare*, 259.
30. See Foulkes, *Ephesians*, 181.

consequence of which they will display the characteristics of the Annointed One in their attitudes, language, and behaviour. In this way they resist the devil, giving him no opportunity to gain an advantage over them.[31]

Therefore, I'll summarize this spiritual warfare move thusly: *disciples are to resist the devil by proactively cooperating with the Spirit's desire to help them maintain a sturdy embrace of the truth of the gospel over against all religious and philosophical alternatives, and then to embody that truth in every aspect of their lives.*[32]

The idea here is that to stand firm against the evil one, we must not only remain true to the apostolic gospel the New Testament presents to us but must also take seriously the apostolic exhortations on how to live it out. Paul calls for his readers not only to be truth-dwellers but truth-tellers and truth-doers as well! This is how we overcome and do damage to the devil!

Paul and *Righteousness*

> Stand firm then, with . . . the breastplate of righteousness in place . . . (Eph 6:14b)

Paul probably had a couple of ancient passages in mind when he exhorted the Ephesians to put on this second virtue. First, Isaiah 59:17 reads:

> He put on *righteousness as his breastplate*, and the helmet of salvation on his head; he put on the garments of vengeance and wrapped himself in zeal as in a cloak.

But, it's also possible Paul may have been thinking about a passage from an apocryphal work known as the Wisdom of Solomon. There's a passage in that work that says:

> He shall put *on righteousness as a breastplate*, and true judgment instead of an helmet. He shall take holiness for an invincible shield. (Wis 5:18–19, KJV, Apocrypha, emphasis added)

---

31. O'Brien, *Letter to the Ephesians*, 474. See also Muddiman, *Epistle to the Ephesians*, 290–91; Barth, *Ephesians*, 767–68; Hoehner, *Ephesians*, 839–40; Schnackenburg, *Epistle to the Ephesians*, 277; Arnold, *Power and Magic*, 110; Murphy, *Handbook for Spiritual Warfare*, 410.

32. See O'Brien, *Letter to the Ephesians*, 474.

Once again, I'm going to side with those scholars who insist, because of the way Paul referred to the Christian disciple's righteousness earlier in this letter (Eph 4:24; 5:1, 8–9) and in his Epistle to the Romans (Rom 3:21–26), this exhortation should be interpreted thusly: *disciples are to resist the devil by allowing the knowledge of their positional righteousness in Christ to motivate them to, in cooperation with the Holy Spirit, pursue a practical righteousness for Christ, thereby depriving the enemy of any opportunity to gain a foothold in their lives.*[33]

I once heard the late Dallas Willard speak of how disappointed he was with the bumper-sticker slogan: "Christians aren't perfect, just forgiven." He felt this saying is used too often by Christians who are seeking to excuse the ongoing (habituated) sin in their lives. It's possible, in other words, to focus all our attention on what Paul had to say about the *positional* righteousness of Christ that's been imputed to his disciples (e.g., Rom 3:22; 4:22–24; 1 Cor 1:30; Phil 3:9; 2 Cor 5:21), while essentially ignoring what the apostle had to say about the *practical* righteousness Christ's followers are called to live into (e.g., Rom 6:1–23; 8:4; Eph 4:17–32; Col 3:1–17). What I'm suggesting is that an understanding of Paul's "armor of God" discussion that's both careful and compelling requires we do justice to everything Paul had to say about righteousness.

One of Satan's go-to moves is to come to us, whispering in our ears words of accusation, recrimination, condemnation: *Who are you to think you can cultivate a moral faithfulness before a holy God?* Our response to this devilish device must be two-pronged: first, we remind ourselves of our positional righteousness in Christ, and then surrender ourselves afresh to the Holy Spirit's work of enabling us to embody a practical righteousness for Christ. This is how, says Paul, we succeed at shutting the door in the devil's face!

Paul and the *Readiness that Comes from the Gospel of Peace*

> Stand firm then . . . with your feet fitted with the readiness that comes from the gospel of peace. (Eph 6:14–15)

---

33 See O'Brien, *Letter to the Ephesians*, 473–75; Barth, *Ephesians*, 796–97; Hoehner, *Ephesians*, 840–41; Murphy, *Handbook for Spiritual Warfare*, 408; Dean and Ice, *What the Bible Teaches*, 160–61.

The third virtue Paul exhorts his readers to put on might very well indicate he had a progression in view. When Christian disciples are enabled by the Holy Spirit to traffic in the truth, and then to embody a practical righteousness, we should expect the result to be an ecclesial environment (church community) so winsome in its proclamation of the gospel of peace that it draws newcomers into it at an amazing pace (see Acts 2:41, 47; 5:14). But, I'm getting ahead of myself. Let's back up a bit.

The truth is scholars are not in complete agreement as to what constitutes the third virtue Paul prescribes in his "armor of God" discussion. Most suggest the virtue in view isn't only the feeling of peace disciples enjoy due to their embrace of the gospel (see Rom 5:1) but is also a "readiness" Paul associates with the gospel of peace. An Old Testament passage that would seem to support this interpretation reads like this:

> How beautiful on the mountains are the feet of those who bring good news, who proclaim peace, who bring good tidings, who proclaim salvation, who say to Zion, "Your God reigns!" (Isa 52:7)

We know Paul was impressed with this passage because of the way he cites it in his Letter to the Romans:

> How, then, can they call on the one they have not believed in? And how can they believe in the one of whom they have not heard? And how can they hear without someone preaching to them? And how can anyone preach unless they are sent? As it is written: "How beautiful are the feet of those who bring good news!" (Rom 10:14–15)

So, was the "readiness" Paul prescribed in his "armor of God" discussion a commitment to keep preaching the gospel? Not a few scholars have come to this conclusion.[34]

I contend, however, it's possible Paul had even more in mind. A really careful treatment of this exhortation requires we consider the possibility that Paul was not only encouraging a readiness to preach the gospel of peace, but also a readiness to proactively engage in the cultivation of an ecclesial community earmarked by the peace the gospel produces.[35]

---

34. For example, see O'Brien, *Letter to the Ephesians*, 478; Muddiman, *Epistle to the Ephesians*, 285–86, 291; Mitton, *Ephesians*, 225–26; Murphy, *Handbook for Spiritual Warfare*, 410–11; Rankin, *Spiritual Warfare*, 260.

35. Some support for this contention can be found in Schnackenburg, *Epistle to the Ephesians*, 278.

Sorry, but the novelty of this exegetical take requires I indicate, briefly, the biblical support for it.

There are four reasons why I'm open to this expanded interpretation of the "readiness that comes from the gospel of peace. First, though the Greek noun translated as "readiness" or "preparation" (Greek: *hetoimasia*) doesn't occur elsewhere in the New Testament, various versions of it do occur in Pauline passages that encourage Christian disciples to be "ready" or "prepared" to *engage in good works* (see Titus 3:1; 2 Tim 2:20–21). Apparently, Paul considered it very important for church members to be *ready* or *prepared* to engage in loving actions toward everyone, but especially toward those who belong to the family of faith (Gal 6:10). In other words, elsewhere in Paul's letters we find him encouraging a "readiness" on the part of church members to engage in Christian community building.

Second, we must also keep in mind the various ways Paul refers in his letters to the phenomenon of *peace*. In some passages, Paul speaks of the peace our participation in Christ provides (e.g., Rom 5:1). In other passages, however, the apostle refers to a pursuit of peace our participation in Christ requires. For example, earlier in his Letter to the Ephesians, Paul had written:

> As a prisoner for the Lord, then, I urge you to live a life worthy of the calling you have received. Be completely humble and gentle; be patient, bearing with one another in love. *Make every effort to keep the unity of the Spirit through the bond of peace.* (Eph 4:1–3)

And, in his Letter to the Colossian Christians, Paul wrote:

> Let the peace of Christ rule in your hearts, since *as members of one body you were called to peace*.... (Col 3:15)

In both of these passages, we find Paul connecting the phenomenon of peace to the dynamic of community building. This connection begs the question: In what sense, if any, did Paul's third exhortation in his "armor of God" discussion have the dynamic of peacemaking in mind? Was Paul calling for his readers here, as he did elsewhere in his writings, to make the pursuit of peace a high priority? Is this, too, a way Christian disciples resist the devil?

Third, Paul devotes an entire chapter in his Letter to the Ephesians to the task of proclaiming and promoting the history-making, world-changing peace the gospel of Jesus has produced. It's a peace so powerful it has accomplished the unthinkable: it has brought together Jews and gentiles into a unified worshipping community! But this peace must be contended for, says Paul, in passages such as Ephesians 4:1–3 and Colossians 3:15. Was he doing so again in his "armor of God" discussion? Why would we not at least be open to this possibility?

Fourth, we must not underestimate the missional value of churches that are earmarked by peace rather than conflict, and an active caring for one another rather than competition. Such communities, empowered by the Holy Spirit, not only enable disciples to render to Jesus a long obedience in the same direction, they also do terrific damage to the devil. Their "readiness" to pursue peace provides a winsome witness to the glory of Christ, a witness Satan would rather unbelievers remain blinded to (2 Cor 4:4). In other words, genuine Christian communities preach the good news even between Sundays. They evidence the reality of God's kingdom through a demonstration of an essential attribute of it (see Rom 14:17)![36] As one commentator puts it, a Spirit-enabled readiness to promote the peace and harmony the gospel produces serves now as a "pledge of future cosmic harmony" and, in so doing, "sounds the death knell for opposing cosmic powers."[37]

It's for these four reasons my summary of Paul's third exhortation in his "armor of God" discussion goes like this: *Disciples, filled with a peace that transcends all understanding (Rom 5:1; Phil 4:7), are to resist and do damage to the devil by boldly sharing the Christian gospel of peace. They do this by means of Spirit-prompted, peace-producing words and actions, thereby evidencing the reality of God's coming kingdom in a missionally impactful manner (Acts 2:42–47).*

In sum, this is the type of presentation that compels us to take Paul's "armor of God" discussion seriously: it encourages us to believe that our heeding Paul's call to put on the virtues of truth, righteousness, and the readiness that comes from the gospel of peace will not only honor God, but highly frustrate Satan at the same time!

---

36. Some implicit support for a connection between a healthy Christian community and the "spreading of the good news of Christ to others" is provided in Arnold, *3 Crucial Questions*, 41, and Boyd, "Ground Level Deliverance Model," 154.

37. See Lincoln, *Ephesians*, 449.

Paul's Calls to "Take Up"

I've suggested the first three exhortations in Paul's "armor of God" discussion call for his readers to cultivate a commitment to three virtues: truth, righteousness, and the readiness that comes from the gospel of peace. The next three, I contend, call for a theologically-real employment of three provisions or gifts: faith, the hope of salvation, and the Spirit-inspired word of God.

PAUL AND *FAITH*

> In addition to all this, take up the shield of faith, with which you can extinguish all the flaming arrows of the evil one. (Eph 6:16)

We don't know for sure what Old Testament passage, if any, lay behind Paul's call for his readers to take up the shield of faith. In one of his psalms, David referred to God as his shield. This passage reads:

> My shield is God Most High, who saves the upright in heart. (Ps 7:10)

The implication is that David, in a fight for his life, was depending upon God to rescue him. The first two verses of this psalm read:

> LORD my God, I take refuge in you; save and deliver me from all who pursue me, or they will tear me apart like a lion and rip me to pieces with no one to rescue me. (Ps 7:1–2)

Reading this, one can't help but call to mind the way the apostle Peter referred to the devil's prowling around "like a roaring lion looking for someone to devour." At the same time, Peter's exhortation called for disciples to do more than cry out to God for divine deliverance. Instead, they were to actively "resist" the devil, by doing the hard work of "standing firm in the faith" (1 Pet 5:8–9).

So, what did Paul have in mind when he exhorted his readers to take up the shield of faith? Was he merely encouraging disciples to cry out to God for deliverance, or was he suggesting something else?

The tension between God's sovereignty and human responsibility is notoriously difficult to maintain, and scholars have a tendency to err toward one or the other. For instance, because Paul in this very letter specifies that faith is a divine gift rather than a product of human effort about which one might boast, it's possible to interpret the faith referred to in Ephesians 6:16 as "an objective, divine reality" which disciples merely thank God for rather than employ (much less cultivate). Over against this view, a biblical scholar I respect a lot, Andrew Lincoln, maintains that the faith referred to in Paul's "armor of God" discussion is "the confident trust in and receptiveness to Christ and his power that protects the whole person."[38] This strikes me as a nuanced, theologically real understanding of faith that maintains the tension referred to above. For sure, faith is a gift, but it's one that's meant to be employed and cultivated. Faith is a door, a divinely enabled response to the gospel that leads somewhere: to the realm of grace and a real give-and-take relationship with God (Rom 5:1–2). Faith is a gift, but it leads to the possibility of transformed human beings becoming responsible actors on the stage of human history.

Put differently, Christian faith is not merely mental assent to the historicity of Christ or his resurrection; it is also a dynamic, personal interaction with him. When we take up the shield of faith—when we proactively cultivate the Spirit-empowered ability to experience the mentoring of Christ in this or that situation—we receive something from him. Exercising faith in the midst of a fierce spiritual battle results in our becoming, like him, essentially impervious to the fiery missiles Satan sends our way. Lincoln puts it this way: "Faith takes hold of God's resources in the midst of the onslaughts of evil and produces the firm resolve which douses anything the enemy throws at the believer."[39] Thus, there is a focus here on faith in both its subjective and objective forms.[40] Yes, Paul considered faith a gift from God that's to be gratefully embraced, but he also indicated it's something to be embodied, employed. According to Paul, the effect a genuine, personal experience of Christ's *faithfulness* can produce in his followers is nothing less than a Spirit-imparted capacity to render to him a spiritual, moral, and ministry *faithfulness* in return![41]

So, here's my summary of the fourth exhortation in Paul's "armor of God" discussion. *It's a call for Christian disciples to resist and do damage to the devil by cultivating and employing their God-given faith. This*

38. Lincoln, *Ephesians*, 449.

39. See Lincoln, *Ephesians*, 449.

40. See also O'Brien, *Letter to the Ephesians*, 479; Foulkes, *Ephesians*, 176; Murphy, *Handbook for Spiritual Warfare*, 411; Rankin, *Spiritual Warfare*, 260; Barth, *Ephesians*, 773–74; Hoehner, *Ephesians*, 846; Schnackenburg, *Epistle to the Ephesians*, 278; Muddiman, *Epistle to the Ephesians*, 293.

41. See Eph 3:16–19; 4:11–13; 2 Thess 3:3–4; cf. Heb 11:32–34.

involves their inviting the Holy Spirit, over and over again (Gal 5:25; Eph 5:18) to do his work of making the love and faithfulness of Christ so persistently real and tangible to them (Eph 3:16–19) that they find themselves compelled to live the rest of their lives serving him rather than themselves (2 Cor 5:14–15). Taking up the shield of faith in this way will dramatically affect the ability of Christ's followers to withstand Satanic temptation to defect from the faith, sin against Christ or his people, and/or keep silent about their faith in and love for their Lord.

I contend we simply must take an exhortation such as this seriously. How can we not?

Paul and the *Hope of Salvation*

Take the helmet of salvation . . . (Eph 6:17a)

According to the prophet Isaiah, the armor worn by the Messiah includes "righteousness as his breastplate" and "the helmet of salvation on his head" (Isa 59:17). Surely, this imagery impacted Paul's understanding of spiritual warfare. In his Letter to the Thessalonians, which predated his Epistle to the Ephesians, Paul encouraged those church members to put on "faith and love as a breastplate, and the *hope of salvation* as a *helmet*" (1 Thess 5:8).

It should be noted straightaway that Christian hope is not wistful in nature but optimistic. The hope the Bible provides those who indwell (or live into) the story it tells is a confident, enthusiastic expectancy regarding the future.[42] It's a rock-ribbed certainty that Jesus is Lord and, in the end, God wins! It's because of the way 1 Thessalonians 5:8 associates hope with the helmet of salvation, and the importance Paul attributes to Christian hope elsewhere in his writings, I'm inclined to believe the apostle's fifth exhortation in his "armor of God" discussion is essentially a call for Christ's followers to lean into the hope/certainty they have in the one who will someday crush Satan's head under their feet (Rom 16:20)!

Providing some scholarly support for this interpretive take, biblical scholar Markus Barth suggests Paul's fifth exhortation "most likely" had "a 'helmet of victory' in mind which is more ornate than a battle

---

42. For more on what it means to indwell the Spirit-inspired Scriptures, and by this means to gain reliable spiritual knowledge, see Tyra, *Holy Spirit in Mission*, 119–20.

helmet and demonstrates that the battle has been won."[43] What's in view here seems to be a helmet worn in the postbellum (after the war) victory parade. Barth believes Paul was encouraging the Ephesian church members to "'take' this helmet as a gift from God. They go into battle and stand the heat of the day in full confidence of the outcome, with no uncertainty in their minds; for they wear the same battle-proven helmet which God straps on his head (according to the original meaning of Isa 59:17)."[44] Once again taking seriously the possibility that Paul's embrace of the tension between God's sovereignty and human responsibility might warrant it, this interpretation seeks to do justice to Christ's assured victory and the need for his followers to nurture a devil-defeating, life-story-shaping reliance upon it.

Andrew Lincoln also provides some implicit support for this interpretation when he suggests the "flaming arrows" referred to in Ephesians 6:16 "represent every type of assault devised by the evil one, not just temptation to impure or unloving conduct but also . . . doubt, and despair."[45] Doubt and despair are deadly. It's currently in vogue for Christian authors to extol the virtues of doubt. A little doubt never hurt anyone and might even be good for us, is the idea. I understand how such rhetoric plays well in an increasingly postmodern cultural milieu, but I'm struck by the fact that nowhere in the New Testament is doubt referred to in a positive manner.[46] There are better ways of helping church members overcome the obsession with certainty and craving for control that can lead to Christian Pharisaism and/or religious formalism rather than a real, messy, grace-and-trust-based relationship with God.[47] It's good to encourage intellectual/spiritual humility and a tolerance for some ambiguity, but encouraging doubt is not the way to do it.

Likewise, we need to recognize postconversion despair for the spiritual cancer it is. Spiritual despair is demonic. While the experience of preconversion despair can lead us to Christ, postconversion despair is a

---

43. Barth, *Ephesians*, 775.

44. Barth, *Ephesians*, 775–76. See also Lincoln, *Ephesians*, 450–51; Murphy, *Handbook for Spiritual Warfare*, 411; Hoehner, *Ephesians*, 848–50; Muddiman, *Epistle to the Ephesians*, 293; Foulkes, *Ephesians*, 176; Rankin, *Spiritual Warfare*, 260.

45. See Lincoln, *Ephesians*, 450.

46. See Matt 14:31; 21:21; Mark 11:23; Jas 1:6; Jude 22.

47. I talk a bit more about the need to do this in Tyra, *Getting Real*, 133–34, and Tyra, *Holy Spirit in Mission*, 164–65, 257–69.

tool Satan uses to cause church members to either suffer silently, complain constantly, drop out of the church, or, sometimes, end their lives.[48]

What Christian authors, pastors, and professors need to be encouraging is not doubt but hope. I can assert this in such a bold manner not only because of my pastoral and professorial experience but also because of the way the apostle Paul referred to the importance of hope in the Christian life. He refers to the possibility of and need for hope (in the sense of a God-given sense of confidence and expectancy regarding the future) no fewer than sixteen times in the sixteen chapters that make up his Letter to the Romans. The culminating appearances of the word "hope" used in this way in Romans is found in its fifteenth chapter. That poignant passage reads:

> May the God of hope fill you with all joy and peace as you trust in him, so that you may overflow with hope by the power of the Holy Spirit. (Rom 15:13)

And there's more. Scattered throughout Paul's literary corpus (i.e., his letters) are dozens of additional references to the importance of Christian hope. Each of these passages are telling, but, focusing our attention here on his Letter to the Ephesians, we find Paul speaking of the vital connection between Christian hope and Christian discipleship in four dramatic ways.

First, in Ephesians 1:11–14, Paul seems to equate what happened when his readers placed their hope in Christ (v. 11) and what occurred when they believed the gospel of Christ (v. 13). Both of these dynamics were involved in their coming to Christ!

Second, in Ephesians 1:17–23, we learn that at the heart of the apostle's intercession for the Ephesian church members was a request that the Holy Spirit enable them to become thoroughly aware of what their hope in Christ entails. He also wanted them to understand why this hope is so certain despite the reality of various spiritual authorities (see Eph 3:10; Col 1:16), and the conflict this current reality results in (see Eph 6:12).

Third, in Ephesians 2:11–13, Paul reminds his readers that prior to their coming Christ, they were "without hope and without God in the world." It's hard to imagine a more striking way for Paul to emphasize the importance of Christian hope, while also encouraging the Ephesian church members to hang on to it.

---

48. We must keep in mind the anti-truth, anti-life, anti-God nature of the devil as discussed in chapter 2 of this work.

Fourth, in Ephesians 4:3–6, Paul begins the *paraenesis* (practical moral and ministry application) section of the letter (4:1—6:9) with a call for his readers to pursue peace and unity. The ground of this unity, Paul explains, is the fact there is "one body and one Spirit, just as you were called to *one hope* when you were called; one Lord, one faith, one baptism; one God and Father of all, who is over all and through all and in all" (Eph 4:4–6). This is another profound indication of the importance Paul attributed to Christian hope!

All this to say I believe Paul's fifth exhortation in his "armor of God" discussion can be summarized as *a call for Christian disciples to resist and do damage to the devil by proactively cultivating a personal lifestyle spirituality that is hope-enabling, one that enables them to keep their eyes on the prize of which the Holy Spirit is a down payment* (Eph 1:13–14; see also 2 Cor 1:21–22; 8:14–17, 22–23). *The hope/certainty that is nurtured by this spirituality will strengthen Christ's followers against the enemy's attempts at engendering within them the discipleship-defeating attitudes of disappointment, discouragement, distraction, doubt, and despair.*[49]

Paul and the *Word of God*

> Take the ... sword of the Spirit, which is the word of God. (Eph 6:14–17)

In a nutshell, Paul's sixth exhortation calls for Christ's followers to imitate the way Jesus and his apostles employed the Spirit-inspired word of God. Let's try to discern what this involves.

Yet another biblical commentator I appreciate, Francis Foulkes, makes the observation that "[t]he Old Testament often refers to speech as a sword." In some passages, "[t]he words of the wicked are said to wound as a sword" (e.g., Ps 57:4; 64:3). In other passages, it's made clear God will sometimes use his word as a weapon (see Heb 4:12; Isa 11:4; Hos 6:5). Finally, Foulkes points out, there are still other passages which indicate God's word can be "wielded by his messengers in the lives of others" (e.g., Isa 49:2).[50] In other words, there are various Old Testament verses that

---

49. Some support for this summary can be found in Barth, *Ephesians*, 775–76. See also Lincoln, *Ephesians*, 450–51; Murphy, *Handbook for Spiritual Warfare*, 411; Hoehner, *Ephesians*, 848–50; Muddiman, *Epistle to the Ephesians*, 293; Foulkes, *Ephesians*, 176; Rankin, *Spiritual Warfare*, 260.

50. Foulkes, *Ephesians*, 184.

may have influenced Paul to suggest that taking up the word of God is an important spiritual warfare move. And, of course, the apostle may have also been aware of the way Jesus successfully wielded the word of God in his duel with the devil in the desert (Matt 4:1–11)!

What we can be certain of is the dynamic connection Paul made between the Holy Spirit and God's word. On the one hand, we know Paul believed the Scriptures came into existence by means of the Spirit (breath) of God (2 Tim 3:16–17; cf. 2 Pet 1:21). But in his "armor of God" discussion, Paul goes beyond this to indicate the word of God is something the Spirit uses in an ongoing manner. The word (Greek: *rhēma*) is the Spirit's sword,[51] by means of which he does his work of empowering God's people to accomplish God's purposes in the world. According to Foulkes, the Holy Spirit puts this sword into the grasp of the Christian disciple, and then "enables him to use it."[52]

This language implies something prophetic is going on: the Spirit speaking and acting on God's behalf to and through God's people. Indeed, the fact the Greek word Paul uses in Ephesians 6:17 to refer to God's word is *rhema* rather than *logos* is significant in this regard for many New Testament scholars. It implies, they suggest, Paul had something prophetic in mind when he enunciated this sixth exhortation—a Spirit-empowered or prophetic wielding of God's word.

For instance, Markus Barth argues that, in Paul's lexicon, the term *rhema*, which is translated here and in Ephesians 5:26 as "word," signifies speech that is "specifically weighty" because of it's "creative, revelatory, *prophetic*" character.[53] Barth goes on to indicate that, because of the prophetic interaction between church members that's alluded to by Paul in Ephesians 4:25, 29–30; 5:13, 18–19, we can't rule out the possibility that when Paul uses the term *rhema* in Ephesians 6:17, "a reference to *prophetic* speech . . . cannot be excluded."[54]

Likewise, another well-respected biblical commentator, Leslie Mitton, has argued the way Paul associates "word" and "Spirit" in his sixth exhortation suggests a prophetic dynamic was on his mind. Mitton writes:

> In Paul's writings those who spoke God's word under the impulse of the Spirit were called *prophets*. It was their function not

---

51. Foulkes, *Ephesians*, 184.
52. Foulkes, *Ephesians*, 184.
53. See Barth, *Ephesians*, 777, emphasis added.
54. See Barth, *Ephesians*, 777, emphasis added.

so much to recall and expound written words from the past as to *speak out what God was saying to them* in the present. "Thus says the Lord" was their characteristic utterance. The Spirit in a Christian can enable him to become *God's spokesman to the situation in which he finds himself.* The Spirit *furnishes him with the word of God,* the spiritual sword in God's advancing cause. In this cause the Spirit, it was believed, would provide the Christian with the word he needs to make an effective answer either as a witness or under interrogation: "The words you need will be given to you . . . It will be the Spirit of God speaking in you" (Matt 10:19–20).[55]

In my book, *The Holy Spirit in Mission: Prophetic Speech and Action in Christian Witness,* I point out that in twenty-one of the twenty-eight chapters that make up the book of Acts, we find some type of prophetic, Spirit-prompted and -enabled speech and/or action.[56] In other words, scattered throughout the book of Acts are passages that portray the first followers of Jesus engaging in evangelistic, edifying, and equipping activities that were prophetic in nature.[57] The Spirit of mission was powerfully enabling church leaders and rank-and-file members (e.g., see Acts 9:10–20) to fulfill the mission Jesus had bequeathed to the church (Matt 28:19–20; Acts 1:8). What I'm suggesting in this work is the phenomenon of prophetic speech and action that's so prominent in the book of Acts shows up in Paul's letters as well. And not just in Romans 8, 1 Corinthians 12, 14, and Ephesians 5,[58] but in his "armor of God" discussion too. The upshot is that the same Holy Spirit who empowers Christian disciples to engage prophetically in missional ministry can and will empower them to function prophetically in the context of spiritual warfare as well. Indeed, sometimes these two dynamics occur at the same time (see Acts 13:6–12; 16:16–18)!

I'll have more to say about the possibility that Paul had something prophetic in mind when he penned his *peroratio*-plus in the next section of this chapter. For now, it's enough to note that not a few scholars believe that, just as the Spirit was involved in Jesus' victory over Satan at the

---

55. See Mitton, *Ephesians,* 227, emphasis added. See also Tyra, *Holy Spirit in Mission,* 39–101.

56. See Tyra, *Holy Spirit in Mission,* 65–67.

57. See Tyra, *Holy Spirit in Mission,* 75–101.

58. See Tyra, *Holy Spirit in Mission,* 68–74.

beginning of his public ministry, he can and will enable Jesus' followers to follow suit.[59] Foulkes speaks for many when he asserts:

> The Lord's use of the word of Scripture in his temptations (Matt. 4:1–10) is sufficient illustration and incentive for Christians to fortify themselves with the knowledge and understanding of the word that they may with similar conviction and power defend themselves by it in the onslaughts of the enemy.[60]

Thus, my summary for this sixth exhortation provided by Paul in his "armor of God" discussion goes like this: *Disciples are to resist and do damage to the devil by obeying the Spirit's promptings to speak the word of God in a prophetic manner to themselves, the devil, and others in an evangelizing, edifying, and equipping manner.*

The cursory summaries we've just worked our way through represent an attempt at an interpretation of the six exhortations presented in Paul's "armor of God" discussion that strives to be both responsible and life-story-shaping. It's my hope that a thoughtful pondering of these interpretations, all of which seek to do justice to the three Pauline perspectives referred to earlier, will empower contemporary Christians to be more than "hearers" of these important spiritual warfare instructions, but "doers" as well (Jas 1:22).

And yet, we must press on. We haven't reached the end of Paul's "armor of God" discussion yet. Two more very important sections remain to be treated.

Paul's Call to Prayer—"Pray In" and "Pray For" (6:18)

> And pray in the Spirit on all occasions with all kinds of prayers and requests. With this in mind, be alert and always keep on praying for all the Lord's people.

Having indicated the important role the Holy Spirit plays in the effective use of the word of God (Eph 6:17), Paul immediately exhorts his readers toward a dynamic, *Spirit-enabled* engagement in prayer as well (Eph 6:18). This succession of references to the Holy Spirit is suggestive of how important Paul considered the Spirit to be to a successful engagement in

---

59. See Barth, *Ephesians*, 777; Mitton, *Ephesians*, 227; O'Brien, *Letter to the Ephesians*, 482; Arnold, *Power and Magic*, 120.

60. Foulkes, *Ephesians*, 184.

spiritual warfare. It makes sense, then, that an interpretation of Ephesians 6:10–20 that strives to be Spirit-sensitive will devote a bit of extra space to its treatment of the call to prayer presented in it.

The Importance of Prayer to Spiritual Warfare

While only some commentators consider the exhortation to pray in Ephesians 6:18 to be a seventh piece of armor,[61] nearly all suggest it's critical to Paul's "armor of God" discussion.[62] For example, after asserting that "[p]rayer is the heart of spiritual warfare," Clinton Arnold goes on to offer this clarification: "The seventh weapon in the believer's arsenal listed by Paul is prayer (Eph. 6:18). It is not seventh in importance, however. It is actually foundational to deploying all of the other weapons. Prayer is the essence and mode of spiritual warfare."[63] It's hard to find a more emphatic indication of the importance of prayer to Paul's "armor of God" discussion than this.

What It Means to Pray in the Spirit

Pressing on, while I very much agree with this assessment of the critical importance of prayer to Paul's "armor of God" discussion, I'm somewhat disappointed at how few scholars describe what it means to pray *in the Spirit* in a way that reflects Paul's pneumatologically real understanding and practice of it. For example, though John Muddiman refers to prayer as "the gift of the Holy Spirit," citing Paul (Rom 8:15) in the process, the conclusion he draws is it's the Spirit "who inspires all prayer (cf. Rom 8:16, 26f)."[64] Now, while this assertion certainly pays attention to the importance of the Spirit to Christian prayer, taken by itself it can prompt the notion that Paul taught that *since the Spirit inspires all prayer, all prayer is necessarily prayer in the Spirit*.

---

61. For example, Arnold, *3 Crucial Questions*, 43; Boyd, *God at War*, 281–82. Brown, *Armor of God*, 91–92, 129.

62. For example, see Lincoln, *Ephesians*, 430–31, 451–52, 457; O'Brien, *Letter to the Ephesians*, 483–84; Arnold, *Power and Magic*, 112; Foulkes, *Ephesians*, 177; Murphy, *Handbook for Spiritual Warfare*, 412; Ingram, *Invisible War*, 175; Corts, *Truth about Spiritual Warfare*, 91.

63. Arnold, *3 Crucial Questions*, 43–44. See also Barth, *Ephesians*, 777.

64. See Muddiman, *Epistle to the Ephesians*, 295.

In essential agreement with this view, other scholars insist that to pray in the Spirit is simply to pray constantly, variously, alertly, perseveringly, universally, biblically, etc.[65] In other words, the only thing that makes praying in the Spirit different is the especially intense or fervent manner in which it's engaged.

To his credit, Clinton Arnold goes beyond this to speak of a special type of prayer that involves a significant amount of sensitivity to the Spirit. He explains that praying in the Spirit actually

> refers to the Holy Spirit's work of guiding and directing us to pray for specific things. Paul calls us to cultivate a sensitivity to *what the Spirit may be prompting us to pray for* and then how we should pray about it. Prayer is more than vocalizing a list of needs to God. Prayer involves asking God how we should pray and then acting on *the promptings and impressions the Spirit places on our minds.*[66]

In another place, Arnold comes even closer to a fully pneumatologically real interpretation of praying in the Spirit when he writes:

> Jesus promised that he would send the Holy Spirit to serve as a counselor and guide for us (John 14:16, 26; 15:26). Part of the ministry of the Holy Spirit is in providing direction and guidance in how we pray (Eph. 6:18). As we seek to reach our community with the gospel or intercede for another country, we should begin by asking the Spirit how we should pray. This is at the basis of what some are calling *"prophetic intercession."* We listen to the Spirit and exercise sensitivity to what he impresses on us to pray for.[67]

Some support for the notion that there may be something *prophetic* about the way Paul understood what it means to pray in the Spirit derives from the way he linked the "Spirit" and the "word of God" in Ephesians 6:17. We've already acknowledged some scholars think it significant that Paul chose to use the word *rhema* in 6:17 rather than *logos* when referring to the "word" of God. This, and the emphasis upon prophetic interaction between church members found elsewhere in the same letter, would seem to indicate there was something prophetic about the way Paul envisioned

---

65. For example, see Brown, *Armor of God*, 91–105. See also Borgman and Ventura, *Spiritual Warfare*, 90–92; Beeke, *Fighting Satan*, 56–58.

66. Arnold, *3 Crucial Questions*, 46, 185, emphasis added.

67. Arnold, *3 Crucial Questions*, 188. See also Barth, *Ephesians*, 780, emphasis added.

the Ephesian disciples wielding the sword of the Spirit (word of God) in the context of spiritual warfare. Pressing on, I contend these observations open the door to a more prophetic understanding of the type of praying Paul immediately called his readers to engage in for themselves and "all the Lord's people" (Eph 6:18). *Why should we not at least consider the possibility that in Ephesians 6:18 Paul may have had a pneumatologically real (more explicitly prophetic) understanding of praying in the Spirit in mind? Isn't it possible praying in the Spirit might involve not only a sensitivity to the Spirit, but the experience of the Spirit praying through us in a prophetic manner?*

The Nature of Spirit-Enabled (Prophetic) Prayer

Not a few reputable New Testament scholars are willing to acknowledge that when Paul referred to praying in the Spirit he had in mind the phenomenon of *glossolalic* prayer—praying in tongues (see 1 Cor 14:2, 14–19).[68] This is an indication of how normative this practice may have been back in the day. But, for many of us, this raises the question: *How would this understanding of prophetic prayer be applicable to contemporary church members who aren't in possession of what's commonly referred to as a "prayer language" (see 1 Cor 14:2, 14–15).*

I deal with this scenario every semester as I lecture on pneumatology and spirituality in the Foundations of Christian Life course I've referred to several times already. On the one hand, I'm not at all reluctant to let my students know that, as a Pent-evangelical, my own praying in the Spirit can and often does take the form of *glossolalic* prayer. Moreover, because I'm aware that even those students who do possess a prayer language may not be using it, I also explain *why* praying in the Spirit each day in this prophetic manner is so important to my cultivation of an ongoing mentoring relationship with the risen and ascended Jesus. In other words, for me, praying in the Spirit is key to a theologically real interaction with Christ that empowers me to remain faithful and fruitful in the spiritual, moral, and missional dimensions of my walk with him.[69]

---

68. For example, see Fee, *God's Empowering Presence*, 731; Bruce, *Romans*, 165; Barrett, *Epistle to the Romans*, 164, 168.

69. For what it's worth, my experience has been that a discernible (though not necessarily direct) correlation seems to exist between my praying in the Spirit (in this prophetic sense) and the likelihood that something prophetic might occur during the preaching, teaching, counseling, or writing activity I'm preparing for.

On the other hand, I go on to indicate I'm also open to the possibility that prophetic praying—the Spirit praying through us—can occur when Christian disciples engage in a viscerally intense waiting on or travailing before God that either *literally* or *virtually* involves "wordless groans."[70] In both 1 Corinthians 14:2, 14–15 (where praying in tongues is referred to) and Romans 8:26 (where Paul refers to prayer occurring through "wordless groans") the apostle seems to be describing a kind of praying that does not originate in, and is not limited by, human understanding. Thus, a realist reading of both passages would suggest the possibility that a genuine partnering in prayer with the Spirit can occur, whether it's by means of *glossolalia* or *wordless groans*. In both prayer methods, the Spirit of Christ is praying through the disciple in a way that bypasses human understanding. In both forms of prayer, therefore, an extraordinary degree of trust and humility on the part of the person praying is required. Perhaps those dynamics which "*glossolalic* prayer" and "praying through *wordless groans*" have in common shouldn't be underestimated. Perhaps there's reason to believe both are pathways to a prophetic, empowering interaction with God!

While it requires a certain degree of exegetical and theological humility on the part of everyone in the contemporary church (both charismatics and noncharismatics), this both/and understanding of praying in the Spirit makes it possible for everyone reading this book to take seriously Paul's call to pray in the Spirit for themselves and one another. It must be quickly asserted, however, that what's not OK is for contemporary church members to be merely "hearers" of Ephesians 6:18, and not "doers" also (see Jas 1:22). I'm in the habit of telling church members, students, and fellow academics: *However we understand what it means to pray in the Spirit, if we want to put on the armor of God, we must actually do it!*

Praying in the Spirit and an Empowering Lifestyle Spirituality

I trust it's apparent now why I can be so hopeful about enabling contemporary Christians to actually put on and keep on the full armor of God. Paul's exhortation to engage in a *special kind of prayer* makes his Ephesians-ending discussion much more than a mere recapitulation. It's this game-changing exegetical observation that lies behind my contention

---

70. For example, see Wallis, *Pray in the Spirit*, 95–96.

that a presentation of Paul's "armor of God" discussion that correctly emphasizes its call to engage in pneumatologically real prayer can't help but be existentially impactful!

To be more specific, I'm suggesting that in Ephesians 6:18 Paul exhorts his readers to make praying in the Spirit a central, ongoing activity in their everyday lives. To pray in the Spirit for ourselves and others doesn't require a dedicated time and space, nor a type of concentration that would prohibit it occurring in between, and even while engaging in, various activities during the day. It's an interaction with God that can occur "on all occasions with all kinds of prayers and requests (Eph 6:18; see also Phil 4:6; 1 Thess 5:16–18)." In other words, praying in the Spirit can become part of *lifestyle spirituality* that enables Christian disciples to experience the divine empowerment that Paul's teaching here and elsewhere infers is not only possible but necessary. Put differently, I contend an important key to successfully heeding all the Pauline exhortations presented in Ephesians 6:10–18 is the cultivation of a lifestyle spirituality that enables us to "keep in step with the Spirit" (Gal 5:25) so we might, on an ongoing basis, "be strong in the Lord and in his mighty power" (Eph 6:10; see 3:16). *Indeed, a lifestyle of prayerfully partnering with the Spirit may very well be the key to obeying all the moral and ministry imperatives included in the second half of all of Paul's letters!* So, once again, whether our praying in the Spirit takes the form of praying in tongues, or allowing the Spirit to (literally or virtually) pray through us via wordless groans, we simply must be doing it!

Paul's Personal Request for Prayer (6:19–20)

> Pray also for me, that whenever I speak, words may be given me so that I will fearlessly make known the mystery of the gospel, for which I am an ambassador in chains. Pray that I may declare it fearlessly, as I should.

There's one last section of the "classic spiritual warfare passage" to be examined before I draw this very full chapter to a close. Some commentators consider Paul's request that the Ephesian disciples pray (in the Spirit) for him and his preaching ministry to be part of the apostle's "armor of God" discussion.[71] I not only concur with this perspective, but contend

---

71. For example, see O'Brien, *Letter to the Ephesians*, 483–84.

the best way to make sense of Paul's personal prayer request is to view it as an invitation for his readers to engage in some *prophetic intercession* on his behalf—that he might experience a *prophetic anointing* upon his own proclamation of the gospel!

The fact that not once but twice in these two verses Paul indicated his desire to proclaim the mystery of the gospel "fearlessly" makes it apparent he was requesting prayer for the *Spirit-imparted boldness* Jesus had promised the apostolic community (Acts 1:8).[72] But Paul's request also indicated another concern: "that whenever I speak, words may be given me. . . ." Even some noncharismatic scholars are willing to suggest Paul was soliciting prayer over the *content* of his preaching as well as its *delivery*.[73] But what does this mean since, in an earlier section of the Ephesian letter, Paul had already indicated a profound degree of familiarity with the "mystery of the gospel" (Eph. 3:1–13)?

The answer to this question may lie in the fact that, in addition to promising his future apostles that the Holy Spirit would provide them with a holy boldness (Acts 1:8), Jesus had also provided them the following word of warning and promise:

> I am sending you out like sheep among wolves. Therefore be as shrewd as snakes and as innocent as doves. Be on your guard; you will be handed over to the local councils and be flogged in the synagogues. On my account you will be brought before governors and kings as witnesses to them and to the gentiles. But when they arrest you, do not worry about what to say or how to say it. At that time you will be given what to say, *for it will not be you speaking, but the Spirit of your Father speaking through you.* (Matt 10:16–20)

Could it be that Paul, who describes himself in Ephesians 6:20 as an "ambassador in chains," had this Jesus-saying in mind when he asked the Ephesians to pray (in the Spirit) for him? What I'm suggesting is the type of *prophetic intercession* Paul solicited in Ephesians 6:19 was for an anointing to rest upon him that would result in preaching that was *prophetic* in nature and therefore transformational (life-story-shaping) in effect (see 1 Cor 14:24–25).[74] Some implicit support for this possibility is provided by biblical scholar Rudolph Schnackenburg, who acknowledges

---

72. See Foulkes, *Ephesians*, 179–80.

73. For instance, see Brown, *Armor of God*, 102.

74. For more on the *transformational* nature of prophetic preaching, see Tyra, *Getting Real*, 168–70.

the phrase "that whenever I speak, words may be given me. . . ." connotes "prophetic speech" and echoes Old Testament passages such as Ezekiel 3:27; 29:21; 33:22; and Daniel 10:16.[75] Therefore, it's my contention that a truly Spirit-sensitive (pneumatologically real) interpretation of Paul's "armor of God" discussion will maintain it was a prophetic anointing upon his preaching that Paul asked the Ephesian disciples to pray for on his behalf. *Moreover, I also contend such an interpretation will be impactful in the sense that it encourages church members to earnestly pray their preaching minister, and missionary preachers everywhere, might experience the same type of prophetic anointing!*

The ultimate aim of this chapter was to explore what a presentation of Paul's "armor of God" discussion that's both careful and compelling might look like. My treatment of this classic spiritual warfare passage was driven by my desire as a university professor (with three decades of pastoral experience) to see the youth of our churches develop a keen awareness of the very real need to put on the spiritual armor that Christ himself used to overcome the evil one in his own life and ministry. By now it should be obvious I believe the most effective way to do this is to expose church members to a Spirit-sensitive interpretation of Paul's epistle-ending discussion. The Spirit of Christ can and will empower us to stand firm against the devices of the devil. But, this empowerment is not automatic. The apostle Paul made clear how very necessary it is for Christian disciples to "keep in step" with the Spirit (Gal 5:25), and to continually "be filled" with him (Eph 5:18–20).[76] This, I suggest, explains why Paul's "armor of God" discussion culminates with a call to develop a lifestyle spirituality, at the heart of which is the phenomenon of partnering with the Spirit in prayer whenever and however he directs (Eph 6:18).

I (at the time of this writing) just finished reading a slew of personal testimonies composed by the students enrolled in this semester's offering of my Foundations of Christian Life course. I encouraged them to be honest. They were. While some are inspirational, others are gut-wrenching. Indeed, I have some tangible proof in my hands of how successful the evil one is at using some truly terrible life circumstances to produce in many young adults huge amounts of skepticism with respect to the notion that "God has a wonderful plan for your life."

---

75. See Schnackenburg, *Epistle to the Ephesians*, 283.

76. For more on the need for Christians to leave themselves "open to be filled constantly and repeatedly by the divine Spirit," see Foulkes, *Ephesians*, 152.

But it doesn't have to be this way. Just think of the alternative: students arriving at Christian and secular colleges and universities already suited up in the armor of God and thereby steeled against the post-Christian impulse that's rife in our culture due to the insidious influence of the world, the flesh, and the devil! We can do this. We can model for our youth what it means to be spiritually, morally, and missionally faithful to God. We can demonstrate what a long obedience in the same direction looks like. But for this to happen, we ourselves have to do more than merely *hear* Paul's "armor of God" discussion; we must *do* it as well. We must put into practice what Paul had in mind when he exhorted his readers to "put on," "take up," "pray in," and "pray for." These four spiritual warfare moves, and the lifestyle spirituality that enables them, are crucial to any disciple's ability to deal with the devil, regardless of their age. What are we waiting for?

Reflection/Discussion Questions:

1. Prior to reading this chapter, would you have said you had been fully trained in what it means to put on and keep on the full armor of God?

2. Do you agree with the chapter's assertion that our approach to Paul's "armor of God" discussion needs to be both exegetically responsible and existentially impactful? Why or why not?

3. How do you feel about this chapter's emphasis on the role of the Holy Spirit in our being able to put on and keep on the full armor of God?

4. How do you feel about this chapter's suggestion that what's needed is a lifestyle spirituality that makes possible an ongoing mentoring relationship with the risen Christ? To what degree is this a current reality in your Christian walk? What might you do to see it go to the next level?

5. To what degree do you embrace the goal of the youth of our church going away to college already suited up in the armor of God and thereby steeled against the post-Christian impulse that's rife in our culture? How might you help this happen? Will you?

8

Crucial Close-Quarters Combat Tactics

Coming Near, Leaning Into, and *Holding Fast*

> Submit yourselves, then, to God. Resist the devil, and he will flee from you. Come near to God and he will come near to you.
>
> —JAMES 4:7-8A

Those reading the title of this chapter and thinking to themselves *"At last, a discussion of what the Bible has to say about casting out demons!"* will be disappointed. Indeed, it may come as a surprise for some to learn that, even though Paul's "armor of God" discussion in Ephesians 6:10-20 emphasizes the personal nature of our conflict with Satan,[1] we look in vain in the New Testament for explicit instructions on how

---

1. The Greek word translated "struggle" in Ephesians 6:12 connotes the idea of a wrestling match—close-up, hand-to-hand combat with an opponent (see Barth, *Ephesians*, 763; O'Brien, *Letter to the Ephesians*, 465-66; Hoehner, *Ephesians*, 825). Scholars comment on how peculiar it was for Paul to shift the imagery from that of a Roman soldier to an athlete competing in a very popular sporting contest (e.g., see O'Brien, *Letter to the Ephesians*, 465). One explanation is that Paul was at pains to have his readers understand how personal and rigorous the spiritual conflict he's referring to in this discussion actually is (see Arnold, *3 Crucial Questions*, 37-38; Foulkes, *Ephesians*, 172).

rank-and-file church members are to exorcise demons.[2] I'm not saying nonapostles casting out demons never happens (see Luke 10:17; Acts 8:4–8), only that the focus in the New Testament letters and Apocalypse is on a different kind of "close-quarters" spiritual warfare: a type in which the "close-quarters" refers to the disciple's proximity to God rather than the enemy, a type in which the devil is defeated, ironically, not by church members hunting down and exorcising evil spirits, but by their being careful to maintain a theologically real—holiness-producing, ministry-engendering, life-story-shaping—relationship with God the Father, through Christ the Son, in the power of the Holy Spirit.[3]

In the previous chapter we learned how important it is for Christ's followers to "be strong in the Lord and in his mighty power" (Eph 6:10). More specifically, we discovered that to *stand our ground* against the devil (Eph 6:11–12) we must put on Christ's armor, take up Christ's weapons, and pray in partnership with the Holy Spirit for ourselves and one another (Eph 6:13–18). In this chapter we'll discuss three more apostolic exhortations that possess spiritual warfare significance: the crucial importance of our com*ing near* to God in praise and penitence, our *leaning into* any Satan-induced pain and suffering God allows us to experience, and our *holding fast* to the testimony of Jesus no matter what the devil does to us. The fact these additional close-quarters combat tactics are being discussed near the conclusion of our endurance training doesn't

---

2. This being said, I'll also point out that, even though it's true that in Paul's "armor of God" discussion the practice of exorcism—casting out demons—is not explicitly addressed, several things need to be kept in mind. First, serving as an implicit connection between Ephesians 6:10–20 and what is often referred to as "deliverance ministry" is the importance of the Spirit to both putting on God's armor and the deliverance ministries of Jesus and Paul (see Matt 12:28; 1 Cor 2:4). Second, another possible connection might be inferred from the fact that the deliverance ministries of Jesus and Paul seemed to derive from the same type of lifestyle spirituality connoted in Ephesians 6:18–20—a spirituality earmarked by a serious devotion to prayer (e.g., Mark 9:25–29 [see Luke 5:16]; Acts 16:16–18 [see Col 1:9; 1 Thess 3:10; 5:17; 2 Tim 1:3]). Finally, for what it's worth, some practitioners have commented on the value of praying in the Spirit with respect to deliverance ministry. (For example, see Wallis, *Pray in the Spirit*, 92–94. See also Basham, *Deliver Us from Evil*, 203–4.) These three observations lead me to wonder if Paul didn't simply presume that his Ephesian readers, with their personal experience of his ministry of deliverance (Acts 19:1–20), would've understood that the "armor of God" spirituality he was encouraging them to cultivate would not only enable them to "resist" the devil, but do so with extreme prejudice.

3. Some implicit support for this provocative observation can be found in Arnold, *3 Crucial Questions*, 26–27.

mean they are lacking in importance. On the contrary, they are absolutely critical to our winning the spiritual war we're engaged in!

Dealing with the Devil by *Coming Near*

Gaining some knowledge about dealing with the devil is one thing; putting it into practice is another. I learned this lesson the hard way during the personal spiritual warfare experience I described in this book's introduction. In that brief recitation I alluded to the fact there was one spiritual warfare move in particular that was critical to my eventually defeating the anxiety demons that had hounded me for a year and a half. The time has come for me to elaborate a bit more on what that crucial spiritual warfare move entailed.

By way of review, at the very beginning of what I'm referring to as my eighteen-month-long "dark night of the soul" experience, I sensed the Lord telling me this ordeal was about my learning how to engage in spiritual warfare so that I, as a young pastor, could teach others how to do so as well. Moreover, I also sensed the Lord indicating to me the importance of James 4:7–10 for my experience. That passage reads:

> Submit yourselves, then, to God. Resist the devil, and he will flee from you. Come near to God and he will come near to you. Wash your hands, you sinners, and purify your hearts, you double-minded. Grieve, mourn and wail. Change your laughter to mourning and your joy to gloom. Humble yourselves before the Lord, and he will lift you up. (Jas 4:7–10)

In a nutshell, it was when I finally realized the way I was to defeat the devil was not by battling him myself, but by running into the arms of God, that I found the deliverance I so desperately needed. I'm not suggesting this is the sum total of what it means to engage in close-quarters combat with the evil one; simply that it was a spiritual warfare move that essentially saved my life as well as my ministry nearly forty years ago. Because of its importance to *my* ability to render to Christ a long obedience in the same direction, there's no way I can avoid spending a few pages discussing how I was led to understand and heed James's exhortation to resist the devil by *coming near* to God.

What My Experience of *Coming Near* Involved

I'll begin this discussion by pointing out there are two different ways this passage impacted me. But please note: I'm not suggesting the passage can't be interpreted and applied differently, only that this was how I was led to apply it to my life back in the day, and have ever since with real effect.

Coming Near Involves Proactive Praise *in the Face of the Devil*

Because of what many psalms have to say about the dynamic of entering God's presence (e.g., Ps 42:4; 95:2; 96:8; 100:1, 4; 116:17; 118:19–21), I had the sense God was telling me that whenever I would feel the soul-chilling experience of anxiety closing in on me I should deliberately draw near to him in worship.[4] To be even more specific, even though some biblical scholars see in this passage an exhortation to devote ourselves to all sorts of devotional activities,[5] I sensed God calling me to come near to him through a deliberate offering of something I refer to as "proactive praise."

The Bible contains many passages which portray this phenomenon occurring. In the middle of a difficult season of adversity someone will, in effect, say something like "But I praise you, God, anyway!" For instance, both Psalm 57 and 71 portray David being careful to praise God and extol his faithfulness *even while he is currently experiencing some distressing adversity.*

Moreover, we should also take note of the fact that in addition to the many times the psalms simply exhort God's people to give thanks to him, some passages more specifically focus on the role proactive "thank offerings" play in our experience of God's deliverance. In other words, there are times when we are to praise God in anticipation of his work in

---

4. Biblical commentator Thomas Lea explains: "'Come near to God' involves approaching God in worship and commitment. Those who approach God in the obedience of worship find that he comes near to them. As our knowledge of the Lord deepens, we learn more fully his strength, power, and guidance for godly living" (Lea, *Hebrews, James*, 321).

5. According to another biblical scholar, coming near to God might take the form of "Bible reading, prayer, private and public worship, feasting at the Lord's Table, devoting ourselves to Christian fellowship, cultivating every appointed avenue whereby we can draw near to him" (Motyer, *Message of James*, 152).

our lives rather than afterward. Consider, for example, these two excerpts from Psalm 50:

> *Sacrifice thank offerings* to God, fulfill your vows to the Most High, and call on me in the day of trouble; I will deliver you, and you will honor me. (Ps 50:14–15)

> Those who *sacrifice thank offerings* honor me, and to the blameless I will show my salvation. (Ps 50:23)

Though Psalms is filled with examples of proactive praise, my favorite Old Testament example of this dynamic is the concluding words of the book of Habakkuk:

> Though the fig tree does not bud and there are no grapes on the vines, though the olive crop fails and the fields produce no food, though there are no sheep in the pen and no cattle in the stalls, *yet I will rejoice in the LORD, I will be joyful in God my Savior.* The Sovereign LORD is my strength; he makes my feet like the feet of a deer, he enables me to tread on the heights. (Hab 3:17–19)

We find some support for the practice of proactive praise in the New Testament as well, in passages such as:

> always giving thanks to God the Father for everything, in the name of our Lord Jesus Christ. (Eph 5:20)

> Rejoice in the Lord always. I will say it again: Rejoice! (Phil 4:4)

> Rejoice always, pray continually, give thanks in all circumstances; for this is God's will for you in Christ Jesus. (1 Thess 5:16–18)

> Through Jesus, therefore, let us continually offer to God a sacrifice of praise—the fruit of lips that openly profess his name. (Heb 13:15; see Isa 57:19; Hos 14:2)

Worthy of some special attention is Philippians 4:7–10, which not only calls for us to rejoice in the Lord in the face of our anxiety but also seems to suggest that doing so is an effective spiritual warfare move. I encourage you to read this familiar passage again with the observation just made in mind:

> Rejoice in the Lord *always*. I will say it again: Rejoice! Let your gentleness be evident to all. The Lord is near. Do not be anxious

about anything, but in *every* situation, by prayer and petition, *with thanksgiving*, present your requests to God. And the peace of God, which transcends all understanding, will guard your hearts and your minds in Christ Jesus. (Phil 4:4–7)

Moreover, my suggested take on this passage from Paul's Letter to the Philippians is buttressed by the fact that perhaps the most prominent New Testament example of an apostle engaging in proactive praise just happened to occur in Philippi! I'm referring, of course, to the way Paul and Silas famously behaved when, having already been arrested and severely beaten with rods, they were confined in chains in a Philippian jail cell. Luke tells us:

About midnight Paul and Silas were praying and singing hymns to God, and the other prisoners were listening to them. (Acts 16:25)

For all these reasons I believed God was instructing me to offer him praise in a proactive, theologically real manner. In other words, I was to develop the habit of intentionally entering into God's spiritual presence through praise and worship whenever I sensed the forces of darkness closing in on me.[6]

Coming Near Involves Sincere Penitence *Before a Holy God*

But I was also aware James 4:7–10 had more to say about what it means to come near to God. Indeed, I received the impression that for the dynamic of proactive praise to be effectual at shutting the door on the devil, so to speak, I must also take seriously those biblical passages which mandate an approach to God that's earmarked by humility and sincere penitence.[7]

To be sure, some scholars believe humility and penitence are all "coming near" involves. Biblical commentator Douglas Moo, commenting on James 4:8a, points out that, in the Greek version of the Old Testament, the verb "come near" (Greek: *engizō*) often refers to approaching

---

6. Of course, there are other ways of entering into a theologically real experience of God's presence: for example, the Eucharist. It's just that, since my most intense battles with the "anxiety demons" took place in the middle of the night, my *coming near* very often took the form of a quiet but intense, solitary engagement in praise and worship. I'll have more to say about the nature of this praise and worship below.

7. For example, see Ps 66:16–19; 145:17–20; Prov 3:34; 18:12; Matt 23:12; Luke 18:9–14; Jas 4:6.

God in worship (e.g., Lev 21:3, 21, 23; Isa 29:13; 58:2; 65:5; Ezek 40:46, etc.), and has this meaning also in Hebrews 7:19. However, because of what James 4:8b–10 has to say about repentance, Moo is convinced James didn't have worship in mind in verse 8 after all. According to Moo, coming near to God is simply the act of returning to God after having, like the prodigal son, spent some time in the far country (Luke 15:17–20; see Hos 12:6).[8] In other words, according to this interpretation, coming near to God is all about penitence, coming correct before the Holy One.

Coming Near Involves Both *Proactive Praise* and *Sincere Penitence*

While I understand and respect Moo's argument, I'm not sure why James couldn't have had both worship and repentance in mind when he wrote James 4:8a. I'm struck by the way passages such as Isaiah 6:1–8 and Psalm 51:1–17 powerfully evidence the connection that exists between prayerful, worshipful repentance and spiritual, moral, and missional renewal. Apparently, New Testament scholar Peter Davids agrees. Having suggested James had Malachi 3:7 and Zechariah 1:3 in mind when he exhorted his readers to "come near" to God, Davids links worship to repentance (returning to God) when he contends, concerning the call in James 4:8a, "[t]he picture is that of a person coming to offer sacrifice in the temple and coming near to God in the ceremony."[9]

In any case, the bottom line is that what I ultimately sensed God saying to me through James 4:7–10 was this: "Gary, the key to your defeating the devil in this trial is not your battling him yourself, but your resisting him by coming near to me via proactive praise, and doing so in a way that precludes his maintaining any kind of a foothold in your life (see Eph 4:27)." Put differently, I got the sense that behind James's spiritual warfare counsel are two realities: (1) the devil is loathe to follow Christ's followers into an experience of sacred encounter; and (2) once he realizes his machinations will only encourage us to draw near to God in praise and penitence, he's liable to cease and desist until another opportunity to tempt us away from a spiritual, moral, and missional faithfulness presents itself (see Matt 4:10–11; Luke 4:13). Thus, to deliberately come near to God in the praiseful and penitent, theologically real manner James

---

8. See Moo, *Letter of James*, 193. See also Moo, *James*, 152–53.
9. Davids, *James*, 1364–65.

4:7–10 prescribes will, very often, succeed in causing the evil one to back off.

What My Experience of *Coming Near* Looked Like

For what it's worth, this is precisely what occurred in my life when I finally began to put into practice what God had impressed upon me at the beginning of my "dark night" experience, and then reminded me of eighteen months later as I cried out to him in a darkened hotel room. Chided by God for having ignored James's spiritual warfare counsel for a year and a half, I returned home from that ministry conference determined to put it into practice. Put simply, the difference this close-quarters combat tactic made in my life was huge!

To be more precise, my practice had been that, after my son Brandon would fall back to sleep in the middle of the night, I'd remain in his room, rocking an already asleep child, wrestling with the anxiety demons, worrying that, like my dad, I'd not live long enough to see him graduate from high school, get married, go to college, begin a family, succeed at a career. But then, after the come-to-Jesus moment described above, and influenced by James 4:7–10, I began the new practice of putting Brandon into his bed and then going into the family room where I'd spend some time praising and worshiping God in the face of my adversity, prayerfully surrendering myself to a fresh in-filling of the Holy Spirit. To be more precise, I'd stand in the center of that darkened room with my hands raised, whispering prayers and softly singing songs of praise. I'd also humble myself, beseeching God to make me aware of any pride, selfishness, and rebellion at work in my life. It was at that time I developed the devotional habit of asking God to forgive me for anything I'd recently said, done, or even thought about doing that was displeasing to him (Ps 139:23–24). Finally, I'd allow the Spirit of Christ to actually pray and worship through me (1 Cor 14:15), and would, on occasion, even dance before the Lord (2 Sam 6:14–15). For sure, I was aware that my rather clumsy dancing before God with arms raised wouldn't have been a pretty sight if someone had been observing. But then again, I was desperate. So I danced anyway—conscious of the fact I was engaging in spiritual warfare, and inspired by the thought that the one I was dancing before was into it. After all, in verse 6 of James 4 we read: "God opposes the proud but shows favor to the humble!"

Amazingly, within a couple weeks of my taking James 4:7-10 seriously in this manner, my eighteen-month-long ordeal was over. As a result, for nearly four decades now I've personally practiced, and often prescribed for parishioners and students, this type of spiritual warfare. Never once have I had someone tell me that employing James 4:7-10 in a theologically real manner failed to provide them with a sense of God's empowering presence in the face of their Satan-induced, anxiety-producing adversity. Mark it down: the evil one simply can't have his way with us when our new (righteous) habit (see Rom 6:13, 16-18) is to engage in prophetic praise and prayerful surrender to God each time we become aware we're being attacked. I don't think it's going too far to say employing this close-quarters combat tactic is what our theologically real experiences of worship, nurture, community, and mission are designed to prepare us for. Coming near to God isn't an alternative to putting on the full armor of God, it's a complement to it!

Dealing with the Devil by *Leaning Into*

And yet, I must hasten to add that coming near is not a silver bullet. There are times when God's empowering presence doesn't immediately chase the evil one away. Indeed, at times it seems God allows Satan to afflict us in an ongoing manner, thus producing within us a lifestyle of coming near! I referred to this reality in an earlier chapter, and I will discuss in the next chapter how the Old Testament story of Job seems to portray God *using* some Satan-supplied suffering in a providential manner. Here I'll simply say that if the experience of Paul described in 2 Corinthians 12:7-10 is any indication, there may be times when the appropriate spiritual warfare move is not to continue to pray for deliverance, but to embrace the pain and suffering instead, allowing it, ironically, to intensify the manner in which our lives speak to others of God's reality. Having alluded to this passage briefly when discussing the need to stay on mission in chapter 6, I want to drill down a bit more deeply here.

What *Leaning Into* Involves

Paul's "thorn in the flesh" discussion reads thusly:

> ... Therefore, in order to keep me from becoming conceited, I was given a thorn in my flesh, a messenger of Satan, to torment

> me. Three times I pleaded with the Lord to take it away from me. But he said to me, "My grace is sufficient for you, for my power is made perfect in weakness." Therefore I will boast all the more gladly about my weaknesses, so that Christ's power may rest on me. That is why, for Christ's sake, I delight in weaknesses, in insults, in hardships, in persecutions, in difficulties. For when I am weak, then I am strong. (2 Cor 12:7–10)

In this somewhat startling passage, the apostle Paul states he has come to the place where he's able to actually embrace or lean into the pain and suffering caused by the "thorn" or "stake"[10] which a "messenger (Greek: *angelos*) from Satan" has pierced him with. I'm using the contemporary English idiom "lean into" to translate the Greek verb *eudokeō* which the NIV translates as "delight in" in verse 10. Because God has made it clear to the apostle that the stake piercing his side is serving a providential purpose—one designed to enhance his ministry effectiveness—Paul is all in. Rather than complain, whine, or become morose about Satan's work in his life, he boasts about and delights in it instead!

Though I've met some disciples who don't like this passage very much because it contradicts their black-and-white understanding of the relationship between God and human suffering, we must deal with it. After all, the focus of this book is what the New Testament (as a whole) has to say about why and how Christians are to deal with the devil.

I'm not saying all suffering should be considered providential, but according to the New Testament some surely is. Some of the suffering God allows his people to experience serves a salutatory purpose. This phenomenon is a major theme of 1 Peter, in which we find the following exhortations:

> In all this you greatly rejoice, though now for a little while you may have had to suffer grief in all kinds of trials. These have come so that the proven genuineness of your faith—of greater worth than gold, which perishes even though refined by fire—may result in praise, glory and honor when Jesus Christ is revealed. (1 Pet 1:6–7)

---

10. According to David Garland: "The word translated 'thorn' (*skolops*) occurs only here in the New Testament. It refers to something pointed such as a stake for impaling, a medical instrument, or a thorn. 'Stake' would be a better translation, though 'thorn' has dominated English renderings of the word. The metaphor carries 'the notion of something sharp and painful which sticks deeply in the flesh and in the will of God defies extracting'" (Garland, as cited in Minn, *Thorn*, 10).

> But even if you should suffer for what is right, you are blessed. "Do not fear their threats; do not be frightened." But in your hearts revere Christ as Lord. Always be prepared to give an answer to everyone who asks you to give the reason for the hope that you have. But do this with gentleness and respect, keeping a clear conscience, so that those who speak maliciously against your good behavior in Christ may be ashamed of their slander. For it is better, if it is God's will, to suffer for doing good than for doing evil. (1 Pet 3:14–17)

> Therefore, since Christ suffered in his body, arm yourselves also with the same attitude, because whoever suffers in the body is done with sin. As a result, they do not live the rest of their earthly lives for evil human desires, but rather for the will of God. For you have spent enough time in the past doing what pagans choose to do—living in debauchery, lust, drunkenness, orgies, carousing and detestable idolatry. They are surprised that you do not join them in their reckless, wild living, and they heap abuse on you. But they will have to give account to him who is ready to judge the living and the dead. (1 Pet 4:1–5)

But Peter doesn't simply refer to the fact that his readers should expect some suffering for Christ's sake in this life; he goes on to exhort them to, like Paul, lean into it, actually praising God in the face of it! The fisherman-turned-apostle writes:

> Dear friends, do not be surprised at the fiery ordeal that has come on you to test you, as though something strange were happening to you. But rejoice inasmuch as you participate in the sufferings of Christ, so that you may be overjoyed when his glory is revealed. If you are insulted because of the name of Christ, you are blessed, for the Spirit of glory and of God rests on you. If you suffer, it should not be as a murderer or thief or any other kind of criminal, or even as a meddler. However, if you suffer as a Christian, do not be ashamed, but praise God that you bear that name. For it is time for judgment to begin with God's household; and if it begins with us, what will the outcome be for those who do not obey the gospel of God? And, "If it is hard for the righteous to be saved, what will become of the ungodly and the sinner?"
>
> So then, those who suffer according to God's will should commit themselves to their faithful Creator and continue to do good. (1 Pet 4:12–19)

Now, it's true the kind of suffering Peter calls his readers to lean into is explicitly referred to as that which results from their being persecuted for their faith. Thus, it might be argued it's one thing to lean into suffering that's directly caused by our commitment to Christ and it's another to think we should ever embrace the kind of suffering that isn't the direct result of our spiritual, moral, and missional faithfulness to God. However, I'll point out while Paul refers in 2 Corinthians 12:10 to his having experienced "persecutions," he also speaks of his having embraced some personal "weaknesses," and the pain that resulted from the "insults," "hardships," and "difficulties" that derived from them. Some scholars are of the opinion that Paul's thorn in the flesh was ultimately personal in nature, and perhaps manifested as a physical illness or deformity in his body. For example, according to biblical scholar David Garland:

> The exact nature of this "thorn in the flesh" has prompted much speculation. Paul does not go into any detail in describing it because the Corinthians apparently were well familiar with what he meant. Some of their number or his competitors may have made it the object of their derision.... Most interpreters through the years have assumed that Paul alludes to some bodily ailment. This view is reinforced by Paul's mention of a physical illness that detained him in Galatia and led to his preaching the gospel to them. He writes that his physical condition was a trial to them (Gal 4:13–14). Assuming that this affliction was something that persisted, the suggestions range from a pain in the ear or head, to malarial fever, epilepsy, and solar retinitis.... Others have claimed that Paul suffered from some psychological ailment or distress, some personal anxiety or torment. Less incapacitating problems have been suggested such as depression over his earlier persecution of the church, a tendency to despair and doubt (see Luther, *Table Talk*, 24.7), or even sexual temptation. Still others interpret the stake to refer to persecution or adversaries—the rise of the Judaizers, for example—who have dogged him throughout his ministry and now supposedly plague him at Corinth.
>
> Since Paul prays so fervently to have the stake removed, it was probably something that he felt interfered with his ministry. [Peter] Marshall identifies it as a "socially debilitating disease or disfigurement which was made the subject of ridicule and invidious comparison." Paul's speech has been the subject of the Corinthians' criticism (10:10), and the stake could have been something that led to some kind of a speech handicap.

The "angel of Satan" could allude to the story of Balaam (Num 22:22–34) where the angel of the Lord gets in his way three times to prevent him from speaking and cursing the nation of Israel, against God's will. In the end we must accept the fact that we will never know for certain what Paul's stake in the flesh was. We can only be certain that initially it caused him considerable annoyance.[11]

The point I'm making is there's more than one way for us to be persecuted for our faith. Any adversity God allows us to experience can be something Satan will use to try to produce in us the kind of disappointment, discouragement, and despair that, unfortunately, causes some professing Christians to throw in the towel. But it doesn't have to be that way. By imitating the apostle Paul, who allowed his unrelieved suffering to produce in him a lifestyle of coming near to God, we can see God's ability to use us in the lives of others expanded in ways we never thought possible.

A Contemporary Example of What *Leaning Into* Looks Like

Joni Eareckson Tada is a powerful contemporary example of what *leaning into* looks like.

Joni suffered a severe injury to her spine in a diving accident in 1967 and became a quadriplegic, paralyzed from the shoulders down. "Today, she is an internationally known mouth artist, a talented vocalist, a radio host, an author of 17 books and an advocate for disabled persons worldwide."[12] In an article written in 2017 commemorating the 50th anniversary of her accident, she summarized the meaning of the many years she's spent in a wheelchair, embracing the pain she's convinced God has allowed her to experience. In this compelling article we read:

> Recently I was at my desk writing to Tommy, a 17-year-old boy who just broke his neck body surfing off the Jersey shore. He's now a quadriplegic. He will live the rest of his life in a wheelchair without use of his hands or legs. When it comes to life-altering injuries, quadriplegia is catastrophic.
>
> Halfway through my letter describing several hurdles Tommy should expect in rehab, I stopped. I felt utterly overwhelmed, thinking of all that lies ahead for him. I've been there. And even

11. Garland, as cited in Marshall, "Metaphor of Social Shame," 315–16.
12. Anonymous, "Joni Eareckson Tada Story," lines 1–3.

though half a century has passed, I can still taste the anguish. Hot, silent tears began streaming, and I choked out a prayer, *Oh God, how will Tommy do it? How will he ever make it? Have mercy; help him find you!* . . .

Like Tommy, I was once the 17-year-old who retched at the thought of living life without a working body. I hated my paralysis so much I would drive my power wheelchair into walls, repeatedly banging them until they cracked. Early on, I found dark companions who helped me numb my depression with scotch-and-cola. I just wanted to disappear. I wanted to die.

What a difference time makes—as well as prayer, heaven-minded friends, and deep study of God's Word. All combined, I began to see there *are* more important things in life than walking and having use of your hands. It sounds incredible, but I really would rather be in this wheelchair knowing Jesus as I do than be on my feet without him. But whenever I try to explain it, I hardly know where to begin.

Yet I know this: I'm *in the zone* whenever I infuse Christ-encouragement into the hearts of people like Tommy. It feels so right to agonize alongside them. Better yet, to participate in their suffering in the spirit of 2 Corinthians 1:6: "If we are distressed, it is for your comfort and salvation." Can I do something for Tommy's comfort and salvation? You bet. . . .

Half a century of paralysis has also shown me how high the cosmic stakes really are. Whenever I fidget in my confinement, I can almost hear Satan taunt God—as he did with Job—"Look at her, see? She doesn't really trust you. Test her with more pain and you'll see her true colors!" When the Devil insists God's people only serve him when life is easy, I have the high honor of proving him wrong. To be on the battlefield where the mightiest forces in the universe converge in warfare? By God's grace, I'm all in.[13]

In 2010 Joni was diagnosed with breast cancer, but was declared cancer-free in 2015. Then, in November 2018, Tada was diagnosed with a malignant nodule on her chest wall near the site of her original cancer.[14] Radiation treatments for the nodule proved successful and in July 2019 she announced she had once again been declared cancer-free. In an announcement regarding this good news, Joni stated:

---

13. Tada, "Reflections," paras. 1–2, 5–7, 18.
14. Ellis, "Joni Eareckson Tada Says She's Cancer Free!," lines 8–9.

Proverbs 25:25 says, "Good news from far away is like cold water to a thirsty soul." That perfectly describes Ken and me today. . . .

But the Lord was gracious and heard the desire of our hearts – last Friday's PET scan shows that my second tumor that was removed last November... did not metastasize! Given the aggressive nature of that reoccurring cancer, this news is quite miraculous.

So, THANK you for lifting us up before the Lord Jesus. For now, we have been spared of more cancer battles. We humbly realize that may well change in the future; but for today, for now, we are rejoicing in those wonderful words from my medical oncologist: "all clear!" Onward and upward...[15]

Joni continues to be a powerful example of someone who is continually *coming near* as she engages in the *leaning into* that drives the devil crazy!

Dealing with the Devil by *Holding Fast*

This is another topic that was briefly addressed in chapter 6 but which deserves a fuller treatment at this stage in our endurance training. The dynamic of holding fast is referred to several times in the New Testament. Writing to the disciples in Thessalonica who were experiencing some pretty severe persecution (2 Thess 1:4), the apostle Paul wrote:

> So then, brothers and sisters, stand firm and *hold fast* to the teachings we passed on to you, whether by word of mouth or by letter. (2 Thess 2:15)

In Revelation 3:3 we find Jesus warning the church in Sardis thusly:

> Remember, therefore, what you have received and heard; *hold it fast*, and repent. But if you do not wake up, I will come like a thief, and you will not know at what time I will come to you. (Rev 3:3)

There are other passages in the New Testament that, while not containing the phrase "hold fast," speak of the importance of Christian disciples holding on to some things that are very important. Such things as:

- Jesus' teaching (John 8:31);
- the traditions passed on by the apostle Paul (1 Cor 11:2);

15. Tada, "Health Update," lines 1–15.

- the word Paul preached (1 Cor 15:2);
- the word of life (Phil 2:16);
- prophetic utterances that pass the test (1 Thess 5:21);
- faith and a good conscience (1 Tim 1:19; 3:9);
- eternal life (1 Tim 6:12, 19);
- the trustworthy message as it has been taught (Titus 1:9);
- our confidence and hope in which we glory (Heb 3:6);
- our original conviction to the very end (Heb 3:14);
- the faith we profess (Heb 4:14);
- the hope set before us (Heb 6:18; 10:23); and
- the spiritual, moral, and missional strength we currently have (Rev 2:25; 3:11).

Though the devil is not mentioned explicitly in any of the passages referred to above, everything we've discovered so far makes clear he's obviously eager to keep us from succeeding at holding fast to all these important aspects of our walk with Christ. Indeed, Revelation 12:17 alerts us to the fact that our holding fast to our testimony—our confession of faith in Jesus[16]—can actually result in our being targeted for a Satanic attack! This sobering passage says:

> Then the dragon was enraged at the woman and went off to wage war against the rest of her offspring—those who keep God's commands and *hold fast* their testimony about Jesus.

So, here's the bottom line: it appears the apostolic authors knew holding fast our Christian testimony would cause the devil to come at us in a ferocious manner, and yet they peppered their writings with exhortations for us to hold fast anyway! Apparently, they were convinced of three realities. First, they understood there's no way to live a godly life and not experience trials and tribulations (see 2 Tim 3:12). Second, they truly believed the glory we will experience for eternity in the presence of our triune God will make any suffering we experience in this present age pale in comparison (see Rom 8:18; 2 Tim 4:7–8; Rev 21:1–4; 22:1–5). Third, they possessed a personal awareness that Jesus wasn't beyond exhorting

---

16. See Matt 24:14; Luke 21:12–13; 1 Cor 1:6; 2 Cor 9:13; 1 Tim 6:12–13; 2 Tim 2:19; Rev 1:2, 9; 6:9; 12:11, 17; 19:10.

his disciples to go the distance, to hold fast even if it means they pay the ultimate price for doing so. After all, they no doubt remembered Jesus saying to them:

> But before all this, they will seize you and persecute you. They will hand you over to synagogues and put you in prison, and you will be brought before kings and governors, and all on account of my name. And so you will bear testimony to me. But make up your mind not to worry beforehand how you will defend yourselves. For I will give you words and wisdom that none of your adversaries will be able to resist or contradict. You will be betrayed even by parents, brothers and sisters, relatives and friends, and they will put some of you to death. Everyone will hate you because of me. But not a hair of your head will perish. Stand firm, and you will win life. (Luke 21:12–19)

Surely an awareness of this *terrible promise* had to have influenced how the original readers of John's *Apocalpyse* (the book of Revelation) interpreted the significance of Jesus' message to the church in Smyrna presented in Revelation 2:10–11. I cited this passage in chapter 6, but, because this bracing word of exhortation may be a word the risen Jesus intended all of his followers to take to heart, I rehearse it here:

> Do not be afraid of what you are about to suffer. I tell you, the devil will put some of you in prison to test you, and you will suffer persecution for ten days. Be faithful, even to the point of death, and I will give you life as your victor's crown.
> Whoever has ears, let them hear what the Spirit says to the churches. The one who is victorious will not be hurt at all by the second death. (Rev 2:10–11)

Coming Near, Leaning Into and *Holding Fast*: An Historical Example

Dietrich Bonhoeffer was a German theologian, seminary leader, and pastor who had been a vocal critic of Hitler's rise to power in the years leading up to World War II. At the risk of greatly oversimplifying a complex story, I'll simply indicate Bonhoeffer surprised some of his theological and ecclesiastical (churchly) colleagues when, just as the struggle between the Confessing (theologically conservative) German churches and Hitler was heating up, he accepted an invitation to pastor two German congregations in London.[17] What was Bonhoeffer thinking? In his biography of Bonhoeffer, Eric Metaxas suggests Bonhoeffer may have sensed God calling him to play a prophetic role in Germany that would lead to his paying the ultimate price. This was a daunting call and he needed some time and space to work some things out. Metaxas offers:

> It's hard to escape the conclusion that Bonhoeffer was somehow thinking prophetically, that somehow he could see what was ahead of him, that at some point he would be able to do nothing more than "suffer patiently" in his cell, praising God as he did so, thanking him for the high privilege of being counted worthy to do so.[18]

Metaxas goes on to suggest a sermon Bonhoeffer preached while in London provides some evidence for the veracity of the theory presented above. According to Metaxas:

> During this tense time of waiting, Bonhoeffer preached his now rather famous sermon on the prophet Jeremiah. It was Sunday, January 21. Preaching on a Jewish Old Testament prophet was quite out of the ordinary and provocative, but that was the least of the sermon's difficulties. The opening words were typically intriguing: "Jeremiah was not eager to become a prophet of God. When the call came to him all of a sudden, he shrank back, he resisted, he tried to get away.
>
> The sermon reflected Bonhoeffer's own difficult situation. It is extremely doubtful whether anyone in his congregations could understand what he was talking about much less accept that it was God's word to them that Sunday. If they had ever been puzzled by their brilliant young preacher's homilies, they must have been puzzled now.
>
> The picture that Bonhoeffer painted of Jeremiah was one of unrelieved gloom and drama. God was after him, and he could not escape. . . . The sermon began to get seriously depressing. What was the young preacher getting at? . . . They continued listening, hoping for an upturn in Jeremiah's fortunes.
>
> But alas, Pastor Bonhoeffer delivered an unrelenting homiletic bummer. . . .
>
> If Bonhoeffer wanted to ensure that his congregation would never dream of following God too closely, this sermon was just

---

17. See Metaxas, *Bonhoeffer*, 195–98.
18. Metaxas, *Bonhoeffer*, 196.

the ticket. He then spoke of God driving Jeremiah "from agony to agony." Could it get worse? . . .

> Bonhoeffer's congregation was lost. God maneuvered his beloved servant and prophet into imprisonment and agony? Somewhere along the line they must have missed a crucial sentence! But they hadn't. And what none of them could know was that Pastor Bonhoeffer was talking, in some large part, about himself and about his future, the future that God was showing him. He was beginning to understand that he was God's prisoner, that like the prophets of old, he was called to suffer and to be oppressed—and in that defeat and the acceptance of that defeat, there was victory. It was a sermon that applied to anyone with ears to hear, but few could actually hear it . . .[19]

Further support for the idea Bonhoeffer was wrestling, coming to terms with, a call from God to render to him a long obedience in the same direction that would likely involve suffering and even martyrdom can be adduced from yet another sermon Bonhoeffer preached while in London:

> No one has yet believed in God and the kingdom of God, no one has yet heard about the realm of the resurrected, and not been homesick from that hour, waiting and looking forward joyfully to being released from bodily existence.
>
> Whether we are young or old makes no difference. What are twenty or thirty or fifty years in the sight of God? And which of us knows how near he or she may already be to the goal? That life only really begins when it ends here on earth, that all that is here is only the prologue before the curtain goes up—that is for young and old alike to think about. Why are we so afraid when we think about death? . . . . Death is only dreadful for those who live in dread and fear of it. Death is not wild and terrible, if only we can be still and hold fast to God's Word. Death is not bitter, if we have not become bitter ourselves. *Death is grace, the greatest gift of grace that God gives to people who believe in him.* Death is mild, death is sweet and gentle; it beckons to us with heavenly power, if only we realize that it is the gateway to our homeland, the tabernacle of joy, the everlasting kingdom of peace.
>
> How do we know that dying is so dreadful? Who knows whether, in our human fear and anguish we are only shivering and shuddering at the most glorious, heavenly, blessed event in the world?

---

19. Metaxas, *Bonhoeffer*, 210.

> Death is hell and night and cold, if it is not transformed by our faith. But that is just what is so marvelous, that we can transform death."[20]

It almost seems as if Bonhoeffer's goal wasn't so much to encourage and embolden the hearts of his parishioners, but his own. (Here's a little secret: sometimes we preachers are not only the prophetic conduit of God's strengthening, encouraging, and comforting word [1 Cor 14:3], but recipients as well. Very often, the most passionate sermons are those that pastors are preaching, either consciously or subconsciously, to themselves.)

While in London, Bonhoeffer became convinced it would take more than mere religion to defeat Hitler.[21] Still, he worked against Hitler's attempts to silence all ecclesial (churchly) resistance to his leadership.

Eventually, Bonhoeffer would return to Germany to lead a seminary for the Confessing Church. When the seminary was shut down by the Nazis, and it became clear Bonhoeffer would be forced to join the German army and fight Hitler's wars, he accepted an offer to teach and pastor in America.[22] Bonhoeffer had become convinced his confession must morph into resistance. But what that meant wasn't as yet clear to him. Metaxas reports:

> Later on in conversations he used an example of a drunken driver killing pedestrians on a main street . . . in Berlin. He said it would be the responsibility of everyone to do all they could to stop the driver from killing more people. A year or two later, Bonhoeffer knew what few others knew, that the killing of Jews was beyond anything they had conceived. He felt a responsibility to stop it, to do anything he could. But now, before he left for America, he was still working these things out.[23]

However, after just twenty-four hours in the states, Bonhoeffer knew in his heart he belonged in Germany and had to return. He was only in America for twenty-six days before he did so.[24]

---

20. Metaxas, *Bonhoeffer*, 531.
21. Metaxas, *Bonhoeffer*, 249.
22. Metaxas, *Bonhoeffer*, 252–53.
23. Metaxas, *Bonhoeffer*, 327.
24. Metaxas, *Bonhoeffer*, 329–44.

Once back in Germany, it was only a matter of time before Bonhoeffer crossed the line from confession to resistance to conspiracy.[25] Metaxas explains:

> A major theme for Bonhoeffer was that every Christian must be "fully human" by bringing God into his whole life, not merely into some "spiritual" realm. To be an ethereal figure [less than fully human] who merely talked about God, but somehow refused to get his hands dirty in the real world in which God had placed him, was bad theology. Through Christ, God had shown that he meant us to be in this world and to obey him with our actions in this world. So Bonhoeffer would get his hands dirty, not because he had grown impatient, but because God was speaking to him about further steps of obedience.[26]

I've devoted the last few pages to some details in Bonhoeffer's story in order to provide some context for the historical fact some readers of this book might not be aware of. Eventually, Bonhoeffer became embroiled in a plot to assassinate Hitler. I encourage those who are tempted to condemn Bonhoeffer for such behavior to try their best to understand he sincerely believed this was something his discipleship to Christ called for him to do. Metaxas explains:

> For Bonhoeffer, the relationship with God ordered everything else around it. . . . To be true to God in the deepest way meant having such a relationship with him that one did not live legalistically [as the Pharisees of Jesus' day did] by "rules" or "principles." One could never separate ones' actions from one's relationship to God. . . . Bonhoeffer had come to see that the evil of Hitler was forcing Christians to go deeper in their obedience, to think harder about what God was asking. Legalistic [Pharisaical] religion was being shown to be utterly inadequate.[27]

Now, as someone who has written on the topic of Christian ethics, I wish Bonhoeffer had done a better job of indicating how passages such as Micah 6:8 can and should inform our ability to understand the heart of God for this or that moral dilemma. It's my opinion that the genius of Jesus' moral manner was he paid attention to rules, results, and virtues

---

25. Metaxas, *Bonhoeffer*, 361, 367.
26. Metaxas, *Bonhoeffer*, 361.
27. Metaxas, *Bonhoeffer*, 366–67.

rather than focusing on only one to the neglect of the others.[28] That said, my conviction that Christian ethics calls for us to strive to hear and honor the heart of God causes me to appreciate Bonhoeffer's desire to make an ethical choice he believed was both responsible and responsive to what God was asking of him.[29] My point is, whether we agree with Bonhoeffer's move or not, we must not doubt the sincerity of his faith.

In sum, sure enough, God allowed this young theologian/pastor/prophet to, like Jeremiah, suffer greatly. When the plot to kill Hitler failed, Bonhoeffer was arrested and imprisoned. In the end, he was hung by the Nazis just days before allied forces liberated the prison camp he had been interned in. But when that day came, we have reason to believe it found Bonhoeffer *holding fast*. Metaxas tells us that, years later, the camp doctor at Flossenbürg gave the following account of Bonhoeffer's last minutes alive:

> On the morning of that day between five and six o'clock the prisoners ... were taken from their cells, and the verdicts of the court martial read out to them. Through the half-open door in one room of the huts I saw Pastor Bonhoeffer, before taking off his prison garb, kneeling on the floor and praying fervently to his God. I was most deeply moved by the way this lovable man prayed, so devout and so certain that God heard his prayer. At the place of execution, he again said a short prayer and then climbed the steps to the gallows, brave and composed. His death ensued after a few seconds. In the almost fifty years that I worked as a doctor, I have hardly ever seen a man die so entirely submissive to the will of God.[30]

While we don't know for sure what Bonhoeffer prayed while kneeling on the floor of his prison cell—a prayer that moved the prison doctor so deeply—we do know the type of prayers he composed during his imprisonment. His letters and prayers were collected and published posthumously. One prayer in particular indicates why Bonhoeffer serves as a prime historical example of what *coming near, leaning into*, and *holding fast* looks like. Peruse the prayer presented below in a quiet, thoughtful

---

28. For more on this, see the chapter titled "So, What *Would* Jesus Do?" in Tyra, *Pursuing Moral Faithfulness*, 205–28.

29. For more on my take on what is involved in ethical deliberation that is both responsible and responsive, see the chapter titled "Responsible and Responsive Decision Making: A Closer Look at 'Drawing in the Dirt,'" in Tyra, *Pursuing Moral Faithfulness*, 229–53.

30. Metaxas, *Bonhoeffer*, 532.

manner, doing your best to see in it indications of Bonhoeffer's coming near in praise and penitence, leaning into the pain and suffering God had allowed him to experience, and holding fast his testimony of Christ. You won't be disappointed:

> O God, early in the morning I cry to you.
> Help me to pray
> And to concentrate my thoughts on you:
> I cannot do this alone.
>
> In me there is darkness,
> But with you there is light;
> I am lonely, but you do not leave me;
> I am feeble in heart, but with you there is help;
> I am restless, but with you there is peace.
> In me there is bitterness, but with you there is patience;
> I do not understand your ways,
> But you know the way for me.
>
> O heavenly Father,
> I praise and thank you
> For the peace of the night;
> I praise and thank you for this new day;
> I praise and thank you for all your goodness
> and faithfulness throughout my life.
>
> You have granted me many blessings;
> Now let me also accept what is hard
> from your hand.
> You will lay on me no more
> than I can bear.
> You make all things work together for good
> for your children.
>
> Lord Jesus Christ,
> You were poor
> and in distress, a captive and forsaken as I am.
> You know all man's troubles;
> You abide with me
> when all men fail me;
> You remember and seek me;
> It is your will that I should know you
> and turn to you.
> Lord, I hear your call and follow;

Help me.

O Holy Spirit,
Give me faith that will protect me
from despair, from passions, and from vice;
Give me such love for God and men
as will blot out all hatred and bitterness;
Give me the hope that will deliver me
from fear and faint-heartedness.

O holy and merciful God,
my Creator and Redeemer,
my Judge and Saviour,
You know me and all that I do.
You hate and punish evil without respect of persons
in this world and the next;
You forgive the sins of those
who sincerely pray for forgiveness;
You love goodness, and reward it on this earth
with a clear conscience,
and, in the world to come,
with a crown of righteousness.

I remember in your presence all my loved ones,
my fellow-prisoners, and all who in this house
perform their hard service;
Lord, have mercy.

Restore me to liberty,
and enable me so to live now
that I may answer before you and before men.
Lord, whatever this day may bring,
Your name be praised.
Amen.[31]

The Nazis may have killed Bonhoeffer's body, but his soul lives on (see Matt 10:28). Indeed, he continues to speak to the church through his writings and the testimonies of those who knew him (see Heb 11:4). His story makes the point: *there's a sense in which the defeat of the devil in this life requires a willingness to go the distance—to suffer and even die rather than allow the evil one to entice us into renouncing our faith in Jesus or even to go off mission.* Once again, the church offers training with respect

---

31. Bonhoeffer, *Letters and Papers*, 139–41.

to many things. What's desperately needed is some endurance training that takes seriously not only the concept of the dark night of the soul—a purposeful season where God seems to withdraw his presence so we might make some important discoveries about ourselves and him—but also those passages which clearly indicate Christian disciples are sometimes called to suffer because of their commitment to Christ (e.g., 2 Cor 4:7–18; 5:1–10; Phil 1:29; 1 Pet 4:1–2, 12–19). The good news is God's grace is sufficient. The words, example, and Spirit of Christ can help the sincere follower of Jesus to endure, and in doing so, to overcome!

So far in part three of the book we've focused on what the New Testament's authors had to say about *how* we are to deal with the devil. In the final two chapters of the work the discussion will shift to the *why* question. Gulp! You know that saying about "Where angels fear to tread?" Yeah, we're going there!

Reflection/Discussion Questions

1. To what degree do you believe praising God in the face of adversity might honor him in a special way? Might it also possess some spiritual warfare value?

2. Have you ever had the sense the Spirit was calling upon you to come correct before God in order to experience his presence in a fresh, renewed, vibrant manner (a la Ps 51)? If so, is this something you've felt the need to do more than once? Care to share how you do so and what the effect has been?

3. How would you explain to someone what the spiritual warfare move I refer to as "leaning into" involves, and why and how Joni Eareckson Tada is a poignant contemporary example of it?

4. How would you explain to someone what the spiritual warfare move I refer to as "holding fast" involves, and why and how Dietrich Bonhoeffer was a provocative yet powerful example of it?

5. What's your biggest personal takeaway from this chapter? Is the Holy Spirit prompting you to do something with it? Will you? How can we be praying for you?

Part Four

Standing Firm in the Faith:
Why the Devil Must Be Dealt with

9

Where Angels Fear to Tread
The Ultimate "Why" Question, Part 1

> But I have calmed and quieted myself, I am like a weaned child with its mother; like a weaned child I am content.
>
> —PSALM 131:2

My daughter, Megan, a senior producer for a major entertainment media company, had come home for a weekend visit. She asked how my work on this book was going. As I spoke about what I'd just completed—the initial drafts of the two chapters that make up part one of the work—I couldn't help myself; I grabbed my laptop and read some excerpts as Megan listened attentively.

Now, since Megan is a very sweet girl, her affirming and even enthusiastic response to my excerpts didn't surprise me. What did take me aback a bit, though, were some questions she put to me in a very eager and animated manner—questions about this and that topic and whether my book would address them. Because she went on to explain these are some questions she knows her friends and colleagues are asking, and because it occurred to me that not a few of my students have wondered aloud about them also, I took them seriously. In fact, I quickly grabbed a pen and notepad and had her repeat them for me as I took notes. Some of these questions ended up informing some of the discussions presented already in this book. But it seemed to me that one issue, in particular, deserved a more substantial treatment. Hence, the two chapters that conclude this work.

Throughout the book, I've focused attention on what the New Testament has to say about why and how Christians must deal with the devil. What Megan helped me become aware of is that some thoughtful readers of this work will read its first eight chapters and continue to wonder about an issue that's not explicitly addressed in the New Testament, or in the Bible as a whole for that matter. I'm referring to the ultimate *why* question: *If God is both great and good, why is there so much pain and suffering in the world?* Or as Megan phrased it: "Why did God create a world in which the devil could gain control and wreak so much havoc in the lives of human beings?" In either form, this is the question at the heart of what's called *theodicy*—the attempt to understand the problem of evil.

More specifically, theodicy is the attempt of those who believe in the God of the Bible to justify this conviction despite the fact that the presence of so much pain and suffering in the world would seem to argue against it.[1] The Bible describes God as *great* (all-powerful),[2] *good* (all-loving),[3] *eternal* (always existing),[4] and *sovereign* (the ultimate authority).[5] Thus, unless we embrace a notion the Bible doesn't support—that God and evil have always coexisted (ontological dualism)—it appears God must have done something to create it. But why would he do that? Is it because he is in truth not completely great, good, eternal, and sovereign? Or could it be he's not there at all?

For those with a biblically informed belief in God, this is the problem of evil—something that, truth be known, not a few church members and university students struggle with. I've referred previously in this work to the phenomenon of confused and hurting Christians wondering about the goodness and whereabouts of God because of some besetting trial he's allowed them or someone they love to pass through. There's a sense in which I've written the final chapters of this book for them.

That said, I want to point out straightaway that the Bible itself doesn't provide us with a theodicy. Instead, passages such as Psalm 131 encourage us to maintain our trust in God despite our inability, at present, to

---

1. See Keller, *Walking with God*, 88.
2. For example, see Jer 32:17.
3. For example, see 1 John 4:8.
4. For example, see Ps 90:2.
5. For example, see Ps 115:3; 119:89.

understand all the mysteries in the world. This poignant passage reads thusly:

> My heart is not proud, LORD, my eyes are not haughty; I do not concern myself with great matters or things too wonderful for me. But I have calmed and quieted myself, I am like a weaned child with its mother; like a weaned child I am content. Israel, put your hope in the LORD both now and forevermore. (Ps 131:1–3)

With this passage in mind, the purpose of these concluding chapters is not to *prove* anything with respect to the problem of evil, but to put forward some ideas that might help readers keep hoping in God in the face of it.[6] Put differently, my goal in this chapter and the next is *not* to provide a philosophical solution to the problem of evil but to try to clarify how the self-revelation of God presented in the Scriptures provides God's people with what they need to keep trusting in and cooperating with what he is up to in the world, despite the presence of so much pain and suffering in it. Please consider the rather substantial two-part essay that makes up these two concluding chapters a humble attempt at a response to the ultimate "why" question, and a final contribution to the reader's endurance training.

What the Bible *Does* Have to Say about the Problem of Evil

In a chapter devoted to the doctrine of God within his theological primer titled *Christianity 101*, Gilbert Bilezikian addresses the problem of evil. In sum, Bilezikian's theodicy asserts that a Christian answer to this question must begin by taking into account what the Bible has to say about:

- *the reality of the devil* (he opposes God in this world so God's will is not always being done on earth as it is in heaven);[7]

---

6. See the helpful distinction Keller makes between a theodicy that must prove to the skeptic the existence of God and the defense which merely explains why "these two statements—'There's a good, omnipotent God.' and 'There is evil in the world.'—are not a direct contradiction" (Keller, *Walking with God*, 95–96).

7. Bilezikian, *Christianity 101*, 40. Likewise, Gregory Boyd argues for the need to take Satan seriously. In his book, *Satan and the Problem of Evil*, Boyd puts forward what he refers to as a "warfare theodicy." According to Boyd, the problem of evil must take into account that "God genuinely strives against rebellious creatures. According

- *the dynamic of human freedom* (the presence of evil in the world is also explained in Scripture as the result of humans abusing the freedom granted to them by God);[8]
- *the true nature of God's greatness* (God's sovereignty doesn't require him to micromanage or control every decision made by human beings);[9] and
- *the true nature of God's goodness* (although God abhors evil, he sometimes utilizes it for beneficial purposes).[10]

At the risk of oversimplifying, I'll point out what Bilezikian is presenting is essentially a "free will" theodicy.[11] At the heart of this understanding of the problem of evil is the contention that, according to the Bible, we humans are directly responsible for what has happened to the good world God created. Humans were created to function as God's viceregents over his creation (Gen 1:26–28). In turning away from God (just as Satan and his fallen angels had), humans opened the door for evil to invade God's good world.[12] According to Genesis 3, the sin of Adam and Eve changed everything: their relationships with God, each other, nature, and themselves. Not just the ground fell under a curse as a result of humanity's rejection of God's loving lordship (Gen 3:17), but creation as a whole (see Rom 8:19–21).[13] Indeed, humanity's rejection of God's loving

---

to Scripture, the head of this rebellion is a powerful fallen angel named Satan. Under him are a myriad of other spiritual beings . . . . The world is literally caught up in a spiritual war between God and Satan" (Boyd, *Satan and the Problem of Evil*, 15).

8. Bilezikian, *Christianity 101*, 40.
9. Bilezikian, *Christianity 101*, 41.
10. Bilezikian, *Christianity 101*, 42–43.
11. For more on this argument, both pro and con, see Keller, *Walking with God*, 90–93.
12. While pastor/theologian Gregory Boyd also places blame on the human misuse of their God-given freedom, he incorporates this into a "warfare theodicy." According to Boyd, Satan and God are engaged in a cosmic conflict. Though evil is entirely the work of the evil one, he was empowered to affect God's creation by us human beings. Boyd explains: "When Adam and Eve fell, they surrendered to Satan the authority over the earth that they and their descendants were supposed to have. Once established as 'ruler' and 'god' of the world (John 12:31; 14:30; 16:11; 2 Cor 4:4), Satan immediately began to exercise his own dominion over the earth" (see Boyd, *Satan and the Problem of Evil*, 312).
13. Boyd explains: "God created the world such that when morally responsible agents fall, everything they are morally responsible for will become adversely affected. . . . Thus, there is no contradiction in saying that God cursed the earth because of

lordship became the source of not only *moral evil* (the pain and suffering which human beings inflict upon each other by means of "oppression, war, crime, and violence"), but *natural evil* as well (the pain and suffering that results from "disease, genetic disorders, famine, natural disasters, aging and death").[14] The upshot of Bilezikian's take is *when it comes to the problem of evil, we human beings need to look in the mirror rather than immediately blame God for all the pain and suffering in the world!*

But, then, Bilezikian seems to throw his readers a curveball when he goes on to make the following observation:

> Undeniably, human abuse of God-given freedom opened the way for evil to appear in a world created good. But as shocking as it may sound, since it was God who created the world into which evil would emerge, his responsibility is also involved. Had God not created the world, there would have been no evil. The real question is: Why did God proceed with creation, knowing that it would become ravaged with evil and that countless numbers of his creatures would doom themselves to eternal death? Or, put differently: Why did God create free will, knowing that it would become self-destructive? . . . Many sincere people cannot believe in God or in his goodness because he knowingly created a world that held the high risk of generating evil and inflicting unspeakable suffering upon itself.[15]

Wow! We might wonder at this point whose side Bilezikian is on! Furthermore, he goes on to make this even more bold assertion:

> So, while acknowledging the fact that human responsibility was definitely involved in the existence of evil, we must honestly face the issue that God bears his share of responsibility for going ahead with the creation of a world that he knew to be corruptible.[16]

Adam's sin and that Satan and his legions also plague the earth because of Adam's sin" (Boyd, *Satan and the Problem of Evil*, 313).

14. See Keller, *Reason for God*, 177.
15. Keller, *Reason for God*, 44.
16. Keller, *Reason for God*, 44.

God in the Dock

The phrase "God in the Dock" alludes to a thusly titled essay penned by C. S. Lewis in which he made the following observation:

> The ancient man approached God (or even the gods) as the accused person approaches his judge. For the modern man the roles are reversed. He is the judge: God is in the dock. He is quite a kindly judge: if God should have a reasonable defence for being the god who permits war, poverty and disease, he is ready to listen to it. The trial may even end in God's acquittal. But the important thing is that Man is on the Bench and God in the Dock.[17]

My point is, having put God in the dock (or on trial), so to speak, Bilezikian then proceeds, rather ironically, to argue on his behalf as a legal advocate might. What we might call his "defense brief" puts forward three main arguments, one of which seems to focus on the question of *God's culpability for the fall*; another on the fact of *God's responsible behavior after the fall*; and the third on the message of the book of Job. As these arguments are considered, we will also pay attention to how pastor/professor Gregory Boyd, author of the books, *God at War: The Bible and Spiritual Conflict*, and *Satan and the Problem of Evil: Constructing a Trinitarian Warfare Theodicy*, also speaks to the matter before us. We might think of Boyd as Bilezikian's co-counsel.

The Defense Brief, Part 1: *God's Culpability for the Fall*

Put simply, the first main argument presented by Bilezikian and Boyd focuses on the question of whether the indictment against God is justified in the first place. In the process, they address three main issues.

Why God Created Humans as Free Moral Agents

First, Bilezikian proffers a succinct but important discussion of why and how God engaged in the act of creation. In the process, he refutes the notion that God is a capricious being who created the world in either a careless or malicious manner. According to Bilezikian:

---

17. Lewis, *God in the Dock*, 268.

> The accusation of cosmic sadism could be justifiably leveled at God if he had whimsically created a world with built-in corruptibility. However ... the world did not derive from a divine caprice, as if in the course of eternity, God had suddenly come upon the idea of creation and decided to put it into effect. Rather ... the disposition to create pertains to the very nature of God. Because he is love, God is by nature a giving God. ... He irresistibly invests in his creation what is most precious to him: he gives himself by giving his own image. Because God cannot go against his own giving nature, he creates human beings endowed with the capacity to make decisions.[18]

What Bilezikian is suggesting is human beings created in the image of a God who creates in freedom will *necessarily* possess the capacity to make free decisions.

Bilezikian then draws our attention to the implications of this fact for the larger discussion. Far from being a malicious act, this was an act of love, of self-giving. It was an ennobling act on God's part to, in freedom, create image-bearers with freedom. Bilezikian puts it this way:

> In other words, God neither willed evil nor did he create it. But because he by nature loves freedom and gives freedom, he was compelled by the necessity of who he is to give the very freedom that would turn against him and against itself. God is neither sadistic nor whimsical. Like a compulsive lover, he is outrageously giving to the point of creating beings whom he allows to function beyond his direct control.[19]

We should note at this point Bilezikian's use of the phrase "was compelled by the necessity of who he is" indicates his belief that, in a sense, God couldn't help himself; if he was true to himself, he had to create, and to do so in freedom, with freedom. This seems to be an implicit appeal to a legal concept which asserts that actions that are involuntary (or unavoidable) are not culpable (or punishable).[20]

Also noteworthy is the fact that Gregory Boyd takes another, though similar, tack in his defense of God. Boyd puts forward the idea that God's *goal* or *desire* was to create creatures with whom he could have a personal, loving relationship. For such a relationship to be real and genuine, Boyd

---

18. Bilezikian, *Christianity 101*, 44–45.
19. Bilezikian, *Christianity 101*, 45.
20. For more on this legal notion, see Robinson, "Brief History," 815–53.

insists, it requires a freedom on the part of the creature to love and trust the creator (or not to).[21] Taking this alternative approach, Boyd explains:

> If God desires a bride made up of people who genuinely love him—who do not just *act* lovingly toward him—he *must* create people who have the capacity to reject him. He *must* endow agents with self-determination. They, not he, must determine whether or not they will love him and each other. And this, I submit, explains why God created a world in which evil was possible. If love is the goal, it could not be otherwise. God chose to create a world in which evil was possible only in the sense that he chose to create a world in which love was possible.... It is, in effect, the metaphysical price God *must* pay if he *wants* to arrive at a bride who says yes to his triune love.[22]

So, while Bilezikian suggests, given his nature as a lover, God had no choice but to create, and, because of his own freedom, to create his image-bearers with freedom, Boyd argues that doing so was *necessary* for God to achieve his desired goal: an eternal love and trust-based relationship with those who bear his image. Both approaches have the effect of arguing, essentially, *God had no real choice but to do what he did: create human beings in freedom, with freedom.*

So, as God's defense attorneys, both Bilezikian and Boyd stipulate the fact that it was indeed God's having created human beings in freedom, with freedom, that made evil possible. At the same time, they insist God's creative activity wasn't performed in a capricious manner, or with anything other than a loving, benevolent motive in place. Their collective argument seems to be this: *How could God have done otherwise?*

God's Creative Activity: Risky Rather than Evil

Moreover, both Bilezikian and Boyd make the assertion that we human beings should not be so quick to presume God knew in advance that the fall would inevitably occur. While I don't want to get too deep into the weeds here, I suppose it's necessary to point out that a significant feature of Boyd's (and Bilezikian's) proposal is *God didn't know for sure the fall would occur, only that it might.*

21. See also Lewis, *Mere Christianity*, 47–48; Keller, *Walking with God*, 90–93.

22. Boyd, *Satan and the Problem of Evil*, 55, emphasis added. It should be noted that elsewhere in his book Boyd clarifies that the bride is the "bride of Christ." See Boyd, *Satan and the Problem of Evil*, 118, 119, 190, 320, 371.

At the risk of oversimplifying, I will summarize the classic understanding of God's foreknowledge thusly: God knows the end from the beginning, regarding all matters, period. Over against this classical view of divine foreknowledge, Boyd contends if we are going to avoid the conclusion that God created people knowing they would fall and engage in behaviors hurtful to others as well as themselves, we have to arrive at an understanding of God's foreknowledge which makes the future from God's perspective a set of possibilities only. Boyd's argument, which is both theological and philosophical in nature, ends up suggesting God's creative activity was simply *risky* rather than evil. Here's how Boyd summarizes his "open view" of God's knowledge of the future:

> In this view, therefore, the future is partly comprised of possibilities. And since God knows all things perfectly—just as they are, and not otherwise—God knows the future as partly comprised of possibilities.
>
> The open view of the future thus affirms that in creating the world God faced the possibility, but not the certainty, that free creatures would choose to oppose him to the extent that they have. This view thereby allows us to consistently affirm that God entered into a somewhat risky endeavor in creating the world.[23]

While Bilezikian is also an advocate of open theism—i.e., the open view of the future—the way he makes the case for it in *Christianity 101* is slightly different. For Bilezikian, the issue is not so much that God *can't* possess an exhaustive knowledge of the future, but that he *chooses not to*. According to Bilezikian, God in his sovereignty has placed some limits on his foreknowledge to protect the ability of humans to make genuinely free decisions.[24] He writes:

> In order to respect the integrity of human freedom and not to interfere with its exercise, God often seems to limit his awareness of their actions—as if he were surrounding them with a bubble of noninterference, sheltering them from the full scope of his omniscience.[25]

Notice Bilezikian suggests a felt need on God's part to *shelter* humans from the "full scope of his omniscience." The assumption seems to be if God *foreknows* something is going to happen, then it is *foreordained*

---

23. Boyd, *Satan and the Problem of Evil*, 91–92.
24. Bilezikian, *Christianity 101*, 29.
25. Bilezikian, *Christianity 101*, 29.

or *predestined* to occur. By this logic, if God knows in advance what humans are going to do in a given situation, then the future is irrevocably decided—human beings aren't really free with respect to their decision-making. They may think they are free, but are actually only puppets acting out God's predetermined will. Thus, apparently embracing the philosophical proposition that foreknowledge equals foreordination, Bilezikian argues that for humans to have free will, God has to place limits on his omniscience—choose not to foreknow all their choices.

Bilezikian and other open theists find support for this revised version of divine foreknowledge in various Old Testament passages that seem to portray God:

- registering surprise, disappointment, and even regret at the discovery of what is happening on the human scene (e.g., Gen 3:9; 6:5–6; 18:20–21);
- discovering a state of affairs that causes him to take action (e.g., Gen 6:5–7; 11:5–7; Exod 3:9–10; 1 Sam 15:11, 35; 2 Sam 24:16; Jer 18:9–10; Joel 2:13; Amos 7:3, 6; Jonah 3:1–4, 10); and
- changing his mind as a result of human prayer or intercession (e.g., Exod 32:7–14; Isa 38:1–6).

Open theists believe passages such as these indicate that, in truth, God relates to human beings in a genuinely reciprocal, interactive manner rather than one in which his predetermined will makes human freedom nothing more than an illusion.[26] Again, what makes God truly great, say Boyd and Bilezikian, is not his ability to micromanage everyone's decision-making, but to take everyone's free choices and cause them to work together for good according to his overarching plan for the cosmos.[27] The larger point this discussion of open theism is making, however, is we can't really blame God for creating a world he knew in advance would become infected with evil. Even from God's perspective, creation was full of possibilities, not already-realized actualities. Though God's sovereignty is such that he can and is guiding human history toward its predetermined *telos* (goal), this doesn't mean every human choice is foreknown and thus foreordained.

26. For a discussion of why passages such as these shouldn't be considered mere *anthropomorphisms* (i.e., the biblical authors simply "portraying God in human like terms") see Boyd, *Satan and the Problem of Evil*, 97–100.

27. Bilezikian, *Christianity 101*, 41.

God Considered the Prize Worth the Cost

Having argued there's no way for such things as love and goodness to be present in God's creation without there also being an alternative,[28] Boyd goes on to suggest God came to the conclusion the invaluable prize he was aiming for was simply worth the risk. Portraying God's decision to create the world as a grand "gamble," Boyd asserts that the "wager" in this case was justified. He explains his reasoning thusly:

> [T]he wisdom of a risk must be judged by the *quality* of the potential prize, on the one hand, and the *probability* of acquiring that prize, on the other.
>
> We continue to love despite painful losses because we intuitively know that the potential reward of love is what makes life worth living. God does not need any love outside his own eternal, triune identity to make life worth living, but the Lord nevertheless regards the reward of created beings joining him in everlasting, triune celebration as worth whatever losses he and his creation might experience along the way. In other words, God deems the risk involved in creation as being *on the whole* worth it. In creating the world God judged that the quality of the prize was worth the possible, and perhaps even inevitable, pain the venture might cause him and others.[29]

According to Boyd, at the end of the day, God in his sovereignty made a fateful choice to create human, free, moral agency despite the risks inherent in his doing so. Why? Because the prize of a genuinely reciprocal love relationship with us was worth any cost that might ensue!

The Lingering Question

Despite the truly vigorous defense for their client Bilezikian and Boyd have thus far presented, they go on to boldly address a question they apparently feel may still be lingering in the minds of many jury members: *Given the way things turned out, isn't it possible to view God's risky decision to create humans (and angels) in freedom, with freedom, as an incredibly irresponsible act?* This brings us to the second principal argument presented by Bilezikian and Boyd in their defense brief.

---

28. See Boyd, *Satan and the Problem of Evil*, 169–73.
29. Boyd, *Satan and the Problem of Evil*, 176–77, emphasis original.

The Defense Brief, Part 2:
God's Responsible Behavior after the Fall

The second part of the defense brief presented in this case is a succinct but powerful response to the lingering question presented above. Bilezikian points out to the jury how willing God has been to personally pay the costs that have accrued from his having created humans and angels in freedom, with freedom. The essence of his argument is it's inappropriate to accuse God of being irresponsible in his creative activity precisely because he has so "lovingly and servant-like, accepted that responsibility and assumed it upon himself."[30] According to Bilezikian:

> The God who created the freedom that would turn against him in pride and rebellion also took it upon himself to come into the world as a baby and to grow up as a servant, perfectly subjected to the Father and submitted to humans to the point of dying at their hand. The God who created beings who chose evil and brought into the world sin, suffering, and death, also took it upon himself to defeat sin through the righteousness of the Son, to bear our suffering on the cross, and to overcome death in the victory of the resurrection. At infinite cost to himself, God initiated a redemptive program that required his own identification with humans at their lowest point. As a result, God is able to offer those who submit to him access to new personhood in Christ, inclusion in God's new community, and deliverance from the eternal consequences of evil.[31]

Bilezikian's reference to "a redemptive program that required his own identification with humans at their lowest point" is an allusion to two very important New Testament passages. In his Letter to the Philippians, the apostle Paul speaks of something theologians refer to as the *kenosis* or self-emptying of Christ. Here's how Paul describes the voluntary self-emptying Christ performed on behalf of God's image-bearers:

> In your relationships with one another, have the same mindset as Christ Jesus: Who, being in very nature God, did not consider equality with God something to be used to his own advantage;

---

30. Bilezikian, *Christianity 101*, 46. Likewise, N. T. Wright observes that "The Gospels thus tell the story, centrally and crucially, which stands unique in the world's great literature, the world's religious theories and visions: the story of the Creator God taking responsibility for what has happened to creation, bearing the weight of its problems on his own shoulders" (Wright, *Evil and the Justice of God*, 94).

31. Bilezikian, *Christianity 101*, 46.

> rather, he made himself nothing by taking the very nature of a servant, being made in human likeness. And being found in appearance as a man, he humbled himself by becoming obedient to death—even death on a cross! Therefore God exalted him to the highest place and gave him the name that is above every name, that at the name of Jesus every knee should bow, in heaven and on earth and under the earth, and every tongue acknowledge that Jesus Christ is Lord, to the glory of God the Father. (Phil 2:5–11)

The second passage that comes to mind when I read about "a redemptive program that required his own identification with humans at their lowest point" is located in the New Testament's Letter to the Hebrews. In chapter 2 of that missive, the author explains:

> Since the children have flesh and blood, he too shared in their humanity so that by his death he might break the power of him who holds the power of death—that is, the devil—and free those who all their lives were held in slavery by their fear of death. For surely it is not angels he helps, but Abraham's descendants. For this reason he had to be made like them, fully human in every way, in order that he might become a merciful and faithful high priest in service to God, and that he might make atonement for the sins of the people. Because he himself suffered when he was tempted, he is able to help those who are being tempted. (Heb 2:14–18)

Considered together, these two passages teach us the eternal Son of God not only took on human flesh, but, in a servant-like manner, also consented to die on our behalf as a sin offering, thus making a reconciliation between a holy God and his sinful progeny possible. Moreover, Christ's resurrection has the effect of freeing us from the fear of death, which is what the anti-God, anti-truth, and anti-life devil uses to keep God's image-bearers in bondage to his tyrannical rule. As a result, we now possess the Spirit-imparted freedom to say "yes" to God and "no" to the evil one! But we must not forget, says Bilezikian, it was at "infinite cost to himself" God brought about this reversal of fortune. Bilezikian's point seems to be this: *How could we ever use the words "irresponsible" and "God" in the same sentence?*

The Defense Brief, Part 3: *God's Message to Job*

Bilezikian and Boyd also make use of the biblical story of Job in their defense of God in the face of human pain and suffering. The book of Job is one of the wisdom writings included in the Old Testament. Its focus is on the sudden, severe, and sustained suffering experienced by its title character even though he is introduced at the very beginning of the work as an especially righteous, God-fearing man (Job 1:1). The question arises: *Why would God allow someone as righteous as Job to experience such horrific suffering?*[32]

Approaching the Job story as a biblical theodicy,[33] some interpreters have suggested it "seeks to justify the arbitrary dispensation of injustice by God for His private ends."[34] In other words, this perspective maintains that, whether we like it or not, the purpose of the book of Job is to function as a bald declaration of God's sovereign right to do whatever he wants with the people he created.

Another move some interpreters make is to suggest the story's purpose is to function as a cathartic (or psychological aid). The message of the book is simply that *ambiguity happens!* According to this view, the question of undeserved suffering that's at the heart of the work is never fully answered. And yet, the reader experiences a strange and ironic comfort as he or she identifies with Job and the bold maintenance of his integrity against all accusers, human and divine. Thus, one proponent of this perspective asserts: "all the hero can do, if he is visited as Job was, is to persevere in the pride of his conviction, to appeal to God against God, and if he is as fortunate as Job, hear his questionings echo into nothingness in the infinite mystery and the glory."[35] Put simply, though the story of Job provides no real answer to the question of the problem of evil, reading it and identifying with Job provides some psychological comfort: we're not alone in our suffering!

---

32. In my book, *Pursuing Moral Faithfulness*, I discuss the manner in which the story of Job illustrates the phenomenon of "purposeful ambiguity"—God's use of ambiguity in our lives to drive us to our knees and into a more theologically real relationship with him (Tyra, *Pursuing Moral Faithfulness*, 258–68). Some of my interaction here with Bilezikian and Boyd regarding "the message of the book of Job" is adapted from that discussion.

33. Wolfers, *Deep Things*, 68. See also Davidson, *Old Testament*, 166–68; Waltke, *Old Testament Theology*, 929.

34. Wolfers, *Deep Things*, 68.

35. See Sewall, "Book of Job," 34.

In contrast to the two views just presented, the conclusion which both Bilezikian and Boyd come to in their respective treatments of this important biblical story is that its ultimate message is Job must recognize he lives in a complex and combative world in which things happen that are not directly caused by God.[36] Thus, all the primary human characters in the story (Job and his three friends) were wrong in their diagnosis of Job's dilemma. Contrary to the insistence of Job's three friends, he wasn't suffering because of some secret, unconfessed sin in his life (see Job 4:1–9). Contrary to Job's own insistence, he wasn't suffering because God was acting in an arbitrary and unjust manner toward him (see Job 34:5). Instead, say Boyd and Bilezikian, Job was suffering simply because *crud happens!* More specifically, because of the way we humans misused our moral freedom, we are now living in a temporary war zone in which Satan can and does do things that are not necessarily willed by God.

According to this perspective, the best God can do at the end of the book is reassure Job he knows of his suffering and is grieved by it. Though God's ultimate victory is assured, there's a sense in which, in the meantime, God and Job are in this difficult dilemma together.[37] Boyd asserts that the message of the book is "[t]he cosmos is far more complex and combative than either Job or his friends assumed in their simplistic theologies,"[38] and "[p]eace comes to Job only when he learns that, though his suffering is a mystery, he can and must nevertheless humbly trust God. His suffering is not God's fault, and God is not against him. God's character is trustworthy."[39]

It must be acknowledged that Bilezikian and Boyd have put forward a hearty defense of God in the face of evil. There's a sense in which I hope they are correct. And yet, I'm also aware they might not be, and some Christians will struggle with certain aspects of their three-part defense brief. For at least some readers of this book, a few still-lingering questions might be: *What if we are not open theists who believe God has placed limits on his foreknowledge? What if God's creating humans and angels in freedom, with freedom, was not really a gamble as Boyd suggests? What if there's another way to understand the message of Job, one that doesn't let God off the hook for human suffering quite so easily? Why would God go*

---

36. See Boyd, *God at War*, 52, 165–66.
37. Boyd, *Satan and the Problem of Evil*, 224.
38. Boyd, *Satan and the Problem of Evil*, 223.
39. See Bilezikian, *Christianity 101*, 45; Boyd, *Satan and the Problem of Evil*, 226.

ahead and create humans and angels in freedom, with freedom, if, in his foreknowledge, he knew with certainty that the fall and all the evil that came of it would inevitably occur?

Bilezikian and Boyd in the Dock

Let's make our way now, so to speak, to the jury room where, in real life, a jury goes to form a verdict with respect to the case before it. Ideally, a jury's verdict is arrived at as its members reflect together on the evidence and arguments presented during the trial and then engage in a discursive (conversational) process of deliberation. In this case, however, the conversation is one-way, as I share in the next few pages some of my musings concerning several key arguments Bilezikian and Boyd have presented on God's behalf.

We've seen that at the heart of their defense brief (theodicy) are the following three suggestions:

1. As a compulsive lover in search of a bride, God was virtually compelled to create the way he did—in freedom, with freedom.
2. God didn't know for sure that evil would result from his creative activity, but did so despite the risk because he considered the prize to be worth it.
3. The ultimate message of Job's story is, since the devil is the direct cause for human suffering, it is wrongheaded for humans to blame God for it.

Honestly, the goal behind my interaction with the defense brief put forward in this chapter is to prepare the way for an alternative proposal I'll present in the next—one that nuances the theodicy of Bilezikian and Boyd in some important and, I think, helpful ways.

The Open View of the Future

From the outset, I want to indicate how appreciative I am for the way Boyd makes clear his warfare theodicy doesn't hinge upon an acceptance of his revised version of divine foreknowledge.[40] I'm also grateful for his willingness to grant it's possible for good-hearted Christians to hold on to

---

40. Boyd, *Satan and the Problem of Evil*, 87.

part or all of a more traditional understanding of God's foreknowledge, even while understanding the need to engage in spiritual warfare.[41]

Going further, I also deeply resonate with the assertion that what makes God so great is not his ability to micromanage every decision made by his image-bearers, but is instead his remarkable ability to cause the free decisions humans and angels make to work toward his overarching plan for the planet. This latter understanding encourages us to recognize the give-and-take nature of our relationship with our heavenly Father, rather than seeing ourselves as puppets being exhaustively determined by him.

That said, I'm not convinced a real, interactive relationship between God and his image-bearers required that he place selective limits upon his foreknowledge. For one thing, I don't see any explicit support for this revision of the traditional understanding of God's foreknowledge in the writings of the New Testament authors.[42] Instead, what I see in the New Testament is much closer to the more traditional conception (see Luke 22:31–32; Acts 2:23; Rom 8:29; 11:2; 1 Pet 1:2).[43]

What's more, given our limited understanding of how time operates in the dimension of light in which God dwells (Ps 104:2; 1 Tim 6:15–16), I'm open to the possibility that God can foreknow and respond to what we do in this or that situation without infringing on our freedom to, in the moment, make an unencumbered choice. After all, doesn't the New Testament (see Rom 8:29; 1 Pet 1:2) seem to make a distinction between foreknowledge (Greek: *proginōskō*) and predestination (Greek: *proorizō*)? What if, in God's economy, his foreknowledge doesn't equal foreordination? This would mean God wouldn't have had to blind himself to what Adam and Eve were going to do vis-à-vis the tree of the knowledge of good and evil in order for them to be able to act freely in their moment of decision.

---

41. Boyd, *Satan and the Problem of Evil*, 86–87.

42. For more on the hermeneutical (interpretive) principle known as *progressive revelation* (the idea that in the Bible we find God revealing the truth about himself and his plan for the planet a bit at a time until it is fully revealed in the person of Christ), see Slick, "What is Progressive Revelation?"

43. I'll also point out by way of footnote that Boyd himself has acknowledged that the traditional view of God's omniscience was "not generally questioned' until a heretical group known as the Socinians did so in the seventeenth century A.D. This would seem to be an admission that explicit support for Boyd's revised view of God's foreknowledge is lacking in the writings of the church fathers. See, Boyd, as cited in Erickson, *What Does God Know?*, 115.

In sum, I'm suggesting that, whereas Boyd only refers to three options with respect to God's foreknowledge—one which has God foreknowing and foreordaining every human choice (exhaustive, definitive foreknowledge); one which has God foreknowing genuinely free human choices and being completely impotent to act responsively in light of this foreknowledge (simple foreknowledge); and the open view of the future described above—there's actually a fourth. What I have in mind is an option that's *not as determining* as the way Boyd describes exhaustive, definitive foreknowledge, that's *more aware* than the way Boyd explains the open view, and that's *much more dynamic/responsive* than the way Boyd defines simple foreknowledge. For instance, in the Gospel of Luke we find Jesus not only speaking in advance of Peter's failing a test Satan will put him through, but also indicating his ongoing prayer support for his disciple, and then encouraging an ultimate, rebounding response from Peter after his foreseen failure (Luke 22:31–32). I consider this passage to be suggestive of a dynamic, responsive, fully aware foreknowledge that doesn't fit into any of the three categories put forward by Boyd.

That said, nowhere is the fourth option I have in mind better illustrated than in what I believe God was up to in the life of Job. This leads us to a consideration of another major argument put forward by Bilezikian and Boyd.

The Message of the Book of Job

To be clear, there are some aspects of their treatment of Job's story I can affirm. In particular, along with Boyd and Bilezikian, I'm convinced the point of the book is not simply to declare that God is sovereign and can do whatever he likes with his creation. I also agree with their observation that Job and his friends were wrong in their respective conclusions about the cause of Job's suffering. That said, I'm concerned the interpretation put forward by Boyd and Bilezikian may be guilty of excessively understating the sovereignty of God. To be more specific, I see in this biblical book an emphasis on God's "use" of Satan in Job's life. There seems to have been a providential *purpose* behind Job's suffering which the interpretation proffered by Bilezikian and Boyd, out of its concern to promote a warfare theodicy, doesn't seem to have room for.[44]

---

44. It should be noted that an additional perspective regarding the reason for human suffering is presented late in the story by a mysterious character named Elihu (Job

While Boyd acknowledges the importance of not ignoring the prologue of Job's story when formulating a perspective on its ultimate message,[45] he and I differ in our understanding of its implications. According to my read of the prologue, Job is portrayed straightaway as a very, *very* pious, righteous person (Job 1:1; 31:1–40). However, the text seems to suggest Job's religiosity wasn't a reflection of his love and trust in Yahweh, but was rooted in fear and an excessive ritualism instead. A key verse in the book's prologue explains:

> His sons used to hold feasts in their homes on their birthdays, and they would invite their three sisters to eat and drink with them. When a period of feasting had run its course, Job would make arrangements for them to be purified. Early in the morning he would sacrifice a burnt offering for each of them, thinking, "Perhaps my children have sinned and cursed God in their hearts." This was Job's regular custom. (Job 1:4–5)

I'm not alone in suggesting the observance of religious ritual described in Job 1:4–5 was *overly scrupulous*. Commenting on Job's "regular custom" of offering sacrifices on behalf of his kids, Old Testament scholar Bruce Waltke observes:

> "Job would have them purified," showing his *"extraordinary scrupulousness* that must cover even unseen sin, that must bestir itself 'early in the morning,' that must offer not one sacrifice but ten, that must never fail in its responsibility but 'do so continually.'"[46]

Moreover, the fact that Job's religiosity—his super-scrupulous obedience to rules and observance of ritual—was driven by a deep-seated

---

32–37). Some commentators question whether these chapters were part of the original story. Others suggest that Elihu's perspective, which is critical of those provided by Job and his three friends, is intended to reflect the position held by the book's author. (For more on this see Genung, "Elihu," 930.) According to pastor/theologian John Piper, Elihu's position can be summarized thusly: the suffering which God allows "righteous sinners" like Job (and us) to experience is not meant to be punitive but curative, to *refine the righteousness* present in our lives even more. (See Piper, "Job," paras. 32–42.) Though the perspective presented below differs some from the one Piper attributes to Elihu, common to them both is the idea that God in his wisdom uses our suffering in a providential manner.

45. Boyd, *Satan and the Problem of Evil*, 225.
46. Clines, as cited in Waltke, *Old Testament Theology*, 930, emphasis added.

sense of fear is indicated not only in Job 1:1, but also by statements he makes later on in the book. For example:

> What I feared has come upon me; what I dreaded has happened to me. (Job 3:25)

> That is why I am terrified before him; when I think of all this, I fear him. (Job 23:15)

> For I dreaded destruction from God, and for fear of his splendor I could not do such things. (Job 31:23)

I consider the last verse just cited to be especially important. While Job 31 as a whole makes it clear Job's life was not lacking with respect to righteous behaviors, verse 23 seems to indicate Job's impeccable piety was not grounded in his love for and trust in God, but a terrible *dread* of him instead. What I'm suggesting is what we find in the prologue to the story of Job is a not-so-subtle indication the main character's extraordinarily righteous lifestyle was rooted in a fear of God that went beyond reverence, and manifested itself in a super-scrupulous, actually obsessive-compulsive obedience to rules and observance of religious ritual.[47]

Taking all of this into consideration, my question is: *What if God wanted to move Job away from a fear-based religion of rules and rituals to a love-and-trust-based personal relationship where rules and rituals are means to an end rather than ends in themselves? How would God go about this?* One way to accomplish this spiritual development would be to throw Job some existential curveballs designed to help him see that true spiritual fulfillment requires more than a scrupulous obedience to religious rules and observance of religious rituals.

This bold suggestion mandates a brief discussion of yet another important feature of the book's prologue: *how it seems to portray God as using Satan to bring about the spiritual development referred to above.* Near the beginning of Job's story we read of two conversations between God and Satan:

---

47. For more on how fear can be a causal factor in religious legalism and ritualism, see Tyra, *Defeating Pharisaism*, 68–75. According to Tim Keller, the development God wanted to see in Job's life was for him to "become more fully someone who serves God for nothing and loves God for him alone," or to move from loving God in a mercenary way toward loving God himself" (Keller, *Walking with God*, 273–75). While this interpretation is on the right track, I will present below a similar but slightly different take on the development God wanted to see take place in Job's spiritual life. What both Keller and I have in common is the belief that God was using Job's suffering in a redemptive manner.

One day the angels came to present themselves before the LORD, and Satan also came with them. The LORD said to Satan, "Where have you come from?" Satan answered the LORD, "From roaming throughout the earth, going back and forth on it." Then the LORD said to Satan, "Have you considered my servant Job? There is no one on earth like him; he is blameless and upright, a man who fears God and shuns evil." "Does Job fear God for nothing?" Satan replied. "Have you not put a hedge around him and his household and everything he has? You have blessed the work of his hands, so that his flocks and herds are spread throughout the land. But now stretch out your hand and strike everything he has, and he will surely curse you to your face." The LORD said to Satan, "Very well, then, everything he has is in your power, but on the man himself do not lay a finger." Then Satan went out from the presence of the LORD. (Job 1:6–12)

On another day the angels came to present themselves before the LORD, and Satan also came with them to present himself before him. And the LORD said to Satan, "Where have you come from?" Satan answered the LORD, "From roaming throughout the earth, going back and forth on it." Then the LORD said to Satan, "Have you considered my servant Job? There is no one on earth like him; he is blameless and upright, a man who fears God and shuns evil. And he still maintains his integrity, though you incited me against him to ruin him without any reason." "Skin for skin!" Satan replied. "A man will give all he has for his own life. But now stretch out your hand and strike his flesh and bones, and he will surely curse you to your face." The LORD said to Satan, "Very well, then, he is in your hands; but you must spare his life." So Satan went out from the presence of the LORD and afflicted Job with painful sores from the soles of his feet to the crown of his head. Then Job took a piece of broken pottery and scraped himself with it as he sat among the ashes. (Job 2:1–8)

Boyd's contention seems to be the prologue to Job's story is crucial to a proper understanding of its ultimate message simply because it refers to Satan, and indicates Satan was the direct cause of Job's suffering. By themselves, these bare facts would seem to support Boyd's concept of a warfare theodicy. Poor Job was caught in the crossfire between God and the devil!

However, such an interpretive move ignores the fact the two passages presented above portray God actually instigating Satan's engagement with Job, and putting limits on it as well. This more careful reading of the prologue has convinced Old Testament scholar Paul House that Job 1:6—2:6 makes it clear, "Yahweh is King in charge of angels, Satan, human affairs and ultimately the tests people endure."[48] N. T. Wright likewise suggests in the first two chapters of the story "we learn both that 'the satan' is the source of Job's problem and that God has given him permission—we might almost say encouragement—to do what he has done."[49]

This more nuanced read of the book's prologue runs counter to the view of Boyd and Bilezikian that the message of God to Job is, "Sorry about your suffering, but I've got my hands full trying to sustain the world while keeping the hounds of evil at bay." But it accords well with my proposal that God sometimes uses our suffering to bring us, like Job, to a place where we recognize we weren't made to fearfully obey rules and observe rituals as ends in themselves; we were made for a real, intimate, interactive, love-and-trust-based relationship with the living God!

I won't treat here the middle section of the book (Job 2:11—37:24), except to say the numerous conversations between Job and his friends have the effect of causing him to become crazy-hungry desperate for a personal encounter with God.[50] The more Job's friends accuse him of being a secret sinner,[51] the more Job asserts his righteousness and suggests that, this time around, God has it wrong. Though Job never actually curses God in his speeches to his "friends," he does come close, essentially accusing God of acting in a capricious/unjust manner toward him and, by extension, the whole world.[52] Moreover, even when Job isn't explicitly expressing misgivings regarding God's faithfulness toward him, he's doing so inferentially by wishing he had never been born (e.g., Job 3:1–26; 10:18–19). I suggest to my students that this is essentially a

48. House, *Old Testament Theology*, 428.
49. Wright, *Evil and the Justice of God*, 69. See also, Keller, *Walking with God*, 273.
50. Gray, "Purpose and Method of the Writer," 40–41. See also Westermann, *Structure of the Book of Job*, 68–69. Indeed, according to Westermann, Job's "main wish" is "for a direct encounter with God. This is the real wish toward which Job has been struggling all along." Westermann also observes that "this is the most elaborate wish in the whole Book of Job" (Westermann, *Structure of the Book of Job*, 69).
51. For more on the belief system and motive of Job's "friends," see Gray, "Purpose and Method of the Writer," 38–41. See also Alden, *Job*, 40.
52. For example, see Job 7:17–21; 9:16–18, 22–24; 10:1–3; 16:7–17; 19:1–7; 23:11–17; 24:1, 12; 27:2–6; 30:20–26; see also 33:8–11; 34:5–6; 40:8.

passive-aggressive way of indicting God for having performed his duties poorly! This is all to say, before it's over, the tension between Job and his friends, and Job and a God whom he accuses of avoiding him,[53] reaches a fever pitch. Again, I'm suggesting God knew what he was doing; by the time these debates are concluded, he has Job right where he wants him: crazy-hungry desperate for a personal encounter!

Eventually, we read, God does shows up, so to speak, and he and Job have it out (Job 38:1—41:34). Actually, we find God delivering two speeches of his own—monologues which communicate to Job that it's not only pointless to try to tame or control him, but unnecessary as well. Though it seems God is saying to Job: "Hey, little man! Shut up and take what I give you," much more than that is going on. Commenting on these two divine speeches, Francis Andersen makes this critical observation:

> There is a kindly playfulness in the Lord's speeches which is quite relaxing. Their aim is not to crush Job with an awareness of his minuteness contrasted with the limitless power of God, not to mock him when he puts his tiny mind beside God's vast intellect. On the contrary, the mere fact that God converses with him gives him a dignity above all the birds and beasts, assuring him that it is a splendid thing to be a man. To look at any bird or flower—and how many of them there are!—is a revelation of God in His constant care for His world.[54]

Likewise, another scholar, Eleonore Stump, suggests: "It is a mistake, then, to characterize God's speeches to Job as demonstrating nothing but God's power over creation. The speeches certainly do show God's power; but, equally importantly . . . . [t]he divine speeches suggest that God's relationship to all his creatures is personal, intimate, and parental."[55]

What I'm suggesting is in his two speeches (Job 38:1—40:2; 40:6—41:34), God is engaged in some crucial self-revelation, essentially saying to Job (and the reader): "The world is more complicated than you think; being God is more involved than you could ever imagine. But because I'm the kind of God I am, it's both inappropriate and unnecessary for you to ever assume that I'm acting capriciously toward you. I'm a good, big and dependable God and I'm here for you!"[56]

---

53. For example, see Job 10:2; 13:3, 15-24; 19:7; 23:3-9; 30:20; 31:35-37; see also 35:12-14.

54. Andersen, *Job*, 271.

55. Andersen, *Job*, 191.

56. Additional support for the idea that this is the message of the story of Job as a

Finally, as the book wraps up, the only resolution to the story offered to the reader is that in the face of this personal, powerful, existentially impactful encounter with God,⁵⁷ Job essentially says of his sufferings: *"It's all good. Once upon a time I knew about you, but now I've seen you up close and personal. I repent of ever having mistrusted you"* (see Job 42:1–6).

In sum, Job has moved from someone exhibiting a hyper-religiosity that was fear-based, to someone with a sense of how radically committed God is to a real, intimate, interactive, love-and-trust-based relationship with the people he created in his own image. Some significant support for this interpretation is provided by several Old Testament scholars. For instance, Anderson et al., pondering the biblical author's intention in Job's story, conclude: "To be sure, the poet wrestles with an inescapable problem of human life: the suffering of the innocent. But the problem of suffering—and its counterpart, the question of divine justice—provides the occasion for probing a much deeper question: *What is a person's relationship to God?*"⁵⁸ Then, this trio of scholars goes on to assert: "the climax of the Job poetry occurs at the very end, when a *false relationship based on a conception of God received from tradition* ("I had heard of you by the hearing of the ear") is converted into a *relationship of personal trust and surrender*—'but now my eye sees you'" (Job 42:5)⁵⁹

G. Buchanan Gray, Professor of Hebrew and Old Testament Exegesis, provides some additional support for this understanding of what God was up to in Job's life. Commenting on the effect his eventual encounter with God had upon Job, Gray writes:

> But the speech of Yahweh accompanies an appearance or direct manifestation of Yahweh to Job, and in this respect is the direct response of Yahweh to Job's deepest desire: Job has at last found Yahweh; and in spite of the rebuke of his words beyond knowledge, he has found Yahweh on his side, no more estranged from him than in the days of his former prosperity, but *more intimately known*; as compared with his former, his present knowledge is as sight to hearing, as direct, first hand personal to second hand and traditional knowledge.⁶⁰

whole can be found in Alden, *Job*, 41; House, *Old Testament Theology*, 437; and Gordis, *Book of God and Man*, 127–34.

57. See Westermann, *Structure of the Book of Job*, 128.
58. Anderson et al., *Understanding the Old Testament*, 545, emphasis original.
59. Anderson et al., *Understanding the Old Testament*, 551, emphasis added.
60. Gray, "Purpose and Method of the Writer," 43, emphasis added.

Going a bit beyond Gray, I'm suggesting the possibility that it's not only true that Job's communion with God has been intensified through this experience of suffering and encounter, but that he has actually moved from a fear-based, legalistic, and obsessively ritualistic religious posture to a personal, interactive, faith-based relationship with God.[61]

In sum, my take is that the purpose of Job's story wasn't simply to assert God's sovereign right to do what he wants with the people he's created, but neither was it to suggest God has his hands full and simply can't keep bad things from happening to good people. Ultimately, it's about how God uses suffering to make us, like Job, crazy-hungry desperate for a personal encounter with the living God that will, in turn, allow us to enter into a whole new type of relationship with him.[62]

As I will spell out in the next chapter, this emphasis on God's desire for an eternal, love-and-trust-based relationship with the people who bear his image is critical to a biblically informed understanding of the problem of evil. However, before we begin that discussion, there is one more aspect of the proposal put forward by Bilezikian and Boyd that I want to interact with in an appreciative yet nuanced manner.

God's Romantic and Risk-Taking Creative Impulse

We've seen that Bilezikian argues against the idea that God is a capricious deity who created human beings in a careless manner. He does this by asserting he's actually a self-giving, "compulsive lover" who essentially couldn't help but endow human beings with his own image, which includes free moral agency. For his part, Boyd emphasizes the idea that God endowed human beings with free will because his grand goal is an

---

61. LaSor et al. opine that: "The answer comes not so much in the flood of new information as in a *new* relationship with the Lord of the universe: 'but now my eye sees thee' (v. 5)" (LaSor et al., *Old Testament Survey*, 568, emphasis added).

62. Some scholarly support for this interpretive take is provided by Anderson et al., *Understanding the Old Testament*, 545, 551; Gray, "Purpose and Method of the Writer," 43. At the same time, some might wonder about the suffering experienced by others in Job's story—for example, his children. Wasn't this apparently "collateral suffering" unjust? On the one hand, we must reckon with the possibility that the disaster Job's kids experienced was, for reasons not made explicit in the story, a just act on the part of God (see Prov 6:12–15; 16:4). On the other hand, read through the eyes of New Testament authors, we may find in Proverbs 14:32 this word of promise: God can be counted on to make right in the age to come any "collateral suffering" the righteous experience in this life (see Rom 8:18; 2 Tim 4:7–8; Rev 21:1–4; 22:1–5).

eternal bride made up of those humans who have *chosen* to love, trust, and honor (be faithful) to him forever. Both approaches seem to portray God as a highly personal, relational, divine being.[63] Indeed, the way Bilezikian refers to God as a "compulsive lover," and the manner in which Boyd speaks of God's ambition to form a "bride" for himself seem to connote there was something almost romantic about God's creative impulse.

But the thing about romance is there are no guarantees. It's the messiness of mutually consenting relationships that causes Boyd to suggest God's creating in freedom, with freedom, was a risky endeavor even for him! Still, he did so anyway. Why? Because just the *possibility* of a genuine love relationship with us was, in his eyes, worth anything it might cost. Together, Boyd and Bilezikian seem to be suggesting, given his radically loving nature and great desire for a bride with which he could spend eternity, God was virtually compelled to take the risk. And, once the fall occurred, both Bilezikian and Boyd emphasize the chivalrous manner in which God as romantic lover has owned the problem. According to this warfare theodicy, ever since the fall God has been engaged in a genuine struggle with the usurper Satan and his demonic hosts. Though God's sovereignty assures his eventual, ultimate victory over evil, in the meantime, we humans must recognize we live in a war zone where God's will is not always done, where bad things happen that simply aren't under God's current control.

This is certainly a highly personal view of God's nature and creative impulse that emphasizes his essential goodness and the worth he places on a real relationship with his image-bearers. Such a view of God and his creative work can't help but be tremendously inspirational at a personal level. It can also be quite encouraging to folks who have suffered greatly and have wondered how they are to, in the aftermath, continue to see God as good.

And yet, while the warfare theodicy put forward by Boyd (and less explicitly by Bilezikian) makes it possible for us to keep worshiping our

---

63. Though not a theologian, per se, C. S. Lewis drew attention to the fact that the God of the Bible, far from being impersonal, is actually superpersonal. (Lewis, *Mere Christianity*, 160.) After all, says Lewis, the Bible speaks of God as having existed eternally in an interpersonal relationship—Father, Son, and Holy Spirit. Thus, the God who created the world should be viewed as both hyperpersonal and ultrarelational—i.e., radically committed to a personal relationship with those he's created in his image. So, there's a sense in which both Bilezikian and Boyd are right. Because of his triune, loving, relational nature, God can't help but create sentient beings capable of a genuine interpersonal relationship with him. It's who he is.

creator in the face of the natural and moral evil that pockmarks human existence, it leaves us with an understanding of God I'm unable to reconcile in a satisfactory manner with the book of Job and the self-revelation of God we find in the rest of the Scriptures. I can't help but wonder about the possibility of a more nuanced understanding of the problem of evil. What I'm after is a biblically informed theodicy that retains the emphasis Bilezikian and Boyd place on the relational nature of God, but doesn't require a revised understanding of the his foreknowledge, or overstate his struggle with Satan. What's more, I have in mind a theodicy that, in addition to offering a defense of God in the face of evil, actually encourages an enthusiastic participation in what the Bible portrays as God's defeat of Satan and the moral and natural evil he engenders.

The psalmist reminds us that to keep hoping in the Lord requires a weaned soul—the ability to remain cool, calm, and collected even in the face of unanswered questions (Ps 131:1–3). Again, the goal of this two-chapter essay isn't to prove anything with respect to God, but simply to provide readers with some reasons to keep trusting in and cooperating with the Lord while they wait patiently, in hope, for his victory over evil to become fully realized. The apostle Paul wrote: "For in this hope we were saved. But hope that is seen is no hope at all. Who hopes for what they already have? But if we hope for what we do not yet have, we wait for it patiently" (Rom 8:24–25). I'd like to think that in the second part of this essay the reader will discover even more reasons to keep trusting in and cooperating with God . . . in hope.

Reflection/Discussion Questions:

1. How important do you think it is for rank-and-file Christian disciples to be able to thoughtfully engage in discussions regarding the problem of evil? Why or why not?

2. What is your reaction to the argument put forward by Bilezikian and Boyd regarding God's limited foreknowledge, and my response to it?

3. What is your reaction to the argument put forward by Bilezikian and Boyd regarding the ultimate message of the book of Job, and my response to it?

4. What is your reaction to the argument put forward by Bilezikian and Boyd regarding God's romantic creative impulse and the risk it entailed, and my response to it?

5. Overall, how satisfied are you with the theodicy put forward by Bilezikian and Boyd? How much value would you place on a theodicy that not only enables an ongoing trust in God, but also encourages an eager cooperation with what he's currently doing about evil?

10

God's Endgame
The Ultimate "Why" Question, Part 2

> The God of peace will soon crush Satan under your feet.
> The grace of our Lord Jesus be with you.
>
> —ROMANS 16:20

My daughter's friends aren't the only ones to wonder: *Why did God create a world in which the devil could gain control and wreak so much havoc in the lives of human beings?* This is a question many church members and Christian university students wrestle with as well. Gilbert Bilezikian and Gregory Boyd are to be commended for the forthright manner in which they address this perplexing issue. As the previous chapter indicated, their response maintains that God created human image-bearers in freedom, with freedom, because he desired a bride who would choose to love him rather than be forced to. Only aware of the possibility that this act of creation might prove problematic, God performed it anyway, considering the prize—a real, mutually consenting relationship with us—worth the risk. Moreover, when things did go south, as the biblical story indicates, God stepped up to the plate and assumed responsibility for the problem of evil by sending his son into the world to make it possible, through his death and resurrection, for people to escape the stranglehold the devil currently has on the human race (Heb 2:14–15). At the same time, we must recognize we currently live in a war zone where a very real battle is taking place between God and Satan. Unfortunately, this means bad things happen to good people. We are to consider it collateral damage that grieves God greatly.

This is certainly a highly relational view of God's nature and creative impulse that emphasizes his essential goodness and the worth he places on a real relationship with his image-bearers. Such a view of God and his creative work can't help but be tremendously inspirational at a personal level. It can also be quite encouraging to folks who've suffered greatly and have wondered how they are to, in the aftermath, continue to see God as good. The message of Job, say Bilezikian and Boyd, is God is good, but he also has his hands full, so to speak.

I concluded the previous chapter affirming the fact that the theodicy put forward by Bilezikian and Boyd goes a long way toward enabling us to keep worshiping our creator despite the evil and injustice that has resulted from his creating humans with free moral agency. I also indicated I can't help but wonder about the possibility of a more nuanced understanding of the problem of evil—one that might enjoy even more biblical support and doesn't require a revised understanding of God's knowledge of the future or even hint at a surrender of some of God's sovereignty to Satan. Moreover, it's my suggestion the answer to the "why" question I'm proposing might do an even better job of inspiring love and trust in our creator, while also motivating us toward an even more active, aggressive participation in his devil-defeating agenda. Articulating this more nuanced proposal is what this chapter is about.

My Suggestion: Two Subtle but Highly Significant Shifts in Focus

In a nutshell, I'm suggesting that, as compelling as the romantic understanding of God's creative impulse is, perhaps it shouldn't be focused on to the exclusion of other possible *motivations*. And perhaps instead of focusing solely on God's loving and freedom-giving *nature*, we should allow a deeper understanding of who God is and what he's up to in the world to impact our approach to the problem of evil. It's my contention the first shift in focus I have in mind makes possible a relational understanding of God without our having to limit his foreknowledge. The second shift not only enables a steadfast trust in God's goodness in the face of evil (while maintaining his sovereignty), it also encourages an enthusiastic participation in God's evil-defeating agenda. It's because both of these shifts of focus are grounded in a biblically informed understanding of God's ultimate endgame that they are potential game-changers in our discussion of why God ended up creating a world in which the devil could acquire authority and introduce so much moral and natural evil in it.

Toward a More Nuanced Understanding of *God's Creative Impulse*

We've seen how Bilezikian points out the remarkable degree to which God assumed responsibility for the problem of evil by assuming human flesh and suffering and dying for humankind in such a way as to defeat the devil's stranglehold on his image-bearers. Once again, this allusion to God's incarnational, self-emptying, self-limiting, redemptive behavior is evocative of Hebrews 2:14–18, a pertinent passage Boyd refers to numerous times in his books *Satan and the Problem of Evil: Constructing a Trinitarian Warfare Theodicy*, and *God at War: The Bible and Spiritual Conflict*. Because I've already cited this important passage in full, I'll simply point out it begins with these three words: "Since the children . . . ." (Heb 2:14). According to this passage, it's God's *children* Christ has gone to great lengths to rescue from the merciless tyranny of the evil one. This portrayal of God sounds less romantic than it does parental, right? Think about it: God's creative activity had him making possible the existence of sentient creatures whose free decisions would impact him, other creatures, and ultimately all of creation. Put differently, God ended up generating creatures who possessed the potential to both bless his heart and break it. And then he remained faithful to these creatures even as they rebelled against him. Sound familiar? Does the image of the father in the story of the lost son (Luke 15:11–32) come to mind?

What if God's creative impulse wasn't exclusively romantic in nature, but parental as well? What if his goal in creating human image-bearers can be understood not only as a spiritual bride but also as a forever family made up of spiritual daughters and sons who could enter into the eternal dance of mutual love and respect enjoyed by the Father, Son, and Holy Spirit? Isn't that what the eternal state (kingdom of God) will essentially involve (see Rev 21:1–7)? And shouldn't we take into account the many passages in the New Testament that refer to Christ's followers as "children of God,"[1] "sons and daughters,"[2] and "heirs?"[3]

These are some important questions. This subtle shift in the way we view God's creative impulse—from romantic partner to responsible parent—carries with it two dramatic implications for how we understand his creative activity.

Parenting, by Definition, Involves Give-and-Take

It's because I believe this shift in focus from the "Creator as romantic partner" to the "Creator as responsible parent" is a game-changer in the discussion of the problem of evil that I want to explore the correlation between God's parenting and our own a bit more. To begin, I'm struck by the *self-encumbering* that God's parenting, and that engaged in by responsible humans, can't help but result in. Surely, this self-encumbering can't have taken God by surprise.

There's no way for a responsible, loving person to enter into a relationship with another sentient being and not be *inconvenienced, limited,* or *encumbered* by it to some degree.[4] Once a genuine interactive relationship with another human being is entered into, it's no longer a simple matter of fulfilling one's own wishes, meeting one's own needs, and seeking one's own welfare. Now there's another person in our world whose wishes, needs, and welfare must be considered and, at times, even prioritized. Ask any young couple who have just brought a newborn home from the hospital about whether their life is the same now as it was just twenty-four hours ago!

---

1. Matt 5:9; John 1:12; 11:52; Rom 8:14, 19, 21; Gal 3:26; Phil 2:15; 1 John 3:1, 2, 10; 5:2, 19.

2. 2 Cor 6:18; Gal 4:6; Heb 2:10; 12:8.

3. Rom 8:17; Gal 3:29; Eph 3:6; Titus 3:7; 1 Pet 3:7.

4. I'm reminded of this quote by C. S. Lewis: "There is no safe investment. To love at all is to be vulnerable. Love anything, and your heart will certainly be wrung and possibly be broken. If you want to make sure of keeping it intact, you must give your heart to no one, not even to an animal. Wrap it carefully round with hobbies and little luxuries; avoid all entanglements; lock it up safe in the casket or coffin of your selfishness. But in that casket—safe, dark, motionless, airless—it will change. It will not be broken; it will become unbreakable, impenetrable, irredeemable. The alternative to tragedy, or at least to the risk of tragedy, is damnation. The only place outside Heaven where you can be perfectly safe from all the dangers and perturbations of love is Hell" (Lewis, *Four Loves*, 155–56).

Put simply, to choose to bring another person into the world who possesses an independent mind and will is not *liable* to change your life; it's *guaranteed* to! When thoughtful humans reproduce, they do so *knowing* their progeny will bring them some pain as well as joy. They can't help but be *aware* that with parenting comes some self-encumbering that's an *inevitability* rather than a mere possibility. Surely God possessed this awareness. *If so, his creative activity really wasn't a risk-taking endeavor after all, and there's no necessity for a revised understanding of God's foreknowledge.* We don't have to embrace an open theism in order to possess a highly relational understanding of God. His decision to create human image-bearers in freedom, with freedom, guaranteed that our relationship with him would be one of give-and-take.

Furthermore, conceiving of God as a responsible parent points us toward yet another theological truth—one that can't help but impact our thinking about the problem of evil.

God's Endgame Requires that His Heart Be Broken!

To reiterate, my assertion is God's creative activity entailed some dramatic *self-encumbering* he had to have known in advance would occur. And yet, God created us human image-bearers anyway. Why? I contend the answer lies in God's *endgame, which I suggest is best conceived of as a forever family made up of progeny who have been enabled by grace to love, trust, and honor their creator (and one another) fully and forever.*[5] It's a simple vision really, and yet breathtakingly beautiful.

It was also quite costly. Indeed, it's the costly nature of this divine dream that makes its realization relevant to a discussion of the problem of evil.

The apostle John made clear our love for God (and others) is *made possible* by a genuine experience of God's prior love for us (1 John 4:19). And how was God's love perfectly evidenced to us? The apostle Paul insists the way we humans become fully and adequately aware of divine love is through the cross work of Christ (Rom 5:8). In other words, our becoming fully aware of God's magnificent, eternal love for us required the incarnation, suffering, and death of God's eternal Son on our behalf *while we were still in rebellion against him!*

---

5. See 2 Pet 1:10–11; Rev 1:6; 21:1–4, 7; see also Rom 8:17; 2 Cor 4:17; Eph 3:20–21; 1 Tim 1:15–17; 2 Tim 2:10; 1 John 2:25; 3:14–15.

Here's my point: evidently, the amazing gift of God creating us—bringing us into existence, giving us the gift of life—was apparently not enough to inspire or inculcate within us human beings the kind of complete love, trust, and faithfulness that will last for eternity. Apparently, it's necessary for God's image-bearers to experience more than *creation* in order to love, trust, and honor their creator the way he deserves. We need to experience *redemption* as well—God's coming after us, reconciling us to himself through the death of his much-loved son. Put simply, *it's only by witnessing and experiencing the amazing, loving act of redemption, which cost God so dearly, that our hearts can now be filled with an amazing ability to love, trust, and honor him (and one another) the way he deserves: fully and forever (see 2 Cor 5:14–15; 1 Thess 4:17)!*

So, the game-changing questions I'm posing are these:

- *What if the presence of evil in our world wasn't simply an unfortunate outcome of God's creative activity as Boyd's divine risk-taking rhetoric might suggest?*

- *What if God always knew giving his human image-bearers the gift of temporal life wasn't enough, by itself, to inspire them as free moral agents to choose to love, trust, and honor him (and one another) fully and forever?*

- *What if God always knew it would take the sacrificial death of his Son to fully communicate to his image-bearers just how much he loves them, and to inculcate within them the capacity to love, trust, and honor him (and one another) the way he deserves (fully and forever)?*

As we are pondering these "what if" questions, we must keep in mind the scenario I'm suggesting finds some support from Revelation 13:8, which speaks of Christ as the sacrificial lamb "slain from the creation of the world" (see also 2 Tim 1:9; Heb 9:26; 1 Pet 1:18–20; John 17:24)!

So, it appears that God—the ultimate parent—created human beings as free moral agents knowing full well that his heart: (a) would be broken by our rebellion against his loving lordship; (b) would be broken by the death of his Son on our behalf; and (c) would be broken by the fact that some of his image-bearers would use their free moral agency in such a way as to never allow themselves to be enabled to love, trust, and honor their creator (and one another) in the way he deserves. Maybe when we humans refer to God as a Father, we're not projecting onto him an aspect of our reality. Maybe, instead, the phenomenon of responsible human parents making the decision to procreate despite the guarantee that doing so will involve some significant self-encumbering and heartache as well as joy is a reflection of God's archetypal reality as an eternal, loving, self-giving Father. If this is granted, then it would seem to be possible to possess a highly relational understanding of our creator without having to redesign the biblical portrayal of his foreknowledge in order to do so.

Toward a Fuller Understanding of God's Nature and What He's Up to in the World

This second suggested shift in focus I'm proposing is related to the first. We need to keep in mind that responsible human parents not only love their kids; they discipline them as well. In fact, the reason why they discipline their kids is precisely because they love them. According to the Epistle to the Hebrews, the loving administration of some needed discipline is yet another point of similarity between human parenting and that which is engaged in by God. To the beleaguered recipients of this letter, its author wrote:

> Endure hardship as discipline; God is treating you as his children. For what children are not disciplined by their father? If you are not disciplined—and everyone undergoes discipline— then you are not legitimate, not true sons and daughters at all. Moreover, we have all had human fathers who disciplined us and we respected them for it. How much more should we submit to the Father of spirits and live! They disciplined us for a little while as they thought best; but God disciplines us for our good, in order that we may share in his holiness. (Heb 12:7–10)

According to this verse, high on God's parenting agenda is the disciplining of his progeny so that they might know and embody one of his divine attributes in particular—one a multitude of biblical passages refers to—his being innately holy, and wholly committed to justice.[6] So impor-

---

6. Some biblical passages which indicate that *holiness* should be considered an attribute of God include: Lev 11:44–45; 19:2; 20:7, 26; 21:8; Josh 24:19; 1 Sam 2:2; 6:20; Ps 71:22; 77:13; 78:41; 89:7; 99:5, 9; Isa 5:16; 29:23; 43:3; 48:17; 54:5; 55:5; 60:9; Jer 51:5; Hos 11:9, 12; Hab 1:12; 3:3; Rev 4:8; 2 Cor 7:1; Eph 4:24; Heb 12:10; 1 Pet 1:16. Some biblical passages which indicate that *justice* should be considered a cardinal virtue possessed by God include: Deut 32:4; Ps 9:16; 11:7; 33:5; 36:6; 45:6; 50:6; 89:14; 97:2; 99:4; 101:1; 103:6; Prov 8:20; 28:5; Isa 5:16; 30:18; 33:5; 51:4; 61:8; Mic 3:8; Zeph 3:5; Luke 11:42; 18:7; Acts 17:31; Rom 12:1; 1 Cor 1:2; 2 Cor 6:14–18; Rev 19:11.

tant is this attribute to who God is and what he's about that Hebrews 12:14–28 goes on to say our learning to share (embody in ourselves) God's holiness is critical to our ability to "see the Lord" (i.e., experience him forever)!

Once again, I sincerely appreciate the arguments Bilezikian and Boyd have put forward in God's defense. But, as we've seen, their focus is primarily on the benevolent rather than capricious motive for God's creative activity. I contend that, to fully process the problem of evil, we must focus not only on the impact God's *self-giving love* had upon his *creative impulse*, but also on the significance of his *holiness and commitment to justice* for *what he's up to in this world, and the one to come*.

God's Justice and the World He Created

Because the divine reality out of which all other realities derive is holy and just, some have suggested the environment in which we human beings find ourselves is best thought of as a "moral universe."[7] Such a world (Greek: *kosmos*) has baked into it not just a cosmic *awareness* of holiness and justice, and not just a cosmic *preference* for holiness and justice, but a cosmic *requirement* for holiness and justice (see Lev 19:1–2; Mic 6:8; 1 Pet 1:15–16; Matt 23:23). Another way to put this is, precisely because holiness/justice is a primary attribute/virtue of the one who formed all creation, holiness/justice can be thought of as integral to the very fabric of the moral universe in which we exist. This metaphysical reality explains why God can't simply excuse sin, but must address it. It's not only about his glory, or his being true to himself; it's also about *sustaining the cosmos*. For God, the sustainer of the universe, to excuse evil would be to allow a metaphysical cancer to go unaddressed. The future of the cosmos requires God to deal decisively with sin and injustice, even if the perpetrators of it are his kids, as the story of the fall related in Genesis 3 so dramatically indicates.[8] Tim Keller provides some inferential support for what I'm proposing when he writes:

> The devastating loss of *shalom* through sin is described in Genesis 3. We are told that as soon as we abandoned living for and

---

7. For example, see Wright, *Evil and the Justice of God*, 158, 160; Lewis, *Reflections on the Psalms*, 32.

8. What I am proposing here is in some respects similar to the "natural law" theodicy promoted by C. S. Lewis. See Lewis, *Problem of Pain*.

enjoying God as our highest good—the entire created world became broken. Human beings are so integral to the fabric of things that when human beings turned from God the entire warp and woof of the world unraveled.... In Romans 8, Paul says that the entire world is now 'in bondage to decay' and 'subject to futility' and will not be put right until we are put right.[9]

On the one hand, we're given to believe, because of human sin, our world is broken and must be put right. On the other, we must also keep in mind our creator can't simply excuse sin but must address it in a holy and just manner. These two observations prompt the questions: *What was God thinking when he situated what he knew in advance to be fallible human image-bearers in a moral universe where the demand for justice is part of its warp and woof? Does his doing so suggest his creative activity was in fact irresponsible at best, or capricious at worst, or is there a sense in which God's endowing his progeny with free moral agency and then placing them in a world that requires justice was, from the beginning, part of his plan?*

God's Justice and the Old Testament Narrative

It's this metaphysical connection between God's justice and his creation that lies behind the contention of N. T. Wright in his book *Evil and the Justice of God* that God's response to what happened in the garden (Gen 3) is what the rest of the biblical story is all about. Wright defines the problem of evil or *theodicy* as an "explanation of the justice of God in the face of counterevidence."[10] In other words, at the heart of the problem of evil is the question: *How can we consider God just when there's so much injustice in the world he created?*[11] Essentially ignoring the question of evil's origin,[12] Wright's focus is on God's holy and just response to it. The justification of God in the face of evil, according to Wright, is the consistently *just* way the Bible portrays him responding to it.

Thus, Wright contends in the Old Testament we find a series of narratives which show God judging rather than excusing evil, even when it's his own people who are responsible for it (e.g., Isa 5:1–30; 59:1–8; Ezek

---

9. Keller, *Reason for God*, 170.
10. Wright, *Evil and the Justice of God*, 45.
11. Wright, *Evil and the Justice of God*, 64–66.
12. Wright, *Evil and the Justice of God*, 45, 71–72, 136, 141.

9:8–9)! Sadly, these narratives make it apparent his own people are not any less capable of the primary sins of idolatry, immorality, and injustice than those not in a covenant relationship with him. However, there is some good news. The Old Testament portion of the story culminates with the prophetic promise of a future act of divine redemption that will not only heal God's people of their propensity toward pride, selfishness, and rebellion (Isa 53), but will make possible a new creation—essentially, a restoration of the health and wholeness of Eden (Isa 55). This is what the Old Testament is about, says Wright. "It's written *to tell the story of what God has done, is doing and will do about evil.*"[13]

God's Justice and the Cross of Christ

Proceeding into the New Testament, we read that the aforementioned act of divine redemption has finally occurred by means of the cross-work of Christ. *Jesus' passion needs to be understood as evidence of not only the full extent of God's love for his image-bearers, but his commitment to cosmic justice as well!* Wright explains:

> The story of Gethsemane and of the crucifixion of Jesus of Nazareth present themselves in the New Testament as the strange, dark conclusion to the story of what God does about evil, of what happens to God's justice when it takes human flesh, when it gets its feet muddy in the garden and its hands bloody on the cross. The multiple ambiguities of God's actions in the world come together in the story of Jesus.[14]

I'm sometimes asked by students: "Why did Christ have to die? Why couldn't God just forgive our sin?" Thus, it might be helpful here for the connection between God's justice and Christ's suffering and death on the cross to be clarified even more. Here's an attempt to do this.

We've already adduced that, for God, the Sustainer of the universe, to excuse evil would be to allow a metaphysical cancer to go unaddressed. This simply can't happen. We must keep this insight in mind when considering those New Testament passages which indicate that the death of Jesus on the cross possessed an *atoning* significance (Rom 3:25; Heb 2:17; 1 John 2:2; 4:10), and those which stipulate a firm connection between Christ's death and "our sins" (Rom 4:25; 1 Cor 15:3; Gal 1:4; Col 2:13; 1

---

13. Wright, *Evil and the Justice of God*, 45, emphasis original.
14. Wright, *Evil and the Justice of God*, 74.

Pet 2:24; 1 John 1:9; 2:2; 3:5; 4:10; Rev 1:4–6). Thus, one way of understanding its atoning significance is that Jesus' death on the cross had the effect of satisfying a spiritual, perhaps even metaphysical, requirement for *justice*. This idea is supported by Romans 3:25–26, where we find Paul asserting the sacrificial death of Jesus on the cross made it possible for God to forgive guilty sinners and yet remain holy and just himself.[15] This critical passage reads:

> God presented Christ as a sacrifice of atonement, through the shedding of his blood—to be received by faith. He did this to demonstrate his righteousness, because in his forbearance he had left the sins committed beforehand unpunished—he did it to demonstrate his righteousness at the present time, so as to be just and the one who justifies those who have faith in Jesus. (Rom 3:25–26)

Tim Keller puts it this way: "On the cross neither justice nor mercy loses out—both are fulfilled at once. Jesus' death was necessary if God was going to take justice seriously and still love us."[16] The implication is some sort of a requirement for justice, perhaps one that's built into the fabric of the moral universe God created, was satisfied through Christ's action on behalf of sinful humanity.[17]

The finally-realized good news is that the vicarious suffering of Yahweh's servant foretold by the prophet Isaiah (Isa 53:4–6, 10–12) found its fulfillment in Jesus of Nazareth. As a result, a healing of the human heart can now occur (1 Pet 2:24). This means it's not only possible for fallen human beings to have their sins forgiven, but for them to be empowered by the Holy Spirit, to live righteously (in a holy manner) before God (Rom 8:1–17). All of this, Wright argues, is part of the biblical story, which in turn is about God's response to the problem of evil! Ultimately, the cross of Christ, the forgiveness of sins, and the in-filling of the Spirit are about God's endgame!

---

15. Gregory Boyd seems to provide some implicit support for this idea when he suggests that God, in his sovereignty, can create what amounts to a "metaphysical necessity" that even he must abide by. See Boyd, *Satan and the Problem of Evil*, 354.

16. Keller, *Reason for God*, 196.

17. Though there are other ways the apostolic authors referred to the experience of salvation—e.g., *redemption* (Mark 10:45; 1 Pet 1:18-19); *reconciliation* (2 Cor 5:18-20); *adoption* (Rom 8:14–17; Gal 4:4-7; Eph 1:5); *spiritual healing* (1 Pet 2:24); and *liberation* (Col 2:15; Heb 2:14–15)—at the heart of all of these various metaphors is the dynamic of atonement.

God's Justice and the Restoration of Creation

This is precisely why Wright proceeds to point out that the biblical record of God's response to evil doesn't end with Christ's death on the cross, as *crucial* as that was. Wright goes on to argue for a connection between Paul's discussion of the justification of God at the personal level in the atonement (in Rom 3:25–26) with his discussion of the future liberation of creation as a whole (in Rom 8:19–27; see also Eph 1:7–10; Col 1:19–20).[18] In doing so, he suggests

> unless creation as a whole is put to rights, it might look as though God the Creator had blundered or was weak and incapable, or was actually unjust. No, declares Paul: the renewal of creation, the birth of the new world from the laboring womb of the old, will demonstrate that God is in the right. Romans 8 is the deepest New Testament answer to the "problem of evil," to the question of God's justice.[19]

So, how can we consider God just in the face of so much injustice currently at work in the world he created? The answer lies in the notion of God's endgame. The creator is not done with the world yet! A restored creation, in which righteousness dwells, is even now in the works (2 Pet 3:13)!

God's Justice and the Future Day of Reckoning

What's more, the New Testament also contains numerous references to a future day of reckoning or judgment in which every person will have to give an account before a holy God for how they've lived their lives.[20] In this way too, God's commitment to justice in an unjust world is evidenced. Tim Keller explains:

> Many people complain that they cannot believe in a God who judges and punishes people. But if there is no Judgment Day, what about all the enormous amount of injustice that has been and is being perpetrated? If there is no Judgment Day, then there are only two things to do—lose all hope or turn to vengeance.

---

18. See also Ladd, *Theology of the New Testament*, 450, 612–13.
19. Wright, *Evil and the Justice of God*, 117–18.
20. For example, see Acts 17:31; Rom 2:5–11; 1 Cor 4:5; 2 Cor 5:9–10; 1 Tim 5:24–25; 2 Tim 4:1; Heb 6:1–2; 9:27–28; 10:26–31; 1 Pet 1:17; 2 Pet 2:4, 9; 3:7; 1 John 4:17; Jude 6; Rev 6:10; 11:18; 14:7; 20:11–15.

> Either it means that the tyranny and oppression that have been so dominant over the ages will never be redressed, and in the end it will make no difference whether you live a life of justice and kindness or a life of cruelty and selfishness, or it means that, since there is no Judgment Day we will need to take up our weapons and go and hunt down the evildoers now. We will have to take justice into our own hands. We will have to be the judges, if there is no Judge.[21]

Likewise, N. T. Wright makes this fundamental observation: "the ultimate answer to the problem of evil is to be found in God's creation of a new world, new heavens and new earth, with redeemed, renewed human beings ruling over it and bringing to it God's wise, healing order."[22] Then, Wright goes on to insist:

> This does not require that all human beings will come to repent and share the joy of God's new world, wonderful though that would be. Indeed throughout the New Testament we are constantly warned that the choices we make in this life, especially the choices about what sort of a person we might become, are real and have lasting consequences which God himself will honor. But we do not have the choice to sulk in such a way as to prevent God's party going ahead without us. We have the right, like the older brother [in Jesus' parable of the prodigal son— Luke 15:11–31], to sit it out; God has the right to come and reason with us; but the fatted calf is going to be eaten whether we join in or not. Those who accept God's invitation to God's party on God's terms will indeed celebrate the feast of deliverance from evil.[23]

Without meaning to take anything away from Wright, I believe I hear in these words the influence of another famous British thinker, C. S. Lewis, who spoke of the fate of the steadfastly unrepentant in several of his books, especially *The Problem of Pain* and *The Great Divorce*. This is significant because Lewis, while reluctantly arguing for the morality of hell,[24] also suggested its purpose is not retribution but isolation (i.e., quarantine). Indeed, he famously suggested people aren't really sent to

---

21. Keller, *Walking with God*, 116.
22. Wright, *Evil and the Justice of God*, 146.
23. Wright, *Evil and the Justice of God*, 146–47.
24. Lewis, *Problem of Pain*, 119–21, 130.

hell; they're there of their own choosing. It's a state of self-exile. While the suffering in hell is real and terrible, its doors are locked from the inside.[25]

Such a view of the final judgment and eternal state, while taking seriously the notion that sin, evil, and injustice constitute a spiritual, metaphysical malignancy that God simply must deal with for the sake of the cosmos, has the potential to mitigate the claim that any form of eternal punishment is both unloving and unjust. A proponent of a view similar to Lewis's explains:

> People are not in hell for the reasons of punishment. People are in hell under their own free will, eternally separated from God because they cannot will freely as God's will [sic]. This state of exile is however, one of eternal pain and sorrow. . . . identical to the traditional concept of hell except for one facet; the primary motivation for hell is not retributive. If hell is instead a place of exile, then hell is no longer incompatible with God's love [and justice].[26]

Some of the best theological minds of the contemporary era suggest our continuing to believe the creator is loving and just isn't something we must do despite the fact there will someday be a day of reckoning during which every image-bearer will give an account for what they did with the freedom they were endowed with, but precisely because this reckoning will occur. Why? Because this too is part of God's response to the problem of evil![27]

---

25. Lewis, *Problem of Pain*, 130. It should be noted that Keller seems to follow Lewis on this point. See Keller, "Importance of Hell," para. 13.

26. See Anonymous, "Deconstructing the Traditional Hell." For a more detailed discussion of how what is referred to as the "quarantine model" of hell can be understood as demonstrating love for the damned, see Stump, "Dante's Hell, Aquinas' Moral Theory," 196–97. For more on the notion that maintaining the existence of the damned is a more loving action than their annihilation, see Spiegel, "Annihilation, Everlasting Torment, and Divine Justice."

27. The astute reader will wonder if the quarantine or self-exile model of hell might leave the door open, so to speak, to the possibility that someone quarantined from the rest of creation might at some point repent, experience a spiritual healing, unlock the door, and be restored to God and the rest of creation. Though the Scriptures as a whole seem reluctant to suggest that this ever has or will occur (cf. 1 Pet 4:6), and many theologians argue that the nature of sin is to eventually turn the human soul into a black hole which engages in an eternal swallowing of itself, we must always keep in mind God's goodness as well as his holiness, thus maintaining some theological humility in the face of mystery.

God's Justice and His Endgame

What we've seen so far is it's possible to argue that perhaps the best defense of God in the face of evil is the consistently just and righteous manner in which the Bible portrays him responding to it. But, having dared to go where angels fear to tread, I'll go ahead and pose a most provocative question: *Was the biblical story, which seems to be all about God's response to evil, a result of the fall or the reason for it?* While Wright essentially ignores this big, bold query, I feel the need to address it, suggesting a possible connection between God's justice and his endgame. To review, God's grand goal is a forever family made up of progeny who have been so impacted by their experience of redemption that they are now capable of loving, trusting, and honoring their creator (and one another) fully and forever. But think about it: *How can we love, trust, and honor God fully and forever if we're not fully aware of who he is and what he's about? Doesn't God's endgame require we possess a profound understanding of not only his mercy and grace, but his holiness and commitment to justice as well? Isn't it true there's simply no way for God's image-bearers to adequately know who their creator is and what he's about without watching how he responds to the problem of evil?*

Put differently, it might be argued it's not possible to genuinely share in God's holiness/justice without a sufficient understanding of what holiness is and isn't. Since such an understanding would seem to require our observing God's rigorous response to evil and injustice as reflected in the biblical story, it stands to reason that *the process of creatures with free will learning to share in their creator's innate holiness and commitment to justice essentially required that the problem of evil become a thing.*[28]

Put differently yet again, what if it were the case that, for his freedom-wielding but naïve image-bearers to properly value the endgame their creator had in mind (an eternal state in which righteousness dwells), they had to experience a dreadful alternative, a provisional existence in which unrighteousness is pervasive (cf. 2 Pet 3:13)? Could it be that in order for God's progeny to value his eternal kingdom enough to make it the main aim of their entire being, they had to first experience a world ruled over by an anti-truth, anti-life, anti-God angelic usurper?

C. S. Lewis famously argued: "If I find in myself a desire which no experience in this world can satisfy, the most probable explanation is that

---

28. A variation of this argument can be found in Lewis, *Mere Christianity*, 38–39.

I was made for another world."[29] I've already suggested God might have allowed the fall to occur in order to inculcate within his image-bearers the capacity to love, trust, and honor him (and one another) fully and forever. What I'm suggesting now is we can find in this Lewis quote some support for yet another bold notion. For God's image-bearers to become sufficiently appreciative of the main event—the new, eternal age in which righteousness dwells—they simply had to experience a provisional world which, though filled with much beauty and many wonderful blessings, could never satisfy the desperate longings of their hearts. How does God help innocent, naïve creatures, not ready for eternity, know they were made for it? How does a heavenly father adequately inculcate within his progeny a passion for the holiness and justice he knows is critical to their immortal existence? It was only by allowing the fall to occur, and then having his image-bearers observe his consistently holy and righteous response to the evil and injustice it caused, that their hearts could be adequately *aroused*, not only toward him, but also toward what his endgame entails: an eternity spent existing in and presiding over a world made right!

Please note: I'm not insisting this must be the case. It's possible Bilezikian and Boyd have it right, that God created human beings in freedom, with freedom, not knowing for sure that they would misuse their moral freedom and empower Satan to affect human history in a manner that's virtually, if not literally, in God's face.

Or, it could be that the two shifts in focus I've proposed are actually game-changers! Together, they enable a perspective on human suffering that does justice to what the Bible has to say about the creator's foreknowledge and sovereignty, and they do this without losing sight of his relational nature in the process! In support of the nuanced defense brief I've proffered, I will cite a couple of passages from Paul's pen, which, though brief, are nevertheless pregnant with problem-of-evil-processing significance:

> I consider that our present sufferings are not worth comparing with the glory that will be revealed in us. (Rom 8:18)

> For our light and momentary troubles are achieving for us an eternal glory that far outweighs them all. (2 Cor 4:17)

---

29. Lewis, *Mere Christianity*, 136–37.

Ultimately, what I'm suggesting is we are back to the book of Job and its message that God will, like responsible human parents, sometimes "play rough" with his kids. Our Creator/Heavenly Father is not only great and good, but infinitely, inscrutably wise as well (see Rom 11:33–36). God is God, and we are not. God is God, therefore we don't have to be. God is God, and we can trust him, as scary as this is to do when we're walking through valleys dark.[30]

The call of the psalmist is not for us, as unweaned children, to clamor for the breast, screaming and squirming, insisting on palatable answers to all our theological and philosophical questions before we will honor God. The call is for us, as those with weaned souls, to keep trusting in Yahweh, the God of the Bible, even in the face of mystery.

And yet, I realize merely posing the philosophical/theological possibility presented above might strike some readers as a gross trivialization of the real pain and suffering evil creates. I trust the next few pages will demonstrate this is not my intent. Instead, behind the ensuing discussion is a very practical question: *Could it be that God's endgame requires we not only understand God's holiness and justice, and value an eternity earmarked by it, but go on to become the kind of Christ-followers who eagerly cooperate here and now with what our creator is up to in the world with respect to the problem of evil?*

God's Justice and His Church

The survey of the biblical story presented above included observations about what God has done and will do about the problem of evil. A question I've yet to address is: *What is God currently doing about it?* The answer to this question is this: the Bible as a whole makes it quite clear our

---

30. Besides, as C. S. Lewis points out, it doesn't do any real good to decide to disagree with God's decision to create in freedom, with freedom. He writes: "Perhaps we feel inclined to disagree with Him. But there is a difficulty about disagreeing with God. He is the source from which all your reasoning power comes: you could not be right and He wrong any more than a stream can rise higher than its own source. When you are arguing against Him you are arguing against the very power that makes you able to argue at all: it is like cutting off the branch you are sitting on. If God thinks this state of war in the universe a price worth paying for free will—that is, for making a live world in which creatures can do real good or harm and something of real importance can happen, instead of a toy which only moves when He pulls the strings—then we may take it it is worth paying" (Lewis, *Mere Christianity*, 48).

holy and just God expects his people, in every era, to pursue holiness and justice in his name![31]

Once again, N. T. Wright is of some assistance here. He reminds us the Bible indicates very clearly that creation was always "designed to function through the stewardship of God's image-bearing creatures—the human race," and that the purpose of the lamb being slain (Rev 5:9–10) was not simply to defeat the dragon, but to do so by ransoming "people from every nation in order to make them a royal priesthood, serving God and *reigning on the earth.*"[32] Moreover, despite the fact the Bible speaks of a renovation of the present creation in passages such as Isaiah 65:17, Matthew 24:35, 2 Peter 3:10, and Revelation 21:1, passages such as Matthew 25:21, 23, 34 and Luke 16:10–12 suggest some continuity exists between our actions/character in this age and our activities/responsibilities in the next.[33] If nothing else, we ourselves are that continuity (see 2 Cor 5:17)! Therefore, if we are going to fulfill the crucial role God has called us to play in the age to come (see Matt 25:21), we can and must begin to embody now the values and realities of the coming kingdom. It's with this thought in mind that Wright continues:

> This theme, so frequent in the New Testament and so widely ignored in Christian theology, is part of the solution to the problem. It isn't that the cross has won the victory, so there's nothing more to be done. Rather, the cross has won the victory as a result of which there are now redeemed human beings getting ready to act as God's wise agents, his stewards, constantly worshipping their Creator and constantly, as a result, being equipped to reflect his image into his creation, to bring his wise and healing order to the world, putting the world to rights under his just and gentle rule. A truly biblical ecclesiology [doctrine of the church] should focus not so much on the fact that the church is the community of the saved but that the church is the community of

---

31. Some biblical passages which indicate that God expects his people to pursue *holiness* include: Lev 11:44–45; 20:7, 26; Eph 1:1, 4; 2:21; 5:25–27; Col 1:22; 3:12–14; 1 Thess 3:13; 4:4, 7; 1 Tim 2:8; 2 Tim 1:9; 2:21; Titus 1:8; Heb 2:11; 3:1; 10:14; 11:4; 12:14; 1 Pet 1:15–16; 2:5, 9; 2 Pet 3:11; Rev 22:11. Some biblical passages which indicate that God expects his people to pursue *justice* include: Lev 19:15; Deut 16:20; Ps 11:7; 112:5; Prov 29:7; Isa 1:17; 56:1; 59:1–8; Jer 9:23–24; 21:12; Hos 12:6; Amos 5:14–15, 21–24; Mic 6:8; Zech 7:8–10; Matt 23:23; Luke 11:42; 2 Cor 7:11.

32. Wright, *Evil and the Justice of God*, 138–39, emphasis original.

33. For more on how some biblical passages emphasize the continuity between the "old and new orders," and others the discontinuity (see 2 Pet 3:10–13), see Ladd, *Theology of the New Testament*, 654–55.

those who, being redeemed through the cross, are now to be a kingdom and priests to serve God and to reign on the earth. Our fear of triumphalism on the one hand, and on the other hand our flattening out of our final destiny into talk merely of "going to heaven," have combined to rob us of this central biblical theme. But until we put it back where it belongs we won't see how the New Testament ultimately offers a solution to the problem of evil.[34]

This is a hugely significant statement, which presents us with a bold idea. Perhaps instead of spending our time *exclusively* devoted to celebrating our own salvation and endeavoring to help others experience eternal salvation as well, Christ's followers should *also* band together as communities of salt and light, learning how to bring to bear upon a fallen, unjust, evil-filled world, the victory of God—the life-giving realities of God's kingdom come and coming.

I have written elsewhere of the need to avoid a false antithesis many churches have fallen prey to: the idea that they *have to choose between the Great Commission and the Great Commandment—i.e., between disciple-making and social action/creation care.*[35] Instead, we can and should see *both* of these ministry endeavors working together to make disciples for Jesus—disciples made through gospel proclamation *and* demonstration for gospel proclamation *and* demonstration.[36] Though some contemporary missiologists and church leaders have suggested the mission of God (*missio Dei*) is all about such things as justice and peacemaking, and actually excludes any evangelistic activity on the part of the church,[37] Lesslie Newbigin, widely recognized as the founder of the missional church movement,[38] once offered this word of warning:

> The concept of *missio Dei* has sometimes been interpreted so as to suggest that action for justice and peace as the possibilities are discerned within a given historical situation *is* the fulfillment of God's mission, and that the questions of baptism and church

---

34. Wright, *Evil and the Justice of God*, 139.

35. See Tyra, *Missional Orthodoxy*, 310–17. Support for this assertion can be found in Hastings, *Missional God*, 99, 149–63.

36. Tyra, *Missional Orthodoxy*, 317.

37. For more on this, see Wright, *Mission of God*, 63.

38. See Van Gelder and Zscheile, *Missional Church*, 36–38.

membership are marginal or irrelevant. That way leads very quickly to disillusion and often to cynical despair.[39]

Appreciative of the insights provided by both Wright and Newbigin, I've put forward an ecclesial model I refer to as the "Great Co-Missional Church." The local church should see itself as a disciple-making community of believers that's committed to a faithful fulfilling of the Great Commission (Matt 28:18–20; Mark 16:15–16), while at the same time being careful to obey the Great Commandment (Matt 22:34–40), and engaging in creation care (Gen 1:28).[40]

Some tacit support for this ecclesial model is provided by Wright in his book *Surprised by Hope*. Though diligent in this work to warn against an unbalanced ministry focus on helping people get ready to go to heaven, Wright never dismisses evangelism out of hand. He does contend, however, that an engagement in evangelism (disciple-making) that takes the concept of new creation seriously will result in a new convert who

> knows from the start that he or she is part of God's kingdom project, which stretches out beyond "me and my salvation" to embrace, or rather to be embraced by, God's worldwide purposes. Along with conversion there will then go, at least in principle, the call to find out where in the total project one can make one's own contribution.[41]

It's in his subsequent work, *Evil and the Justice of God*, that Wright refers to the "total project" as "God's project of justice within a world of injustice," arguing the big picture of what God is up to in the world, and wants his people to be up to here and now, ultimately relates to the problem of evil.[42] Wright is right about there being a dynamic connection between the Bible's theology of atonement and the new creation. Both are about the problem of evil—moral and natural. Both are about healing—souls and creation. Making disciples and pursuing justice here and

---

39. Newbigin, *Gospel*, 138, emphasis original.

40. See Tyra, *Missional Orthodoxy*, 314–15. For a thoughtful discussion of the "authority" of both the Great Commission and the Great Commandment, and how behind them both is the Great Communication—"the revelation of the identity of God, of God's action in the world and Gods' saving purpose for all creation"—see Wright, *Mission of God*, 59–60.

41. Wright, *Surprised by Hope*, 229.

42. Wright, *Evil and the Justice of God*, 73.

now in anticipation of the age to come are both part of God's *total project*. We can and should be involved in both. God's endgame requires this too!

You and I in the Dock!

So, where does this leave us jury members? I contend Bilezikian and Boyd are to be commended for helping us recognize God's creating his human image-bearers in freedom, with freedom, wasn't done in a capricious, irresponsible manner; and for reminding us of how responsible God was in his personally owning the problem of evil after humanity's fall. At the same time, this two-part essay has suggested a shift in focus from God as romantic lover to God as responsible parent renders a revised understanding of divine foreknowledge unnecessary, and results in an understanding of God's endgame that's not only profoundly inspirational but critically transformational as well. And this is a good thing since, as the previous section of this essay indicated, the presence of evil in our world isn't simply a theological conundrum to be solved; it's a problem to be owned, and not just by God, but by his people as well.

The verse that serves as the epigraph of this chapter—Romans 16:20—tells us God will crush Satan's head *under the feet of those who make up his church!* With this in mind, I'm suggesting, instead of continually complaining about the presence of evil in our world, those of us who own the moniker "Christian" should keep trusting God and seize the opportunity to actively and aggressively cooperate with him and his efforts to overcome the evil which his image-bearers have unleashed into the good world he created. As the old saying goes, we can either spend our days cursing the darkness or we can begin lighting some candles. In the end, it's not God who's in the dock, but us!

I don't know of any sincere Christ-follower who doesn't want to someday hear Jesus say to them: "Well done, good and *faithful* servant" (Matt 25:21)! But what if, in addition to our avoiding sin, attending church, sharing our faith, and giving to missions, a truly faithful Christian discipleship is, in Christ's eyes, earmarked by a serious engagement in God's justice project (Matt 23:23)? Moreover, what if, with God's help, we might actually alleviate or even avert someone's suffering in this fallen world? While it's true God can use suffering for good in people's lives, our default must always be to try to reduce suffering in this world rather than ignore it.[43]

The last two chapters have been about the ultimate *why* question: *If God is both great and good, why is there so much pain and suffering in the world?* Or as my daughter Megan phrases it: "Why did God create a world in which the devil could gain control and wreak so much havoc in the lives of human beings?" Once again, I'm not asserting God is the direct cause of evil writ large or of anyone's pain and suffering in particular. Satan and the misuse of the moral freedom provided us human beings are the direct causes for the evil and injustice all around us. What I'm suggesting is there is a way to possess a relational understanding of God without having to limit his foreknowledge, and it's possible to continue trusting in his goodness in the face of evil without even appearing to cede any of his sovereignty to Satan. Both of these problem-of-evil-processing moves are accomplished when we: (1) allow for a more nuanced understanding of God's creative impulse; and (2) are careful to keep in mind all the Bible has to say about who God is and what he's about. Most importantly, both moves are grounded in a biblically informed understanding of our creator's ultimate endgame.

At the end of the day, it's my hope I've provided the readers of these chapters with some encouragement to keep trusting God in the face of the current darkness, and to participate in the lighting of some candles. After all, a vibrant, fruitful, enduring walk with Christ requires not only a spiritual faithfulness, but a moral and missional faithfulness as well. That's why it's called a long *obedience* in the same direction.

Reflection/Discussion Questions:

1. How would you explain to someone how the shift in focus from God as romantic lover to responsible parent renders unnecessary a revised understanding of his foreknowledge regarding the fall? Do you resonate with this suggestion? If so, why?

2. What are your thoughts concerning the notion that God always knew that for his people to come to possess a love and trust that's

---

43. See Prov 21:13; 24:11–12; 31:9; Matt 25:31–46; Luke 10:25–37; Jas 2:14–17; 1 John 3:18.

full and will last forever would require they experience the gift of redemption as well as creation?

3. How would you explain to someone why God can't simply excuse human sinfulness?

4. What are your thoughts about the philosophical/theological suggestion that the process of creatures with free will learning to share in their creator's innate holiness and commitment to justice essentially required the problem of evil to become a thing? If you consider this argument helpful in understanding the problem of evil, how would you explain it to someone else? What would you be careful not to say?

5. How would you explain to someone this chapter's focus on the importance of lighting some candles? Has God spoken to you at all through this chapter? If so, would you care to share?

Conclusion

What I've referred to in this work as the dark side of discipleship is difficult. Endurance training, whatever the type, is not an easy or pleasant process. Growing in our ability to render to Christ a long obedience in the same direction is especially challenging. I'm reminded of the way the esteemed Old Testament scholar Walter Brueggemann described the real relationship God was committed to bringing his servant Job into: it is "a demanding way to live," and "no enterprise for wimps or sissies."[1] So, if you've made it this far in your endurance training you are to be congratulated!

We've covered a lot of territory together. Chapters 1 and 2 endeavored to help us understand what the authors of the New Testament had to say about the need to take the devil seriously, always keeping in mind his reality, nature, and what his deal seems to be. Chapters 3 through 6 presented us with thick discussions of the four cardinal components of the Christian life, endeavoring to help us better understand why they're so important to our walk with Christ and how we can expect the devil to come at them. An important excursus discussion appended to chapter 3 focused on the importance of a "lifestyle spirituality" that makes possible an ongoing experience of Christ's empowering presence. Indeed, all of the chapters in part two of this book emphasized the need for a theologically real experience of worship, nurture, community, and mission if we want to render to God the spiritual, moral, and missional faithfulness he desires and deserves. Moving into part three of the work, chapter 7 was essentially a deep dive into what scholars consider the ultimate spiritual warfare passage presented in the New Testament: Paul's "armor of God" discussion (Eph 6:10–20). Ultimately, we learned the key to putting on

---

1. Brueggemann, *Introduction to the Old Testament*, 302, emphasis original.

and keeping on the full armor of God is the "lifestyle spirituality" referred to earlier in the work. We also learned that at the heart of this devil-defeating spirituality is a prayer partnership with the Holy Spirit that Paul referred to as "praying in the Spirit." In chapter 8 we focused on three more "close-quarters" combat tactics, contemplating what it means to obey the New Testament's exhortations for us to resist and defeat the devil by "coming near," "leaning into," and "holding fast." Finally, chapters 9 and 10 were my humble attempt at an answer to a question which the New Testament doesn't explicitly address but which many people have pondered: *Why did God create a world in which the devil could gain control and wreak so much havoc in the lives of human beings?* It's my hope these two concluding chapters might encourage readers not only to keep trusting and hoping in God, but also to take their cooperation with his evil-ending agenda to the next level.

I'm also hopeful, now that we've come to the end of our endurance training, the book's readers won't make the mistake of thinking I'm suggesting dealing with the devil will now be a walk in the park. It's anything but, as the story of my extended "dark night of the soul" experience alluded to at various places in the book should serve to indicate.

That said, I want to conclude our training experience with some final words of encouragement: *enduring is possible; shutting the door on the devil is doable; we really can render to Christ a long obedience in the same direction and hear him say to us:* "Well done, good and faithful servant!" But to do so, we must cultivate a lifestyle spirituality which enables us to continually:

- remind ourselves (and others) it's never just us and God;
- engage in theologically real versions of the four cardinal components of Christian discipleship: *worship, nurture, community,* and *mission*;
- clothe ourselves in the full armor of God by *putting on, taking up, praying in,* and *praying for*;
- employ the close-quarters combat techniques of *coming near, leaning into,* and *holding fast*; and, finally,
- participate in God's justice-pursuing, evil-ending agenda.

If we allow the risen Christ to enable us, by his Spirit, to do these things—to heed all the references to discipleship's dark side the apostolic authors embedded in the New Testament—the promise of Paul to the Roman Christians will apply to us as well: *the God of peace will soon crush Satan under our feet!*

May the grace of our Lord Jesus be with us all (Rom 16:20)!

Bibliography

Aaron, Charlene. "'Losing My Religion': What We Can Learn from Celebrity Christians Who Walk Away from the Faith." *CBN News* (August 23, 2019). https://www1.cbn.com/cbnnews/us/2019/august/losing-my-religion-what-we-can-learn-from-celebrity-christians-who-walk-away-from-the-faith.

Akin, Daniel L. *1, 2, 3 John*. New American Commentary. Nashville: Broadman & Holman, 2001.

Alden, Robert L. *Job*. New American Commentary. Nashville: Broadman & Holman, 1993.

Allison, Gregg R. *Historical Theology: An Introduction to Christian Doctrine*. Grand Rapids: Zondervan, 2011.

Andersen, Francis I. *Job: An Introduction and Commentary*. Downers Grove, IL: InterVarsity, 1976.

Anderson, Bernhard W., et al. *Understanding the Old Testament*. Upper Saddle River, NJ: Pearson Prentice Hall, 2007.

Anderson, Paul. "Balancing Form and Freedom." *ChristianityToday.com*. https://www.christianitytoday.com/pastors/1986/spring/86l2024.html.

Anonymous. "2 Enoch." *Wikipedia*. https://en.wikipedia.org/wiki/2_Enoch#Content.

———. *The Book of Enoch*. Translated by R. H. Charles. Overland Park, KS: Digireads.com, 2018.

———. "Book of Jubilees." *Wikipedia*. https://en.wikipedia.org/wiki/Book_of_Jubilees#Origins.

———. "Circles of Support and Accountability." *Justice Center: The National Reentry Resource Center.* https://csgjusticecenter.org/nrrc/circles-of-support-and-accountability/.

———. "Deconstructing the Traditional Hell." *Matthew2262 (Blog)* (October 2012). https://matthew2262.wordpress.com/2012/10/14/deconstructing-the-traditional-hell/.

———. "The History of Alcoholics Anonymous: C. G. Jung / Bill W. Letters - Spiritus contra Spiritum." *Sacred Connections*. https://12wisdomsteps.com/related_topics/history/carl_jung.html.

———. "Joni Eareckson Tada Story." *Joni Eareckson Tada Story*. http://www.joniearecksontadastory.com/.

———. "Nurture." *Google.com*. https://www.google.com/search?q=Nurture+def&rlz=1C1GCEB_enUS860US860&oq=Nurture+def&aqs=chrome..69i57j0l5.3701j1j7&sourceid=chrome&ie=UTF-8.

———. "Paradise Lost – A Brief Summary." *New Arts Library* (1999). http://www.paradiselost.org/5-sum-short.html.

———. "Watchers/Nephilim." *DeliriumsRealm*. https://www.deliriumsrealm.com/watchers/#1Enoch1.

Arnold, Clinton E. *3 Crucial Questions about Spiritual Warfare*. Grand Rapids: Baker Academic, 1997.

———. *Power and Magic: The Concept of Power in Ephesians*. 1989. Reprint, Eugene, OR: Wipf and Stock, 2001.

———. *Powers of Darkness: Principalities and Powers in Paul's Letters*. Downers Grove, IL: IVP Academic, 1992.

Augustine of Hippo. *Confessions*. New York: Oxford University Press, 2009.

Barrett, C. K. *The Epistle to the Romans*. Harper's New Testament Commentaries. New York: Harper & Row, 1957.

Barth, Karl. *Church Dogmatics. I/1: The Doctrine of the Word of God*. Translated by G. W. Bromiley. Peabody, MA: Hendrickson, 2010.

———. *Church Dogmatics. III/3: The Doctrine of Creation*. Translated by G. W. Bromiley. Peabody, MA: Hendrickson, 2010.

———. *Church Dogmatics. IV/1: The Doctrine of Reconciliation*. Translated by G. W. Bromiley. Peabody, MA: Hendrickson, 2010.

———. *Homiletics*. Louisville: Westminster John Knox, 1991.

———. "The Need and Promise of Christian Preaching." In *The Word of God and the Word of Man*, translated by Douglas Horton, 97–135. New York: Harper & Row, 1957.

———. *Prayer*. Louisville: Westminster John Knox, 2002.

Barth, Markus. *Ephesians: Translation and Commentary on Chapters 4–6*. Anchor Bible Commentary. Garden City, NY: Doubleday, 1974.

Basham, Don. *Deliver Us from Evil: A Pastor's Reluctant Encounters with the Powers of Darkness*. Minneapolis: Chosen, 1972.

Baudelaire, Charles. *The Prose Poems and La Fanfarlo*. New York: Oxford University Press, 2001.

Beeke, Joel R. *Fighting Satan: Knowing His Weaknesses, Strategies, and Defeat*. Grand Rapids: Reformation Heritage, 2015.

Belleville, Linda L. *2 Corinthians*. IVP New Testament Commentary Series. Westmont, IL: IVP Academic, 1996.

Bilezikian, Gilbert. *Christianity 101*. Grand Rapids: Zondervan Academic, 1993.

Blomberg, Craig. *Matthew*. New American Commentary. Nashville: Broadman & Holman, 1992.

Bonhoeffer, Dietrich. *Letters and Papers from Prison*. New York: Touchstone, 1997.

Borgman, Brian, and Rob Ventura. *Spiritual Warfare: A Biblical and Balanced Perspective*. Grand Rapids: Reformation Heritage, 2014.

Bosch, David J. *The Transforming Mission: Paradigm Shifts in Theology of Mission*. Maryknoll, NY: Orbis, 2011.

Boyd, Gregory A. *God at War: The Bible and Spiritual Conflict*. Downers Grove, IL: IVP Academic, 1997.

———. "The Ground Level Deliverance Model." In *Understanding Spiritual Warfare: Four Views*, edited by James K. Beilby and Paul Rhodes Eddy, 129–57. Grand Rapids, Baker Academic, 2012.

———. *Satan and the Problem of Evil: Constructing a Trinitarian Warfare Theodicy.* Downers Grove, IL: IVP Academic, 2001.

———. *Trinity and Process: A Critical Evaluation and Reconstruction of Hartshorne's Di-Polar Theism Towards a Trinitarian Metaphysics.* New York: Peter Lang, 1992.

Braaten, Carl E. *That All May Believe: A Theology of the Gospel and the Mission of the Church.* Grand Rapids: Eerdmans, 2008.

Brown, Gregory. *The Armor of God: Standing Firm in Spiritual Warfare.* 2nd ed. BTG, 2017.

Bruce, F. F. *Romans.* Tyndale New Testament Commentaries. Downers Grove, IL: InterVarsity, 1985.

Brueggemann, Walter. *An Introduction to the Old Testament: The Canon and Christian Imagination.* Louisville: Westminster John Knox, 2003.

Bultmann, Rudolf. *New Testament and Mythology and Other Basic Writings.* Translated by Schubert M. Ogden. Philadelphia: Fortress, 1984.

Buttrick, David G. "Foreword." In *Homiletics*, by Karl Barth, translated by Geoffrey W. Bromiley and Donald E. Daniels, 7–11. Louisville: Westminster John Knox, 1991.

Carter, Joe. "Survey: Majority of Americans Believe in the Existence of Satan and Demon Possession." https://www.thegospelcoalition.org/article/survey-majority-of-americans-believe-in-the-existence-of-satan-and-demon-po/.

Charles, R. H. *The Book of Jubilees.* London: Black, 1902.

Chastain, Tim. "The Fall of Satan in the Book of Enoch." *Jesus Without Baggage.* https://jesuswithoutbaggage.wordpress.com/2013/10/10/the-fall-of-satan-in-the-book-of-enoch/.

Clement of Alexandria. *Fragments from Cassiodorus.* In *The Ante-Nicene Fathers*, edited by Alexander Roberts et al., 2:571–76. New York: Cosimo Classics, 2007.

Clines, David J. A. *Job 1–20.* Word Biblical Commentary. Waco, TX: Word, 1989.

Coe, John H. "Musings on the Dark Night of the Soul: Insights from St. John of the Cross on a Developmental Spirituality." *Journal of Psychology and Theology* 28.4 (2000) 293–307. https://journals.sagepub.com/doi/10.1177/009164710002800408.

Corts, C. Mark. *The Truth about Spiritual Warfare: Your Place in the Battle between God and Satan.* Nashville: B&H, 2006.

Currie, Thomas Christian. *The Only Sacrament Left to Us: The Threefold Word of God in the Theology and Ecclesiology of Karl Barth.* Eugene, OR: Pickwick, 2015.

Cyprian. *Treatise* 10.4. In *The Ante-Nicene Fathers*, edited by James Alexander Roberts et al., 5:421–562. New York: Cosimo Classics, 2007.

Dahl, Gordon. *Work, Play and Worship in a Leisure-Oriented Society.* Minneapolis: Augsburg, 1972.

Davids, Peter H. *James. New Bible Commentary: 21st Century Edition.* Edited by D. A. Carson et al. 4th ed. Downers Grove, IL: Inter-Varsity, 1994.

Davidson, Robert. *The Old Testament.* Philadelphia: Lippincott, 1964.

Dean, Kenda Creasy. *Almost Christian: What the Faith of Our Teenagers is Telling the American Church.* New York: Oxford University Press, 2010.

Dean, Robert, Jr., and Thomas Ice. *What the Bible Teaches about Spiritual Warfare.* Grand Rapids: Kregel, 2000.

de Sales, Francis. *Introduction to the Devout Life.* New York: Doubleday, 1966.

DeVine, Mark. "Can the Church Emerge without or with Only the Nicene Creed?" In *Evangelicals and Nicene Faith*, edited by Timothy George, 179–95. Grand Rapids: Baker, 2011.

Dyck, Drew. *Generation Ex-Christian: Why Young Adults are Leaving the Faith . . . and How to Bring Them Back.* Chicago: Moody, 2010.
Eddy, Paul Rhodes, and James K. Beilby. "Introducing Spiritual Warfare: A Survey of Key Issues and Debates." In *Understanding Spiritual Warfare: Four Views*, edited by James K. Beilby and Paul Rhodes Eddy, 1–46. Grand Rapids: Baker Academic, 2012.
Elgvin, Torleif. "Belial, Beliar, Devil, Satan." In *Dictionary of New Testament Background*, edited by Craig A. Evans and Stanley E. Porter, 153–57. Downers Grove, IL: IVP Academic, 2000.
Ellis, Mark. "Joni Eareckson Tada Says She's Cancer Free!" *God Reports* (July 15, 2019). https://godreports.com/2019/07/joni-eareckson-tada-says-shes-cancer-free/.
Enns, Peter. *Inspiration and Incarnation: Evangelicals and the Problem of the Old Testament.* Grand Rapids: Baker, 2005.
Erickson, Millard. *What Does God Know and When Does He Know it?* Grand Rapids: Zondervan, 2003.
Eskridge, Larry. "The 'Praise and Worship' Revolution." *Christian History* (October 29, 2008). https://www.christianitytoday.com/history/2008/october/praise-and-worship-revolution.html.
Fee, Gordon D. *God's Empowering Presence: The Holy Spirit in the Letters of Paul.* Peabody, MA: Hendrickson, 1994.
———. *Paul, the Spirit, and the People of God.* Grand Rapids: Baker Academic, 1996.
Fee, Gordon D., and Douglas Stuart. *How to Read the Bible for All its Worth: Fourth Edition.* Grand Rapids: Zondervan, 2014.
Filson, Floyd V. *A Commentary on the Gospel According to St. Matthew.* London: Black, 1960.
Fink, Michael. "Apostasy." In *Holman Illustrated Bible Dictionary*, edited by Chad Brand et al., 87–88. Nashville: Holman, 2003.
Flett, John G. *The Witness of God: The Trinity, Missio Dei, Karl Barth, and the Nature of Christian Community.* Grand Rapids: Eerdmans, 2010.
Foster, Richard. *The Celebration of Discipline: Pathway to Spiritual Growth.* San Francisco: HarperSanFrancisco, 1998.
Foulkes, Francis. *Ephesians.* 2nd ed. Tyndale New Testament Commentaries. Downers Grove, IL: InterVarsity, 1983.
———. *Ephesians: An Introduction and Commentary.* Tyndale New Testament Commentaries. Grand Rapids: Eerdmans, 1989.
France, Richard T. *Matthew: An Introduction and Commentary.* Tyndale New Testament Commentaries. Downers Grove, IL: InterVarsity, 1985.
Gallagher, Richard. "As a Psychiatrist, I Diagnose Mental Illness. Also, I Help Spot Demonic Possession." *The Washington Post* (July 1, 2016). https://www.washingtonpost.com/posteverything/wp/2016/07/01/as-a-psychiatrist-i-diagnose-mental-illness-and-sometimes-demonic-possession/?noredirect=on&utm_term=.7da5329239bc.
Garland, David E. *2 Corinthians.* The New American Commentary. Nashville: Broadman & Holman, 1999.
Genung, John Franklin. "Elihu." In *International Standard Bible Encyclopedia*, edited by James Orr et al., 930. Chicago: The Howard-Severance Company, 1915.
Gonzalez, Inigo. "Your Entire Idea of Satan and Hell are Based on 'Paradise Lost' You Just Didn't Know." *Graveyard Shift.* https://www.ranker.com/list/satan-in-paradise-lost-facts/inigo-gonzalez.

Gordis, Robert. *The Book of God and Man: A Study of Job*. Chicago: University of Chicago Press, 1965.
Gray, G. Buchanan. "The Purpose and Method of the Writer." In *Twentieth Century Interpretations of the Book of Job*, edited by Paul S. Sanders, 36–45. Englewood Cliffs, NJ: Prentice-Hall, 1968.
Green, Michael. *The Message of Matthew: The Kingdom of Heaven*. The Bible Speaks Today. Downers Grove, IL: InterVarsity, 2001.
Guder, Darrell, ed. *Missional Church: A Vision for the Sending of the Church in North America*. Grand Rapids: Eerdmans, 1998.
Guthrie, Donald. *Hebrews: An Introduction and Commentary*. Tyndale New Testament Commentaries 15. Downers Grove, IL: InterVarsity, 1983.
———. *Pastoral Epistles: An Introduction and Commentary*. Tyndale New Testament Commentaries 14. Downers Grove, IL: InterVarsity, 1990.
Hastings, Ross. *Missional God, Missional Church: Hope for Re-Evangelizing the West*. Downers Grove, IL: IVP Academic, 2012.
Herman, Nicholas (Brother Lawrence). *The Practice of the Presence of God with Spiritual Maxims*. Grand Rapids: Revell, 1967.
Hill, Alec. "The Most Troubling Parable: Why Does Jesus Say We are Like Slaves?" *Christianity Today* 58.6 (July/August 2014) 76–79.
Hoehner, Harold W. *Ephesians: An Exegetical Commentary*. Grand Rapids: Baker Academic, 2002.
House, Paul R. *Old Testament Theology*. Downers Grove, IL: InterVarsity, 1998.
Huie, Bryan T. "Fallen Angels and Demons." *Here a Little, There a Little*. http://www.herealittletherealittle.net/index.cfm?page_name=Demons.
Hunsberger, George R. "Starting Points, Trajectories and Outcomes in Proposals for a Missional Hermeneutic: Mapping the Conversation." Paper presented at the annual meeting of the Society of Biblical Literature. Boston, MA, November 22, 2008.
Ignatius of Antioch. "The Epistle of Ignatius to the Ephesians." In *The Ante-Nicene Fathers*, edited by Alexander Roberts et al., 1:49–58. New York: Cosimo Classics, 2007.
Ingram, Chip. *The Invisible War: What Every Believer Needs to Know about Satan, Demons, and Spiritual Warfare*. Grand Rapids: Baker, 2015.
Jackman, David. *The Message of John's Letters: Living in the Love of God*. The Bible Speaks Today Series. Downer's Grove, IL: InterVarsity, 1988.
Johnson, Jan. *Enjoying the Presence of God*. Colorado Springs: NavPress, 1996.
Keener, Craig S. *Matthew*. IVP New Testament Commentary Series. Downers Grove, IL: InterVarsity, 1997.
———. "Who Comes to Steal, Kill, and Destroy?" *Christianity Today* (March 17, 2017). https://www.christianitytoday.com/ct/2017/april/thief-steal-kill-and-destroy-john-10.html.
Keller, Timothy. "The Importance of Hell." *Redeemer Churches and Ministries* (August 2009). https://www.redeemer.com/redeemer-report/article/the_importance_of_hell.
———. *The Reason for God: Belief in an Age of Skepticism*. New York: Dutton, 2008.
———. *Walking with God through Pain and Suffering*. New York: Penguin, 2015.
Kelly, Thomas. *A Testament of Devotion*. New York: Harper and Row, 1941.

Kinnaman, David, and Gabe Lyons. *unchristian: What a New Generation Really Thinks about Christianity—And Why it Matters*. Grand Rapids: Baker, 2007.

Kraft, Charles H. *The Evangelical's Guide to Spiritual Warfare: Scriptural Insights and Practical Instruction on Facing the Enemy*. Minneapolis: Chosen, 2015.

Kruse, Colin G. *2 Corinthians: An Introduction and Commentary*. Tyndale New Testament Commentaries. Downers Grove, IL: InterVarsity, 1987.

———. *The Letters of John*. Pillar New Testament Commentary. Grand Rapids: Eerdmans, 2000.

Ladd, George E. *A Theology of the New Testament*. Grand Rapids: Eerdmans, 1974.

Larkin, William J., Jr. *Acts*. IVP New Testament Commentary Series. Westmont, IL: IVP Academic, 1995.

LaSor, William Sanford, et al. *Old Testament Survey: The Message, Form, and Background of the Old Testament*. Grand Rapids: Eerdmans, 1982.

Lea, Thomas D. *Hebrews, James*. Holman New Testament Commentary. Nashville: Broadman & Holman, 1999.

Lee, Morgan. "Responding to Josh Harris's Announcement." *Christianity Today* (July 31, 2019). https://www.christianitytoday.com/ct/2019/july-web-only/leaving-faith-church-christianity-falling-away-josh-harris.html.

Lewis, C. S. *The Four Loves*. New York: HarperOne, 2017.

———. *God in the Dock*. Grand Rapids: Eerdmans, 2014.

———. *The Lion, the Witch and the Wardrobe*. New York: HarperCollins, 2000.

———. *Mere Christianity*. New York: HarperOne, 2015.

———. *The Problem of Pain*. New York: HarperOne, 2015.

———. *Reflections on the Psalms*. New York: HarperOne, 2017.

———. *The Screwtape Letters*. New York: HarperOne, 2015.

Lincoln, Andrew T. *Ephesians*. Word Biblical Commentary. Dallas: Word, 1990.

Long, Thomas G. *Testimony: Talking Ourselves into Being Christian*. San Francisco: Jossey-Bass, 2004.

Longenecker, Richard. "Acts." In *The Expositor's Bible Commentary (Volume 9) - John and Acts*, edited by Merrill Tenney, 205–573. 12 vols. Grand Rapids: Zondervan, 1981.

Marshall, Peter. "A Metaphor of Social Shame: *Thriambeuein* in 2 Cor. 2:14." *NovT* 25 (1983) 302–17.

Mays, Anthony. "Greater Is He that Is in Me: The Real Meaning of 1 John 4:4." *Medium* (June 1, 2015). https://medium.com/@anthonymays/greater-is-he-that-is-in-me-the-real-meaning-of-1-john-4-4-f43adb82d813.

McGuckin, John Anthony. *The Westminster Handbook to Patristic Theology*. Louisville: Westminster John Knox, 2004.

McKnight, Scot. "From the Shepherd's Nook: Preaching as Encounter." *Jesus Creed* (blog). http://www.patheos.com/blogs/jesuscreed/2013/05/17/from-the-shepherds-nook-preaching-as-encounter/.

Melick, Richard R. *Philippians, Colossians, Philemon*. New American Commentary. Nashville: Broadman & Holman, 1991.

Metaxas, Eric. *Bonhoeffer: Pastor, Martyr, Prophet, Spy*. Nashville: Thomas Nelson, 2011.

Minn, Herbert R. *The Thorn that Remained*. Auckland: Institute, 1972.

Mitton, C. Leslie. *Ephesians*. New Century Bible Commentary. Grand Rapids: Eerdmans, 1973.

Moo, Douglas J. *James: An Introduction and Commentary*. Tyndale New Testament Commentaries. Downers Grove, IL: InterVarsity, 1985.
———. *The Letter of James*. Pillar New Testament Commentary. Grand Rapids: Eerdmans, 2000.
Morris, Leon. *The Gospel According to Matthew*. Pillar New Testament Commentary. Grand Rapids: Eerdmans, 1992.
Motyer, John A. *The Message of James: The Tests of Faith*. The Bible Speaks Today. Downers Grove, IL: Inter-Varsity, 1985.
Muddiman, John. *The Epistle to the Ephesians*. Black's New Testament Commentaries. New York: Continuum, 2001.
Murphy, Ed. *The Handbook for Spiritual Warfare*. Nashville: Thomas Nelson, 2003.
Newbigin, Lesslie. *The Gospel in a Pluralist Society*. Grand Rapids, Eerdmans, 1989.
O'Brien, Peter T. *The Letter to the Ephesians*. Pillar New Testament Commentary. Grand Rapids: Eerdmans, 1999.
Origen, *First Principles*. In *The Ante-Nicene Fathers*, edited by Alexander Roberts et al., 4:239–382. Peabody, MA: Hendrickson, 1994.
Ortberg, John. *The Life You've Always Wanted*. Grand Rapids, Zondervan, 2002.
Peck, M. Scott. *Glimpses of the Devil: A Psychiatrist's Personal Accounts of Possession*. New York: Simon and Schuster, 2009.
———. *People of the Lie: The Hope for Healing Evil*. New York: Simon and Schuster, 1983.
Peterson, Eugene. *A Long Obedience in the Same Direction: Discipleship in an Instant Society*. Downers Grove, IL: InterVarsity, 1980.
Piper, John. "Job: Rebuked in Suffering." *Desiring God*. https://www.desiringgod.org/messages/job-rebuked-in-suffering.
Powlison, David. "The Classical Model." In *Understanding Spiritual Warfare: Four Views*, edited by James K. Beilby and Paul Rhodes Eddy, 89–111. Grand Rapids: Baker Academic, 2012.
Pratt, Dwight M. "Apostasy." In *The International Standard Bible Encyclopaedia*, edited by James Orr, 1:190. 4 vols. Chicago: The Howard-Severance Company, 1915.
Rankin, Jerry. *Spiritual Warfare: The Battle for God's Glory*. Nashville: B&H, 2009.
Robinson, Paul H. "A Brief History of Distinctions in Criminal Culpability." *Hastings Law Journal* 31.4 (1980) 815–53. https://repository.uchastings.edu/hastings_law_journal/vol31/iss4/2.
Routledge, Robin. "'An Evil Spirit from the Lord' – Demonic Influence or Divine Instrument?" https://biblicalstudies.org.uk/pdf/eq/spirit_routledge.pdf.
Russell, Jeffrey Burton. *Mephistopheles: The Devil in the Modern World*. Ithaca, NY: Cornell University Press, 1986.
Schnackenburg, Rudolf. *The Epistle to the Ephesians: A Commentary*. Edinburgh: T. & T. Clark, 1991.
Sewall, Richard B. "The Book of Job." In *Twentieth Century Interpretations of the Book of Job*, edited by Paul S. Sanders, 21–35. Englewood Cliffs, NJ: Prentice-Hall, 1968.
Shannon-Missal, Larry. "Americans' Belief in God, Miracles and Heaven Declines." *The Harris Poll* (December 16, 2013). https://theharrispoll.com/new-york-n-y-december-16-2013-a-new-harris-poll-finds-that-while-a-strong-majority-74-of-u-s-adults-do-believe-in-god-this-belief-is-in-decline-when-compared-to-previous-years-as-just-over/.

Slick, Matt. "What is Progressive Revelation and is it Scriptural?" *Christian Apologetics & Research Ministry*. https://carm.org/what-is-progressive-revelation-and-is-it-scriptural.

Smith, Christian, and Melinda Lundquist Denton. *Soul Searching: The Religious and Spiritual Lives of American Teenagers*. New York: Oxford University Press, 2005.

Smith, Christian, and Patricia Smith. *Souls in Transition: The Religious and Spiritual Lives of Emerging Adults*. New York: Oxford University Press, 2009.

Smith, Christian, et al. *Lost in Transition: The Dark Side of Emerging Adulthood*. New York: Oxford University Press, 2011.

Spiegel, James S. "Annihilation, Everlasting Torment, and Divine Justice." *International Journal of Philosophy and Theology* 76.3 (August 2015) 241–48. http://dx.doi.org/10.1080/21692327.2015.1077469.

Stott, John R. W. *The Contemporary Christian*. Downers Grove, IL: InterVarsity, 1992.

———. *The Message of Acts: The Spirit, the Church & the World*. The Bible Speaks Today. Downers Grove, IL: InterVarsity, 1994.

Stump, Eleonore. "Dante's Hell, Aquinas' Moral Theory, and the Love of God." *Canadian Journal of Philosophy* 16.2 (1986) 196–97.

Tada, Joni Eareckson. "Health Update: All Clear!" *Joni and Friends* (July 9, 2019). https://www.joniandfriends.org/health-update-all-clear/.

———. "Reflections on the 50th Anniversary of My Diving Accident." *The Gospel Coalition* (July 30, 2017). https://www.thegospelcoalition.org/article/reflections-on-50th-anniversary-of-my-diving-accident/.

Taylor, Jeremy. "Holy Living." In *Jeremy Taylor: Selected Writings*, edited by Charles H. Sisson, 42–92. Manchester, UK: Carcanet, 1990.

Towner, Philip. *1–2 Timothy & Titus*. IVP New Testament Commentary Series. Downers Grove, IL: InterVarsity, 1994.

Twain, Mark. *The Mysterious Stranger 7*. Los Angeles: University of California Press, 1970.

Tyra, Gary. *Christ's Empowering Presence: The Pursuit of God through the Ages*. Downers Grove, IL: IVP, 2011.

———. *Defeating Pharisaism: Recovering Jesus' Disciple-Making Method*. Downers Grove, IL: IVP, 2009.

———. *Getting Real: Pneumatological Realism and the Spiritual, Moral, and Ministry Formation of Contemporary Christians*. Eugene, OR: Cascade, 2018.

———. *The Holy Spirit in Mission: Prophetic Speech and Action in Christian Witness*. Downers Grove, IL: IVP Academic, 2011.

———. *A Missional Orthodoxy: Theology and Mission in a Post-Christian Context*. Downers Grove, IL: IVP Academic, 2013.

———. "Paul's 'Armor of God' Discussion: A Pneumatological Engagement with a Critical Formation Text." *Journal of Spiritual Formation and Soul Care* (December 20, 2019). https://journals.sagepub.com/doi/abs/10.1177/1939790919894555.

———. *Pursuing Moral Faithfulness: Ethics and Christian Discipleship*. Downers Grove, IL: IVP Academic, 2015.

Tyra, Gary, and Patti Tyra. *Beyond the Bliss: Discovering Your Uniqueness in Marriage*. Eugene, OR: Wipf & Stock, 2018.

Van Gelder, Craig, and Dwight J. Zscheile. *The Missional Church in Perspective: Mapping Trends and Shaping the Conversation*. Grand Rapids: Baker, 2011.

Wallace, J. Warner. "Updated: Are Young People Really Leaving Christianity?" *Cold Case Christianity* (January 12, 2019). https://coldcasechristianity.com/writings/are-young-people-really-leaving-christianity/.
Wallis, Arthur. *Pray in the Spirit*. Fort Washington, PA: CLC, 1970.
Waltke, Bruce. *An Old Testament Theology*. Grand Rapids: Zondervan, 2007.
Warren, E. Janet. *Cleansing the Cosmos: A Biblical Model for Conceptualizing and Counteracting Evil*. Eugene, OR: Pickwick, 2012.
Weatherhead, Leslie. *The Transforming Friendship*. Nashville: Abingdon, 1977.
Weber, Stuart K. *Matthew*. Holman New Testament Commentary. Nashville: Broadman & Holman, 2000.
Westermann, Claus. *The Structure of the Book of Job: A Form-Critical Analysis*. Minneapolis: Fortress, 1981.
Wilson, Jim. *Future Church: Ministry in a Post-Seeker Age*. Nashville: Broadman & Holman, 2004.
Wolfers, David. *Deep Things Out of Darkness: The Book of Job*. Grand Rapids: Eerdmans, 1995.
Wright, Christopher J. H. *The Mission of God: Unlocking the Bible's Grand Narrative*. Downers Grove, IL: IVP Academic, 2006.
Wright, N. T. *Evil and the Justice of God*. Downers Grove, IL: IVP, 2006.
———. *Surprised by Hope: Rethinking Heaven, the Resurrection, and the Mission of the Church*. Grand Rapids: Zondervan, 2008.

General Index

Aaron, Charlene, 86n6
accountability, interpersonal. *See* community (Christian), earmarks of genuine.
addictions, blinding, 51
See also lifestyles, addictive.
agreement, spiritual, prayerful, 110, 112, 120, 121, 124, 127
See also symphōnēsis (spiritual agreement).
Akin, Daniel L., 104–5, 105n35, 105n36, 105n37, 105n38, 106, 106n39–40
Alcoholics Anonymous, 50, 51n21
Alden, Robert L., 246n51, 248n56
alienation, the devil and, 114
Allison, Gregg R., 25n12, 50n20
ambiguity,
  tolerance for, 183
  purposeful, 238n32
anointing, prophetic, 112, 123, 194–95
Andersen, Francis I., 247n54, 247n55
Anderson, Bernard W., 248, 248n58, 248n59, 249n62
Anderson, Paul, 74n12
anxiety, 11–13, 199–201, 202n6, 204–5, 208
angel(s), x, 22–23, 29n22, 30, 30n25, 33, 40, 43, 73, 140, 144–45, 221, 225, 235–37, 239–41, 245–46, 267

fallen, 22–23, 25–29, 29n23, 30, 30n25, 31n26, 32-33, 36, 50n20, 228, 285
See also devil, fall of.
See also watchers.
Apocrypha, the, 26, 26n13, 27–29, 99, 167, 175
apostasy, 5n10, 86, 86n5, 87, 92, 92n20, 101
apostles (teachers), false, 87, 92–94, 101–2, 102n29, 102n31, 103, 105, 105n37, 106
See also teaching(s), false.
armor of God, x, 4, 10, 163, 163n2, 164–74, 176–82, 185–89, 189n61, 190n65, 192-93, 194n73, 195–97, 198n2, 205, 277–78
Arnold, Clinton E., 2n4, 3n7, 4n9, 47n15, 74, 74n11, 87, 87n10, 99, 99n26, 101, 101n28, 163n1, 164n3, 164n4, 167n10, 170n20, 171n24, 172, 172n28, 175n31, 179n36, 188n59, 189, 189n61–63, 190, 190n66, 190n67, 197n1, 198n3
Augustine, Saint, 49n19

Barrett, C. K., 191n68
Barth, Karl, 38–39, 39n1, 40, 40n2–3, 42, 46, 46n14, 54, 108, 108n41, 108n43, 108n44, 109–10, 110n45, 110n46, 111, 111n50

Barth, Markus, 167n9, 168n12, 170n19, 171n22, 171n25, 175n31, 176n33, 181n40, 182–83, 183n43–44, 185n49, 186, 186n53, 186n54, 188n59, 189n63, 190n67, 197n1
Basham, Don, 198m2
Baudelaire, Charles, 9, 9n20
Beeke, Joel R., 190n65
Beilby, James K., 22n7
Belleville, Linda, 41n4
biblical inspiration, theologically nuanced version of, 96
Bilezikian, Gilbert, 47n16, 111, 111n49, 227, 227n7, 228, 228n8–10; 229–31, 231n18–19, 232, 232n24, 232n25, 234, 234n27, 235–36, 236n30–31, 237–38, 238n32, 239, 239n39, 240, 242, 246, 249–50, 250n63, 251–55, 260, 268, 273
Blomberg, Craig, 117, 118n3, 143, 143n8, 145, 145n11, 147, 147n16, 148n18
boldness, Spirit-imparted, 194
Bonhoeffer, Dietrich, 213–31
Borgman, Brian, 190n65
Bosch, David J., 140n1, 140n2, 140n3
Boyd, Gregory A., 21n5, 22n6, 23n10, 25n12, 32n27, 44, 44n7–10, 45, 47n16, 131, 131n11, 131n12, 132, 132n13, 132n14, 132n15, 179n36, 189n61, 227n7, 228n7, 228n12, 228n13, 229n13, 230–32, 232n22, 233, 233n23, 234, 234n26, 235, 235n28, 235n29, 238, 238n32, 239, 239n36, 239n37, 239n38, 239n39, 240, 240n40, 241n41, 241n43, 242–43, 243n45, 245–46, 249–50, 250n63, 251–55, 258, 260, 263n15, 268, 273

Braaten, Carl E., 22n7
Brown, Gregory, 189n61, 190n65, 194n73
Bruce, F. F., 191n68
Brueggemann, Walter, 277, 277n1
Bultmann, Rudolf, 20, 20n3
Buttrick, David G., 111, 111n48

Carter, Joe, 5n11
Charles, R. H., 29n24
Chastain, Tim, 23n8
Christian(s),
    almost (lukewarm), 51, 52, 55, 87n9
    de-churched (ex-), 84–85
        See also Christian(s), post-.
    lone-ranger, 118, 121
    post-, 14, 75, 85, 85n4, 86, 92, 96–97, 112–13, 116, 196
        See also Christian(s), de-churched (ex-).
Christianity,
    non-apostolic versions of, 99n25
    orthodox(y) (biblical, historical, missional), 6n14, 63n3, 85, 90, 91n19, 94, 98n24, 100n27, 104–6, 151, 271n35, 271n36, 272n40
Christology, high, 106, 113
church(es),
    Confessing German, 213, 216
    contemporary, 92, 166
    God's justice and his, 269
    "Great Co-Missional" model of, 272
    megachurch model of, 88
    multisite, 88
    Spirit-filled, 123
churchianity, 86
Circles of Support and Accountability (COSA), 138n19
Clement of Alexandria, 50n20
Clines, David J., 243n46
Coe, John H., 11n21
commands, "one another," 115, 125, 130, 139
Commission, Great, 271–72, 272n40

GENERAL INDEX   293

See also mission (Christian).
commitment,
   volitional-intellectual (to
      Christ), 90–91, 113
communion,
   with God, 61, 63,
   mystical-experiential (with
      Christ), 90, 90n18, 91, 113
community (Christian),
   earmarks of genuine, 114, 127,
      135, 138
   Jesus and the importance of,
      117–20
   pseudo, 135
   theologically real experience of,
      117, 120–22, 123, 124–25,
      126–27, 135, 138, 205,
      277–78
connection (to Christ), head-and-
   heart, 89, 91–92
Corts, C. Mark, 189n62
cultural milieu, postmodern, 183
Currie, Thomas Christian, 110,
   110n47, 111n50
Cyprian, Saint, 43, 43n6

Dahl, Gordon, 62n2
dark night of the soul, 11, 11n21,
   12–13, 15, 199, 221, 278
Davids, Peter H., 203, 203n9
Davidson, Robert, 238n33
Dean, Kenda Creasy, 87n9
Dean, Robert Jr., 167n10, 171n22,
   174n29, 176n33
deception, the devil and, 84
demon(s),
   anxiety, 13, 199, 202n6, 204
   lustful, driven nature of, 50n20
   and possession, 21, 21n5, 45,
      45n12
   prince of, 3, 33
demonic, impulse of, 9, 45–46, 114
demythologization, 7, 20, 20n2
Denton, Melinda Lundquist, 86n9
de Sales, Frances, 80, 81n21, 81n22
despair, spiritual, 183
   See also hope, Christian.

devil (Satan),
   creaturely attributes and
      behaviors of, 40
   deal of (motivation), 43–44, 46,
      52, 68
   devices of, 9, 14, 40n3, 56, 61,
      73, 83, 91, 195
   existence of, 5–7, 20, 29, 40,
      47n15
   fall of, 22–25, 29, 44, 228, 228n7
   nature of, 37, 39, 41–43, 46, 54
   origin of, 19–20, 22–27, 32, 34,
      37–38, 40, 54
   personal, 6, 20–21, 47n15
   reality of, 2–3, 5, 7–9, 19–22,
      33n28, 35, 37, 40, 44, 54, 56,
      184, 227, 277
   stock and trade of, 143
   and his tyranny over creation,
      143, 255, 265
DeVine, Mark, 100n27
discipleship,
   cardinal components of, 9–10,
      61–63, 88, 114, 122, 127,
      138, 141, 152, 277–78
   dynamics. *See* discipleship,
      cardinal components of.
   fruitfulness, 52
discipline(s),
   ecclesial, 119
   See also disfellowship, practice
      of.
   spiritual, 53, 78–79
disfellowship, practice of, 119, 134
   See also discipline(s), ecclesial.
distance,
   geographical, 128, 130
   relational, 130
   spiritual, 133, 139
doctrines,
   false, 94, 99
   See also teachings, false.
doubt, the New Testament portrayal
   of, 183
dragon, the, 33, 52, 212, 270
   See also serpent, the.
Dreyfus, Richard, 35

dualism,
  metaphysical, 40
    See also dualism, ontological.
  ontological, 226
    See also dualism, metaphysical.
dynamic,
  post-Christian, 85, 85n4, 86, 92
    See also posture, post-Christian.
  prophetic, 186
Dyck, Drew, 84, 85, 85n2

Eddy, Paul Rhodes, 22n7
Elgvin, Torleif, 26n14, 27n17,
  28n18, 28n19, 28n20, 28n21
Ellis, Mark, 210n14
encounter,
  existentially impactful, 65, 72,
    77, 107, 110, 248
    See also encounter, life-story
      shaping.
  life-story shaping, 63, 63n4, 65,
    77, 89, 107, 122n8, 166, 169,
    171, 194, 198
  prophetic, 12–13, 125–26, 194
  sacred, 203
endurance,
  spiritual, 6, 8, 15, 20, 56, 86, 89,
    159
Enns, Peter, 98n24
entendre, double, (double coding),
  25, 25n12, 46
environment,
  discipling, 88n13, 91
    See also environment, nurturing/
      discipling (ministry).
  nurturing/discipling (ministry),
    87–89, 92, 94, 97, 100n27
    See also environment, discipling.
Erickson, Millard, 241n43
Eskridge, Larry, 64n5
Eucharist, the, 202n6
exorcism(s), 9n19, 45, 45n12, 143,
  198n12
expectancy,
  confident, enthusiastic, 182
  corporate sense of, 111
  eager, 111
  God given, 184
  holy, 76–77, 98, 110–13
  pneumatological, 122n8, 166
  spiritual, 98
experience,
  nurturing, 88
  theologically real, 79, 83, 124,
    126, 135, 138, 154, 191, 198,
    202n6, 205
evil,
  moral, 47, 229, 251, 255
  natural, 47, 229, 251, 255
  problem of, 5, 10, 47, 47n16,
    131, 226–30, 238, 249, 251,
    253–57, 260–61, 263–67,
    269, 271–73, 275

faith, theologically real
  understanding of, 185.
    See also experience,
      theologically real.
    See also realism, theological.
faithfulness,
  Christian, 5, 89
  spiritual, moral, and missional,
    xii, 1, 2, 9, 15, 52, 54, 65, 68,
    89, 121, 127–28, 135, 141,
    157, 159, 172–73, 203, 208,
    274, 277
  threefold, 1, 2, 9, 9n19, 52, 89,
    89n16, 92, 172
fall, the, 25, 48, 230, 232, 236, 240,
  250, 260, 267–68, 274
Fee, Gordon D., 89n14, 167, 167n8,
  168–69, 169n15, 169n17,
  169n18, 191n68
fellowship, See community
  (Christian).
  theologically real. See
    community (Christian),
    theologically real experience
    of.
Filson, Floyd V., 148n18,
Fink, Michael, 86n5
fix, religious, 75–76
Flett, John G., 140n2–3
formalism,
  religious, 63n4, 183
  Spiritless, 74n12

See also spiritualism, formless.
formation, spiritual, 75, 87n9, 96,
    125, 164–65, 172
Foster, Richard, 64n6, 76, 77n15
Foulkes, Francis, 170n21, 171n22,
    171n23, 174n30, 181n40,
    183n44, 185, 185n49,
    189n50, 186, 186n51–52,
    188, 188n60, 189n62,
    194n72, 195n76, 197n1
France, Richard T., 145n9, 147n15
freedom (free will),
    God-given, 22, 25, 228n12, 229
    human, 228, 233–34
future, open view of, 233, 240, 242
    See also theism (theists) open,

Gallagher, Richard, 21, 21n4, 21n5
gamble, the grand, 235, 239
Garland, David E., 206n10, 208,
    209n11
Genung, John Franklin, 243n44
glance, quick, sharp, 38–40, 54
Gnosticism, 102n31, 102n31,
    105n37
God,
    creative impulse of, 249–50, 252,
        254–56, 260, 274
        See also parent, the ultimate.
    dancing before, 204
    endgame of, 253, 255, 257,
        263–64, 267–69, 273–74
    devil-defeating agenda of, 254
    evil-defeating agenda of, 255
    foreknowledge of, the, 233–34,
        239–41, 241n43, 242, 251,
        254, 257, 259, 268, 273–74
        See also God, omniscience of.
    freedom-gving nature of, 254
    holiness of, 175, 198, 259,
        259n6, 260, 266n27, 267–70,
        270n31, 275
    hyperpersonal and
        ultrarelational nature of,
        250n63
        See also God, loving and
            freedom-giving nature of.
    See also God, relational nature
        of.
    justice of, 42, 47, 142, 158, 248,
        259, 259n6, 260–66, 266n26,
        267–70, 270n31, 271–75,
        278
    image of, 42–43, 45, 47, 49,
        72, 231–32, 241, 248–49,
        250n63, 270
        See also image-bearers, God's.
    kingdom of. *See* kingdom, of
        God.
    loving nature of, 65, 79, 142,
        226, 228, 232, 236, 250,
        250n63, 254, 258–59, 266,
        266n26,
        See also God, hyperpersonal and
            ultrarelational nature of.
        See also God, relational nature
            of.
    missionary, 140, 159
    mission of. *See missio Dei*
        (mission of God).
    omniscience of, 233–34, 241n43
        See also God, foreknowledge of.
    parenting nature (agenda) of,
        256, 259
    relational nature of, 251, 268
        See also God, freedom-giving
            nature of.
        See also God, hyperpersonal and
            ultrarelational nature of.
        See also God, loving nature of.
    realist understanding of, 111
        See also realism, theological.
    sovereignty of, 6, 40, 48, 63, 180,
        183, 201, 226, 228, 233–35,
        238, 242, 249–50, 254,
        263n15, 268, 274
Gonzalez, Inigo, 23n8
Gordis, Robert, 248n56
gospel (or Jesus story),
    apostolic version of, 95, 99
        See also witness (to Christ),
            apostolic.
        See also witness (to Christ), New
            Testament's.

296 GENERAL INDEX

gospel (or Jesus story) (continued)
  legalistic and antinomian
    perversions of, 99, 100
Gray, G. Buchanan, 246n50–51, 248,
    248n60, 249, 249n62,
Green, Michael, 119n6
Guder, Darrell, 142n5
Guthrie, Donald, 103n31, 151n21,
    151n22

habit(s), righteous, 68, 70
Hastings, Ross, 140n3, 271n35
hell,
  See also reckoning, future day of.
Herman, Nicholas (Brother
    Lawrence), 79, 79n17,
    79n18, 80n19, 82n24
Hill, Alec, 158, 158n26
Hitler (Adolf), 213, 216–18
Hoehner, Harold W., 171n22,
    175n31, 176n33, 181n40,
    183n44, 185n49, 197n1
Holy Spirit,
  and personal, phenomenal, life-
    story shaping interactions
    with, 122n8, 166
  See also mission, Spirit of.
  See also realism,
    pneumatological.
  See also Spirit, of Christ.
  See also Spirit, of God.
hope, Christian, 182, 184–85
  See also armor of God, hope.
  See also despair, spiritual.
House, Paul R., 246, 246n48, 248n56
Huie, Bryan T., 31n26
humility, 30n25, 33n28, 41, 73–74,
    116, 118n4, 183, 192, 202,
    266n27
Hunsberger, George R., 140n2
hurry sickness, 53–54, 56
Hussein, Suddam, 19

Ice, Thomas, 167n10, 171n22,
    174n29, 176n33
Ignatius of Antioch, 69, 69n9, 70
image-bearers, God's, 43, 47, 48,
    50n20, 53, 231–32, 236–37,
    241, 250, 253–55, 257–58,
    261–62, 266–68, 270, 273
  See also God, image of.
impact (punch, effect),
  transformational, life-story
    shaping, 63, 65, 77–78,
    98, 100n27, 107, 110, 123,
    124–26, 164–66, 169, 170,
    193, 195–96, 248, 267
Ingram, Chip, 189n62
intercession, prophetic, 190, 194

Jackman, David, 104n33
Job,
  friends of, 239, 242, 246
  message of, 230, 238, 238n32,
    239–40, 242, 246, 247n56,
    251, 254
  religiosity of, 243, 248
  spiritual development of, 244
John of the Cross, 11n21
Johnson, Jan, 81, 82n23
Jung, Karl, 50–51, 53

Keener, Craig S., 46n13, 120n7,
    150n19
Keller, Timothy, 48n18, 49, 226n1,
    227n6, 228n11, 229n14–16,
    232n21, 244n47, 246n49,
    260, 261n9, 263, 263n16,
    264, 265n21, 266n25
Kelly, Thomas, 81n22
King, Martin Luther, Jr., 158
kingdom,
  of God, 34, 142–43, 169, 215,
    255
  of Satan (rebel, demonic), 3, 34,
    44, 68
Kinnaman, David, 84, 84n1
Kraft, Charles H., 7n15, 7n16
Kruse, Colin, 102n29, 104n34

Ladd, George E., 143n7, 168,
    169n16, 264n18, 270n33
Larkin, William J., Jr., 123n9,
    153n23,
LaSor, William Sanford, 249n61
Lea, Thomas D., 200n4

Lee, Morgan, 85n3
legalism (legalistic), 73, 99–100,
    100n27, 102–3, 103n31, 217,
    244n47, 249
Lewis, C. S., 7n17, 8, 67n7–8, 71,
    71n10, 158, 158n25, 230,
    230n17, 232n21, 250n63,
    256n4, 260n7–8, 265,
    265n24, 266n25, 267,
    267n28, 268, 268n29, 269n30
lifestyle(s),
    addictive, 50
    See also addictions, blinding.
    spirituality. See spirituality,
        lifestyle.
Lincoln, Andrew T., 164n3, 165n5,
    168n13 168n14, 170n19,
    171n22, 179n37, 181n38,
    181n39, 183n44, 183n45,
    185n49, 189n62,
liturgy (liturgical), 64, 70, 74, 74n12
Long, Thomas G., 136n17
Longenecker, Richard, 153n23
Lyons, Gabe, 84n1

Macchia, Frank, xi, 38
manner, prophetic, 188, 191
    See also dynamic, prophetic.
Marshall, Peter, 208, 209n11
Mays, Anthony, 113n51
McGuckin, John Anthony, 151n20
McKnight, Scot, 108n42
Melick, Richard R., 102n30, 102n31,
    103n32
mentality,
    elitist, 106
    "I-It," 98
    spectator, 71
Metaxas, Eric, 214, 214n17, 214n18,
    215n19, 216, 216n20,
    216n21, 216n22, 216n23,
    216n24, 217, 217n25,
    217n26, 217n27, 218, 218n30
Minn, Herbert R., 206n10
Milton, John, 23, 34, 132
ministry,
    teaching, 88, 88n14, 91–92, 94,
        99, 107, 112

missio Dei (mission of God), 141,
    271
mission (Christian), 65, 88, 123,
    125, 127, 140, 152, 154, 156–
    57, 159, 172, 205, 277
    of Jesus, 141–52
    Spirit of, 187
    theologically real experience of,
        138, 191, 198, 205, 277
    See also experience,
        theologically real.
    See also realism, theological.
mistakes, mother of all, 19–20, 37
Mitton, C. Leslie, 164n3, 170n19,
    171n23, 177n34, 186,
    187n55, 188n59
Moo, Douglas J., 202–3, 203n8
Morris, Leon, 117, 117n2, 118n5,
    119n5, 119n6, 120, 120n7,
    145, 145n10, 146n12, 148,
    148n17, 148n18
Motyer, John A., 200n5
Muddiman, John, 168n12, 170n20,
    175n31, 177n34, 181n40,
    183n44, 185n49, 189,
    189n64
Murphy, Ed, 175n31, 176n33,
    177n34, 181n40, 183n44,
    185n49, 189n62
Murray, Bill, 35

National Study of Youth and
    Religion (NSYR), The, 86n9
Nephilim, 26–28, 28n21
Newbigin, Lesslie, 271–72, 272n39
Nichtige, das. See "nothingness, the."
"nothingness, the," 40, 42, 46, 54
nurture (Christian),
    communal approach to, 125
    theologically real experience of,
        91, 98, 110, 123, 125, 127,
        138, 205, 277–78

obedience, long, 15, 15n23, 52, 88,
    112, 114, 116, 141, 156, 159,
    179, 196, 199, 215, 274,
    277–78

O'Brien, Peter T., 164n3, 165n5, 170n21, 171n22, 175n31, 175n32, 176n33, 177n34, 181n40, 188n59, 189n62, 193n71, 197n1
offerings, thank, xii, 65, 200–1
Origen, 25n12
Ortberg, John, 53, 53n23, 54n24
overcorrection, 6–7
orthodoxy, missional, 6n14, 63n3, 91n19, 98n24, 100n27, 271n35, 271n36, 272n40

paraenesis, 164, 185
parent, the ultimate, 258
   See also God, creative impulse of.
peacemaking, 178, 271
Pearce, Lisa, 86n9
Peck, M. Scott, 21n5, 45n12
penitence, 198, 202–3, 219
peroratio, 165, 170, 173, 187
Peterson, Eugene, 15, 15n23
Pharisaism, 78n16, 88n13, 137n18, 183, 217, 244n47
   See also Pharisees.
Pharisees, 33, 143, 217
   See also Pharisaism.
Piper, John, 243n44
posture, post-Christian, 6
   See also dynamic, post-Christian.
Powlison, David, 163n1, 165n6
praise, proactive, 200–203
Pratt, Dwight M., 92n20
prayer,
   glossolalic (in tongues), 191–93
   in the Spirit, 106, 164, 188–91, 191n69, 192, 192n70, 193–94, 198n2, 278
   See also prayer, glossolalic (in tongues).
   See also prayer, prophetic (Spirit-enabled).
   See also prayer, and wordless groans.
   Jesus' life of, 150
   Lords, the, 118
   pneumatologically real, 189–91, 193
   prophetic (Spirit-enabled), 188, 191–92
   theologically real experience of, 110, 112, 116, 118n4, 123–24
   See also experience, theologically real.
   See also realism, theological.
   and wordless groans, 192–93
preaching,
   anointed (Spirit-empowered, sacramental, encounter-effecting, transformational), 107–10, 112, 125, 194, 194n74
   See also Scripture, transformational capacity of.
   apostolic, 93, 122
   prophetic, 108, 108n41, 108n44, 109, 125, 186–88, 194, 194n74, 195, 216
presence,
   empowering, 53, 61n1, 78, 90n18, 120, 139, 167n8, 169, 205, 277
   real, 63, 72, 78–79, 110, 125

Rankin, Jerry, 174n29, 177n34, 181n40, 183n44, 185n49
realism,
   theological, 63, 122n8
   See also experience, theologically real.
   pneumatological, 75, 122n8, 166, 166n7, 168, 169, 172, 189–91, 193, 195
reckoning, future day of, 264, 266
   See also hell.
relationship (with God), 49, 55, 63n4, 67–68, 74, 89, 104, 181, 183, 198, 217, 249
   See also relationship (with God) real.
   intimate, trust-based, 55, 65, 67–68, 89, 110, 183, 232, 244, 246–47, 248–49

life-story shaping, 55, 63, 63n4, 89, 122n8, 166, 198
mentoring, 61n1, 78, 191, 196
real, 74, 238n32, 250, 254, 277
See also relationship (with God).
responsibility, human, 6, 180, 183, 229
revelation, progressive, 241n42
rhema, 186, 190
Robinson, Paul H., 231n20
Routledge, Robin, 24n11
Russell, Jeffrey Burton, 47n15

sabotage,
    satanic, 48
    self, 5, 13, 48–49, 51–52, 114, 135
Schnackenburg, Rudolf, 168, 168n13, 171n22, 175n31, 177n35, 181n40, 194, 195n75
Scripture,
    high view of, 95–96, 112
    transformational capacity of, 95–96, 98, 113
    I-Thou vs. I-it approach to, 98
seduction, the devil and, 61, 65–66
serpent, the, 3, 23, 25, 33, 37, 41n4, 52, 66–68, 101, 103
    See also dragon, the.
Sewall, Richard B., 238n35
shalom, 42, 67, 260
Shannon-Missal, Larry, 5n12
Slick, Matt, 241n42
Smith, Christian, 86n9, 87n9
Smith, Patricia, 86n9, 87n9
speeches,
    Job's, to his friends, 246
    divine, the, 247
Spiegel, James S., 266n26
Spirit,
    of God, 34, 109, 187
    of Christ, 94, 169, 192, 195, 204, 221
    See also Holy Spirit.
    See also mission, Spirit of.
    See also realism, pneumatological.

spirituality, lifestyle, 61–62, 69, 78–79, 81–83, 91, 99, 116, 122, 141, 151–52, 166, 185, 192–93, 195–96, 198n2, 277–78
spiritualism, formless, 74n12
    See also formalism, Spiritless.
spiritus contra spiritum, 50–51
St. John of the Cross. *See* John of the Cross.
steps, baby, 35
stones, sharp, 45, 48, 50, 54, 56
Stott, John R. W., 123n9, 140n1
Stuart, Douglas, 89n14
Stump, Eleonore, 247, 266n26
suffering, 4, 8, 11–12, 44, 48, 68, 155–57, 159, 198, 205–10, 212, 215, 219, 226–27, 229, 236, 238–40, 242, 242n44, 243n44, 244n47, 245–46, 248–49, 249n62, 255, 257, 262–63, 266, 268–69, 273–74
support, interpersonal. *See* community (Christian), earmarks of genuine.
symphōnēsis (spiritual agreement), 110, 112, 120–21, 127
    See also agreement, prayerful.

Tada, Joni Eareckson, 209, 209n12, 210, 210n13, 219n14, 211, 211n15, 221
Taylor, Jeremy, 79–80, 80n20
teachers, false, 87, 92–94, 101–2, 102n29, 102n31, 103, 105, 105n37, 106
teaching(s),
    anointed (Spirit-empowered, sacramental, encounter-effecting, transformational), 96, 107, 109–10, 112, 125
    See also preaching, anointed.
    See also Scripture, transformational capacity of.
    false, 87, 93, 99–100, 100n27, 101–2, 102n31, 104–5, 105n37, 106, 112

teaching(s) (*continued*)
See also apostles (teachers), false.
See also doctrines, false.
theologically real experience of, 123
See also nurture (Christian), theologically real experience of.
temptation, the devil and, ix, 66–67, 92, 117, 140–41, 144–46, 146n12, 147–48, 150–52, 157, 159, 171, 182–83, 188, 208
testimony, Christian, 198, 212–13, 219
thanatophobia, 11
theism (theists), open, 233–34, 239, 257
See also future, open view of.
theodicy, 226–27, 227n6, 240, 251–52, 254, 261
biblical (story of Job as a), 238
biblically informed, 251
free will, 228
natural law, 260n8
warfare, 227n7, 228n12, 230, 240, 242, 245, 250, 255
thorn, Paul's, 31, 44, 157, 205–6, 206n10, 208
Towner, Philip, 103n31
tradition(al),
Christian, 20, 22, 74, 77, 78, 108, 211, 241, 241n43, 266, 266n26,
human, 93, 102, 248
training, endurance, 6, 8, 9n19, 11, 15, 20, 34–35, 37, 52, 54, 56, 83, 86, 91–93, 130, 154, 156, 156n24, 157, 159, 163, 198, 211, 221, 227, 277–78
transformation, 5, 65, 72–74, 76, 95–96, 98, 100n27, 107, 109, 113, 135–36, 138, 138n19, 139n4, 194, 194n74, 273
universe, moral, 260–61, 263
verities, Christological, 100n27
Twain, Mark, 41, 41n5

Tyra, Gary, 2n3, 6n14, 12n22, 14, 52n22, 61n1, 63n3, 75n13, 76n14, 78n16, 86n7, 87n9, 88n13, 89n16, 90n17, 90n18, 91n19, 98n24, 100n27, 108n41, 116n1, 122n8, 136n16, 163n2, 166n7, 172n27, 182n42, 183n47, 187n55, 187n56, 187n57, 187n58, 194n74, 218n28–29, 238n32, 244n47, 271n35–36, 272n40
Tyra, Patti, 136n16

Van Gelder, Craig, 140n1–2, 271n38
Ventura, Rob, 190n65

W. Bill, 50
Wallace, J. Warner, 85n4
Wallis, Arthur, 192n70, 198n2
Waltke, Bruce, 238n33, 243, 243n46
warfare, Jesus' wilderness, 67, 144–45, 147, 152
Warren, E. Janet, 40n2,
watchers, 26–27, 28n21
See also angel(s), fallen.
Weatherhead, Leslie, 82, 82n25
Weber, Stuart K., 146n13, 147n14
Wesley, John, 137n18
Westermann, Claus, 246n50, 248n57
"why" question, the ultimate, x, 10, 225, 227, 253–54
Willard, Dallas, 81, 176
Williams, Roger, III, 75
Wilson, Jim, 75, 75n13, 76, 76n14
whisper test, the, 136
witness (to Christ),
apostolic, 94–95
See also gospel, apostolic version of.
See also witness (to Christ), New Testament's.
New Testament's, 133
Wolfers, David, 238n33–34
worldview(s),
modern, anti-supernaturalistic, 21
premodern, 97

worship (Christian),
  as encounter (encounter-
    oriented type of), 202,
    202n6
  See also worship (Christian),
    theologically real experience
    of.
  corporate, 69–70, 78, 128
  personal, 69, 78
  secularization of, 75
  theologically real, 63, 65, 71–74,
    74n12, 76, 78–83, 88, 123,
    125, 127–28, 138, 202,
    202n6, 203, 205, 277–78
  See also worship (Christian), as
    encounter.

wrappings, linen, 77
Wright, Christopher, J. H., 140,
  140n1, 141n4, 271n37,
  272n40
Wright, N. T., 40n3, 47, 47n15,
  48n17, 49, 236n30, 246,
  246n49, 260n7, 261, 261n10,
  261n11, 261n12, 262,
  262n13–14, 263–64, 264n19,
  265, 265n22, 265n23, 267,
  270, 270n32, 271n34, 272,
  272n41, 271n42

Zscheile, Dwight J., 140n1–2,
  271n38

Ancient Document Index

OLD TESTAMENT

Genesis
1:26–28	43, 228
1:28	148, 272
1:31	43, 47
3	25, 33, 55, 65, 67, 228
3:1–13	66
3:4	25
3:5	67
3:9	234
3:15	33n29
3:17	228
4—11	67
5:24	28–29n22
6	27, 28, 33
6:1–2	30n25
6:1–8	29
6:2	27
6:4	27
6:5–6	234
6:5–7	234
11:5–7	234
18:20–21	234

Exodus
3:9–10	234
32:7–14	234

Leviticus
11:44–45	259n6, 270n31
19:1–2	260
19:2	259n6
19:15	270n31
20:7	259n6, 270n31
20:26	259n6, 270n31
21:3	203
21:8	259n6
21:21	203
21:23	203

Numbers
19:11–22	77
22:22–34	209

Deuteronomy
6:10–25	147
6:13	67, 148
6:16	67, 147
8:1–5	146
8:3	67, 146
14:1	45n11
16:20	270n31
32:4	259n6

Joshua
24:14	1n2
24:19	259n6

1 Samuel
2:2	259n6
6:20	259n6

1 Samuel (continued)

15:11	234
15:35	234

2 Samuel

6:14–15	204
24:16	234

1 Kings

18:28	45n11

1 Chronicles

21:1	28n19

Job

1:1	238, 243, 244
1:4–5	243
1:6–7	23n10
1:6–12	245
1:6—2:6	246
1:9	28n19
2:1–8	245
2:4	28n19
2:11—37:24	246
3:1–26	246
3:25	244
4:1–9	239
7:17–21	246n52
9:16–18	246n52
9:22–24	246n52
10:1–3	246n52
10:2	247n53
10:18–19	246
13:3	247n53
13:15–24	247n53
16:7–17	246n52
19:1–7	246n52
19:7	247n53
23:3–9	247n53
23:11–17	246n52
23:15	244
24:1	246n52
24:12	246n52
27:2–6	246n52
30:20	247n53
30:20–26	246n52
31:1–40	243
31:23	244
31:35–37	247n53
33:8–11	246n52
34:5	239
34:5–6	246n52
35:12–14	247n53
38:4–7	43
38:1—41:34	247
38:1—40:2	247
38:7	43
40:6—41:34	247
40:8	246n52
42:1–6	248
42:5	248

Psalms

7:1–2	180
7:10	180
9:16	259n6
11:7	259n6, 270n31
25:8–10	89
33:5	259n6
36:6	259n6
36:9	63
42:1	51
42:4	200
45:6	259n6
50:6	259n6
50:14–15	201
50:23	xii, 65, 201
51	221
51:1–17	203
51:6	174
57	200
57:4	185
64:3	185
66:16–19	202n7
71	200
71:22	259n6
77:13	259n6
78:32–37	89
78:41	259n6
89:8	1n1
89:7	259n6
89:14	259n6

95:2	200	14:12–15	24, 29, 40, 43
97:2	259n6	14:13–14	40
96:8	200	14:14	25
99:4	259n6	29:13	203
99:5	259n6	29:23	259n6
99:9	259n6	30:18	259n6
100:1	200	33:5	259n6
100:4	200	38:1–6	234
101:1	259n6	43:3	259n6
103:6	259n6	48:17	259n6
104:2	241	49:2	185
112:5	270n31	51:4	259n6
116:15	46	52:7	170, 177
116:17	200	53:4–6	263
118:19–21	200	53:10–12	263
131	226	54:5	259n6
131:1–3	227, 251	55:5	259n6
131:2	225	55:10–11	110
139:23–24	204	56:1	270n31
141:1–2	71	57:19	170, 201
145:17–20	202n7	58:2	203
		59:1–8	261, 270n31
		59:17	182, 183
		60:9	259n6
		61:8	259n6
		65:5	203
		65:17	270

Proverbs

3:34	202n7
6:12–15	249n62
8:20	259n6
11:2	25
14:32	249n62
16:4	249n62
16:8	25
18:12	202n7
21:13	274n43
24:11–12	274n43
25:25	211
28:5	259n6
29:7	270n31
31:9	274n43

Jeremiah

9:23–24	270n31
18:9–10	234
21:12	270n31
23:29	110
51:5	259n6

Ezekiel

3:27	195
9:8–9	261–62
28	33, 46
28:12–19	24–25, 29, 40
28:13	25
28:14	25
29:21	195
33:22	195

Isaiah

1:17	270n31
5:1–30	261
5:16	259n6
6:1–8	65, 110, 203
11:4	185
11:5	170, 174
14	33, 46

Daniel

10:16	195

Hosea

4:1	1n2
6:5	185
11:9	259n6
11:12	259n6
12:6	203, 270n31
14:12	201

Joel

2:13	234

Amos

5:14–15	270n31
5:44–45	270n31
7:3	234
7:6	234

Jonah

3:1–4	234
3:10	234

Micah

3:8	259n6
6:8	217, 260, 270n31

Habakkuk

1:12	259n6
3:3	259n6
3:17–19	201

Zephaniah

3:5	259n6

Zechariah

1:3	203
3:1	28n19
7:8–10	270, 270n31

Malachi

3:7	203

APOCRYPHA

1 Enoch

1:9	28
6	27
6:1–2	30n25
7	27
8	27
9	27
10	27
10:13	32
15	28n21

2 Enoch

1–22	28–29n22

Jubilees

1:10	29n23
22:17	29n23
10	28
11:11	29n23

Wisdom

5:18–19	175

NEW TESTAMENT

Matthew

4:1–11	144–45, 186
4:2–3	67
4:5–7	67
4:8–9	67
4:10	149
4:10–11	203

4:11	61, 152	24:9–10	92
4:23	143	24:10–13	5n10, 6n13, 86n8, 93n22
5:9	256n1		
5:11–12	154	24:11	92
6	117	24:14	212n16
6:1–18	78	24:35	270
6:2–4	154	25:21	1, 52, 172, 270, 273
6:9–13	116		
6:13	150	25:23	52, 270
6:19–34	154	25:31–46	274n43
7:15	93n22	25:34	270
9:34	33	25:41	29
9:35	143	26:36–46	150–51
10:16	68	28:18–20	272
10:16–20	194	28:19–20	187
10:16–22	155		
10:19–20	187	**Mark**	
11:1–6	143	1:12–13	144
12:24	33	1:13	152
12:25–28	34	1:14–15	142
12:26	4n8	1:35	150
12:28	143, 198n2	3:22	33
12:29	68, 143	3:26	4n8
13:4	29n23	5	45, 143
13:18–19	52	5:1–20	45
13:19	29n23	6:46	150
13:20–21	52	7:22	154
13:22	52	9	45
13:22–23	52	9:21–22	46
14:15–21	146n12	9:25–29	198n2
14:23	150	9:29	50
14:31	183n46	10:45	263n17
15:32–38	146n12	11:23	183n46
16:13–17	149	16:15–16	272
16:14–15	130		
16:21	150	**Luke**	
16:23	140, 149	4:1–13	144
18	124	4:13	149, 203
18:15–18	118	4:18–19	142
18:19–20	120	4:43	142
18:21–35	130	5:16	150, 198n2
21:21	183n46	6:12	150
21:33–44	52	6:38	154
22:34–40	272	8:13	5n10, 92
23:12	202n7	8:31	28n22, 29n23
23:23	260, 270n31, 273	9:28	150
23:25	154		

Luke (continued)

10:17	198
10:17–18	32
10:25–37	274n43
11:1	150
11:15	33
11:15–32	255
11:17–26	34
11:18	4n8
11:39	154
11:42	259n6, 270n31
12:15	154
14:25–27	154
15:17–20	203
16:10–11	270
17:21	143
18:7	259n6
18:9–14	202n7
21:12–13	212n16
21:12–19	213
21:19	3n6
22:20	89
22:31–32	241, 242
22:43	152
24:49	121

John

1:1	97
1:7	135
1:12	256n1
1:14	97, 141
1:18	141
8:31	211
8:32	47n16
8:44	42, 46n13
10	46, 46n13
10:10	46
11:32–35	46
11:52	256n1
12:31	143, 228n12
12:44–46	141
13:34	115
13:34–35	106
14:8	172
14:16	190
14:17	172
14:26	190
14:30	143, 228n12
15	90, 91
15:1–6	5n10
15:1–8	52, 90
15:16	52
15:18–21	154–55
15:26	190
16:11	228n12
17:3–6	141
17:11	48
17:15	48, 150
17:24	258
20:1–10	77
20:30–31	91
20:31	100n27

Acts

1—28	123
1:8	121, 187, 194
1:14	121
2	121, 122
2:1–4	121, 128
2:23	241
2:37–41	153
2:41	177
2:42–47	122, 123, 179
2:47	177
3:19–21	143
4:23–31	123
4:23–25	153
4:36–37	153
5	153
5:1–2	153
5:3	153
5:3–4	153
5:11	154
5:14	177
5:42	92
8:4–8	198
9:10–20	187
9:22	95
10:36–38	68
11:23	6n13
11:27–29	124
12:1–4	155
12:5–11	155

13:1–3	112
13:1–4	124
13:6–11	89n15
13:6–12	187
14:21–22	92, 93n21
14:32	6n13
15:1	102
15:1–5	124
15:5	102
15:6	124
15:6–29	124
15:7	124
15:12	124
15:22	124
15:24	102
15:25	124
15:28	124
16:16–18	187, 198n2
16:22–34	155
16:25	202
17:1–15	128
17:2–3	95
17:31	259n6, 264n20
18:9–11	155
20:35	154
27:21–25	155

Romans

1	64
1:18–25	64
1:25	49
1:26	49
1:29	154
2:5–11	264n20
3:21–24	141
3:21–26	176
3:22	176
3:25	262
3:25–26	263, 264
4:22–24	176
4:25	262
5:1	177, 178, 179
5:1–2	181
5:8	257
5:10–11	141
5:20	55
6:1–23	176
6:13	205
6:16–18	205
6:18	68
8	187
8:5–8	2
8:14	256n1
8:14–17	263n17
8:15	189
8:16	189
8:17	256n3, 257n5
8:18	212, 249n62, 268
8:19	256n1
8:19–21	228
8:19–27	264
8:21	256n1
8:24–25	251
8:26	189, 192
8:29	241
8:34–39	44
8:38–39	30
10:9–10	100n27
10:14–15	177
11:2	241
11:17–22	5n10
11:33–36	264n20
12:1	259n6
12:1–2	79
12:2	2, 99
12:4–8	126
12:6–8	88
12:10	115
12:16	115
13:8	115
13:14	171
14:9–12	100n27
14:13	115
14:17	179
15:1–2	30n25
15:4	6n13, 86n8
15:7	115
15:13	184
15:14	115
15:30–33	156
16:16	115
16:16–18	134
16:20	33n29, 34, 253, 279
16:25–26	95

1 Corinthians

1:2	259n6
1:6	212n16
1:9	1n1
1:30	141, 176
2:4	198n2
3:9	52
4:2	191, 192
4:5	264n20
4:14–15	191, 192
4:14–19	191
5:1–13	119
5:1–14	134
5:9–11	154
6:3	30
6:9–11	154
8:1–13	30n25
9:16	108n44
9:24—10:12	5n10
10:12	3n6, 15
10:20	29n23, 67
10:23–33	30n25
11:2	211
11:10	30
11:25	89
12	187
12:3	100n27
12:7–20	126
14	187
14:1–3	100n27
14:3	109, 125, 216
14:15	204
14:24–25	109, 125, 194
14:25	125
14:26	125
15:1–2	5n10, 93n21
15:2	212
15:3	262
15:45a	65
15:45b	67
15:58	3n6, 141, 172
16:13	4n9, 5n10, 93n21
16:20	115

2 Corinthians

1:21	3n6
1:21–22	185
1:24	3n6, 5n10
2:5–7	119
2:10–11	130
2:11	5, 9, 41, 61
3:17–18	72
3:18	99
4:3–4	49
4:4	44, 179, 228n12
4:7–11	158
4:7–18	221
4:16–18	158
4:17	257n5, 268
5:1–10	221
5:7	159
5:9–10	264n20
5:14–15	159, 182, 258
5:17	72, 127, 270
5:18–20	141, 263n17
5:21	176
6:14–18	259n6
6:18	256n2
7:1	259n6
7:11	270n31
8:14–17	185
8:22–23	185
9:6–10	154
9:13	212n16
10:10	208
11	101, 102
11:1–15	100, 101
11:1–3	101
11:2–3	5n10
11:2–4	93
11:3	33, 37, 41, 52, 102, 135
11:4	101, 102n29
11:4–15	101
11:13	93n22, 94, 101, 102
11:13–15	93
11:14	31, 42, 101
11:22	102n29
11:23–28	155

12	101	1:5	263n17
12:2	28n22	1:7	141
12:7–10	157, 205–6	1:7–10	264
12:8	31	1:13	174
12:10	207	1:13–14	185
13:5	93n21	1:15–21	170
13:11	115	1:17–23	184
13:12	115	2:2	44
		2:21	270n31

Galatians

		2:11–13	184
1—6	103, 104	3:1–13	194
1:1	95	3:6	256n3
1:4	262	3:10	184
1:6	102n29	3:14–19	170
1:6–9	93n21, 95	3:16	193
1:11–12	95	3:16–19	172, 181n41, 182
1:13—2:10	95	3:20–21	257n5
2:1–5	93n22	4:1	171
2:12	102	4:1–3	178, 179
3:29	256n3	4:1—6:9	164, 167, 185
3:26	256n1	4:2	115
4:4–5	141	4:3–6	185
4:4–7	263n17	4:4–6	185
4:6	256n2	4:11–13	181n41
4:8–20	5n10	4:11–16	88
4:13–14	207	4:14	172
5:1	3n6, 4n9	4:14–15	135, 174
5:2–6	5n10	4:15–16	125–26
5:5–6	103	4:17–19	49, 154
5:13	115	4:17–32	171, 176
5:13–14	103	4:19	49
5:16	103	4:20–21	174
5:16–17	137	4:24	171, 176, 259n6
5:19–21	2	4:25	186
5:22–23	171	4:26–27	114, 130
5:22–25	103	4:27	203
5:25	122n8, 166, 171, 182, 193, 195	4:29–30	186
		4:32	115
6:1–2	118	5	187
6:10	178	5:1	176
6:12	102	5:3–5	154
6:14–16	103	5:8–9	176
		5:8–10	174

Ephesians

		5:13	186
1:1	1n2, 270n31	5:18	122n8, 172, 182
1:4	270n31	5:18–19	186

Ephesians (*continued*)

5:18–20	195
5:19	115
5:20	201
5:21	115
5:25–27	270n31
5:26	186
6:10	193, 198
6:10–11	170
6:10–12	74
6:12	184
6:12–13	171
6:10–13	4
6:10–18	193
6:18–20	198n2
6:10–20	10, 163–64, 167, 168, 170, 171, 172, 198n2, 277
6:11	3n6, 9, 128, 163
6:11–12	198
6:11–14	4n8
6:12	31
6:13–18	198
6:14	3n6, 168, 174, 175
6:14–15	176
6:14–17	173, 185
6:16	180, 181, 183
6:17	168, 182, 186, 188, 190
6:18	188, 189, 190, 191, 193, 195
6:19	194
6:19–20	193
6:20	194

Philippians

1:27	3n6, 4n9, 93n21, 172
1:29	221
2:4	30n25
2:5–11	237
2:9–11	100n27
2:15	256n1
2:16	212
3:1–2	133
3:2–3	102
3:9	176
3:17–21	133
4:1	3n6, 4n9
4:4	201
4:4–7	201–2
4:6	193
4:7	179
4:7–10	201
4:12–13	154

Colossians

1—4	102, 103
1	102
1:2	1n2
1:9	198n2
1:9–12	6n13, 86n8, 172
1:13	74
1:13–14	141
1:16	184
1:19–20	264
1:19–22	141
1:21–23	5n10, 90
1:22	270n31
1:28–29	92
2	73
2:1–8	172
2:5	4n9
2:6–7	93n21
2:6–8	103
2:8	93, 102
2:11–14	102
3:13	262
2:15	68, 74, 263n17
2:16–17	103
2:16–23	73–74
2:17–19	93n22
2:18	103
2:20	74
2:20–22	103
3:1–4	103
3:1–10	171
3:1–17	61, 176
3:5	154
3:5–17	103
3:12–14	270n31
3:13	115, 130

ANCIENT DOCUMENT INDEX   313

3:15	178, 179
3:16	88, 115, 126
4:12	3n6

1 Thessalonians

1:3	6n13, 86n8
2:17–18	70, 128
3:5	5n10
3:8	3n6, 4n9
3:10	198n2
3:12–13	172
3:13	270n31
4:4	270n31
4:7	270n31
4:17	258
4:18	115
5:8	168, 182
5:11	115
5:16–18	193, 201
5:17	198n2
5:21	212
5:26	115

2 Thessalonians

1:3–5	6n13, 86n8
1:4	211
2:5	39
2:13	3n6
2:15	3n6, 4n9, 93n21, 211
3:1–2	156
3:3	48, 156
3:3–4	181n41

1 Timothy

1–6	102
1:3	94
1:3–5	92
1:3–7	93n22
1:4	94
1:15–17	257n5
1:18–19	5n10, 93n21
1:19	212
2:8	270n31
2:20–21	178
3:6	32–33, 40

3:6–7	5n10
3:8–9	93n21
3:9	212
4:1	73, 84, 93, 93n21, 94, 99
4:1–3	74
4:1–10	5n10
4:2–3	73
4:6	91, 92
4:7	94, 103
4:11–16	92
5:8	5n10
5:15	37
5:24–25	264n20
6:3–5	93n22
6:9–10	93n22
6:9–12	5n10
6:10	154
6:11–12	6n13, 86n8
6:12	93n21, 212
6:12–13	212n16
6:15–16	241
6:19	212
6:20	94
6:20–21	5n10, 93n21

2 Timothy

1—4	102
1:3	198n2
1:9	258, 270n31
1:13–14	93n21
2:1–2	92
2:2	88
2:10	257n5
2:11–13	5n10, 6n13, 86n8
2:14–18	93n22
2:16	94
2:16–21	5n10
2:19	212n16
2:21	270n31
2:23–26	134
2:24–25	92
2:24–26	5n10
2:25–26	42, 93
3:10–11	156
3:12	155, 212

2 Timothy (continued)

3:16	92, 98
3:16–17	96, 186
4:1	264n20
4:4	92
4:6–8	154
4:7–8	5n10, 52, 212, 249n62
4:10	159

Titus

1:1	73
1:8	270n31
1:9	212
1:10–11	102
2:1	92
2:1–2	6n13, 86n8
2:13–14	141
2:15	92
3:1–2	178
3:3	50
3:7	256n3
3:9–11	134
3:14	52

Hebrews

1:1–3	141
2:1–4	5n10
2:10	256n2
2:11	270n31
2:14	68, 255
2:14–15	143, 150, 263n17
2:14–18	146, 237, 255
2:17	262
2:17–18	68
3:1	100n27, 270n31
3:1–6	90
3:6	212
3:6–14	5n10
3:12	92
3:12–14	90, 93n21
3:13	115
3:14	212
3:15	100n27
4:1–2	5n10
4:12	185
4:12–13	98, 99
4:14	90, 93n21, 212
4:15–16	68
5:7–10	151
6:1–2	264n20
6:4–6	92
6:4–12	5n10
6:18	212
7:19	203
8:6–13	89
9:12	141
9:15	141
9:15–28	89
9:26	258
9:27–28	264n20
10:14	270n31
10:19–39	90
10:23	1n1, 212
10:24	116
10:25	115
10:25–31	92
10:26–31	264n20
10:26–39	5n10
11:4	270n31
11:32–34	181n41
12:1–3	6n13, 86n8, 155
12:7–10	259
12:8	256n2
12:10	259n6
12:14	270n31
12:14–28	260
12:15–17	5n10
13:1	115
13:15	201

James

1:6	183n46
1:16–18	62
1:22	188, 192
2:14–17	274n43
3:13–16	41, 134
4:6	15, 202n7, 204
4:6–10	33n28
4:7–8	197
4:7–10	199, 202, 203, 204, 205
4:8	203

ANCIENT DOCUMENT INDEX 315

4:11	116	1:19	95
5:8	3n6, 4n9, 48	1:20–21	96
5:9	116	1:21	186
5:14–16	127	2	104
5:19–20	5n10	2—3	100
		2:1	94

1 Peter

		2:1–3	93n22
		2:1–22	93
1:2	241	2:4	31, 264n20
1:6–7	206	2:9	264n20
1:15–16	260, 270n31	3:7	264n20
1:16	259n6	3:10	270
1:17	264n20	3:10–13	270n33
1:18–19	263n17	3:11	270n31
1:18–20	258	3:13	264, 267
1:22	115	3:14–18	93
2:5	270n31	3:17	5n10
2:9	270n31	3:17–18	93n21, 106–7
2:24	262–63, 263, 263n17		

1 John

3:7	256n3		
3:8	115	1—5	101, 103, 104, 104n33, 105, 106
3:14–17	207		
3:18–20	31	1:1–3	94, 95, 104
4:1–2	221	1:6	106
4:1–5	207	1:6–10	105
4:9	116	1:9	263
4:10–11	126	2:2	100n27, 105, 262, 263
4:12–13	155		
4:12–19	207, 221	2:3–4	106
5:5	116	2:5–6	106
5:5–9	33n28	2:9	106
5:8	19, 34, 42	2:11	106
5:8–9	4, 4n8, 5n10, 68, 93, 93n21, 180	2:15–17	2
		2:18	94, 106
5:9	3n6, 4n9	2:18–28	104
5:10	4n9	2:25	257n5
5:14	115	2:28–29	106
		2:19	92, 104

2 Peter

		2:20	106
1—3	104n33, 106	2:22	94, 105
1:1–21	94, 186	2:22–23	106
1:5–11	5n10	2:24–28	5n10
1:10–11	257n5	2:26	104, 105
1:10–12	95	2:26–27	106
1:16	94	3:1	256n1
1:16–18	95	3:2	256n1

1 John (continued)

3:5	263
3:7–8	106
3:8	68, 105, 143
3:10	256n1
3:10–11	106
3:11	115
3:14	106
3:14–15	257n5
3:16–18	106
3:18	274n43
3:23	115
3:24	106
4	72
4:1	93n22
4:1–3	105
4:1–6	91, 93, 104, 106
4:2–3	105, 106
4:4	35, 55, 113
4:7	115
4:7–21	106
4:10	100n27, 105, 262, 263
4:11	115
4:13	106
4:15	105
4:17	264n20
4:19	257
4:19–20	72
4:21–24	72–73
5:2	256n1
5:5	100n27
5:5–12	105
5:6–7	104
5:6–8	106
5:11–12	100n27
5:19	44, 256n1
5:19–20	107

2 John

1:1–13	101, 103, 104, 104n33, 104n34, 106
1:5	115
1:7	105, 106
1:7–9	100n27
1:7–11	91, 93
1:8–10	106
1:9	5n10

3 John

1:1–14	104n33, 104n34

Jude

1–25	100, 104, 104n33, 106
3	93n21
3–5	5n10
3–24	93
6	31, 50n20, 264n20
14–15	28
20–21	107
22	183n46
20–25	5n10

Revelation

1:2	212n16
1:4–6	263
1:6	257n5
1:9	6n13, 86n8, 212n16
2—3	108
2:2	93n22, 94
2:3	6n13, 86n8
2:7	156
2:8	52
2:10	42, 52, 157
2:10–11	213
2:11	156
2:13	6n13
2:17	156
2:24	52
2:25	212
2:26	156
3:1–6	5n10
3:3	211
3:5	156
3:8	6n13
3:9	52
3:10	6n13, 86n8
3:11	5n10, 212
3:12	156
3:14–18	51

3:15–16	5n10	14:12–13	157
3:21	156	17:8	28n22
4:8	259n6	19:10	212n16
5:9–10	270	19:11	259n6
6:9	212n16	19:11–16	143
6:10	264n20	20:1	32
6:12–17	44	20:2	33, 52
9	44	20:3	42
9:1–2	28n22	20:7	52
9:7–11	44	20:8	42
9:11	28, 28n22, 32, 44	20:10	42, 52
11:7	28n22	20:11–15	264n20
11:18	264n20	21:1	270
12:1–17	52	21:1–4	143, 212, 249n62, 257n5
12:3–4	42	21:1–7	255
12:7–9	33	21:7	257n5
12:9	42	22:1–5	143, 212, 249n62
12:11	212n16	22:11	270n31
12:17	42, 212, 212n16		
13:4–6	40		
13:4–10	42		
13:8	258		
13:9–10	157		
13:10	1n2, 6n13, 86n8, 89		
14:7	264n20		
14:12	6n13, 86n8, 89		

www.ingramcontent.com/pod-product-compliance
Lightning Source LLC
Chambersburg PA
CBHW030744230426
43667CB00007B/833